Press Freedoms

Press Freedoms

A Descriptive Calendar
of Concepts, Interpretations,
Events, and Court Actions,
from 4000 B.C. to the Present

Louis Edward Ingelhart

GREENWOOD PRESS
NEW YORK • WESTPORT, CONNECTICUT • LONDON

Library of Congress Cataloging-in-Publication Data

Ingelhart, Louis E. (Louis Edward)
  Press freedoms.

  Bibliography: p.
  Includes index.
  1. Freedom of the press—Chronology. I. Title.
PN4735.I56 1987   323.44'5   86-31834
ISBN 0-313-25636-5 (lib. bdg. : alk. paper)

Library of Congress Catalog Card Number: 86-31834
ISBN: 0-313-25636-5

First Published in 1987

Greenwood Press, Inc.
88 Post Road West, Westport, Connecticut 06881

Printed in the United States of America

The paper used in this book complies with the
Permanent Paper Standard issued by the National
Information Standards Organization (Z39.48-1984).

10 9 8 7 6 5 4 3 2 1

Dedicated to all those who have
or are using the press fully and
freely, wisely or foolishly,
responsibly or irresponsibly.

Contents

Preface   xi

A Descriptive Calendar of Press Freedoms   xvii

1. The Challenge to Understand   1

2. From Prehistory to the Age of Printing, 500,000 BC through 1499 AD   4

3. Legacy of England 9 through 1499   12

4. Printing in a World of Irreverence, 1500 through 1599   15

5. The Crown as Stern Entrepreneur, 1500 through 1599   23

6. The Invention of the Newspaper, 1600 through 1643   32

7. Schismatism, Puritans, and Levellers, 1600 through 1643   36

8. The Milton Legacy, 1644 through 1693   46

9. England Tries Limited Freedom, 1644 through 1699   49

10. The Newspaper World Expands, 1644 through 1699   63

11. The Colonial Manner, 1619 through 1699   65

12. Great Britain Defines Libel, 1700 through 1759   73

13. Press Freedom in the Colonies, 1700 through 1759   87

14. Holding Hands with Repression, 1700 through 1759   98

15. The Patriots Lead the Way, 1760 through 1786   101

16. The King, His Ministers, and Parliament, 1760

through 1786   112

17. The Reluctant Tyrants, 1760 through 1786   120

18. The Triumph of Freedom and Its Destruction, 1787
     through 1799   123

19. Thomas Paine Goes Home, 1787 through 1799   142

20. The French Travesties, 1787 though 1799   149

21. The Jefferson and Madison Legacies, 1800
     through 1824   152

22. New Reasons for Suppression, 1800 through 1824   165

23. Napoleon's Destruction of Liberty, 1800
     through 1824   178

24. The Great and Bitter Causes, 1825 through 1867   182

25. Stamp Taxes and Blasphemy in Great Britain,
     1825 through 1867   192

26. False Promises of Freedom, 1825 through 1867   200

27. The Fourteenth Amendment, 1868 through 1899   206

28. Great Britain Attacks Vice, 1868 through 1899   213

29. Tentative Improvements, 1868 through 1899   217

30. Censorship American Style, 1900 through 1924   221

31. Censorship European Style, 1900 through 1924   241

32. The Triumph of the Fourteenth Amendment,
     1925 through 1949   252

33. Laggards and Totalitarians, 1925 through 1949   278

34. Concepts from the U.S. Supreme Court, 1950
     through 1959   285

35. Press Suppression in Asia and Latin America,
     1950 through 1959   294

36. Postwar Adjustments, 1960 through 1969   298

37. The World-Wide Struggle Continues, 1960
     through 1969   316

38. The White House Offensive, 1970 through 1974   321

39. International Agreements and Repressions, 1970
     through 1974   340

40. Individual, Corporate, or Penumbral Right,
     1975 through 1979   344

41.   An International Debate, 1975 through 1979   354

42.   Events in America, 1980 and Beyond   357

43.   Viewpoints and the Courts, 1983 through 1985   370

44.   Press Control and New Dictators, 1980 and Beyond   378

45.   The Promise of the Twenty-First Century   385

Selected Bibliography   391

Index   403

Preface

This reference volume on <u>Press Freedoms</u> has been several years in the making. It results from a lifelong concern for a free press and from lengthy study of the First Amendment to the U.S. Constitution.

This calendar of concepts, interpretations, events, and court actions from earliest times to the present has been prepared so that readers may have a further understanding of what a free press involves. This record of thousands of pertinent pieces of information has been compiled so that readers may appreciate the many aspects of press freedoms more thoroughly.

<u>Press Freedoms</u> has attempted to find and report the many concepts, viewpoints, and events having had considerable impact on creating freedom of the press. Both proponent and antagonist views and efforts are presented. American, European, Asian, South American, African, and Australian actions, events, and court decisions are presented. The book presents in chronological order, the origin, growth, and status of the free press world-wide.

National interest in the Bicentennial of the U.S. Constitution from 1987 to 1989 should foster a renewed interest in basic concepts such as freedom of the press. The bicentennial of the First Amendment on December 15, 1991, is a significant time to give detailed attention to defining what press freedoms mean.

This volume has grown out of an interest in the intriguing history of an emerging free press and in the entangled relationships in strivings and beliefs in all parts of the world. This reference seemed important to develop since so few sources really explore the development of freedom of the press as a concept in any depth and in practical terms.

It is hoped that this volume will serve as a source book to be used by students and teachers alike in a number of disciplines for a variety of purposes. It is hoped also that this reference will provoke enough concern, agreement, or disagreement to stir others to write in greater detail about aspects that they feel have been slighted or perhaps misinterpreted in this study.

The length of a work of this kind always poses a serious constraint on the selection of data. Originally the manuscript contained more than a half million words; heavy and careful editing reduced it by a third. One criterion called for the elimination of material referring exclusively to speech matters rather than just to press matters. Another criterion was the recognition that this book is not intended to be a general history of the press but is limited to a history and analysis of the emergence and development of the concept of a free press. Nevertheless, historical events directly affecting press freedom have been included. Freedom of expression episodes and views, including both press and speech, have also been covered, especially if the speech was subsequently printed or broadcast.

Press Freedoms provides more information about persons and subjects when information is not found readily in standard sources. Less information is given about lives and heroes involved in the struggle for a free press when information is not easily available.

Special attention is given to avoiding the common pitfall of overlaying opinions and views on top of accounts about people and events. An effort is made throughout the book also to show that the concept of a free press is an ever evolving and developing concept.

Whereas "freedom of the press" became an important war cry in the American Revolution, it was not fully grown, legally provided for, or operational at that date in U.S. history. The 1787 Constitutional Convention assumed that freedom of the press was such a strong natural right that no mention of it was needed in the Constitution. Wiser views prevailed to produce the First Amendment free press clause, ratified in 1791, as part of the Bill of Rights. Before the Eighteenth Century ended, however, the Sedition Act in effect destroyed the free press.

Freedom of the press has evolved in the United States and continues to develop, even to the present. Here are several major steps:

1791 -- Ratification of the First Amendment

1801 -- Expiration of the Sedition Act

1868 -- Ratification of the Fourteenth Amendment

1925 -- The Gitlow decision placing First Amendment rights within the provisions of the Fourteenth Amendment

1957 -- The Roth decision and the 1973 Miller
        decision establishing the dimensions of
        obscenity

1964 -- The New York Times-Sullivan decision creating
        a First Amendment defense against libel
        accusations

1986 -- A Supreme Court decision requiring that
        private individuals would have to prove the
        falsity of content they claimed to be
        libelous.

Frequent efforts have been made to thwart the expanded
freedom provided by these events. World War I and World War
II saw the return of seditious prosecutions. Strong efforts
to rid the press of pornography, violence, intrusiveness,
government criticism, radical political views, and other
devils surfaced and continue to have strong support. The
courts, including the Supreme Court, remain unimpressed by
the rhetoric of protagonists and continue to observe the
freedom of the press guarantees of the U. S. Constitution.

When difficult problems arise it is not unusual to hear
proposals to muzzle the press, especially television. The
tragedy of the Challenger shuttle explosion was followed by
criticism of the press for sensational, intrusive, and
critical coverage. Subsequent investigations of NASA
bungling blunted much of this criticism.

The onslaught of terrorism has aroused severe criticism
of the press for its detailed coverage. Paul B. Henze, a
Rand Corporation official, said in urging government controls
of media reports of terrorist actions, that "what has been
gained by all of the minute media reporting on terrorism?
Whose interest have been served? Who has learned something?
I find it very hard to think of what good has been done by
just simply tantalizing people. If the media had had as much
deleterious impact as many of the media think, we'd all be
finished." Stansfield Turner, a former head of the Central
Intelligence Agency, said, "While I decry the media releasing
secrets as much as they do, I would never think of trying to
organize a government censorship bureau."

President Ronald Reagan and CIA Director William Casey
became involved in efforts to restrain press reports
concerning submarine eavesdropping activities in Russian
ports. Information about such activities had been published
much earlier, but a trial of an accused espionage agent
aroused their efforts. NBC used some information on a
television newscast and The Washington Post published some
material. President Reagan pressured The Post not to
publish, and Casey asked the Justice Department to consider
prosecution of NBC under a rather vague 1950 law.

While government officials and others were wont to
criticize the American press for its coverage of government
mistakes, those same officials became eloquent in condemning
Soviet Russia for being slow and guarded in reporting the
Chernobyl atomic energy plant disaster.

Press Freedoms demonstrates that the press is not a monolithic entity that can be controlled by codes of ethics, pressures, associations, or even by government regulations. The press is far too diverse in form, purpose, viewpoint, and vigor to expect anything approaching harmony, unity, or agreement on any subject. It functions in the highest tradition of First Amendment debate.

Perhaps the best beginning for a person eager to go beyond the information given in Press Freedoms would be two remarkable volumes produced by Ralph Edward McCoy. In 1968 he authored Freedom of the Press: An Annotated Bibliography and a second volume in 1979 Freedom of the Press: A Bibliocyclopedia.

More than 2,000 sources were used in the preparation of Press Freedoms. Literally hundreds of books, articles, publications of all kinds were reviewed carefully. Locating sources and analyzing them required a great amount of time and study. As a result, a bibliography of 5,000 or more important sources could be assembled.

However, a bibliography of the 200 most important references has been compiled at the end of the book. The list consists of books that are available in most university or most large libraries. Hopefully Press Freedoms will intrigue its readers and challenge them to look further and to read more deeply in order to learn more about the freedom of the press. The bibliography has been designed as a reading regime to launch a dedicated person into a vigorous study program.

The author's concern for freedom of the press was kindled by Frank Luther Mott at the University of Missouri and Edwin Emery at the University of Minnesota, two deans in the history of journalism. The author is known as a fierce champion for a free student press and as a writer about major issued in student press law. He is proud to have served on the Freedom of Information Committee of the Society of Professional Journalists and in executive and advisory board positions for the Student Press Law Center, College Media Advisers, and the First Amendment Congress.

Much of the work on this volume was made possible by a grant provided by the Gannett Foundation.

The author owes much to his family who have been tolerant and supportive. Margaret managed home fires well while the author was closeted with books and papers. Daughter Sharon did much typing made especially difficult by her having to read her father's handwriting. Son Jim was an excellent audience with his knowledge of history to help evaluate the work in progress. Caroline Britt and the Fred Ingelharts were helpful in providing writing space and a platform in Colorado.

David and Jacquie Tolbert, proprietors of Professional Word Processing, were diligent, skilled, and helpful.

Greatest gratitude of all belongs to the faculty, students, and staff of the Department of Journalism of Ball State University. These marvelous colleagues listened to the author, assisted him in practical ways, provided office space, and administrative assistance.

A Descriptive Calendar of Press Freedoms

4000 BC to 1499 AD

As early as 4000 BC, language and alphabets created written records in many cultures. Devices and procedures were soon developed to make multiple copies. Empires appeared and ended to be replaced by others, some of which were driven by new religions and new ambitions. When Europe escaped from the great invasions from the east, its awakening to new knowledge included the art and machinery of printing in the mid-1400s. Nation states quickly began suppressing printed expression which challenged government dogma.

1500 to 1599

Printing became available throughout Europe and was used vigorously in the Reformation. Martin Luther engineered the world's first media event with his heavy and widespread use of pamphlets, books, and tracts. Kings decided to control the press by owning it or by creating a licensed government monopoly of patents.

1600 to 1643

New hunger and political movement led to the invention of the newspaper as a communications media in Europe. England was embroiled in religious schismatism, Puritan domination, and the nuisance of the Levellers, who demanded a free press.

1644 to 1699

Newspapers became more sophisticated, and England abandoned some press controls during the Commonwealth and because of its Glorious Revolution late in the Century. John Milton produced his respected essay "Areopagitica" which has been used as a clarion call for a free press ever after. In North America, the colonial holdings grew to significant size and the first free expression contentions arose.

1700 to 1759

Great Britain became hypersensitive about libelous expression which it defined very broadly. John Peter Zenger of New York Colony managed to defy the legal definition of libel in a famous trial. In Europe the kings became more repressive of press content.

1760-1786

The American Revolution began at the end of the French and Indian War when the English king, his minister, and both houses of Parliament instituted repressive measures to raise revenues to pay war debts. Free press became a major war cry of the Patriots. In Europe, the tyrants were reluctant to ease press controls.

1787-1799

The proposed constitution for the United States almost was rejected because it did not provide for a free press. The new Congress did propose a Bill of Rights, ratified in 1791, to guarantee such freedom from federal interference. But President Adams and Congress imposed the Sedition Act as the century ended to virtually negate the First Amendment. France was even more repressive, Thomas Paine, propagandist for revolution, returned to England to launch free press efforts.

1800 to 1824

Thomas Jefferson made freedom of the press a central part of his political movement. The Sedition Act expired, and he and James Madison protected free press rights. England was inventing new reasons to supress free expression, and Napoleon taught modern dictators that destruction of liberty was essential to tyranny.

1825-1867

The U.S. Civil War posed great challenges to freedom of the press from government and private agencies. Great Britain imposed stamp taxes on printing, and the rest of Europe heard promises of freedom which proved false.

1868-1900

The Fourteenth Amendment provided the means for extending protection of free press rights against state and local governments, but the U.S. Supreme Court would not accept its provisions. Great Britain attacked vice as forbidden expression. Elsewhere in Europe there was improved opportunities for press freedom.

1900-1924

Censorship and propaganda became two press control factors as World War I arrived. American and European goverments alike repressed the press. In the United States, Anthony Comstock finally meet adverse court decisions in his fifty year control of alleged obscenity campaign.

1925-1949

The U.S. Supreme Court in its 1925 Gitlow decision recognized the power of the Fourteenth Amendment to protect press freeom at all government levels. The totalitarianism of Europe intensified press control and propaganda through World War II and beyond.

1950-1969

Post war adjustments saw the U. S. Supreme Court define the dimensions of a free press much more clearly. A worldwide struggle to free the press or to control the press continues. Central and South American nations were extremely repressive as opportunistic dictatorships arose.

1970-1979

The Nixon White House corps launched bitter attacks on the American Press as the Nixon era self-destructed. The U.S. Supreme Court examined free press issues to establish the right as an individual one or a corporate one, which could be affected by penumbral meanings attached to Constitutional phrasing. International debates about the role of the press led to early agreements enhancing freedom, but governments became repressive to promote government goals.

1980-1986

Events and court decisions strengthened press freedom in the United States, but new dictators and fearsome regimes lessened the level of free press rights elsewhere.

1987-2050

The United States should observe the bicentennial of its First Amendment on December 15, 1991. Attention to the meaning and significance of its free press clause could perpetuate this American principle for the twenty-first century. New technology as well as old tyranny might become an obstacle to freedom, or could become a great boon to freedom of expression.

Press Freedoms

1
The Challenge to Understand

Americans believe they have guaranteed constitutional rights
of freedom of the press and freedom of speech. They read the
First Amendment which directs that Congress shall make no law
abridging the freedom of speech or of the press. Should this
not be clear and sufficient unto the Twenty-First Century?
The answer is suprisingly no. Much has been written and
said, much litigation has marched to decisions in many
courts, and much has been contended by proponents and
opponents of free press and free speech.

The discussion becomes confusing because persons use
freedom of speech and freedom of press as synonyms to mean
freedom of expression. Speech means content, rather than
delivery mode, to some who then use it to encompass all modes
of delivery of content, including the mass communications
media of print and electronic media.

Congress represents only one of three branches of the
federal government. The courts and the executive areas are
not included in the First Amendment. Neither are state
governments. Neither are cities or counties.

Constitutional law from 1791 to 1868 did little to
affect freedom of the press. But the Fourteenth Amendment,
inspired by the post-Civil War reconstruction era, provided a
foundation for a great change in the application of the First
Amendment. The new amendment directed that all laws be
applied equally to all persons, that no constitutional rights
be denied unless full due process procedures were followed,
and that all governmental agencies -- federal, state, county,
or municipal -- must observe constitutional restrictions of
their powers. The Supreme Court considered this concept as
not including the First Amendment from 1873 until 1925. The
landmark view of the 1925 Gitlow decision had to occur before
freedom of the press could actually be fully protected in the

United States, nearly 150 years after the Declaration of Independence.

Judicial history between 1925 and the Twenty-First Century has enhanced and clarified the strength of the free press guarantee. But the Supreme Court had difficulty in doing so because the Constitution lists 85 rights which can conflict with one another. The Court balances rights against rights to determine which should prevail. This means that none of the rights can be considered absolute. The Court has believed that a significantly compelling state interest could set aside a constitutional right on occasion. The Court has demonstrated that the freedom of the press clause of the First Amendment provides a right more nearly absolute than the other rights specified in the Constitution.

This view frequently is disputed by people who do not attach transcendent consequence to freedom of the press. There is a lively debate about the nature of or the desirability of a free press which began in 1787 when the proposed Constitution was submitted. The debate has resurfaced with vigor in the late Twentieth Century. This clash poses a challenge to the hope of the Twenty-First Century for the nation and its citizens.

The purpose of this book and its chronological account is an effort to understand the beginnings of the concept of freedom of the press, its development, growth, and status as the centuries changed. If a person believes in a free press, that person should know about the heritage which created it. Much of the information about freedom of the press appears in isolated sources. There are perceptive books that give excellent overviews, but which remain incomplete in showing the centuries' long struggle for freedom of the press. Press Freedoms is based upon information found in more than 2,000 sources including contemporary books, old books, court decisions, special reports, conference reports, lectures, conversations, journals, magazines, newspapers, and special publications.

Press Freedoms would be much too long if the book were truly comprehensive. A more crushing fault could be that it overlooks major episodes, persons, or developments in the freedom of the press story. Sources used conflicting dates, and spellings of names of people, places, and titles. Press Freedoms presents a logical compromise of the information. The work is generally conversational in tone; it might suffer from stuffiness when court decisions are discussed. Readers who have more precise information or additional material can add or subtract to make the account more meaningful.

The Press Freedoms can claim strengths. It focuses an historical perspective on an important aspect of American life. Its extensiveness presents a thoroughness not readily available elsewhere and draws together the elements of a panorama of the growth of the human spirit and mind in a free society. It depicts an epic struggle with courageous heroes and martyrs. The struggle is filled with dramatic impact worthy of long-running television series, great books, and the dedication of Americans to constitutional principles.

Views about freedom of the press are not restricted to those in favor of the concept. This survey includes the enemies and opponents, the in-betweeners, the almost absolutists, the totally absolutists; the entire continuum of viewpoints is explored. The reader will meet heroes and villians, saints and scoundrels, kings and philosophers, and the Eighteenth Century marvelous democratic-republican. The protagonists for freedom of the press, men and women, stubbornly and obdurately persevered in their media, and even sacrificed homes, families, wealth, fingers, hands, arms, ears, noses, tongues, skins, legs, heads, bowels, lives, carcasses, bones, skeletons, and graves to judges, juries, church officials, government officials, mobs, and assorted tyrants. The reader will walk into this carnage and then into the era of enlightenment, public debate, and freedom of speech and press.

The reader can join with the cavalcade walking from savagery through tyranny to democratic government. The trip can be thrilling and provocative. Perhaps a good time to take the trip would be between 1986 and 1991, years during which America celebrates its bicentennial observance of the United States Constitution and of the Bill of Rights, the foundations of the form of government and the method of government of the most enlightened democratic republic the world has known.

2
From Prehistory to the Age of Printing,
500,000 BC through 1499 AD

Humans developed articulate speech by 500,000 BC. Subsequent
systems of recording speech and communication included horns,
smoke signals, knotted cords, notched sticks, paintings, and
ideographs. The oldest pictograph discovered by 1983 and
dating back to 15,000 BC was found in Italy.

A technological and cultural neolithic revolution in
10,000 BC established the beginning stages of what became
modern civilization. Words could be written in Mesopotamia
in 4,000 BC. The Sumerians used pictorial signs and signals
for things, numbering, and even abstract ideas and terms.
The Armeoid Sumerians invented writing in 3,500 BC. They
established schools and the cylinder seal which might be
considered the first form of printing. Cuniform writing
developed in Babylon. The Egyptians developed hieroglyphics,
a picture language, in 3,400 BC and developed papyrus paper
in 2,500 BC. Urukagina, who was king of Lagash, used a
Sumerian word meaning <u>freedom</u> in 2,100 BC. The Minoans had a
script language in Crete in 2,000 BC. The Egyptians
developed an alphabet, which was used from 1,900 to 400 BC.
A phonetic alphabet and lettering existed in Canaan in 1,800
BC. Books existed during the Chang dynasty in China in 1765
BC. Syrians began using a purely phonetic alphabet in 1,600
BC. The Phoenicians, however, developed the first modern-
type alphabet and introduced it in Rome by 800 B.C. The
Olmecs, an Indian civilization, developed a writing system on
Mexico's gulf coast in 1,500 BC. The 600 BC royal library at
Ninevah was one of several established by the Babylonians and
the Assyrians. Ancient Rome had libel laws in its <u>Twelve
Tables</u> in 451 BC.

Euripedes wrote in 409 BC, "This is true liberty when
free born men, having to advise the public, may speak free;
which he who can and will, deserves high praise; who neither

can nor will, may hold his peace; what can be juster in a state than this?"

His characters in his play <u>Ion</u> said:

> <u>Jocasta</u>: Where for exiles lies its sting?

> <u>Polyneices</u>: This most of all -- a curb is on the tongue.

> <u>Jocasta</u>: This is the slave's lot, not to speak one's thought!

> <u>Polyneices</u>: The unwisdom of his rulers must one bear. Of Athen's daughters may my mother be, that by my mother may free speech be mine. The alien who entereth a burg of pure blood, burgher though he be in name, hath not free speech, he bears a bondman's tongue."

Socrates was executed in 399 B.C. by Athens authorities. His unrelenting questioning of popular ideas were believed to encourage young men to disrespect traditional values. The jury asked Socrates to moderate his method; when he refused he was sentenced to drink poison.

> Socrates said:
> "In me you have a stimulating critic, persistently urging you with persuasion and reproaches, persistently testing your opinion and trying to show you that you are really ignorant of what you suppose you know. Daily discussions of the matters about which you hear me conversing is the highest good for men. Life that is not tested by such discussion is not worth living.

> "Men of Athens, I honor and love you; but I shall obey the god rather than you, and while I have life and strength I shall never cease from the practice and teaching of philosophy, exhorting any one whom I meet, after my manner, and convincing him.

> "I tell you that virtue is not obtained by money, but that from virtue come money and every other good of man, public as well as private. This is my teaching, and if this is the doctrine which corrupts the youth, my influence is ruinous indeed.

> "For if you kill me you will not easily find another like me, who, if I may use such a ludicrous figure of speech, am a sort of gadfly, given to the state by the god; and the state is like a great and noble steed, who is tardy in his motions owing to his very size, and requires to be stirred into life. I am that gadfly which the god has given the state, and all day long and in all places am always fastening upon you, arousing and persuading and reproaching you.

> "Some one will say: 'Yes, Socrates, but cannot you hold your tongue; and then you may go into a foreign city and no one will interfere with you?' If I tell you

that this would be disobedience to a divine command, and therefore that I am serious; and if I say again that the greatest good of man is daily to converse about virtue and all that concerning which you hear me examining myself and others, and that the life that is unexamined is not worth living--that you are still less likely to believe."

Plato wrote in 387 BC that "the poet shall compose nothing contrary to the ideas of the lawful, or just, or beautiful, or good, which are allowed in the state; nor shall he be permitted to show his compositions to any private individual until he shall have shown them to the appointed censors and the guardians of the law, and they are satisfied with them." He suggested The Odyssey be expurgated to protect immature minds.

Zeno, leader of the Greek Stoic concept of philosophy, said in 268 BC that natural law is based on a strong belief in an over-riding power of a divine providence. Stoicism proclaimed a universal, unchangeable standard of right and just thought and action. Since it recognized that customs varied from place to place, it contended that two legal systems existed simultaneously. One was the customary law and the other was the natural law. The concept of natural law appeared in many ages and civilizations thereafter.

The ruler of China burned books pertaining to Confucius in 250 BC, and had hundreds of the philosophers' disciples buried alive. This persecution of Confusicianism continued for many years. The Analects written by Confucius were burned. Since Emperor Shih Huang Ti's purpose was to destroy the traditional culture of China, he also burned all other books except those about medicine, agriculture, science, and divinations, which he put in his imperial library.

Callimachus, an Alexandrian poet and librarian, warned in 210 BC symbolically that "a big book is a big evil."

"The office of the Censors was one of the noblest institutions of the ancient Roman Commonwealth; their chief province was to direct and preserve the public discipline and manners, to preside at the Tribunal of Fame, to reward the brave and virtuous with masks of honour and distinction and to brand the degenerate and corrupt with dishonour and ignominy. This institution was of admirable use in maintaining the morals and virtues of the people; and at the same time highly contributed to support the vigour of the laws, and to preserve or restore the Roman Constitution to its first principles."

Walter Mayle thus analyzed the old Roman function of the Censors of 200 BC in An Essay Upon the Constitution of the Roman Government published in 1726.

Writing materials used in various areas included rocks, stones, cliffs, clay tablets, hides, bones, bamboo, silk, wool fibers, old linen, and papyrus. The king of Pergamum had parchment devised when he couldn't get Egyptian papyrus.

During the Han dynasty in China, there was a monthly periodical record called <u>Miscellanies</u>. The Chinese had developed soft paper by 100 BC.

Julius Caesar used his <u>Acta Diurna</u> in 59 BC, which were news bulletins posted in public places in Rome, to expose the malingering of Roman senators who were causing the government to function poorly. This glare of publicity was used to discipline government officials.

Cicero, Roman statesman and writer, believed in 50 BC in a constant, eternal law or "right reason in agreement with natural law."

The <u>Acts of the Apostles</u>, XIX, 19, of about 100 indicates, "Many of them also which used curious arts brought their books together, and burned them before all men." This was later considered religious dictum to burn books. Taticus pointed out in the Second Century that "things forbidden have a secret charm."

The Roman Church forbade Christians in 300 in Carthage to own or circulate the writings of pagans or unbelievers, or of other anti-religious works.

Arius, the presbyter of Alexandria, was condemned in 325 by the Council of Nicea for his <u>Thaleia</u>. Constantine ordered its destruction. This was among the first writing banned by the Catholic Church. Rome made blasphemy and heresy state crimes in 380.

Papyrus paper rolls were largely replaced by vellum and parchment in 400 because such materials could be folded and sewn into books. Printing of pages from blocks of wood was used in many places in Asia beginning in 450. A catalog of prohibited books call <u>The Decretum Gelascanium</u> was issued in Rome in 496.

The Chinese produced a court journal in 500 called the <u>Tsing Pao</u> in Peking. It was distributed to governmental officers throughout the nation to assist in the operation of the empire. <u>Pao</u> is the modern Chinese word for newspaper.

More than 700,000 manuscripts in the library at Alexandria were burned in various attacks by Romans, Christians, and Arabs. In 642, Omar, the Arabian leader, used the burning books to heat bath water. He said, "These books are either in accordance with the teaching of the Koran or they are opposed to it. If in accord, then they are useless since the Koran itself is sufficient, and if in opposition, they are pernicious and must be destroyed."

In Europe, the production of manuscript books and other materials occurred in monastaries from 700 to 1,300.

The first known printed words or text was the printing of one-million copies of dharani, or thanksgiving prayers, ordered by Empress Shokutu of Japan in 767.

Wang Cheih produced in 868 a book, <u>The Diamond Sutra</u>, either from page blocks or movable type. Copies of this Chinese book still exist as the oldest printed book. The soft paper developed in China was supplanted in 900 by hard surface paper produced in Damascus and Samarkand for European use. The T'ang dynasty prohibited witches, wizards, and sorcerers from cheating ignorant people, and meted out punishments for distributors of their writing in 906. Feng Tao, a court official, explained wood block printing to the Chinese emperor in 932, and printing of Chinese documents by this process became widely used.

Al-HaKam, caliph of Cordova, Spain, built a library of 400,000 volumes. His successor, Ibn Abi Amir, destroyed the library in 975 to placate fanatical Islamic sects he was courting for political support. These sects feared books and learning.

Koreans were using movable type made of clay by 1020 and Pi Sheng began using movable type in China in 1041; Marco Polo described similar Chinese printing when he returned to Venice in 1295 from his travels in the Far East. Su Che reported to the Che T'sung emperor that "people of this dynasty make blocks for printing. Many of the books thus produced are circulating there. Ignorant, common people have been printing even obscene literature in order to make a profit. If books were allowed to spread freely to the north, they might either reveal national secrets or arouse the barbarians' contempt and disgust. Either would be bad." The Board of Rites set up censorship procedures and punishments in 1090.

A series of rulings designed to suppress rumors affecting local governments was issued in 1100 as the Medieval Scandalum Magnatum. Its concepts included provisions that a prosecutor had to prove the falsity of any writings that were objected to and that dissemination of any information against the government was a crime. Inventing such information was an even graver criminal offense. "From henceforth none be so hardy to tell or publish any false news or tales, whereby discord or occasion of discord or slander may grow between the King and his people or the Great Men of the Realm."

Europeans printed books from page-size carved wooden blocks in 1245. Chinese playing cards were introduced in Europe and created a revival of learning. Writing and reading had been obliterated when barbarian tribes burned most of the existing vellum books during the Dark Ages.

Pope Innocent IV forbade translating the Bible into vernacular languages in 1252. Thomas Aquinas produced his Summa Theologica in 1273. It presented the philosophy of scholasticism which believed knowledge came from the truths of the Christian faith and the truths of human reason, but the revelation which comes from faith is the greatest and consists of mysteries to be believed rather than understood. Natural law as conceived by Aquinas provided that "man has a right to live as a human person, to perfect his moral nature and to live as a free, intelligent individual. These rights do not depend upon the authority of human government. Laws

3
Legacy of England 9 through 1499

A fiercely independent tribe in northwestern Germany defeated the Roman army commanded by Varus in the battle of Teutoburg forest in 9 AD. These Saxons had developed a society of freedom and equality for each person and fought vigorously to maintain that society. In 209, they and neighboring Germanic tribes formed a nation based on the fierce tradition of freedom and independence.

At a Saxon convention in 460, a major emigration to England was planned since so many Saxons had gone earlier to England to answer a request of the English King to help resist the Scot and Pict invaders from the north. The Saxons soon took over the government, slaughtering many of the natives, and set up a government similar to the tribal one of Saxony with its traditions of freedom and equality. When Augustine began christianizing the English people in 597, he installed rules against heresy and blasphemy.

Charlemagne conquered German Saxony in 785 and subjected the Saxons to harsh controls. Many Saxons emigrated to England or to Transylvania, taking along their traditions of independence, freedom, and equality.

Before the Norman conquest of 1066, an author or spreader of false rumors amongst the people had his tongue cut out. The Salisbury Oath, imposed on the English by William the Conqueror, demanded allegiance to him, and vested absolute sovereignty in the Norman king.

The Magna Carta was issued at Runnymede in June 1215 by King John under military and political pressure by English nobles. It is the primary source of English civil and political liberties. Henry III, successor to King John, promptly reissued the Magna Carta in 1216 with several

monumental Bible, the financier of the firm, John Fust, took a dozen copies to the University of Paris where 10,000 or more students were studying at the Sorbonne. A powerful guild of the book-trade, the Confrerie des Libraries, Relieurs, Enbimineurs, Ecrivains, et Parcheminiers, became alarmed by such a treasure of books. They called the police because they said only the devil could have provided them, and Fust had to run for his life to save the Bibles from a bonfire.

A handbill printed in Strasbourg in 1460 was the first printed advertisement. An enemy sacked the city of Mainz where Gutenberg and his associates worked. They fled and carried the new art of printing to other cities. Johann Mentelin published a German-language Bible.

Berthold Ruppel, who had learned printing from Gutenberg, set up the first press in Switzerland at the University of Basle in 1463. Arnold Panartz and Conrad Schweinheim, two Germans, set up a printing press in Subisco, Italy, in 1464. They developed and used the roman type design for printing in Italy, instead of the germanic text design. The first printing press in Czechoslovakia was set up in Pilsen in 1468. Johann Von Speyer was granted a 5-year privilege to do all the printing in Venice in 1469.

The Sorbonne housed the first printing press in France in 1470. The earliest printed Italian news-sheets appeared in Rome, Bologna, and Trieste. A printing press was set up at Cracow, Poland. There were printing presses in 19 European cities and towns.

Gerardus Leept and Nicholas Kitalaer printed Holland's first books at Utrecht in 1473.

The first printed book in Poland was produced in Cracow in 1474. The first Spanish book, <u>Verses in Praise of the Virgin Mary</u>, appeared in Valencia. The Pope licensed the University of Cologne to censor books in 1475. A German printer set up a press in Austria to produce religious works in 1480. The Spanish Inquisition was used as a means to regulate the press in 1482. Sweden had its first printed books in 1483. King Corvinus Mathias produced <u>Dracola Waida</u> in 1485, which Hungarians claim was the oldest news publication in the world.

The archbishop of Mainz set up a committee in 1486 to examine all books. The Catholic Church required in 1487 all books be approved by the church before publication. Printing unions base their "chapel" organization plan on the procedure involved to obtain the approval.

The first printed advertisement with an illustration appeared in 1491. It advertised <u>The Lovely Melusina</u>, and the illustration showed the heroine in her bath. The Antwerp printer started the cheesecake that still engulfs the world.

A printing press operated in Sinj, Croatia. The archbishop of Treviso set up a legal code demanding church authorization of any book concerning religion. A news sheet

called a <u>relation</u> appeared in Vienna and described the 1493 funeral of Frederick III. Portugal sent printers to the African Congo in 1494 and established printing in its Far East colonies soon thereafter. The archbishop of Mainz threatened excommunication in 1496 to persons publishing unauthorized books.

that are destructive of the natural rights of man or that are destructive of the common good deny natural justice, and therefore are not laws at all." Reading habits changed in the 1,300s from religious and Latin classical authors to law, politics, science, morals, romances, and translations.

Norway had two handwritten newssheets called <u>Cedula Novitatis</u> and <u>Tidende</u> in 1326. Booksellers, copyists, and stationers were dependent upon universities for their books whose content was tightly controlled by the universities in 1342.

<u>De Republica</u> was published in 1366 as the scholastic natural law manual and contained the elements of the natural law of Rome, (<u>Ius Gentium</u> and <u>Ius Naturale</u>) stemming from Stoic philosophers. <u>Ius Gentium</u> imposed on every man the duty to play his allotted part in society, whatever it might be.

Paper use and manufacturing, introduced into Europe from Arabian areas, expanded greatly in the 1400s to make books cheaper and pressure arose for making multiple copies quickly, first from wood cuts or carvings of entire pages and finally from movable metal type. Movable type made from copper was invented in 1400. Newly established universities throughout Europe demanded many more books.

In 1403, King Sejong of Korea said, "To govern, it is necessary to spread knowledge of the laws and the books so as to satisfy reason and to reform men's evil nature; in this way, peace and order may be maintained. Our country is in the East beyond the sea and books from China are scarce. Wood blocks wear out easily and, besides, it is difficult to engrave all the books in the world. I want letters to be made from copper to be used for printing so that more books may be made available. This would produce benefits too extensive to measure." The first book printed from movable type probably was the <u>Sun-tzu-shi-chu</u>, published in Korea in 1409. Lawrence Coster developed printing from movable type in 1446 in Haarlem, Holland, but his invention languished and was soon forgotten. At least fifteen European cities claim to be the birthplace of printing.

Johann Gutenberg perfected and operated a printing press using movable type in Mainz, Germany, in 1450. The first book he printed was <u>The Donatus Latin Grammar</u> in 1451. It was followed by <u>Appeal of Christianity Against the Turks</u> in 1454.

Michael Clapham said in 1957, "A man born in 1453, the year of the fall of Constantinople, could look back from his fiftieth year on a lifetime in which about eight million books had been printed, more perhaps than all the scribes of Europe had produced since Constantine had founded his city in 330 A.D."

Johann Gutenberg printed his famous Bible in 1456, which demonstrated fully the practicality of printing even major works. E.P. Goldschmidt in 1967 reported this legend: When Gutenberg and Schoeffer had finished the last sheet of their alterations.   In 1217 it was again reissued with additional changes.   The final revision of the Magna Carta was completed in 1225.

Roger Bacon was suspected by religious authorities of dealing in the black arts in 1257.   He was ordered not to write anything for publication for ten years.

The first known document written in the English language was Henry III's Oxford Provision in 1258.

Punishing libel began in the statute of Westminster I of 1275.   King Edward I ruled that a person arrested for distributing discordant or slanderous stories would have to identify the originator or go to jail.   Parliament outlawed "any false news or tales whereby discord or occasion of discord or slander may grow between the king and his people or the great men of the realm."

Edward I confirmed the Magna Carta in 1297, which was afterward placed on the great roll of English statutes.   An English medieval society of writers of court hand and text letters was in existence in 1366.   John Wycliffe translated the Bible into English in 1384.

De Scandalis Magnatum law was strengthened in 1388 with a provision for punishing offenders when advised by the Privy Council.

The court hand and textletter writers, along with illuminators, binders, and book sellers, formed a guild in 1404 to provide "good rules and governance."   These people became known as the "Stationers".   English Catholic church leaders prohibited translating the Bible into English in 1408 unless the proposed translation was examined and approved by church authorities.   The Provincial Council took this action because of the Wycliffe heresies in 1382.   The synod of Canterbury in 1408 forbade translating scriptures from one tongue to another.   More than 200 works of Wycliffe were burned in 1410 in the courtyard of a Prague palace.   The synod of Pisa condemned John Wycliffe's works, and they were burned at Oxford in 1412 as heretical.   Parliament confirmed in 1414 that ecclesiastical officials had the right to prosecute writers of heretical books.   The bones of Wycliffe were dug up in 1428 and burned to punish him for the heresy of translating the Bible, and for denying transsubstantiation.

Corsellis, a workman trained by Gutenberg, was said to have set up a printing press at Oxford in 1468.   William Caxton, a servant of the Mercer's Company, set up his press in the Almonry of Westminister Abbey in 1471.

The first English language book printed was The Recuyell of the Histories of Troye, published by Caxton in Bruges in 1474.   Several printers set up presses in England during the next few years, but it took nearly 50 more years before printing became a social force.   One of the earliest books printed by Caxton in 1481, Mirrour of the World, contained the prophetic adage Vox Audita perdit, littera scripta manet

(The spoken word passes away, the written word remains).

England added a provision to the Act of 1484 to encourage foreign printers to import books and come to England to set up printing business. Henry VII appointed Peter Actors in 1485 as stationer to the king as recognition of the value of printing. Actors was empowered to import books from the continent for sale in England. Next year, Henry VII issued a warning against "forged tydings and tales."

England established its Court of Star Chamber in 1487 which used the oath ex-officio to obtain quick convictions. The Star Chamber supplemented the de Scandalis Magnatum law with the Roman laws of injuria and libellous famosis, which treated verbal insults as crimes.

4
Printing in a World of Irreverence, 1500 through 1599

At least 255 European cities had printers in 1500. Twenty-million copies of books had been printed in Europe by 1500.

1501

Pope Alexander VI proclaimed that unlicensed printing would not be permitted, so that publicity would not be given to evil. He set up preventive censorship in Germany.

1502

Printers began producing newsletters in Rhine valley cities. These changed to crude news sheets in Nuremburg, Augsburg, and Cologne. The <u>Newe</u> <u>Zeitung</u> was an early newspaper produced that year.

1505

Erhard Oreglin, an Augsburg printer, put out a news sheet broadside, announcing the discovery of Brazil.

1507

Rumanians set up printing presses in monasteries to produce religious works and histories, but by 1565 the Turkish rulers stopped all printing and enslaved the Rumanians.

1510

The Holy Roman Empire appointed a censor and superintendent of printing, but the plan was never effective.

1513

In Poland, a publication call New Zeitung Auss Litte and Von den Moscowitter (News from Lithuania and concerning the Muscovites) appeared.

Niccolo Machiavelli, author of The Prince, qualified the right of every man to think all things, speak all things, write all things by pointing out that popular governments suffer because the people are free to speak ill of them. He said princes were wise to allow the citizen to have opinions which please the prince.

1515

Pope Leo X ordered censorship applied to all translations from Hebrew, Greek, Arabic, and Chaldaic into Latin and from Latin into vernacular languages, under the bishops or their delegates or by the inquisitores haereticae provitatis. The decree said readers were being sold books which promoted errors in faith and daily life. Even though the Church and its bishops issued many censorship edicts between 1480 and 1515, the invention of printing was believed to have been divinely inspired.

1517

Martin Luther's religious activities and writings launched a religious publishing avalanche. Three separate editions of Luther's Theses were published by printers in three different cities in December. The Theses were known throughout Germany within two weeks and all of Europe within a month. Louise Halborn reported in 1942 that "scholars complained that the whole book market was devoted to books by Luther and his followers and that nobody wished to print anything for the Pope or any material that would offend Luther."

Martin Luther wrote 92 works and these were re-published 220 times in 1518 and 1519.

1520

Pope Leo X denounced the works of Luther as heretical and ordered them burned. Imperial edicts condemned Lutheran tracts in efforts to stop Protestant heresies. Arthur Dicken said in 1968 that "between 1517 and 1520, Luther's publications sold over 300,000 copies. Through printed books and pamphlets Luther was able to reach the minds of Europe. For the first time in history a large reading public judged revolutionary ideas through mass media which used vernacular languages with the arts of the journalist and the cartoonist." Luther described printing as "God's highest and extremist act of grace, whereby the business of the gospel is driven forward."

Pope Leo X issued the bull Contra Errores in an effort to control and censor Martin Luther's publications. Luther showed his disdain for the Pope's order by burning it publicly.

Desiderius Erasmus wrote In Praise of Folly in efforts to reform the Catholic Church. The Inquisition listed him as an author of the second class which meant objectionable material in his humanist writings had to be expurgated by a church censor before they could be read.

1521

Charles V of the Holy Roman Empire in his Edict of Worms prohibited the printing, sale, possession, reading, illustrating, or copying of any of Martin Luther's works. Luther asked the Elector of Saxony to censor works by Andreas Bodenstein von Karlstat, who was more anti-Catholic than Luther. Charles V made church laws about publishing, the law of the state and put the printing press under the control of the Holy Roman Empire. When Luther traveled through Germany to the Diet of Worms, he disdainfully posted the emperor's edicts that all his books be burned.

King Francis directed Parlement to set up a system of control for publishing. Parlement used the faculty of the Sorbonne as the agency to approve publications.

1523

Catholic censors excised the words strange and gentile from a Jewish law code which discussed the prohibition of idolatry. Martin Luther wrote 58 works which were re-published 285 times. The Sorbonne refused to censor books the king wanted censored, and censored books he didn't want censored. Parlement burned Louis de Berquin's books, but the king protected him from Parlement. The king and Parlement also argued about the works of Erasmus. Berguin was tortured in 1528 by the Sorbonne.

1524

Charles V of Belgium issued a list of censored books, relying on church advice as to what books should be prohibited.

1525

The Sorbonne faculty of theology condemned four works by Erasmus, including his Colloquies.

1526

King Francis reasserted his authority over censorship. The Sorbonne's authority wavered and was almost ended by the French Reformation of the 1530's.

1527

Nuremburg censored Erhard Schon's Eyn Wunderlich Weyssagung von dem Babstum for its attack on the Roman Catholic Pope. Officials confiscated 600 copies, required the printer thereafter to obtain approval of works to be printed, and told Schon to retire to his shoe shop. Other works censored in Nuremburg included Lucas Cranach's The

<u>Papal</u> <u>Coat</u> <u>of</u> <u>Arms</u> and <u>Passionale</u> <u>Christ</u> <u>and</u> <u>Anti-Christ</u>.

1530

The Edict of the Diet of Augsburg stiffened censorship rules in the Holy Roman Empire. This led to trickery and falsehoods by many printers. Presses were set up in Serbia by monks to produce religious materials. Neuchatel became a major publishing center for John Calvin and the French Reformation.

1531

An Anabaptist book by Johannes Setzer which was printed in Haguenau, Germany, was seized by the authorities.

1532

French theologians were authorized to inspect books and to ban those containing false doctrine, but Parlement found it necessary to restrain them for being too strict.

1534

Antoine Augereau was burned at the stake for having printed <u>Miroir</u> <u>de</u> <u>l'ame</u> <u>percheresse</u>. Both Catholics and Protestants suppressed publications of the Anabaptists.

1535

The French burned piles of books. King Francis I forbade the printing of any books on pain of death by hanging. But this decree was never enforced.

1539

French authorites would not allow King Henry to print his <u>Great</u> <u>Bible</u> in France. Henry had to have the manuscript smuggled out in hats to get it back to England for printing.

Fray Juan de Zumapraga, first bishop of Mexico, established a press to help convert the Indians, with Juan Pablos as the printer who produced the first of the 37 books he managed before his death in 1560. Giovanni Paoli, an Italian, set up a press in Mexico City under license from the Spanish Government and the Catholic Church. He printed a news sheet about a Guatemalan earthquake in 1541, and produced a religious book in 1543.

1540

Between 1520 and 1540, the Sorbonne had condemned only eleven printed books, and twelve manuscripts, despite religious contentions and fears of heresy.

1542

Denmark's first news sheets appeared. Pope Paul III set up the Congregation of the Holy Office which systematized the banning of books. Although the Sorbonne condemned Francois Rabelais' <u>Pantagruel</u> in 1535, there had been seven editions

produced by 1542. Parlement described what types of books
and manuscripts were unacceptable, and it reaffirmed its
power to ban publishing after John Calvin's Institution
Chretienne was published. The catalog of censored books in
France contained 394 works.

Johann Sleiden, German historian, said, "As if to offer
proof that God had chosen us to accomplish a special mission,
there was invented in our land a marvelous new and subtle
art, the art of printing. This opened German eyes even as it
is now bringing enlightenment to other countries. Each man
became eager for knowledge, not without feeling a sense of
amazement at his former blindness."

1543

The Roman Catholic Church condemned On the Revolution of
the Heavenly Bodies by Copernicus and listed it as a
prohibited book in the Church's Index.

1544

The Church, using advice from university religious
faculties, drew up lists of heretical books. A listing was
issued in Venice and one was produced in Paris. Although the
Sorbonne faculty of theology condemned French language New
Testaments in 1525, one produced by Publisher Jean Lefevre
had issued seventeen editions by 1544.

1545

Even though the French king authorized Francois Rabelais
to print his works, the Sorbonne condemned them. The King
extended the license for them until 1560. Parlement
meanwhile accepted the Sorbonne's list of condemned books,
thus making them illegal in France. Thereafter, edicts were
poorly enforced. Only obscure printers or boy helpers were
arrested or burned at the stake.

1547

Francois Rabelais was listed as a first-class author by
the Inquisition. This meant his books, including Gargantua,
were completely banned.

1548

France banned books from Geneva, but because of this and
other edicts banning books, a large underground distribution
of books developed throughout France.

1550

Spain issued at least 78 press control decrees between
1550 and 1800. Baron Ungnad started a press in Slovenia.

1551

The Edict of Chateaubriant continued the authorization
of French universities to control publishing within their

geographic areas.

1553

Italy burned copied to the Talmud and other Hebrew books because they were supposedly anti-Christian. Ivan the Terrrible, first czar of Russia, set up Russia's first printing press.

1554

The Pope forbade the possession of books in the Hebrew language. The first book printed in Finnish was a prayer book produced by a Stockholm printer.

1559

The Index Librorum Prohibitorum was issued under papal authority. This impeded the circulation of forbidden books if a vigilant bishop insisted, but it failed to prevent the books which it condemned from penetrating areas obedient to Rome.

1560

Burning at the stake for distributing forbidden books did not effect any substantial reduction of that literature. At least 900 different printed news sheets appeared in Switzerland between 1560 and 1587.

1562

The Notized Scritte was printed and sold in Venice for a gazetta coin. Newspapers were called Gazettes thereafter. An anonymous broadsheet called The Pope A Rich Man published in Germany, depicted lechery, drunkeness, and gluttony as vices of the Roman Catholic clergy. It was censored and a book seller was jailed, tortured, and punished for selling it.

1563

An Albanian set up a press in Scutari. The Turks stopped all Albanian printing in 1571. King Charles IX of France required that all books be licensed.

1564

The Roman Catholic Church Index librorum prohibitorum authorized by the Council of Trent listed books which contained religious doctrinal error, or anti-clerical, lascivious, pornographic, political, magic, demonology, and occult arts materials.

1565

Italian avvisi (newsletters) were being printed instead of handwritten by the Italian menati, forerunners of modern journalists.

1566

The French ordinance of Moulins said no one could print, or cause to have printed, any book or treatise without the permission of the king.

1570

Charles V of the Holy Roman Empire issued the Edict of Speyer to forbid printing in out-of-the-way localities.

1571

Pope Pius V forbade the writing of _avvisi_ because he and other church officials had become incensed with the gossip and scandals reported in many of them. It was even illegal to possess a copy of one.

1579

Vindiciae _Contra_ _Tyrannos_, a pamphlet published by the Hugenots, was printed in Edinburgh, Scotland. It proclaimed to its French readers a right to revolt against unjust princes and was widely circulated despite suppression efforts by French authorities.

1584

Niccolo Machiavelli's _The_ _Prince_ was actually printed in London rather than in Italy as purported, and circulated secretly in Europe.

1585

Pope Sextus issued a _bando_ strengthening Pope Pius' earlier rule which was ineffective in controlling _avvisi_. Here is how the _bando_ was enforced in one instance: Hannibal Capello was accused of slander and arrested for an _avviso_ he produced in Pesano. He was brought to Rome and taken to the Bridge of St. Angelo. First, one of his hands was cut off, then his tongue was cut out, then he was hanged because he had been judged "a false _menati_ and had for many years been a detractor of the honor of persons of every kind, and because he kept and exhibited obscene figures in various postures and libidinous acts, in despaire of God and the saints, and because he wrote _avvisi_ to heretic princes." His body and its parts were tossed into the Tiber river. In sixteenth and early seventeenth centuries all _menati_ were regarded as criminals.

1590

Rome and Venice banned publication of prohibited books and nearly bankrupted booksellers and publishers in Venice.

1595

An extensive and well-organized system to evade censorship and to distribute forbidden books provided circulation from London to Cracow to Rome. Many works were printed in Holland and used this international system.

1598

   Hugo Grotius, a Dutch lawyer and statesman, was
sentenced to life imprisonment for his part in pleading for
religious toleration in Holland just after his nation had won
its independence from Spain. While in prison he wrote his
Introduction to Dutch Jurisprudence. His wife managed his
escape by hiding him in a large box that supposedly contained
his research reference books. They escaped in a frantic dash
to France where he entered diplomatic service. He later
wrote his Law of War and Peace, which is the basis for
international law.

5
The Crown as Stern Entrepreneur, 1500 through 1599

William Faques became the first official printer for England in 1504 when he was granted an English royal printing patent. Richard Pyson was appointed royal printer in 1508. Henry VII introduced printing in Scotland in 1507 and the first English copyright was issued in 1510.

1513

An English law prohibited use of William Tyndale's translation or any other annotated Bible in English.

1518

Cum privilegio appeared on the colophon of a book printed in England.

1521

English clergy demonstrated against Martin Luther's books and burned them publicly. Henry VIII published his answer to Martin Luther and won the title "Defender of the Faith."

1524

Bishop Cuthbert Tunstall warned printers and booksellers about penalties for importing books.

1525

The first protest of the Crown's control of the press followed the printing of the first English New Testament. Bishops abolished the Scriptures and other books in English. John Gough, a London printer, was jailed in Fleet prison for such books; all Lutheran books were banned and burned.

William Tyndale's translation of the New Testament was the first to be printed in English. He fussed with the clergy in Gloucestershire and found London just as antagonistic to his idea to make the Bible so understandable that even a plough boy would know more scripture than most clergymen. He went to the continent, finished his translation, was driven from Cologne, but finally had it printed in Worms. It was bitterly opposed by ecclessiastical authorities.

1526

Thomas Berthelet was arrested by church authorites for publishing three harmless works because he had not submitted them for censorship before printing. Under the most comprehensive order yet issued, the Bishop of London and the Archbishop of Canterbury became the sole licensers of all books.

1527

Henry VIII helped circulate Reformation books to set up a ploy in which he would later stamp them out. This was supposed to please the Pope and trick him into granting Henry a divorce from Queen Catherine.

1529

Between 1488 and 1529 at least 200 occasionnels, or news leaflets, had been published. Political leaflets were called canards. Henry VIII, in an effort to fight the rising tide of protantism, established a list of prohibited books, thus establishing the authoritarian concept of press control. His control of foreign printers a year earlier set up England's press controls, which led to licensing next year.

1530

Thomas Hitton was executed in England for selling books by William Tyndale. Richard Bayfield and John Teukesbury, English booksellers, were burned in 1531 at the stake for selling heretical publications. The Supplication of Beggars by Simon Fish was suppressed. Thomas Bilney and James Bainham, English booksellers, were burned in 1532 for reading a prayer book in English and for having English scripture books hidden under floor boards.

1533

King Henry VIII ordered Thomas Cromwell to act against Edward Thwaites' The Nun's Book which told of miraculous cures by Sister Elizabeth Barton. The book criticized Henry's divorce and marriage to Ann Boleyn. Seven hundred copies of the book were destroyed and Sister Elizabeth and five clerics were executed.

1534

Henry VIII established "The King's Proclamation for Seditious Books" which required that no one print an English book without a license from the Privy Council or from a licenser appointed by the king.

1538

Thomas Cromwell produced a new translation of the Bible which was heavily edited to eliminate protestant theology. It was known as the "Great Bible", but its democratic and socialistic tone finally lead to Cromwell's execution.

Henry VIII set up comprehensive regulations of the press with licensing, privilege, and censorship. A proclamation made publishers and possessors of some religious works having "divers heresies and erroneous opinions" liable to punishment. Parliament made Henry VIII's press control rules official English law in 1539.

1540

The Privy Council made arrests for the printing of sheet ballads and broadsides for and against Thomas Cromwell. In 1541, Richard Grafton confessed printing part of the broadsides. He was imprisoned by the Privy Council.

1542

Parliament gave legal power to the Crown to regulate the press and public discussions with abolute authority. Records of the Privy Council show proceedings against individuals for "unfitting words" or seditious utterances. Using or publishing English Bibles was restricted. The Stationers attempted to incorporate under Henry VIII to obtain civic honors, as well as to control scandalous, malicious, schismatical, and heretical printing.

1543

Six printers were finally released from prison where they had been jailed by the Privy Council for printing unlawful books. The council forced 25 printers to pay a bond to assure they would not print forbidden material. The use of the bonds to assure compliance was heavily used thereafter. Printers were imprisoned frequently.

Henry VIII personally inspected and approved his official primer book used in schools and ordered it the only one permitted.

1547

The press control law based upon the Henry VIII proclamation of 1538 was repealed by Edward VI. The repeal had little effect on the king's control of the press. A May proclamation against seditious rumors was the first of several issued by Edward VI. The Treason Act included the words "by printing". English licensing was aimed primarily against papistical books.

1551

The Scottish estates forbade all printing "Unto the Tyme the Samin be sene, vewit and examit by sum wyse and discreit persons." The licensing system provided that no printer print or sell any matter in the English language, nor sell abroad any matter printed in foreign languages unless approved in advance by the crown, upon pain of imprisonment or fine.

1554

The revision of De Scandalus Magnatum added seditious words; even vague or general words could support a common law action if spoken of a magistrate, and truth could not be used as a defense. The statute was administered by the Court of Star Chamber.

1555

A proclamation by Queen Mary commanded "no books, paper, etc., in the name of Martin Luther, John Calvin, Miles Coverdale, Desiderius Erasmus, William Tyndale, etc., or any books containing doctrines against the Catholic faith" be brought into England.

The Stationers Company was incorporated by Queen Mary to provide more supervision and regulations of the press. This agency controlled the printing industry by making it a monopoly. The directors of the company were responsible for any abuses contained in printed materials. Printers organized the company, which was granted a charter by the Crown, but having special royal patents made it possible to ignore the company's rules, as did the universities who claimed they were outside the company's control. Part of the Charter's motivation was to control the spread of heresy, as indicated thus:

> "Know ye that we, considering and manifestly perceiving, that several seditious and heretical books, both in verse and prose, are daily published, stamped and printed by divers scandalous, schismatical, and heretical persons, not only exciting our subjects and liegemen to sedition and disobedience to us, our Crown, and dignity, but also to the renewal and propagating of very great and detestable heresies against the faith and sound Catholic doctrine of holy mother the church."

1558

Christopher Goodman's How Superior Powers Oght to be Obeyd was the chief source of political disobedience theories. One hundred twenty-five years later it was deemed treasonable and burned at Oxford. Queen Mary issued a strong proclamation against heretical books; she used the licensing system to keep Protestants from publishing their views.

1559

Queen Elizabeth reversed Queen Mary's control of Protestants. In her Injunctions, she consolidated her control of the press. She appointed churchmen as licensers, thus assigning control of printing to the Protestant Episcopal Church. As head of the Church, Elizabeth decreed that all new books, pamphlets, plays, ballads, and reprints of works on religion and government had to be approved prior to printing by appropriate officials. Even though licensing was weakly enforced, thirteen printers were fined and imprisoned. The Court of High Commission supplemented the Star Chamber in punishing heresy and sedition.

1566

The Star Chamber issued a decree limiting printers to publishing only the most innocuous material. The Privy Council ordered enforcement of licensing provisions and added heavier penalties; each printer had to help finance the enforcement efforts and had to provide sums of money to guarantee they would observe all rules and regulations controlling printing. The company could search for and seize printing matter, including that on ships. Elizabeth issued a Star Chamber decree authorizing it to punish unlicensed printing since so many secret presses were in operation.

1567

The Stationers investigators caught six people dealing in prohibited Catholic works. John Stow was accused of possessing unlicensed books after a search found unlawful, papist books in 1569.

1570

The Ecclessiastical Court of High Commission handled libel cases. It used a device called the "oath ex-officio" which meant the accused could be imprisoned for contempt or convicted by his required confession. The Licensing Act of Queen Elizabeth required that everything printed had to be submitted to a censor "to stop the Press from publishing anything that might discover the Corruption of the Church or State."

1572

John Field and Thomas Wilcocks were sentenced to a year in jail for sponsoring a Puritan pamphlet pointing out errors in ecclesiastical government. They argued that they wrote it during Parliament time, thus interpreting the right to petition Parliament as an argument for the free press.

1573

Although Queen Elizabeth ordered all Puritan books be brought to the Episcopal bishop of London for destruction, no books were turned in by anyone. John Whitgift published a reply to a second Puritan Admonition written by Thomas Cartwright. The public debate delighted the Puritans, but the government arrested Printer John Strand and his assistants. His presses were destroyed.

1575

Peter Wentworth told the House of Commons that "The liberty of free speech is the only salve to heal all the sores of this common-wealth. There is nothing so necessary for the preservation of the prince and state as free speech."

1576

The Stationers Company adopted an order for the weekly search of London printing houses where printing was concentrated. Pairs of searchers reported on work in progress, the number of orders on hand, the identity of customers, the number of employees, and the wages paid. These searchers were an effective check on extensive bootleg printing.

1577

William Lombarde's proposed establishment of the Governors of the English Print and suggested a 12-member committee instead of the Bishop of London.

1579

Queen Elizabeth became infuriated by a pamphlet discussing her possible marriage. Author John Stubbes had his right hand cut off, but Printer Hugh Singleton was spared even though also sentenced to lose his right hand.

John Wolfe, a fishmonger, set up several secret presses to publish non-political and non-religious books. He refused to agree to the queen's rules saying he would print any lawful book. He insisted upon his liberty to publish and make a living therefrom. The Privy Council jailed him but doing so caused such an uproar that he was released, promoted, and granted publishing privileges. He called himself "The Father of the Book-trade."

1580

Arthur Hall was fined 500 pounds, imprisoned five months, and dismissed from Parliament for publishing a pamphlet criticizing the speaker of the House of Commons.

1583

Stationers company master printers alone had the right to print, and no one could be named a master except through attrition. Twenty-three master printers operated 53 presses.

1584

William Carter was hanged in 1584 after a search of his house found "other naughty papysticall bookes" He had earlier been called a lewd fellow and been imprisoned several times "for printinge of lewde pamphlettes." He was "drawne from Newgate to Tibourne and there hanged, bowelled, and quartered." Carter was hanged for printing Dr. Gregory Martin's <u>A</u> <u>Treatise</u> <u>of</u> <u>Schism</u>, which authorities said would incite women of the court to assassinate Queen Elizabeth.

1586

The 1586 Star Chamber decree gave vast powers of search and seizure to the government, backed printing monopoly, and required the licensing of all books. The Archbishop of Canterbury and the Bishop of London were appointed licensers and all printing had to be done in London or by Cambridge or Oxford universities. The Stationers Company seized unlawful books, and could not elect new printers unless the licensers approved. Severe penalties for violating the rules were stipulated.

Archbishop John Whitgift believed that many scurrilous libels were daily published against the government and the church. The archbishop thought it necessary to have a strict watch to stop any copies going to the press before they had been seen by the bishop of the diocese, or some reverend. He also forbade printing or publishing anything that impinged on doctrine or discipline, or that made any unworthy reflections upon the queen or the state. In spite of this decree, books about religious or political issues, were printed secretly in Britain or smuggled in from abroad.

1588

A printer reported that the bishops handled printers by:

"Daily spoilinge, vesing, molesting, hunting, pursuynge, imprisoninge, yea barringe and locking them up close prisoners in the most unwholesome and ugle prysones, and their deteyninge them, without bringing them to their answeres, untyl the Lord by death put an ende to their myseries. Some they have haled from their honest labours in their trades and caste them loaden handes and feete with boultes and fetters of yron into cold and noysome prysons close prisoners. Some they have cast into the "Little Ease": some they have put into the "Myll" causing them to be beaten with Cudgels in their prysones; others in the nighte tyme they have been apprehended and drawen out of their houses yea separatinge them most ugodbye ffrom their wiefes, laboures to their utter undoinge, and the affanishemente of their poor wiefes and children. All this barbarous havacke they make without regard of age, sexe, estate or Degree as may appeare by the lamentable estate of those which remayne, and by the deathes of others by them murthered in the persons, whose blood cryeth out ffrom under the aulter; some of us have bin kepte prysoners these 19 monethes for hearinge the scripture read unto us in one of our houses uppon a Lordes day mornings in all godly and peaceable maner, neyther have we bin all this tyme once produced to our answere, or had either errour or cryme obieted against us."

1589

A series of anonymous tracts were distributed in England which attacked the bishops of the Church of England. They were signed by "Martin Marprelate". The Privy Council summoned John Udall to answer for the tracts, which he had not written, although he had written criticism of the church and did know who Martin Marprelate was. Udall refused to take the <u>oath ex officio</u> and was jailed. After a farcical trial he was found guilty, but the judges were hestitant to sentence him to death, so they put him in jail for six months, after which he was called up for sentencing again. Sir Walter Raleigh interceded and Udall's sentence was turned over to Whitgift. After two years of imprisonment, Udall was given a pardon by the queen and died soon thereafter from the illnesses he endured while imprisoned. The Puritan printers of the tracts used a secret press which they moved frequently, but they were finally apprehended.

1590

Roger Ward had his presses and type destroyed by the Stationers for printing forbidden religious works for a Reformed Church.

1592

Abell Jeffries was imprisoned for refusing to cooperate with authorites collecting books he had printed. The books were to be burned. The bishop had said "Whosoever wrote books to the defamation of her majesty, and to raise rebellion, doe offende against the statute and are felons. They that wrote for Reformation, make books to diffame the Queen and raise rebellion. Therefore the writers for Reformation offends against this statute, and are felons." A petition to Queen Elizabeth asked that these strict rules be changed, since the actions of the bishops were really the disloyal acts.

1593

John Penry, a Welsh Puritan, was executed for his part in the Marprelate religious tracts which attacked the Presbyterian control system of the church. Penry was probably the chief author of the tracts.

1594

Edward White was fined five shillings for printing a ballad and violating licensing procedures in 1595. Andrew Wyse was fined 40 shillings for twice reprinting a sermon without authorization.

1597

The Stationers Council seized printing materials of Simon Stafford because he had not been admitted as a master printer. Edward Aldee had his type smashed for printing a popish book.

Sir Francis Bacon said that if "libels and licentious discourses against the state became frequent it is a sign of trouble. We make them live longer if we try to stop them -- instead we should correct the cause of the complaints."

Queen Elizabeth removed the deposition scene from William Shakespeare's <u>King Richard II</u> because it concerned royal illegitimacy.

1599

The Archbishop of Canterbury and the Bishop of London ordered the burning of many works, including Christopher Marlowe's translation of Ovid's <u>Elegies</u>. These were probably burned because they had been printed and bound in the volume that contained Sir John Davies' <u>Epigrammes</u>, which satirized contemporary authorities.

6
The Invention of the Newspaper,
1600 through 1643

Persons who published Italian <u>gazettas</u> in 1600 were called <u>menanti</u>; writers of "such base papers intended defamatory reflections." Pope Gregory XIII prohibited these <u>gazettas</u>.

<u>L'Ecole des Filles</u>, a pornographic book, was internationally known and read throughout the Sixteenth and Seventeenth centuries.

The Inquisition tried to destroy copies of a book by Giordino Bruno, which urged worship of a natural god instead of the dogma of Roman Catholcism or of the Protestant Reformation. The Catholics burned Bruno at the stake.

The catalog of the book fair at Frankfurt, Germany, contained 20,000 titles before 1600, more than 35,000 by 1650, and nearly 44,000 between 1650 and 1700.

1603

Earliest known news sheet put out in Germany was a zeitung about the funeral of Emperor Frederick.

1605

Abraham Verhoven obtained a royal privilege to publish news about victories. He produced his <u>Nieuwe Tyding</u> in Antwerp. It became weekly in 1617, and was published three times weekly by 1620. In 1610 a French edition was produced. <u>Mercure de France</u> was the first regular French publication.

1608

The first German newspaper was founded in Wolfenkuttel, Lower Saxony; called <u>Avisa Relation oder Zeitung</u>, it was produced by Johann Carolus. Some reports indicate this first true newspaper might have actually started in Nuremburg, Augsburg, or Brunswick.

1609

Johann Kepler's The New Astronomy was prohibited and placed on the Catholic index of prohibited books.

1610

Switzerland's first regular newspaper began as a weekly in Basle.

1616

Japan developed courtly gossip sheets, complete with sex scandals. These were called yomiuri (newspapers) or Kawarabau (tile sheets) because of the production methods used. The Niuew Tydingen newspaper began in Antwerp, Belgium.

A Catholic Church decree stated Nicholas Copernicus was contrary to scripture and his views were not to be believed or defended. Paolo Antonio Foscarini, head of the Carmelite order, was silenced by the Catholic Church for arguing, in his Carmelite Letters, that Copernicus' views agreed with scripture. Tommaso Campanella was jailed in Naples for his writings, but managed to escape and go to France. His Apologia Pro Galileo was smuggled to Germany and was published by the Rosicrucians.

1617

Nicholas Copernicus' Epitome was placed on the Catholic index of prohibited books. Astronomer Johann Kepler was afraid that Austrian censorship would make it impossible for him to find a printer for his books.

1618

Earliest known copies of printed corantos came from Amsterdam and were produced weekly for 40 years.

1620

The first Austrian regular newspaper was The Ordinari Zeitung.

1621

Andnes de Alma y Mendoza began his Correas de Francia, Flanders, y Alemania in Spain.

A bando generale of the Italian government relaxed the rule against avvisi by allowing written government permission to produce an avviso. If a menanti did not have permission he could be punished by scourging, a heavy fine, and five years in prison. The punishment for libel was death. The relaxation, slight as it was, led to the rise of the professional menati in Italian society, and thus to the profession of journalism.

1624

Olof Olofzson Enaeo was the first publisher in Sweden and produced his Hermes Cynthirus in Strangnas as propaganda for King Gustavus II Adolphus. Sweden's first newspaper was Hermes Gothicus.

1625

Hugo Grotius explained natural law in Protestant terms as serving the maintenance of a social order which had to be consonant with human intelligence and free will of God, "to which beyond all cavil our reason tells us we must render obedience." Grotius reflected deist thought by pointing out that the power of God does not extend over certain things.

1626

Printing began in Ecudor. All printing and publishing were carefully supervised by the government in all Spanish areas. There were at least 140 separate news publications produced by the Dutch by 1626.

1629

The French Code Michaud required submission of two copies of a book prior to publication. One copy was marked up by the censor and returned to the printer for corrections. The other was retained for possible post-publication legal procedures.

1631

Cardinal Duc de Richelieu established the French newspaper, the Gazette de France. His editor, Dr. Theophaste Renaudot, said, "In one thing only will I yield to nobody -- I mean in my endeavor to get at the truth." Renaudot was given the sole privilege to publish news in France. Jean Martin and Louis Vendome started Nouvelles Ordinaires de Divers Endroits as France's first weekly newspaper. The first royal license for printing in Denmark was given to Peter Morsing at the University of Copenhagen.

1632

Galileo Galilei had to defend his support of Copernicus to the Roman Catholic Inquisition. It appeared in his Dialogo, which also was placed in the index of prohibited books. Galileo submitted his book Discourses to the Vatican censor who required him to add a preface indicating the ideas of the book did not advocate the theories proposed earlier by Copernicus. The Church fired the censor and convicted Galileo of heresy but allowed him to recant his views which he did quite willingly. Discourses was on the Vatican's list of prohibited books for at least two centuries, but was widely distributed in countries beyond the control of the Catholic Church.

1633

Rene Descartes stopped work on a cosmological treatise when he heard about Galileo's imprisonment.

1634

Melchoit Matzan and Joachim Moltke acquired the first royal commission to publish news for Denmark in Copenhagen.

1636

Galileo's <u>Discourses</u> could not obtain an Italian imprimatur approval, so it was smuggled to Germany where it was published by the Elseviers in Leiden. Italy's first weekly newspaper began in Florence.

1641

In describing the kingdom of Macaria, Gabriel Plattes said, "The art of printing will so spread knowledge, that the common people, knowing their rights and liberties, will not be governed by the way of oppression and so, little by little, all kingdoms will be like Macaria."

1642

<u>The Gazeta</u> was Portugal's first news sheet after Portugal gained its independence from Spain. But it was suppressed for being untruthful and in bad taste.

7
Schismatism, Puritans, and Levellers, 1600 through 1643

Sir John Hayward was tried for treason in 1600 because Queen Elizabeth objected to his Life of Henry IV. The Bishop of London had the book burned. Hayward was jailed but Sir Francis Bacon interceded to save his life.

In England, censorship turned to indecent or obscene matter as well as political or religious writing. Sir Walter Raleigh said, "Books are written to be read by those who can understand them; their possible effect on those who cannot is a matter of medical rather than literary interest."

John Wolfe couldn't get a London printing license but he printed and sold whatever he wanted until his presses were seized and he was imprisoned.

1601

Queen Elizabeth announced that the Common Law Courts would handle printing patent questions. She revived the powers of ecclesiastical officers and added the authority to fine, imprison, and excommunicate persons deemed guilty of heretical writings or seditious opinions.

1605

In the De Libellis Famosis law, Attorney General Edward Coke and the Star Chamber said that libels made against a private person, and libels made against magistrates or public persons are different in effect because the latter is a greater offense because it concerns not only a breach of the peace, but also the scandal of government.

"For what greater scandal of government can there be

than to have corrupt or wicked magistrates to be
appointed and constituted by the king to govern his
subjects under him?   And greater imputation to the state
cannot be than to suffer such corrupt men to sit in the
sacred seat of justice.   It is not material whether the
libel be true or whether the party against whom it is
made be of good or ill fame, for in a settled state of
government the party grieved ought to complain for every
injury done him in any ordinary course of law, and not
by any means to revenge himself either by the odious
course of libelling or otherwise."

1610

James I promised to appoint commissioners to investigate
"what shall be put to the presses, either concerning our
Authorities Royall, or concerning our government or the lawes
of our Kingdome."   The law-making power of Parliament was
thought limited by the existence of fundamental natural law.

1611

Ecclesiastical courts had complete control of all
printed materials.   King James I ruled, "And also we do give
full authority to inquire and search for all heretical,
schismatical, and seditious books, libels, and writings, and
all other books, pamphlets, and portraitures offensive to the
state or set forth without sufficient and lawful authority,
and to seize and dispose of the presses and books thus
found."

1613

James I assigned jurisdiction to the High Commission
over books, pamphlets, and portraitures offensive to the
state, and of persons producing them.

1614

England regulated location of advertising signs.

Leonard Busher, an obscure Baptist layman in England
wrote, "Even as the chaff before the wind cannot stand, so
error before truth cannot abide."   He told King James I that
"It ought to be lawful for every person or persons, yea, Jews
and Papists, to write, dispute, confer and reason, print or
publish, any matter touching religion, either for or against
whomsoever; always provided they allege no fathers for proof
on any point of religion, but only the holy scriptures."
George Wither was jailed for four months by the Privy Council
for his Abuses Stript and Whipt, even though the licenser had
approved it for publication.

1615

William Martin was forced to remove passages objected to
by the king in Historie and Lives of the Kings of England.

1619

Typical of early "relaciouns" publications was one
produced by Nathaniel Newberry headlined "Newes out of

Holland" concerning Barnevelt and his fellow prisoners; their conspiracy against their "Native Country". These "relaciouns" were replaced by the "corantos" which in turn were replaced by "diurnalls" which in turn yielded to the "mercuries" and the "intelligencers". Each of these were progressive steps leading to the "newspaper".

1620

The first known news sheets or <u>Dutch</u> <u>Corantos</u> in English appeared in Holland. They were printed there by British exile William Brewster who had been driven out of England.

A publisher of an English coranto said, "Custom is so predominant in everything that both the Reader and the Printer of these pamphlets agree in their expectations of Weekly Newes, so that if the Printer have not the werewithall to afford satisfaction, yet will the Reader come and aske every day for new Newes. I can assure you that there is not a line printed nor proposed to your view, but carries the credit of other Originalls, and justifies itself from honest and understanding authority."

1621

News sheets and newsbooks were published in England, but James I tried to suppress both Dutch and English corantos. The first coranto approved by the clerk of the council appeared in England. It bore the inscription "Published by Authority." Thomas Archer published a coranto newspaper in Cornhill, but was arrested for adding material that had not been approved by the licenser.

1622

Oxford authorities burned a book by David Pareus because he advocated that rulers should be called to account for their actions.

1623

George Wither won a printing patent for hymns and church songs, but only after years of efforts and two imprisonments for political allusions in his satirical poetry. He fought with the Stationers in 1625 because they wouldn't sell his songs. He claimed the booksellers had enslaved printers, binders, claspmakers, and authors.

King James I ordered observing the 1586 press control regulation of the Star Chamber after disturbances at the beginning of the thirty-years war. A second proclamation in 1624 re-instated the licensing rules.

William Phillips was jailed for translating a small French pamphlet for printer Nathaniel Newberry; and William Stansby had his presses destroyed for printing a tract for bookseller Nathaniel Butter. Butter was fined in 1624 for printing corantos contrary to order and fined again in 1625 for unfitting speeches.

1625

The House of Commons recommended punishment for Chaplain Richard Montagu for his book <u>An Appeal to Cesare</u> because it offended the Archbishop of Canterbury and encouraged papacy. Bonham Norton and 13 of his associates were fined for reporting that the Lord Keeper had accepted a bribe to keep Robert Barker as the King's printer instead of Norton.

Roger Manwaring, the king's chaplain, was sentenced by Parliament to imprisonment, suspended from the ministry, had his books burned, and had to pay 1,000 pounds for preaching sermons justifying the king's right to levy taxes without Parliament's consent. Although Charles I upheld the sentence, he immediately re-instated Manwaring to the ministry.

Francis Bacon said the invention of printing changed the appearance and the state of the whole world. "We should note the force, effect, and consequences of inventions which are nowhere more conspicuous than in those three which were unknown to the ancients, namely, printing, gun powder, and the compass."

1627

Thomas James, Bodley's librarian, published <u>Index generalis librorum prohibitorium a Pontificibus</u> because he believed it was a recommendation for a library to buy all books condemned by the Pope.

1629

Printers Michael Sparke, Nathaniel Butter, William Jones, and Augustine Matthews were accused of printing four works without license. Sparke, who had been imprisoned, challenged the Star Chamber's legality as "directly intrenching on hereditary liberty and being contrary to the Magna Carta, the Petition of Right, and other statutes." He proposed the firm foundation for freedom of the press which John Milton reiterated ten years later. He was arrested many times, and continued his free press contention; no person of his time waged such a sustained and persistent warfare against regulation of the press.

1630

Physician Alexander Leighton, for his pamphlet entitled <u>An Appeal to the Parliament</u>, or <u>Sion's Plea Against the Prelaige</u> criticizing the English clergy as anti-Christian and satanical, was tried by the Star Chamber and found guilty without being given a chance to appear or speak in his own defense. He was degraded from the ministry, pilloried, whipped, one ear cut off, his nose slit, his face branded, and imprisoned. He escaped for awhile, but the sentence was carried out when he was captured. Its severity infuriated the people. The Long Parliament released him.

Robert Barker, the king's printer, complained that the importation of English Bibles from the continent fostered heresy. Edmond Peacham, was executed for having written a sermon which displeased the authorities even though he never had it published. Nicholas Bourne, James Bowler, and Michael Sparke were arrested for selling controversial pamphlets.

1631

The Archbishop of Canterbury was angered by mistakes made in the 1631 edition of the Bible. Two read "Thou shalt commit adultery" and "The Lord hath shewed us his glory and his great arse." The archbishop said, "I knew the tyme when great care was had about printing, the Bibles especially, good compositors and the best correctors were gotten being grave and learned men, the paper and the letter rare, and faire every way of the beste, but now the paper is nought, the composers boyes, and the correctors unlearned."

1632

William Prynne was fined 5,000 pounds, had his university degrees taken away, and his ears cut off by the Star Chamber and Bishop William Laud for a book which had been passed by the licenser and produced by a registered printer, because Laud and the other judges believed the book contained veiled threats to the crown. Michael Sparke, printer of the book, was fined 500 pounds and had to stand in the pillory. The High Commission had earlier sentenced three men for having false ideas which they blamed on William Prynne, a Puritan. The licenser was fined 50 pounds. Prynne managed to keep up pamphleteering though he was imprisoned for life. One of his ears was cut off at Westminister and the other at Cheapside. The book, Historio Mastrix, had criticized a stage play in a manner considered to cast aspersions on the king and queen.

The Star Chamber prohibited the printing, publishing or selling of gazettes and news pamphlets.

Efforts to license one-page printed pieces began. Earlier news sheets, ballads, and almanacs were published without license.

John Hern's press in Shoreditch was discovered and destroyed, as was one owned by William Harris in the Minorie, on orders of the Court of Assistants of the Stationers Company because they had been installed without permission.

The Spanish ambassador complained to English King Charles I about news books which had offended the Austrian Court. So Charles forbade publication of news from abroad in England. Nicholas Bourne and Nathaniel Butter were suppressed by Charles I who didn't want people to know about reverses on the continent. Charles I ended corantos in England.

1635

A corrector from the king's printing house proposed books be examined before distribution because printers changed the approved manuscripts to insert unlawful views.

John Egerton, a searcher for unlawful books for the crown, took a bribe to keep quiet about an unlawful cache of Bibles. To stop corruption and abuses of searchers, boxes of printed material had to be opened under the licensers' supervision.

1637

When William Laud became Archbishop of Canterbury he had the Star Chamber issue a decree for complete control of printing so he could prevent and punish unauthorized materials. Laud's efforts failed, so in 1637 the Star Chamber issued its most repressive decree to control printing. All books and pamphlets, including title, epistle, proem, preamble, introduction, table, and dedication, had to be licensed. Printers had to deposit 300 pounds as surety not to print anything unlicensed, and only 20 printers were authorized for London. The Star Chamber decreed it unlawful to make, buy, or keep type or presses or to practice printing, publishing, or bookselling without a license from the Company of Stationers. This decree was unpopular and led to the abolishment of the Star Chamber in 1641. The Star Chamber regulations were largely efforts to control Puritan pamphlets. A law was passed limiting what printed materials could be imported into England, and nothing deemed injurious to the church, religion, or the government was allowed to enter the country. These rules generally failed.

Henry Burton, an English Puritan minister, was sentenced to jail by Bishop Laud and the Star Chamber for libelous books against the church hierchy. Parliament released him in 1640.

John Lilburne was arrested on a London street by the Star Chamber which accused him of importing forbidden Puritan books and pamphlets. He was not guilty of the charge, and refused to take the oath ex officio. Lilburne, 20, was accused of importing thousands of illegal books into England from Holland. The Star Chamber sentenced him to pay 500 pounds, be whipped through the streets, stand in the pillory and stay in prison until he would take the oath ex officio. But Lilburne shouted his defiance from the stocks and had his books distributed to the crowd watching him. He was then imprisoned for 30 months without funds or friends.

John Bastwick, Henry Burton, and William Prynne were sentenced by the Star Chamber to pay fines of 5,000 pounds and be degraded from their professions, be pilloried, lose their ears, and be imprisoned for life for their writings. The people turned the public execution of the sentence into a demonstration of sympathy for the three men. Prynne was fined another 5,000 pounds, sentenced to perpetual imprisonment and had his ears shaved off again. In symbolic support people strewed flowers in his path and roared in agony as each ear was shaved. William Laud condemned Puritan writers and praised the king and the Star Chamber in a speech during the trial of the three men. The king ordered the speech printed and distributed, but most people bitterly denounced it.

1638

Nathaniel Butter and Nicholas Bourne were given the privilege of printing corantos. The ancient right of foreign printers to sell books in England was continued until at least 1638.

While in prison John Lilburne produced a report of the trial that put him there. Lilburne became the principal crusader for freedom of the press throughout the Puritan Revolution. He had been convicted of sedition.

1639

The King warned against infamous libels and calumnies against his royal authority, and warned of traitorous intentions of the Scots. But the Scots became more active in distributing materials in defiance of the king and the Star Chamber.

1640

Adrian Vlack, an Amsterdam printer, and many others smuggled books into England in defiance of Star Chamber decrees. Pirated books and anti-bishop books were popular and lucrative.

The Scots descended on London to demand concessions and money from King Charles I. Since he didn't have the money, he summoned Parliament. It set the press free and ended ecclesiastical tyranny. The High Commission Court could no longer seize books or decide on matters about printing. Parliament reversed the convictions of exiles Prynne, Bastwick, and Burton. They returned to England and entered London in triumph. John Lilburne was released immediately from Fleet prison. Lilburne said he was an honest, true-bred, free-born Englishman that never in his life loved a tyrant nor feared an oppressor. Almost all materials published by the English Leveller faction during the 1640's contained a passage condemning censorship and the licensing system, saying that freedom of speech and the press were essential. Parliament was resolved that the press should be free, especially to Puritans, but maybe not to Papists. Parliament ordered many books returned to their owners, and allowed some to be sold to choice persons, but it said some should be burned.

1641

The Long Parliament abolished the Star Chamber and Court of High Commission, which markedly reduced the number of libel prosecutions, but it continued orders for a licensing system for the next two years. John Thomas began publishing parliamentary reports called Diurnal Occurences. Samuel Pecke issued a newsbook entitled Heads of Several Proceedings in both Houses of Parliament on November 29. Its title was soon changed to Diurnal Occurences and later to the Perfect Diurnal. In July, Parliament forbade members giving out notes of proceedings.

Michael Sparke was involved in almost all of the seditious printing of his time and went to jail eleven times. He fought Robert Barker, the king's printer and holder of the lucrative Bible patent, as well as the authority of the church and the crown. John Pocklington published two popish pamphlets which displeased the church. It defrocked him and had the hangmen burn the book. William Bray, who had inadvertently licensed the books, had to preach a recantation sermon.

When Nicholas Bourne, representing the Stationers Company, asked Richard Herne who the publisher was of a "scandalous" pamphlet he was printing, Herne threatened to kill Bourne if he tried to enter the printing establishment.

Committees of the House of Commons on Printing were assigned the duties of prosecuting Archbishop Laud for treason, examining the authority under which he had suppressed books, and examining all abuses in printing. The committees were combined and heard a number of complaints about pamphlets and published sermons, especially those of the royalists and high churchmen. The committee chairman was imprisoned, dismissed, and tossed out of Parliament for printing a collection of speeches about religion. His book was burned. After proceeding against several printers, the committee developed an ordinance passed by the House to control printing. The House printed and distributed reports of its votes to repudiate printers' reports.

In 1642, Thomas Walker, who was in prison already, was tried for printing libels. Several printers were jailed and forced to post surety bonds to obtain release. Richard Herne was jailed but managed to continue publishing pamphlets thereafter. Five mercury women (hawkers of pamphlets) reported they sold the pamphlets for Herne.

Samuel Hartlib said, "The art of printing will so spread knowledge that the common people, knowing their own right and liberties will not be governed by way of oppression."

Publishable news was defined as nothing dishonoring princes even if true. Nothing about English home affairs was permitted. The Stationers Company continued to search out unlicensed printing; for example, they tried to search John Ashton's home for secret presses, but he and his associates fought off the Stationers with swords, guns, and pistols for two hours until they could burn all the contraband printing in the house.

1642

James Boyd wrote a witty pamphlet indicating that writers simply manufactured news when real news was scarce. He said the government was too busy to bother about such news.

Parliament issued a declaration to suppress seditious and scandalous pamphlets aimed at its members; it outlawed all diurnals which ceased publication for awhile, but reappeared in a few months. The House of Commons issued an

order for licensing printing. The House of Lords joined the
House of Commons to erase all of the Star Chamber
proceedings. They even awarded Lilburne 3,000 pounds which
was stolen by bureaucrats. Lilburne continued to defy the
government, including Parliament and Oliver Cromwell.

Newsbooks appeared everywhere and contained
Parliamentary proceedings. Parliament ordered that every
publication had to include the name of the author, because of
false information being published about the civil war. The
Stationers Company was almost destroyed by independent secret
presses.

Henry Walker, once an ironmonger, became England's
funny-man printer. He published nearly 200 things which he
thought could be sold and which would "rend or shake the
piece of either church or state." He evaded one trial for
publishing offensive items by promising to go back to his
iron works. Soon, however, he tossed handfuls of smart aleck
tracts at the king's coach. A rabble from the streets
rescued him from the police so he could spend several
additional months publishing without license or paying any
publishing taxes. He spent this time disguised as a priest
and even conducted mass for St. Mary Magdeline Church. The
king scolded about his libelous pamphlets and he was jailed
in the London Tower. He admitted being guilty of libeling
the king but begged for mercy; the king allowed the
conviction be only a misdemeanor eligible for a light
sentence.

1643

In June, the Ordinance for the Regulations of Printing
was passed by the Long Parliament. This ordinance assured
that the Stationers Company would continue. Religious books
were to be licensed by Presbyterian ministers, minor
publications by the clerks of the Stationers, Parliament
proceedings by each house, and books by the Stationer's
Register. Parliament and the Stationers could search and
seize unlicensed publications and presses with nut, spindle,
and materials. Royalists and non-royalist printers alike
badgered Parliament which found it could not control the
press in 1643.

The Committee dealing with delinquent printers "bunged
up all our mouths at one," according to Samuel Butler.
Samuel Pecke spent several months in Fleet prison for
printing unapproved reports even though he normally was a
careful servant of Parliament. The committee zealously cited
printers for violating rules; nonetheless, the ordinance
proved ineffective. Women found selling pro-Royalist
pamphlets were dragged off to Bridewell prison and whipped.
Sir John Berkenhead published his <u>Mercurius</u> <u>Auclicus</u> to
present the king's side in the gathering civil war.

The Scottish church, disturbed by newspapers, decided
"to attempt some supervision over what might reach the ears
of the people either through the news sheets or by the more
careless methods of the "jade rumour." Parliament was asked
to employ parish ministers to spread news:

"because thruch want of sure and tymous intelligence a
greate pairt of the people are ather left to uncertane
rumoures or flichted by the negligence of common
beareres, or abuseit with malignant imformationes that
thei nather know thair awin danger nor the danger of
religion in the countrey. A solide ordour would be set
down whereby intelligence may goe furth from Edinburgh
to Everie Shyre and so to everie particular pastor that
the people may be informed both of thair danger and
dewtie."

Parliament empowered Henry Walley, clerk to the Company
of Stationers, to be the sole licenser of publication. Thus,
although the Star Chamber was abolished, control of the press
remained in the hands of the government. The Stationers
looked for irregular printers to protect its property rights,
and to help the government suppress seditious publications.
The newsbooks licensed included "Printed according to order"
or "This is licensed and entered according to order."

Henry Robinson, an English merchant said, "No man can
have a natural monopoly of the truth. (Religious opinion
should be) fought out upon eaven ground, on equall termes,
neither side must expect to have greater liberty of speech,
writing, or printing than the other." Reason, and argument
were the only allowable weapons for "Papists, Jewes, Turkes,
Pagans, Hereticks, Infidels, Misbelievers, and all others."
He recommended freedom of speech and press as a logical
extension of the Laissez-faire economic doctrine.

Francis Coles and Francis Leach were jailed for printing
The Continuation of Special and Remarkable Passages Diurnal.
They served three months until they could put up surety bonds
for release. Also jailed were Bernard Alsapp and Thomas
Fawcett who confessed to printing scandalous pamphlets.
Nathaniel Butter was jailed for seditious works.

8
The Milton Legacy, 1644 through 1693

William Walwyn produced The Compassioniate Samaritae in 1644, an anti-printing-regulation pamphlet, before Milton wrote Areogapitica. Walwyn attacked the regulations since they also infringed upon religious liberty.

"No man can have a natural monopoly of truth, and the more freely each man exercises his own gifts in its pursuit, the more truth will be discovered and possessed," was a position by Henry Robinson, another pamphleteer.

Areogapitica was a criticism of the existing law of libel as proclaimed by English court decisions. "To say that the press is free when punishment of publication is certain is to place on trial virtue, honor, and good conduct." John Milton, an English poet and political writer, wrote Areogapitica, which has been considered ever since an eloquent and effective plea for freedom of the press. Actually, Milton had considerable difficulty because of his writing favoring divorce. He had married a 16-year-old girl who could not stand him and ran away for two years. Areogapitica grew out of his fuss over divorce laws.

He was an active proponent of Puritanism and became secretary of foreign tongues during the Commonwealth. He also supervised the licenser of the press. In some reports he appears as a censor; in others, he is said not to have interferred with content. He was arrested but not punished after the restoration in 1660, although he could have been put to death.

In Areogapitica, Milton wrote:

"Truth and understanding are not such wares as to be

monopolized and traded in by tickets and statutes and standards. We must not think to make a staple commodity of all the knowledge in the land, to mark and licence it like our broad cloth and our wool packs. I could recount what I have seen and heard in other countries where this kind of inquisition tyrannizes when I have sat among learned men. That this was it which had dampt the glory of Italian wits; that nothing had bin there written now these many years but flattery and fustian. There it was that I found and visited the famous Galileo grown old a prisoner to the Inquistion for thinking in astronomy otherwise than the Franciscan and Dominican licensers thought. Where there is much desire to learn, there of necessity will be much arguing, much writing, many opinions; for opinion in good men is but knowledge in the making.

Should ye suppress all this flowery crop of knowledge and new light sprung and yet springing daily in this city? Should ye set an oligarchy of twenty ingrossers over it, to bring a famine upon our minds again.

Give me the liberty to know, to utter and to argue freely, according to conscience, above all liberties. And though all the windes of doctrine were let loose to play upon the earth, so Truth be in the field we do injuriously by licencing and prohibiting, to misdoubt her strength. Let her and falsehood grapple. Who ever knew Truth put to the worse in a free and open encounter? Her confuting is the surest and best suppressing. For who knows not that Truth is strong next to the Almighty? She needs no policies, nor stratagems, nor licensings to make her victorious; those are the shifts and defences that error uses against her power; give her but the room and do not bind her when she sleeps."

1651

Milton served as one of Oliver Cromwell's licensers or censors and the works he handled were corantos or newsbooks which were partisan sheets of current news.

1657

Milton wrote in A Treatise of Civil Power in Ecclesiastical Causes that the right of a free and open debate should be reserved to all Protestants including Anabaptists, Socinians, Anglicans, and Puritans, but papists -- the only heretics -- were to be barred from participation.

1660

One of the first actions taken by Charles II after the restoration of the monarchy was to suppress two books written by John Milton.

1673

Milton as late as 1673 was still using Bible authorities

as the standard for truth. In his tract on <u>True Religion,</u>
<u>Heresie, Schism, and Toleration</u>, he insisted that the
Catholic religion could not be tolerated because it was
idolatrous.

1683

Oxford University burned the books written by Milton.

1693

Charles Blount used much of Milton's <u>Areogapitica</u> as the
basis for his pamphlet urging a free press. John Locke in
turn used Blount's work in his demand in Parliament to end
the licensing of the press.

9
England Tries Limited Freedom,
1644 through 1699

The House of Commons Committee of Sequestrations suppressed the sale of pamphlets printed at the king's Oxford headquarters in 1644.

1645

The Parliamentary licensers could not keep up with newsbooks or other printing. Printing was denied to anyone not espousing an exclusive belief in Presbyterianism. The Stationers Company had to expose printers of non-conformist pamphlets. But secret presses produced forbidden books.

Marchamont Nedham, publisher of The Mercurious Britanicus newsbook, was jailed for two weeks for publishing attacks on the House of Lords, the queen, the king, and Sir John Berkenhead (the king's propagandist) who Nedham ridiculed in a false obituary. In 1647 he became disgusted with the Cromwellites and defected to the Royalists. When the king was executed, Nedham was captured and imprisoned, but subsequently was authorized to publish news for the Commonwealth. When the Commonwealth collapsed, he fled to Holland, but managed to obtain a pardon a year later.

Poet John Cleaveland was charged with libel for his satirical condemnation of Parliamentary newsbooks.

John Lilburne produced his A copie of a letter to Mr. William Prynne, Esq. in which he demanded freedom of the press as a privilege of a free-born English subject. Prynne had him arrested and imprisoned in the Tower until 1648. Lilburne continued with other pamphlets and said the Magna Carta was the supreme charter of popular liberty, including liberty of conscience, freedom of the press, and economic justice.

Richard Overton was a Leveller pamphleteerer who supported the natural rights of man concept, popular government, and freedom of the press. He wrote about them while imprisoned at Newgate for supporting and refusing to answer questions about John Lilburne. He urged Parliament to "let the imprisoned presses at Liberty, so that all men's understanding may be more conveniently formed" in a pamphlet which the government declared scandalous. Overton believed the law of God should be translated into the principles of democracy. In a pamphlet he called the licensing system an absurdity.

Archbishop William Laud was found guilty of treason and executed after a 4-year trial. His guilt was partly determined by the testimony of printers and his suppression of books.

John Dillingham was jailed by Parliament for an article critical of the Earl of Essex in Parliament Scout. Richard Royston, a printer, was jailed for vending books from Oxford, a city where Royalist publications were issued.

1646

Petitions were signed by 98,064 persons asking the English government to free John Lilburne. Lawrence Clarkson was banned from England by the House of Commons for his Anabaptist book The Single Eye, All Light, No Darkness, or Light and Darkness One. Abigail Rogers, a mercury woman, refused to name the supplier of pamphlets she was selling. She was jailed but beat the rap because she was pregnant.

Thomas Audley licensed an issue of Mercurious Britannicus in 1645 which contained an article critical of Parliament, which jailed Audley but not the author Marchamont Nedham. In 1946 Nedham sneaked an issue past Audley and was jailed.

1647

The Committee of the Militia of London was assigned the job of suppressing criticism of Parliament. The militia was ordered to investigate George Wharton's Almanac which disturbed government officials. Six people were imprisoned, fined, and placed on life-time good behavior for having published false reports of government proclamations. The ordinance of 1647 was designed to stamp out Royalist publications, especially two newsbooks, Pragmaticus and Elencticus. The Houses of Lords and of Commons Assembled in Parliament passed an ordinance against unlicensed and scandalous pamphlets, and for better regulation of printing.

1648

The printer of Pragmaticus and Parson Hackluyt, author of Melancholicus, mercury newsbooks, were jailed. Friends kept the publications going. Hackluyt escaped and returned to publishing. Parliament call in the militia to control the press since the licensing system had failed.

Sir William Petty, an English physician, proposed that all books be condensed into one set of volumes and that all that was "nice, contentious, and merely fantastical be suppressed and brought into contempt with all men."

Parliament prohibited publication of any of its proceedings unless authorized by one of its Houses. The House of Lords prosecuted several printers until it was abolished. William Walwyn was convicted and jailed for circulating Leveller pamphlets.

1649

Puritans reprinted the Hugenot pamphlet <u>Vindiciae Contra Tyrannos</u> to lead to the revolt that included the execution of King Charles I of Great Britain and set up the Puritan Commonwealth.

The Printing Act of 1649 presented the most detailed list of regulations of the press for the century. Printing was limited to London, Cambridge, Oxford, York, and Finsbury. No house could be rented to a printer nor could any printing equipment be made without notice to the Stationers Company. Scandalous and seditious material was prohibited. All books and pamphlets had to be licensed. All newsbooks were suppressed. The Stationers Company enforced these and other provisions with searches, seizures, fines, and imprisonment. The licensers ignored the views of Parliament and licensed Royalist publications, Leveller publications, the <u>Koran</u>, and even <u>The Man in the Moon</u> attack on Cromwell. Licenser Mabbott resigned in disgust because his name was counterfeited on publications; he believed licensing was being used illegaly and unjustly, because it created a monopoly, and because he believed any person should be allowed to print whatever book he desired.

The army took over the control of printing and deputies of the marshall were authorized to search and seize all unlicensed printing presses with or without the consent of the Stationers Company. The oath of only one witness was sufficient for conviction. Half the fine imposed was awarded the arresting officer and the other half went to the poor of the parish.

The Leveller party petitioned Parliament to revoke all ordinances against free printing, saying:

"by giving freedom to the press and in case any abuse of their authority by scandalous pamphlets, they will never want advocates to vindicate their innocency. And therefore all things duly weighed, to refer all books and pamphlets to the judgment, discretions, or affection of Licensers, or to put the least restraint upon the press, seems altogether inconsistent with the good of the Commonwealth, and expressly opposite and dangerous to the liberties of the people. And if you and your army shall be pleased to look back a little upon affairs you will find you have bin very much strengthened all along by unlicensed printing. That you will precisely hold yourself to the supreme end -- the freedom of the people -- as in other things so as in that necessary and essential part of speaking, writing, printing, and publishing their minds freely without setting of masters, tutors, and controulers over them and for that end to revoke all orders and ordinances to the contrary."

John Lilburne proposed An Agreement of the Free People of England. This plan was heavily used by William of Orange after the Glorious Revolution of 1688.

1650

The government suppressed news books. The Ranters was a group of Englishmen in the 1650s demanding freedom of the press.

The Searchers, or Beagles, looked for unlicensed printing. They included "Parliament Joan, a fifty-year-old fat woman; Smith a tall, thin chapt knave and printer; Holt, who had a trim pair of scratched chaps; Matthews, a cheat; Jack Rudd, a figger-flinger; and John Harris, an actor and printer." Joan Cromwell, the middle-aged woman, was so efficient that Oliver Cromwell and Parliament were able to destroy much Royalist printing.

Lawrence Clarkson spent a month in jail and was banished from England for publishing an impious book call The Single Eye and Mr. Rainborow's Carriages. John Fry was dismissed from Parliament for writing a book which attacked a fellow member and for a second book which was considered a scandalous attack upon the clergy. The Committee for Plundered Ministers brought the action against Fry.

1651

William Bell in a pamphlet said that:

"the most Christian potencies (or Republicks) and Illustrious potentates have thought fit to comprehend the liberty of printing (even as of coyning) within the sphere of their several powers; well perceiving that the eye of understanding might be subject to be deceived by erroneous principles in Print, as may the bodily eye by counterfeit coyne; In regard whereof they propagated wholesome orders and decrees for the regulating of printing and printers; which rightly considered, cannot be defaced nor blemished by the notion of Tyranny."

Not only were authors, printers, and publishers of unlawful books prosecuted, but so were the buyers and readers, until the Printing Act of 1649 expired in 1651.

John Lilburne was fined 7,000 pounds and banished for having been present when a petition had been written about a colliery swindle. The petition author, Joseph Pymatt, also was fined 7,000 pounds and jailed in Fleet Prison.

1652

Presbyterian printers and stationers protested popish and sectarian books with a publication, A Beacon Set on Fire. The printers were called the "Beacon Firers" and wanted a strong licensing system. The Levellers retorted with a publication called Beacons Quenched and became the "Beacon Quenchers." Samuel Chidley, a Leveller, said publications which printed falsehoods should not be permitted. Lodowick Muggleton, a religious fanatic, was given six months in jail for blasphemy for his book Transcendent Spiritual Treatise because it denied the trinity.

1653

Parliament established a new control of printing act which embodied all the regulations of the 1649 Act and resembled earlier Star Chamber decrees. The Council of State was the main agency controlling the press. Printers James Wayte, Robert Hanham, Thomas Locke, Henry Barnes, John Clowes, and Robert Austin were arrested and charged with high treason against Oliver Cromwell.

A printer blamed the government for not suppressing John Lilburne's charges against Oliver Cromwell in a pamphlet entitled Sedition Scourg'd, or A View of the Rascally and Venemous Paper, Entituled A Charge for High Treason Exhibited Against Oliver Cromwell, Esq., for Several Treasons by Him Committed. John Lilburne returned to England and was immediately arrested and placed in the tower. He had supposedly accepted 10,000 pounds from the Duke of Buckingham to destroy the Commonwealth, murder Oliver Cromwell, and restore the monarchy, all within six months. This was to be done by importing publications. The printing licensing system failed again because of Lilburne's defiance and leadership. The Council of State indicted him with a 164-page document. Lilburne fought all tyranny including that of the bishops, the Presbyterians, and Cromwell. He thought himself as championing the rights of common people and as being both a folk hero and a martyr. The Council of State called him the greatest libeler of all; but many others said he was the greatest champion of press freedom.

1655

Oliver Cromwell disregarded criticism aimed toward him and was somewhat tolerant of press attention. He took over as Lord Protector and instituted his own control system of the press; his Council of State became the chief regulation agency. Cromwell suppressed all news books, street hawkers, and mercury women.

John Goodwin's defense of freedom of the press, Fresh Discovery of the High Presbyterian Spirit, indicated that suppression was absurd. His pamphlet was one of the landmarks in the progress of press freedom from governmental control. Goodwin, in reply to the Beacon Firers, said, "The setting of watchmen with authority at the door of the press to keep errors and heresies out of the world is as weak a project and design, as it would be to set a company of armed men about a house to keep darkness out of in the night season.

1656

The Cromwellian government banned "merry books," which were droll, sporty humor containing scandalous, lascivious, and profane matter. Printed ballads, however, were acceptable. The government prohibited the circulation of printed petitions publicly before they had been presented and approved by Parliament.

Giles Calvert was convicted for publishing a merry book and several Quaker publications. The press control managers tried to suppress the Quaker pamphlets but failed. Cromwell ordered the release of seven Quakers from Hosharn Jail where they had been imprisoned for Quaker books.

Sir Henry Vane was imprisoned on the Isle of Wight for making seditious comments in his books which he wrote to help solve England's problems after the government had invited such thought and discussion. His pamphlet Healing Question was considered seditious.

When a plot to kill Oliver Cromwell failed, Colonels Sexby and Titus smuggled in a pamphlet entitled Killing No Murder to carry on the plot against Cromwell. John Stargess was jailed for having copies of the pamphlet and died in the Tower of London. He confessed to the plot and responsibility for the pamphlet.

1657

Cromwell's position was that books or ideas could not be destroyed by punishment or burning. The best way to handle the opposition was to answer their books. Cromwell refused to accept 100 persons elected to be members of Parliament. They produced a pamphlet protesting the action after regular use of the press was denied them. The government confiscated the pamphlets. Henry Muddiman began publishing newsbooks as the official voice of the Council of State, after the Long Parliament had fired Marchamont Nedham as editor of the two official newsbooks of the Protectorate.

1659

John Croope, a member of the Liberty of Conscience Party, spoke vigorously for dissenters to have the freedom to publish their opinions without prosecution during the time of the Protectorate. John Biddle, father of Unitarianism, was prosecuted by the Presbyterian Beacon Firers for his books. He was jailed several times for publishing blasphemous doctrines. He and two printers were imprisoned for publishing A Twofold Catechism which Parliament had declared blasphemous. His books were burned and he was banished to Sicily.

1660

Parliament suppressed all newsbooks but Muddiman's since

he had a three-year monopoly until 1663. John Garfield was imprisoned for writing The Wandering Whore. Answer to Plain English was condemned as a traitorous and fanatic pamphlet by the Council of State, and was suppressed.

For four consecutive weeks from February 21 to March 16, 1660, excepting on Sundays and on one Tuesday, Oliver Williams published A Perfect Diurnal of the Dayly Proceedings in Parliament. It was newsbook size and was the first daily news publication in England.

After the restoration of Charles II occurred, a "patent" system authorizing publication of the news developed. Ultimate control was divided between the crown and Parliament. The press edicts of 1637 were reaffirmed. Appearing in 1660 was a work entitled The London Printers Lamentation or The Press Opprest and Over Prest.

1662

A licensing act specified a printer's code and established a surveyor of the press who could suppress unauthorized publications. It limited the number of printing presses in its efforts to control schismatical, blasphemous, seditious, and treasonable material. Roger L'Estrange wrote Truth and Loyalty Vindicated from the Reproaches and Clamours of Mr. Edward Bagshaw Together with a Further Discovery of the Libeller Himself and His Seditious Confederates. The act for preventing the abuses of printing unlicensed books lasted until 1694. Enforcement included the use of general warrants and surety bonds from printers.

1663

Roger L'Estrange wrote Considerations and Proposals in order to the Regulation of the Press Together with diverse instances of treasonous and seditious pamphlets, proving the necessity thereof. L'Estrange, who was a Tory pamphleteer and licenser of the press, was appointed Surveyor of Imprimery. He inspected printing establishments and strictly enforced the 1662 Licensing Act. He had the monopoly of publishing a newspaper, The Intelligencer, which lasted until 1666.

L'Estrange said:

"Supposing the press in order, the people in their right wits, and news or no news to be the question, a Publick Mercury should never have my vote; because I think it makes the Multitude too Familiar with the Actions and Counsels of their Superiors; too Pragmatical and Censorious, and gives them not only an Itch, but a kind of Colourable Right and License to be meddling with the Government. A paper of quality may be both safe and Expedient; truly if I should say, Necessary, perhaps the case would bear it, for certainly there is not anything, which at this Instant more Imports his Majesty's service and the Publick Than to Redeem the Vulgar from Their Former Mistakes and Delusions, and to preserve them from the like for the time to come. The prudent Menage of

Gazett may contribute in a very high Degree to the Genius, and humor of the common people, whose affections are much more capable of being turned, and wrought upon, by convenient Hints and Touches in the shape and Ayre of a Pamphlet, than by the Strongest Reasons, and best Notions imaginable under any other, and more sober form whatsoever."

The Printing Act of Charles II became known as the Licensing Act. It required that all writing be submitted to an official licenser prior to publication. It was intended to establish a system of control far more comprehensive than a simple censorship. It subjected the whole printing trade to a series of restrictions so severe as to make expansion impossible. Printing was confined to London, Oxford, and Cambridge and no one could set up a printing press anywhere else in England. Master printers were limited to twenty and the number of presses and apprentices allowed was rigidly controlled.

Simon Dover, Thomas Brewster and Nathan Brooks were sentenced to prison and the pillory and fined on the basis of testimony given by L'Estrange. The judge said they would have been executed for treason for publishing seditious pamphlets but for the king's compassion

1664

William Twyn was hanged, drawn and quartered at Tyburn because he would not reveal the name of the author of a book titled A Treatise of the Execution of Justice. The book endorsed the right of revolution and was held to be a threat to the king's life. The trial was reported in An Exact Narrative of the Tryal and Condemnation of John Twyn for Printing and Dispersing of a Treasonable Book. Chief witness against Twyn was Roger L'Estrange.

Benjamin Keach, an Armenian Baptist, was fined, imprisoned, and pilloried in London and his book about infant baptism and criticism of the Church of England was burned.

1665

Henry Muddiman was summoned to Oxford where the court had gone to escape the London plague. He produced The Oxford Gazette. When the plague ended, the newspaper was transferred to London and became The London Gazette, official government newspaper. Under the licensing law, secretaries of state had a monopoly of news until 1688.

1668

John Wickham and Sam Mearne, Stationers Company officials, stole a press belonging to Elizabeth Calvert, but were accused of giving it back to her and of selling unlicensed books for her. Other messengers of the company also were corrupt and frequently took bribes. The company was no longer considered effective by the crown.

1669

Thomas Hobbes's <u>Leviathan</u> was suppressed by the king when the English monarchy was restored. Roger L'Estrange was ordered to arrest those responsible for <u>The Whore's Petition</u>.

1670

A British court drew the first distinction between libel and slander, concluding that libel was the greater evil.

1675

Henry Oldenburg resigned in disgust as licenser. Roger L'Estrange did most of the licensing, but the process became so difficult that other licensers would not serve.

1676

English judges were pronouncing publications as being blasphemous under the law laid down by Sir Matthew Hale, who said:

"That such wicked and blasphemous words were not only an offense to God and religion but a crime against the laws of the state, and government, and therefore punishable in the court; for to say 'Religion is a cheat' is to dissolve all the obligations whereby the civil societies are preserved and Christianity is parcel of the laws of England, and therefore, to reproach the Christian religion is to speak in subversion of the law."

1677

John Donne, son of the poet, complained that many scandalous pamphlets were being attributed to his father but that none of them were written by him. Lodowick Muggleton was sentenced to six months for blasphemy for his book <u>Neck of the Quakers Broken</u>.

1678

Titus Oates, reported a Catholic plot to murder the king. His testimony led to the execution of Edward Coleman, a Catholic writer. The judge who questioned Oates was murdered; newsletters supporting the Popish plot report appeared. The affair was actually concocted by opponents of James II, a Catholic, from becoming king. The newsletters inflamed the nation so much that Charles II dismissed Parliament in 1679. This dismissal ended licensing of the press.

1679

Chief Justice William Scroggs invented the theory that the king had the common law right of licensing and declared it a criminal act to publish without royal consent. A bench of twelve English judges declared it a cardinal offense to publish anything derogatory about the government without a license. Chief Justice Scroggs told the king it was criminal to publish any news without first having obtained a license whether the news was true or false, in praise or in censure. Scroggs said the court had "to take care to prevent and punish the mischiefs of the Press; otherwise the country would be at the mercy of the libels of the Papists, the factions, and the mercenaries."

Charles Blount wrote A Just Vindication of Learning or An Humble Address to the High Court of Parliament in Behalf of the Liberty of the Press. The Stationers Company was reorganized. The first political party papers appeared and supported views about the succession of Charles II. A score of independent newspapers began publishing.

Benjamin Harris was arrested for articles about the Popish Plot in his Appeal from the Country to the City in which the king was openly criticized. Harris was jailed because he had no money to pay the fine, but the Printing Act had expired so he escaped punishment. He then published Triumphs of Justice over Unjust Judges which he dedicated to Justice Scroggs who had sentenced him.

1680

Henry Care was judged guilty of libel for publishing without a permit when he criticized the Pope in his Weekly Paquet of Advice from Rome. He escaped punishment because Parliament was prorogued.

Charles II suppressed all newsbooks to placate the Spanish Court. The House of Commons ordered the clerk to publish an official report of its votes. Elizabeth Cellier was found guilty of scandalous libel for publishing her Malice Defeated, a book celebrating her acquittal of plotting to kidnap the king.

Francis "Old Frank" Smith was a favorite target of Roger L'Estrange, who tricked Smith's arrest and trial by "mean" Judge Scroggs for Tom Ticklefoot, a satire on the trial of Sir George Wakeman. Jane Curtis also was tried for publishing and selling a libel called A Satyr upon Injustice, or Scroggs on Scroggs. When he attempted to suppress the Whig press, Chief Justice William Scroggs was "a wild bull who roared that whoever invented the heretical art of printing should be frying in hell."

1681

Edward Fitz-Harris was executed for high treason for publishing a pamphlet critical of the king, The True Englishman Speaking Plain English in a Letter to a Friend from a Friend. Edmund Hickeingill, rector of All Saints Church in Colchester, was tried for blasphemy for his book The Naked Truth, which criticized the jurisdiction and ritual of the Church of England. Later he said, "No books vend so nimbly as those that are sold (by Stealth, as it were) and want Imprimaturs." William Denton criticized the Catholic Church imprimatur requirement as "stifling books in the womb and injuring truth as a trick to keep the laity ignorant."

An essay on The Tears of the Press said "the tears of the press were but the livery of its guilt. The ink has poison in it. The cure lies not so much in breaking the press but in using it as a battering ram to destroy and overthrow the mighty walls of heresy and error and to communicate wholesome knowledge and science".

Stephen Colledge, a fanatical anti-papist, was executed, drawn, and quartered for threatening the king and riding armed to Oxford where Parliament was meeting. His "scandalous" pamphlets led to his arrest. Joseph Hindmarsh was convicted of blasphemy for printing The Presbyterian Paternoster.

1682

Nathaniel Thompson, publisher; William Pain, writer; and John Farewell, writer, were sentenced to the pillory for letters they published which defended Catholics against murder charges in an episode of the Popish Plot. In addition to having garbage hurled at them, they each had to pay a 100 pound fine.

1683

Oxford University issued a decree authorizing the burning of books by Milton, Goodwin, Baxter, Knox, and Hobbes following the Rye House Plot to kill Charles II. Algernon Sidney was beheaded in 1683 for high treason for writing an unpublished manuscript which stated the king was subject to the laws of God. It was found in his study at his home. Thomas De Laune, a Baptist layman, wrote A Plea for the Non-Conformists. He was arrested, convicted, fined, and the pamphlets burned. He couldn't pay the fine so he, his wife, and two children went to prison where they all died because of its foul conditions.

1686

Samuel Johnson, a clergyman, was convicted of publishing anti-Catholic pamphlets. He was whipped with 317 lashes by the common hangman from Newgate to Tyburn. The Ecclesiastical Commission revoked his clerical status so as not to embarrass the church by whipping a clergyman. In 1689, Parliament declared the sentence, the proceedings, and the commission all illegal and the punishment cruel. Johnson was thereupon given a pension by the king.

1688

James II ordered suppression of seditious and unlicensed books and limited selling to Stationers Company printers. A second order forbade writing, printing, or speaking any false news or meddling with affairs of state. Book vendors were punished for selling the English version of a French book, The School of Venus.

Richard Baxter's book on The Holy Commonwealth was burned at Oxford. Earlier he had spent two years in prison for failure to pay a 500 pound fine assessed in 1865 for his criticism of orthodox Christianity in his A Paraphrase of the New Testament.

The archbishops of Canterbury, St. Asaph's, Ely, Chicester, Bath and Wells, Peterborough, and Bristol were acquitted of publishing a seditious libel. This verdict pushed England's Glorious Revolution forward. The Glorious Revolution in 1688 brought a change in the monarchial institution, which in turn brought more freedom to journalists. English journalists were instrumental in building public opinion which put William and Mary on the throne.

1689

The Bill of Rights joined the Magna Carta and the Petition of Right to form the basis of the unwritten English constitution. After the Glorious Revolution, the crown relinquished its authority governing the press. Although the Bill of Rights in 1689 provided for freedom of speech in Parliament, no mention of freedom of the press was made. The House of Commons ordered the printer of Mr. Duncombe's Case be burned by the hangman. Richard Janeway was arrested for printing a committee action of the House of Commons.

John Selden said:

"A lie will make the circuit of the globe while truth is putting on its boots to follow. Tho some make slight of Libels, yet you may see by them how the wind sits; as take a straw and throw it into the Air, you shall see by that which way the Wind is, which you shall not do by casting up a Stone. More solid things do not show the Complexion of the times so well as Ballads and Libels."

1692

The Society for the Reformation Of Manners was founded to monitor and control the press.

1693

William and Mary extended the 1685 Press Control Law and continued the policies of the Stuart kings and queens in press matters.

Charles Blount, relying on Milton's Areogapitica, produced a pamphlet attacking licensing and arguing for a free press. John Locke relied on Blount's pamphlet for his document asking the House of Commons to end licensing. Blount probably had more to do with ending licensing than did Locke and Milton combined. Through trickery, he even got licenser Edmund Bohun fired. In 1697, Bohun wrote The Diary and Autobiography of Edmund Bohun, Licenser of the Press in the Reign of William and Mary and Subsequently Chief Justice of South Carolina.

William Anderton was hanged for refusing to name the authors of two books considered treasonable. The investigator had to fight off the printer's wife and mother-in-law when he found Anderton's secret press and the books titled <u>Remarks</u> <u>upon</u> <u>the</u> <u>present</u> <u>confederacy</u> <u>and</u> <u>late</u> <u>revolution</u> <u>in</u> <u>England</u> and <u>A</u> <u>French</u> <u>conquest</u> <u>neither</u> <u>desirable</u> <u>nor</u> <u>practicable</u>.

1694

Parliament refused to re-enact the Printing Act. The English common law as declared by the courts prevailed in press and libel law after the Licensing Act expired. In William and Mary's reign the House of Commons did more for liberty than the Magna Carta and the English Bill of Rights; from that time onward, no English government had claimed or practiced the right to license the press. Charles Blount, a diest and republican who had his tracts burned by the hangmen, summarized the Seventeenth Century English thought on the scope of permissible writing. His writings such as <u>Reasons</u> <u>Humbly</u> <u>Offered</u> <u>for</u> <u>the</u> <u>Liberty</u> <u>of</u> <u>Unlicensed</u> <u>Printing</u> in 1693 aided in ending preventative censorship in 1694. John Locke told the House of Commons that there were at least 18 reasons to end government censorship. The House of Lords wanted to renew the Printing Act, but the House of Commons would not agree. Locke objected to government prior censorship because it injured the printing trade, was administratively cumbersome, and was unnecessary because the common law gave adequate protection against licentiousness.

1695

The printing act of 1662 was renewed every two years until 1679, but even then no one had the right to print political news. In 1685 the act was renewed until 1692, but Parliament would not renew it in 1695. The press had been licensed for 157 years in England. Newspapers multiplied and became political party advocates. Strong opposition to these newspapers developed among governing classes. From 1695 until the end of Queen Anne's reign, publishers of domestic news were comparatively free.

1697

The House of Lords reprimanded John Churchill for publishing a report of proceedings and issued an order that reserved such rights to the House only. This order was effective until the end of the 1700s. A London jury condemned John Toland's <u>Christianity</u> <u>not</u> <u>Mysterious;</u> <u>or</u> <u>a</u> <u>Treatise</u> <u>Shewing</u> <u>That</u> <u>There</u> <u>Is</u> <u>Nothing</u> <u>in</u> <u>the</u> <u>Gospel</u> <u>Contrary</u> <u>to</u> <u>Reason</u> <u>Nor</u> <u>Above</u> <u>It</u>, as being blasphemous because it said the mysteries were only nonsense.

1698

Francis Gregory, rector of Hambleden, said in his <u>A</u> <u>Modest</u> <u>Plea</u> <u>for</u> <u>the</u> <u>Due</u> <u>Regulation</u> <u>of</u> <u>the</u> <u>Press</u> that a toleration of all opinions and practices in matters of religion was never thought to be lawful, and consequently such an unlimited liberty of the press, as tends to bring in, and spread errors and heresies, ought not be allowed. This contention was a reply to Matthew Tindal's anonymously published <u>A</u> <u>Letter</u> <u>to</u> <u>a</u> <u>Member</u> <u>of</u> <u>Parliament</u> <u>Shewing</u> <u>That</u> <u>a</u>

<u>Restraint of the Press Is Inconsistent with the Protestant</u>
<u>Religion, and Dangerous to the Liberties of the Nation</u>.
Tindal reproduced Milton's <u>Areogapitica</u> and parts of Charles
Blount's adaptation of it in the 32-page document which
created considerable Parliamentary opposition to licensing
the press.

1699

The Privy Council refused to censor newspapers prior to
publication. Daniel Defoe published a <u>Letter to a Member of</u>
<u>Parliament Shewing the Necessity of Regulating the Press</u>,
"chiefly from the necessity of Publick establishments in
Religion, from the rights and Immunities of a national church
and the trust reposed in the Christian magistrate to protect
and defend them."

John Locke believed the natural state of man provided
absolute independence, freedom, and equality because all men
were ruled only by natural law. Men could judge and punish
those who took these away from him. This concept justified
revolution from the improper application of punishment by the
crown. The purpose of government is the good of mankind.
This concept became the creed of the American revolutionists
in 1776.

10
The Newspaper World Expands,
1644 through 1699

Private news agencies in China during the Ch'ing period printed newspapers in 1644 called <u>Ching pao.</u> This practice continued until at least 1928.

1650

The first daily newspaper was <u>Einkommenden Zeitungen</u> at Leipzeig. It was started by Timotheus Ritzsch.

When Swedish theologians asked the government to condemn local scientists for saying the Baltic Sea shape was changing, the government said that God had made both the Baltic and Genesis. Any contradiction between the two works indicated errors in copies of the Bible, since they had the original Baltic Sea to see.

1656

Warren Chappell in his <u>A Short History of the Printed Word</u> believed the oldest newspaper still existing and being published is the <u>Nieuwe Haarlemsche Courant</u> founded in 1656 as the <u>Weekelyeke Courant.</u>

1660

Antoine Vincent published thousands of copies of the <u>Psalms</u> for non-Catholics. The government jailed many booksellers who soon relocated in other countries and continued publishing there instead of France.

Oslo's postmaster began his <u>Postmaster's Paper.</u>

1661

Spain's first news publication appeared, but it contained news of other nations, rather than Spain.

The first newspaper in Poland was <u>The Merkurguez Polski</u> of Cracow.

The Boaganzas suppressed Portugal's second news sheet and forced Editor Antonio Macedo into exile.

1672

Louis XIV invaded Holland partly because he was disturbed by materials published in Dutch gazettes which he considered libelous. The first magazine was the <u>Mercurie Galant</u> of Paris.

1674

Louis Moceri produced <u>Le Grand Dictionnaire Historique</u> in 1674, which launched the appearance of modern encyclopedias as part of the Age of Enlightenment.

1676

Paolo Sarpi said, "There is no need of books, the world hath too many already, especially since printing was invented; and it is better to forbid a thousand books without cause, than permit one which deserves prohibition."

1677

The K'ang-hsi emperor forbade pornography and dangerous writings.

1685

Pierre Bayle reported that French censors sometimes held up publication of books for as long as five years.

1688

The Dutch published the French language <u>Noveau Journal Universel</u> from 1688 to 1792, while the France called its successful daily newspaper which began in 1777 a journal.

1694

Two men were executed in France for publishing an engraving showing the king and four women who had been his mistresses.

1697

Pierre Bayle produced his <u>Dictionaire Historique and Critique</u> in France. The Catholic Church forced him to revise the second edition to eliminate supposed obscenities.

11
The Colonial Manner,
1619 through 1699

The Virginia House of Burgesses judged Captain Henry Spellman guilty of treasonable words and stripped him of his rank in 1620. Throughout the colonies, hundreds of persons were tracked down by various messengers and magistrates and dragged into legislative houses to make confessions for words or writings which had given offense throughout the 1600s.

The Mayflower Compact was the first document concerning human liberty to be established in the new world.

1622

William Bradford and Plymouth colony checked dissent and seditious practices.

1629

John and Samuel Browne were expelled from Massachusetts by Governor Endicott for their dissent from ecclesiastical pronouncements made in Salem.

1633

Roger Williams had to recant his opinion that the titles to lands taken from the Indians were illegal to the New Plymouth Council.

1635

Roger Williams was brought before the General Court for his views about English churches. His Salem church sent letters to other churches condemning the magistrates. The Salem church leaders were punished; Williams fled to the wilderness to avoid punishment. The Massachusetts legislature, sitting as the General Court, banished Williams for the crime of disseminating "news and dangerous opinions, against the authority of the magistrates."

1637

Thomas Morton published his New English Canaan as part of his effort to have the Privy Council revoke the Massachusetts charters of the Puritans and Pilgrims. He had founded Merry Mount in 1624 as a non-religious and boistrous settlement near Boston, which the Puritans hated and harrassed. After the Puritans lost their charter, Morton returned to Boston and was arrested in 1644 for the book but the Puritans had to let him go.

1639

Joseph Glover died enroute to Boston and his press arrived in the city that year. Several months later Stephen Daye began production on the press in Cambridge. Harvard College had the press set up to produce almanacs, sermons, catechisms, psalters, law books, and broadsides. When a second press was added, a Bible in an Indian language was printed. A book written by Thomas Lochford was submitted for printing in Cambridge, but Thomas Dudley condemned it as dangerous, erroneous, and heretical.

1640

The first book printed in America, commonly called The Bay Psalm Book, was entitled The Psalms in Metre, Faithfully Translated for the Use, Edification, and Comfort of Saints in Publick and Private, especially in New England.

1642

Richard Saltonstall was forced by the Massachusetts Council to apologize and recant his treatise on a proposed Council of Life. Governor John Winthrop believed several passages offensive and unwarranted.

1643

Stephen Daye was arrested in Boston for printing material which displeased the authorities who forced him to post a 100-pound bond not to do so anymore.

1644

Roger Williams wrote The Bloudy Tenent of Persecution, for Cause of Conscience, exempting all matters of conscience, even scandalous doctrines opposing the government, from prosecution except for sedition, or perhaps opinions leading directly to the commission of a crime. Williams, in pleading for toleration, cautioned that "I speak not of scandals against the civil state, which the civil magistrate ought to punish."

1645

A seven-page pamphlet printed at Cambridge was the first effort at news publication in the colonies. It was entitled "A declaration of former passages and proceedings betwixt the English and the Narrowgansets, with their confederates, wherein the grounds and justice of the ensuing warre are opened and cleared. Published by order of the Commissioners for the United Colonies: at Boston the 11 of the sixth month 1645."

1646

Samuel Gorton was tried for blasphemy in Massachusetts, confined at hard labor, and forced to wear heavy irons. If he repeated any of the ideas in his two books, he would be executed. He was banished back to England where he published an expose of his treatment. His book was called Simplicities Defence against Seven Headed Policy.

1647

In Massachusetts, John Wheelwright, Anne Hutchison, a half-dozen or more of their Antinomican followers, Peter Hobart, and others involved in the Hingham affair, Robert Child and his six associates, and Samuel Gorton all were convicted of seditious sermons, petitions, or remonstrances against the civil authority.

1648

In the Cambridge Platform adopted at the third session of a special synod, Massachusetts was authorized to continue restraining offenders from "venting corrupt and pernicious opinions."

1649

The General Court in Massachusetts tried but failed to set up a board of licensers for the press.

1650

James II instructed his governor, Thomas Dongan, of New York, "And for as much as great inconvenience may arise by the liberty within our province of New York, you are to provide by all necessary orders that no person keep any press for printing, nor any book, pamphlet or other matters whatsoever be printed without your special leave and license."

Massachusetts authorities began prosecuting Baptists and Quakers for their tendency to disturb the peace with seditious utterances.

Three members of the Mather family of Boston produced at least 621 written works in the 1650s. Cotton Mather wrote 444 works in seven languages. Many were translated into Indian languages. Jepeosa Mather wrote 102 and Richard Mather wrote 75.

1652

William Pynchon of Springfield had to flee to England to escape punishment from the General Council of Massachusetts for his religious tract, The Meritorious Price of Our Redemption. The authorities considered it "erronyous and hereticall" even though it had been licensed in England. When Sir Henry Vines from England admonished the council not to censure religious views, the council retorted it was its duty under God's will to proceed against such authors for pernicious and dangerous writing.

1654

Henry Dunster, president of Harvard College, was convicted of breaking the peace with his sermon on infant baptism. He was prosecuted under common law process for religious speech. Since he would not retract his statements, the General Council asked for his resignation. Its reasoning was that anyone holding unsound doctrines shouldn't be allowed to teach youths. He sold his printing presses to the College.

The Massachusetts General Court prohibited Quaker books and ordered fines for those who possessed them.

1656

Quakers Mary Fisher and Ann Austin were banished from Massachusetts and the books they owned were seized and burned.

1661

John Eliot, a distinguished Massachusetts leader, was forced to retract statements scandalizing the government. His book, The Christian Commonwealth, which advocated that rulers be elected, was suppressed because the General Court wanted to establish good relations with Charles II.

1662

The Massachusetts legislature set up a licensing law to control the press and censor bothersome religious books that had appeared. Two licensers were appointed to control such publications.

President Henry Dunster and then President Charles Chauncey of Harvard had supervised the Harvard press so closely that formal censorship was unnecessary.

Aggressive Quakers, the royal command for ending religious persecution, and controversy about the Massachusetts synod inspired the General Court to issue rules to censor the press under two licensers -- Daniel Gorkin and Jonathan Mitchell. For a long while the only two printing presses were controlled by Chauncey of Harvard College.

1663

The General Court repealed the press control order and said the press was at liberty in Massachusetts.

1664

For printing of "Irregularities and abuse to the authority of this country, by the printing presse, it is ordered by this court and the authority thereof, that there shall be no printing presse allowed in any towne within this jurisdiction, but in Cambridge, nor shall any person or persons presume to print any copie but the allowance first had and obtayned under the hands of such (persons) as this court shall from tyme to tyme impower." Thus Boston authorities set up a control mechanism for the press, to regulate liberal religious materials that appeared in 1662.

1667

Imitation of Christ, a book by Thomas Kempis, was considered too popish and heretical; consequently, work on the book was stopped, but in 1669 the General Court ordered several revisions for a reprint of the Kempis book.

1668

Marmaduke Johnson and Samuel Green were called before the General Council to prove they had permission to publish books. Green was able to do so, but Johnson had one he couldn't clear and was fined.

1671

Sir William Berkeley, governor of the colony of Virginia, said "I thank God we have not free schools nor printing; and I hope we shall not these hundred years. For learning has brought disobedience and heresy, and sects into the world; and printing has devulged them and libels against the government. God keep us from both."

1674

The Boston General Court, having relaxed its rule about where printing presses could be, appointed additional licensers to evaluate the suitablility of proposed printed materials.

1681

Samuell Seawall was granted a press monopoly in Boston.

1682

John Buckner printed the 1680 laws of Virginia and was required to post a 100 pound bond as a pledge never to print anything again, since he had not obtained Lord Thomas Culpepper's permission to publish the laws.

1683

Lord Effingham was ordered not to allow the use of printing presses in the colonies. Printing was forbidden in Virginia from 1683 to 1729. William Penn presided over a Pennsylvania council meeting when it ordered that the laws of the colony not be printed.

1684

Charles II proclaimed that nothing be printed in New England without the allowance of the governor. But Charles died, and his appointee never served as governor.

1685

William Bradford set up the first printing press in Philadelphia. His first publication was an almanac which was censored in manuscript. He was warned not to print anything but what "shall have lycence from ye Council." The Quaker censor wouldn't let him print a Bible translation, brought him before the governor twice, and censured him three times at Quaker meetings. The council forced him to post a bond for his printing behavoir, and even jailed him.

1686

Benjamin Harris fled from London to Boston after English authorities had confiscated 5,000 copies of English Liberties, a book he had published.

1687

John Wise (known as the first great American democrat) five of his associates, and several other persons were tried and convicted of seditious libel for declaring a tax not levied by the Assembly was contrary to Magna Carta and did not have to be paid.

1689

William Bradford, pioneer printer in Pennsylvania, published an unauthorized anonymous pamphlet in which the writer told settlers about their rights. Governor Blackwell tried to force Bradford to reveal the name of the author, but Bradford refused. He was so harrassed by the government that he went back to England in 1692, and returned a year later to set up printing in New York colony. The material the governor and his Provincial Council objected to was the 8-year-old Charter of Pennsylvania which was thus printed for the first time.

John Coode led the Protestant Association in a revolt against Lord Baltimore's Maryland government, especially because of a law "against all sense, equity, reason, and a law punishing all speeches, practices, and attempts relating to his lordship and government, that shall be thought mutinous and seditious." Among the punishments actually used were "whipping, branding, boreing through the tongue, fine, imprisonment, banishment, or death" making unsafe the words and actions of everyone.

A broadside printer in Boston so disturbed the officials that they issued a warning because "many papers tending to the disturbance of the peace had appeared and that such like papers would be handled with the utmost severity."

Governor Edmund Andros tried to suppress John Winslow for news distribution of William of Orange fighting James II. Andros was dismissed from office, and the General Court again supervised printing in Massachusetts. The legislature issued a stern warning against all unauthorized printing. A news sheet, The Present State of New English Affairs, was published in Boston.

1690

In Boston, Benjamin Harris produced Publick Occurences, the first attempted colonial newspaper. One of the news item concerned atrocities committed by Indian allies of the British. Four days after publication the paper was suppressed. The governor and his council warned that they would "strickly forbide any person or persons for the future to set forth anything in print without license first obtained."

1692

Ben Harris was appointed public printer by Massachusetts Governor William Phipps. Harris printed the acts of the Great and General Court, and of the Assembly. He also printed The New England Primer, a school book. The Cambridge press which originated at Harvard College ceased production after having produced 200 books, pamphlets and broadsides. The Province Charter of 1692 placed control of the press in the hands of the royal governor of Massachusetts until 1730.

William Bradford, first printer in Pennsylvania, became involved in a Quaker dispute. He supported George Keith who was condemned in city meetings but appealed to the General Meeting of Friends; Bradford printed his appeal address which the Quakers judged seditious. Bradford was jailed, but released when the government said the matter was a dispute among Quakers. The frame (or chase) holding the type of the condemned article was brought to court for the jurors to examine. (Bradford had been released from imprisonment by then.) But the jurors couldn't read the backward type. The form was placed perpendicularly so they could see better. One juror poked at the type with his cane; the type spilled to the floor, completely scrambled. Thus, all the evidence was destroyed. Even though Bradford won this way, he left for New York State because the Pennsylvania Quakers disliked him so much. Bradford set up the first printing press in New York in 1693.

1695

Thomas Maule, a Quaker merchant, won a victory for freedom of the press in the American colonies with his book criticizing Massachusetts civil and ecclesiastical authorities. He was imprisoned and disrupted his trial by repeating his charges and saying he was not afraid of the courts since he had been arrested five times and whipped twice. He was kept in jail with high bail. In 1696, he was finally tried and won acquittal with an impassioned and clever plea to the jury, not on free press values, but as a matter of conscience. Massachusetts and the church seized and burned Maule's <u>Truth</u> <u>Held</u> <u>Forth</u> <u>and</u> <u>Maintained</u> as an unauthorized publication.

12
Great Britain Defines Libel,
1700 through 1759

John Erskine argued in 1700 that people seeking to enlighten others, and not intending to mislead, should be able to address the universal reason of a whole nation on what is believed to be true.   Matthew Tindal, England's leading deist, was interested in an unlicensed liberty of the press in religious controversy, and believed freedom of the press was a natural right.

1701

Many newspapers, including The Observer of John Tutchin and the Courant of Samuel Buckley, were cited by the House of Commons for uncomplimentary references to it.   Commons attempted to suppress pamphlets for accusing its members of abominable crimes.

1702

Daniel Defoe devoted his talents to political propaganda.   From the Whigs he obtained government appointments for such service: later he catered to the Torys. He was imprisoned in 1702 for The Shortest Way With Dissenters, and his works were suppressed but he was pardoned in 1703 for helping the Torys. He shifted again to the Whigs after the queen's death.

The English bishops refused to censor John Toland's Vindicious Liberius which the House of Commons considered a pernicious and theistical book.

1703

Charles Devenant, an English political economist, said it was not right nor safe in a free country to restrain the tongues and pens of men to prevent just public censure of private person, but censure of the government and its officers would be intolerable.

The House of Commons prohibited publication of its proceedings. The House had permitted publication of its votes from 1680 to 1703, with brief suspension in 1689 and 1703. The House of Lords ordered one of its officials to publish its votes.

Daniel Defoe wrote A Hymn to the Pillory extolling freedom of the press and proclaimed it an honor to stand in the pillory as did Prynne, Burton, and Bastwick. While he was in the pillory for his Shortest Way with Dissenters, his pamphlet was being sold on the streets. Londoners treated him like a hero as he sat in the pillory by drinking toasts to him and bringing him flowers. On the last day of his sentence, the pillory itself was decorated with plants.

Commons was infuriated by articles in the Flying Post in 1697 and the Observer in 1702 and 1703. When arrested, the Observer printer, publisher, and author absconded in 1703.

Abel Bayer published The Political State of Great Britian, a monthly publication he continued until 1729. His reports of Parliament were delayed until after adjournments so he did not violate publishing prohibitions.

1704

Daniel Defoe started his Review which lasted nine years wherein his editorials were the prototype of contemporary newspaper editorials. Defoe said licensing lent itself to arbitrary actions and bribery. He suggested a law with specific indication of non-publishable items instead of relying on the whims of a magistrate. Defoe's An Essay on the Regulation of the Press said taxing printed news would only encourage newswriters to vent their own opinions and the sum collected would be too small to mention.

Matthew Tindal produced a pamphlet entitled Reasons Against Restraining the Press in which he indicated neither religious nor civil reasons were sufficient to license or restrain the press.

Roger L'Estrange died at the age of 84 after having been associated with printing and newspapering most of his life. He had owned several newspapers and had championed liberty of the press, but as soon as he became licenser he brutally controlled the press as he had proclaimed in the first issue of his Intelligencer which he established as one of his first acts. He had spent six years in prison for his earlier papers, and had been under sentence of death at Newgate prison for four. His plan to destroy liberty of the press included death, mutilation, imprisonment, banishment, corporal pains, disgrace, the pillory, stocks, whipping, carting, standing under the gallows with a rope about the neck at a public execution, wearing some badge of infamy, condemnation to work in the mines, or others. In 1688 he was jailed at Newgate prison for publishing treasonable papers, three years after he had been knighted by James II.

John Tutchin, charged in The Observer, that French gold was bribing national leaders. A jury convicted him of composing and publishing the material but not having written it; however, he was dismissed on a technicality. His works were suppressed, and he died as a debtor in 1707 in the Queen's Bench Prison.

Chief Justice John Holt defined seditious libel thus:

"This is a very strange doctrine to say that it is not a libel reflecting on the government, endeavoring to possess the people that the government is maladministered by corrupt persons. To say that corrupt officers are appointed to administer affairs is certainly a reflection on the government. If people should not be called to account for possessing the people with an ill opinion of the government, no government can subsist. For it is very necessary for all governments that the people should have a good opinion of it. And nothing can be worse to any government than endeavor to procure animosities as to the management of it; this has always been looked upon as a crime, and no government can be safe without it."

The Common Law criminal libel definition meant the press was free of advance censorship, but was subject to subsequent punishment. Judge Holt established the court view that the judge would determine if something was libelous, and the jury would only determine the fact of publication.

1705

James Duke in his Mercurius Politicus about the wide-spread reporting about Parliament in the press said:

"that to have the most weighty and important affairs and the conduct of the Great Council of the Nation canvassed in the public manner, is an invasion of the prerogatives of the Crown and the authority of Parliament, which may prove fatal to 'em both. To answer these views, they meddled with subjects which in strictness ought not to be prostituted in this manner, to the censure and examination of the indiscreet, incompetent rabble."

The Privy Council forced the publisher of the Edinborough Evening Courant to promise to print "nothing concerning the government till first the same be revised by the clerks of Her Majesty's Privy Council."

1707

An Act of Parliament made it high treason to print or write that the Pretender to the Crown or his offspring had a legitimate claim to the crown, or that the queen was not the lawful heir to the crown. The House of Lords arrested several person in London coffee houses for distributing newsletters about its proceedings.

In his _Rehearsal_, Charles Leslie said:

"But the law will not allow private men to asperse and villify those in post and quality, though their accusations were true. For private men are not judges of their superiors. This would confound all government. And the honour and dignity of our governors is to be preserved without which they could not govern, nor would they be obeyed as they ought to be if they were rendered contemptible to their subjects."

Irishman John Asgill was expelled from the Irish Parliament in 1703 and from the English Parliament in 1707 for publishing a heretical book arguing that a person may be translated into eternal life without passing through death. He was nicknamed "Translated." In _An Essay for the Press_, he ignored the law of seditious and blasphemous libel under which he had been censured and his books burned. He believed freedom of the press was the natural right of mankind.

1708

The publisher of _The Fifteen Plagues of a Maidenhead_, was freed from a civil court because obscenity had to be tried in an ecclescastical court. The disappearance of the Privy Council was a great step toward emancipation of the press.

1709

London authorities tried Richard Sare, a London bookseller, and the author of the book, Matthew Tindal, for _Rights of the Christian Church Asserted_.

1710

Sir Robert Walpole said:

"The great licentiousness of the press, in censuring and reflecting upon all parts of the government, has of late been given too just a cause of offence; but when any pamphlets and common libels are matters of complaint; when none but mercenary scribblers, and the hackney pens of a discontented party, are employed to vent their malice, it is fit to leave them to the common course of the law, and to the ordinary proceedings of the court."

The English Revenue Act of 1710 imposed a tax on printed matter. It was aimed primarily at almanacks and calendars.

1711

Queen Anne set up a stamp act to restrain and crush small newspapers. Queen Anne told the House of Commons that "Her majesty finds it necessary to observe, how great license is taken in publishing false and scandalous libels, such as are a reproach to any Government. This evil seems to be grown too strong for the laws now in force. It is therefore recommended to you to find a remedy equal to the mischief." The House of Commons responded to the queen in this statement by Gilbert Dolben: "We are very sensible how much the liberty of the press is abused, by turning it into such a licentiousness as is a just reproach to the nation; since not only false and scandalous libels are printed and published against your Majesty's government, but the most horrid blasphemies against God and religion." The House of Commons attempted to pass a bill to control the press but the House of Lords would not join it.

1712

George Ridpath and William Hurt were jailed in Newgate for printing and publishing the <u>Flying-Post</u>. Ridpath was convicted of three libels published in the paper; in the next year he paid a fine of 600 pounds.

Joseph Addison, a moderate, believed with the Whigs that "there never was a good Government that stood in fear of freedom of speech which is the natural liberty of mankind; nor was ever any administrations afraid of satire but such as deserved it." Addison opposed requiring the identification of authors of even scurrilous works since such law would destroy all learning and "root up the corn and the tares together."

Daniel Defoe did not believe that the 1712 stamp duty on printing would improve news journals and said that taxing any trade so it could not subsist under the payment was not a means to raise money, but to destroy the trade. As a source of revenue the stamp duty would be futile and there is no doubt that the intentions were to suppress the newspaper. The stamp tax was a substitute for the defunct Regulation of Printing Act and was instituted by Queen Anne at the request of ecclesiastic authorities to control license and falsehood in the press. The tax covered newspapers and pamphlets, advertising, and paper, and set up regulation and enforcement provisions. Real purpose of this stamp tax was suppression of the Whig press.

Jonathan Swift wrote:

"Do you know that Grub Street is dead and gone last week? No more ghosts or murders now for love or money. I plied it pretty close the last fortnight and published at least seven penny papers of my own, besides some of other people's; but now every single half sheet pays a half penny to the queen. The <u>Observator</u> is fallen; the <u>Medlays</u> we jumbled together with the <u>Flying Post</u>, the <u>Examiner</u> is deadly sick; the <u>Spectator</u> keeps up and doubles its price; I know not how long it will hold. Have you seen the red stamp the papers are marked with? Methinks the stamping it is worth a half penny."

Henry St. John, who was Viscount Bolingbroke, suppressed the press when in power but became a libertarian and free press advocate to launch political criticism when he established <u>The Craftsman</u>.

Sir Richard Steele, in commenting on the stamp act, said: "This is the day on which many eminent authors will publish their last words."

1713

Printers found so many loop holes in the stamp act that it was largely ignored. Attempts to create a press registration act failed in Commons.

Lord Bolingbroke offered a reward of 100 pounds for the discovery of George Ridpath. William Hurt, the printer, was jailed two years, pilloried, and fined 50 pounds for printing the British Ambassador's Speech to the French King. Publisher Baker escaped prosecution because he was a Tory for a pamphlet about the French Commerce Bill.

Daniel Defoe was accused of treason, but managed only to be convicted of a common law information, and won a pardon so he could write in favor of the French Commerce Bill in his publication, the Mercator.

1715

Daniel Defoe believed in laws against seditious libel and tried to destroy the principal Whig paper (The Flying Post) by trying to get the attorney-general to bring sedition charges against it.

A pamphlet urged that argumentative political papers not be made available to the English populace. "It would be better to cut off the diseased member of the body called liberty of the press, than to infect the whole."

1716

For publishing The Shift Shifted, George and Mary Flint and Isaac and Mary Dalton were convicted as Jacobite sympathizers. Flint managed to escape to France.

1717

John Toland proposed a plan for regulating newspapers to control attacks on the king and villifying his administration, or for defrauding the government by not paying stamp and advertising duties. He proposed several changes to plug loopholes in newspaper tax laws to control seditious and scandalous newspapers, without enroaching on the liberty of the press otherwise.

1718

Richard Steele made most of his money as a political writer and a partisan journalist. The Whigs gave him government positions as a reward after Queen Anne's death.

Thomas Emlyn, Unitarian minister, was sentenced to a year in jail, fined heavily, and put on life probation by a court in Dublin, for publishing An Humble Inquiry into the Scripture Account of Jesus Christ. He wasn't even allowed to speak in his own defense at the trial.

John Matthews, an 18-year-old printer, was hanged for high treason for publishing a pamphlet, <u>Vox</u> <u>Populi</u>, <u>Vox</u> <u>Dei</u>, which said the Pretender to the English throne had a legitimate claim. Two apprentices had tattled on him. When one apprentice died, a huge crowd of printers and editors came to the funeral to insult his body.

1719

Only one of the thirty persons arrested on general warrants for publishing was actually convicted. John Lowden was fined 50 pounds and sent to jail for three months which was considered a light sentence.

James Craggs wrote the English ambassador in Paris that the liberty of the press in England "arises even to a licentiousness, and that we have no redress against the impertinent reasonings of any writer, the law having only provided against false matters of fact."

1720

Lord George Grenville said, "The seditious writers of the present day, who deluge the country with their wicked and blasphemous productions, do not make it a question of whom the government is to be administered by but whether government should exist at all."

John Trenchard and Thomas Gordon writing as "Cato" produced 158 essays between 1720 and 1723 first published in the <u>London</u> <u>Journal</u>, to espouse the libertarian theory of a free press. Their essay "Of Freedom of Speech: That the same is inseparable from Publick Liberty" was especially popular. It said:

"Without Freedom of Thought, there can be no such Thing as Wisdom; and no such Thing as publick Liberty, without Freedom of Speech: Which is the Right of every man, as far as by it he does not controul the Right of another; and this is the only Check which it ought to suffer, the only Bounds which it ought to know.

"This sacred Privilege is so essential to free Government, that the Security of Property; and the Freedom of Speech, always go together; and in those wretched Countries where a Man cannot call his Tongue his own, he can scarce call any Thing else his own. Whoever would overthrow the Liberty of the Nation, must begin by subduing the Freedom of Speech; a Thing terrible to publick Traytors.

"That Men ought to speak well of their Governors, is true, while their Governors deserve to be well spoken of; but to do publick Mischief, without hearing of it, is only Prerogative and Felicity of Tyranny: A free People will be shewing that they are so, by their Freedom of Speech.

"The Administration of Government is nothing else, but the Attendance of the Trustees of the People upon the

Interest and Affairs of the People. And as it the Part
and Business of the People, for whose Sake alone all
publick Matters are, or ought to be, transacted; so it
is the Interest, and ought to be the Ambition, of all
honest Magistrates, to have their Deeds openly examined,
and publickly scanned: Only the wicked Governors of Men
dread what is said of them.

"Misrepresentation of publick Measures is easily
overthrown, by representing publick Measures truly:
when they are honest, they ought to be publickly known,
that they may be publickly commended; but if they be
knavish or pernicious, they ought to be publickly
detested. Freedom of Speech is the great Bulwark of
Liberty; they prosper and die together: And it is the
Terror of Traytors and Oppressors, and a Barrier against
them. It produces excellent Writers, and encourages Men
of fine Genius.

"All Ministers, therefore, who were Oppressors, or
intended to be Oppressors, have been loud in their
Complaints against Freedom of Speech, and the Licence of
the Press; and always restrained, or endeavored to
restrain, both. In consequence of this, they have brow-
beaten Writers, punished them violently, and against
Law, and burnt their Works. By all which they shewed
how much Truth alarmed them, and how much they were at
Enmity with Truth."

1721

The British government suppressed the _True_ _Briton_ and
the _Freeholder's_ _Journal_. Publishers of the _Evening_ _Post_ and
of the _Weekly_ _Journal_ were fined for libel by Commons.

1722

Cato (Trenchard and Gordon) ridiculed government officials

who call:

"every opposition and every attempt to preserve the
People's Rights, by the odious names of Sedition and
Faction; libels rarely foment causeless discontent
against the government; the benefits from what the law
denominated libels, by keeping great men in awe and
checking their behavior, outweigh their mischiefs.
Without freedom of speech and press, there could be
neither Liberty, Property, true Religion, Arts,
Sciences, Learning, or liberty of expression. There may
be a risk in allowing freedom of expression. Let men
talk freely about philosophy, religion, or government,
and they may reason wrongly, irreligiously, or
seditiously; but to restrain their opinions would simply
result in Injustice, Tyranny, and the most stupid
Ignorance. They will know nothing of the Nature of
Government beyond a Servile Submission to Power."

Parliament ordered "no publication of its minutes or
other items, and that the press not intermeddle with debates

or proceedings of either house, or any committee."

1726

The Craftsman in its No. 4 issue of Friday, December 16, said Lord Bolingbroke had this press attitude:

"I must do the persons then in power the justice to own that they generally suffered writings against them to be published with impunity, and contented themselves with applying argument to argument, and answering one piece of wit and satire with another. The only instances of any severity which we meet with, are burning the Bishop of St. Asaph's immortal Preface, and expelling Sir Richard Steele from the House of Commons; but we meet with no grievous imprisonments, no expensive prosecutions or bothersome fines, in the history of that Administration."

The House of Commons attempted to arrest David Jones as author of A New Description of England and Wales with the Adjacent Islands which it believed libelous. But Jones had died, so the publishers and printers were reprimanded and fined.

Anthony Collins, an English diest, believed:

"as it is every man's natural right and duty to think, and judge for himself in a matter of opinion; so he should be allowed freely to profess and publish his opinions and to endeavor, when he judges proper, to convince others of their truth; provided these opinions do not tend to the disturbance of society. Suppressing opinions that differ from one's own only sheds doubt on the opinions of the suppressor."

1727

An English court ruled that Edmund Curll's Venus in the Cloister or The Nun in Her Smock was an obscene book that could be punished as a common law crime and said:

"Destroying morality is destroying the peace of the government, for government is no more than publick order which is morality. My Lord Chief Justice Hale used to say, Christianity is part of the law, and why not morality too?' I do not insist that every immoral act is indictable, such as telling a lie, or the like; but if it is destructive of morality in general, if it does, or may, affect all the King's subjects, it is then an offense of a publick nature."

The king's attorney-general ruled that a thing is offensive against common law if it goes against the constitution or the government, reflects upon religion, or destroys morality. Curll was condemned to the pillory. This conviction established the English civil law misdemeanor of obscene libel.

1728

Twenty-two persons were arrested in London for letters they had written in support of Nathanial Mist and published in Mist's Weekly Journal on August 24.

Robert Raikes, publisher of the Gloucester Journal, and Informant Edward Cave were fined and imprisoned for publishing Parliament proceedings. The next year his printers published a similar item, and Parliament fined a postal clerk and the distributor for the item. Mist's Weekly Journal, No. 175, earned the pillory and six month's jail for three printers and one month's jail for three apprentices for printing reflections on the government.

1729

Thomas Woolston said that the liberty of publication provided the opposition of others which sharpens wit and brightens truth. He was sent to jail for a year for his A Moderator Between an Infidel and an Apostate and his A Defense of the Thundering Legion. Since he had no money to pay his fines, he remained in the English jail until his death in 1733. John Clarke and Robert Knell were jailed and pilloried for publishing A Letter by Amos Dudge criticizing King George II. Joseph Carter and Richard Nutt, apprentices, were jailed for a month and had to wear paper hats depicting their offenses; publisher Nathaniel Mist already was in jail.

A writer told Sir Robert Walpole that "the fall of this one particular instance of liberty will soon be followed by the fall of others. Even if the government should hang or starve all the printers in England, I shall find means to convey ideas to future ages."

John Wickliffe in Middlesex, England, said he was shocked that:

"there should be any men so deaf to Religion and Common Sense, so regardless of the natural rights of mankind as to attempt to break in upon that Liberty which every man ought freely to enjoy, of thinking of himself, and of publishing such thoughts to the World, in all instances where such Publication is not prejudicial to society. I do not write in behalf of infidelity; but I contend for a Liberty for other men to unite in behalf of it, if they think fit."

1730

Robert Nixon was imprisoned for publishing acts passed by Parliament. Edmund Curll was tried for libel for his Ker of Kersland's Memoirs. Nathaniel Mist, publisher of Mist's Weekly Journal, changed the name to Fog's Weekly Journal when the authorities were after him. He escaped to Boulogne and continued his publication for several years. Mist's Journal had a circulation of more than 10,000 in London. He had been arrested several times from 1717 on for objectionable articles.

1731

An indictment for seditious libel was made against Richard Francklin, publisher of The Craftsman, wherein he published "A letter from the Hague" critical of the government's foreign policy. A Bolingbroke partisan wrote a tract condemning the government's practice of stretching phrases to find an innuendo to base sedition charges upon. Francklin was jailed a year for criticizing the treaty in The Craftsman. The Lord Chief Justice would allow the jury to decide only if Francklin were the publisher and if the article referred to the king and his ministers. He was fined 100 pounds and had to post 2,000 pounds for good behavior. He was frequently prosecuted and imprisoned by the courts and Parliament for libel.

1732

The phrase "freedom of the press" became popular and appeared in English courts in 1732 and in Commons in 1738. Reports of the John Peter Zenger trial in New York and republishing Milton's Areogipatica led to this movement.

1733

James Bramston, English playwright, asked, "Can statutes keep the British press in awe, when that sells best, that's most against the law?"

1736

The Privy Council set up rules "to prevent the dispersing of prophane or scandalous Papers, none shall presume to expose to sale any papers or pamphlets (except as are published by authority) until they be seen or approved of by the magistrates or any whom they shall appoint for that purpose, on pain of imprisonment." Actually, the Privy Council was generally ignored and its "thunderings were as the sound of a shot in an empty barrel."

Samuel Buckley, proprietor of the Daily Courant of London, received large rewards for his support of the government. Actual payments to newspapers were recorded under Robert Walpole's administration in the findings of the Secret Committee of 1742.

Henry St. John, Viscount of Bolingbroke, a Jacobite politician, writer and philosopher, contributed to the 18th Century thought used by American revolutionaries. Bolingbroke, in his weekly or every two-week issues of The Craftsman, taunted Robert Walpole's administration with ridicule and denunciation.

The London Magazine said:

"Every subject not only has the right, but is duty bound, to enquire into the publick measures pursued; because by such enquiry he may discover that some of the publick measures tend towards overturning the liberties of his country; and by making such a discovery in time, and acting strenuously according to his station, against them, he may disappoint their affect. This enquiry ought always to be made with freedom and even with jealously."

1737

Robert Nixon was found guilty of ridiculing five acts of Parliament and was sentenced to tour the law courts with a label on his head indicating his offense, fined 200 marks, imprisoned five years, required to post bonds totaling 750 pounds, and put on good behavior until death.

Henry Haines, printer of The Craftsman was jailed for an article comparing King George II with Shakespeare's King John. He was sent to jail for a year, but faced perpetual imprisonment because his employer wouldn't pay a fine for him. The editor of The Craftsman said, "The great benefit of the Liberty of the press consists in the freedom of discussing matters of religion and government, all disputable points, with a proper regard for decency and good manners, though even they ought to give place in case of extremity, to the publick good."

1738

An anti-Whig publication argued that a free press makes it possible for people to vote wisely in selecting officials. This freedom of expression concept was a significant advance in libertarian theory.

The House of Commons ruled:

"that it is an high indignity to, and a notorious breach of the Priviledge of, this House, for any News-Writer, in Letters or Other Papers, or for any printer or publisher to presume to insert in the said Letters or Papers, or to give therein any account of the Debates, or other proceedings of this House or any committee thereof, as well during the recess, as the setting of Parliament; and that this House will proceed with the utmost severity against such offenders."

1739

Samuel Johnson wrote a satirical pamphlet attacking the Robert Walpole government and the Lord Chamberlain thus:

"Let the poets remember, when they appear before the licenser, or his deputy, that they stand at the tribunal from which there is no appeal permitted, and where nothing will so well become them as reverence and submission. A more sure and silent way to control the spread of ideas without a direct attempt on freedom of the press would be to make it a felony to teach children to read without a license from the Lord Chamberlain."

1740

David Hume said a free press would allow the employment of all learning, wit, and genius to foil tyrants. John Hervey probably wrote the statement appearing in London which said, "Freedom of the press was not intended to protect scandal, defamation, falsehood. And to poison minds of mankind with idle thoughts; nor was it intended to teach disrespect and disobedience of the law. The freedom of the press was given to instruct, not to destroy."

1742

Lord Chancellor Hardwicke began the practice of fining and punishing newspaper editors for publishing remarks critical of judges.

1743

When some English religious leaders objected to a woman author as being contrary to God's will, Anne Dutton said, "If it is the duty of women to seek the edification of their brethren and sisters, then it is their duty to use the means of it, whether it be in speaking, writing, or printing."

1746

Edward Cave was fined and reprimanded for reporting Parliament proceedings concerning the treason trial of Lavat. His Gentlemen's Magazine had managed to report Parliament directly at first, then figuratively from 1731 on as its competitor, The London Magazine, did beginning in 1732. The figurative reporting was developed in 1738 when Parliament also forbade reports during times when it was not in session.

1747

Henry Fielding said:

"In a free country the people have a right to complain of any grievance which affects them, and this is the privilege of an Englishman; but surely, to canvass those high and nice points, which move the finest wheels of state, matters merely belonging to the royal prerogative in print, is in the highest degree indecent, and a gross abuse of the liberty of the press."

1748

Horace Walpole said:

"The press is dangerous in a despotic government, but in a free country may be very useful, as long as it is under no correction, for it is of great consequence that the people should be informed of every thing that concerns them; and without printing, such knowledge could not circulate either so easily or so fast. And to argue against any branch of liberty from the ill use that may be made of it, is to argue against liberty itself, since all is capable of being abused."

1750

"Freedom of the Press" became the popular phrase in essays and publications in Ireland as a result of the Charles Lucas trial for seditious and scandalous papers about the House of Commons.

1757

The Stamp tax was made more efficient to help raise revenue for the Seven Years War, but London printers still found ways to evade it.

1758

Samuel Johnson said, "A newspaper writer is a man without virtue, who writes lies at home for his own profit. For mere composition is required neither genius or knowledge, neither industry nor sprightliness; but contempt of shame and indifference to truth are absolutely necessary."

John Shebbeare, an English physician, was sentenced by Lord Mansfield to three years in jail for his Sixth Letter to the People of England because satires of dead kings were punishable. Shebbeare had served a sentence for his novel The Marriage Act, a criticism of Parliament.

1759

Thomas Hayter, Bishop of London, believed freedom of speech was "a hierachy of nonreligious values, a right belonging to and essential to liberty. Printing being only a more extensive and improved kind of speech, freedom of the press was to be cherished because it derived from the Natural Right and Faculty of Speech." Hayter believed even noxious opinions with which he disagreed should not be punished. He believed the benefits of free expression outweighed its mischiefs and should not be sacrificed merely to ward off imaginary dangers to peace and security.

13
Press Freedom in the Colonies,
1700 through 1759

Publication began in 1704 of the first continuous colonial
newspaper, the <u>Boston</u> <u>News-Letter</u>, by Postmaster John
Campbell. Although it bore the statement "Published by
Authority" it still received frequent rebukes from government
officials.

1705

The Virginia House of Burgesses punished ten men for
signing a seditious paper. In 1710 the Burgesses failed in a
search for an anonymous author of a seditious paper.

1715

By the time Governor Joseph Dudley's administration came
to its end, the press was used for partisan politics. The
Massachusetts Council ordered the sheriff to seize all copies
of an anti-Dudley booklet.

1716

The Massachusetts Council ordered William Drummer not to
distribute a political broadside.

1718

John Checkley, a prominent Anglican minister in the
Massachusetts Bay Colony, was prevented from publishing a
tract critical of Calvinism. He refused to take a loyalty
oath and was convicted, fined six pounds, and bound to good
behavior. Later, Checkley went to England and returned to
Boston with copies of his booklet and other materials to
distribute. The court fined him 50 pounds, and the appeals
court added another 50 pounds and ordered him to post 100

more pounds to guarantee good behavior. The courts said his
"sundry, vile insinuations against his majesty's rightfull
and lawfull authority and the Constitution of the Government
of Great Britian consisted of false, seditious, wicked
words."

1719

Until the appointment of Governor William Burnet in 1720
of New York, every colonial governor had been instructed to
allow no press, book, pamphlet, or other printed matter
"without your especial leave and license first obtained."
Massachusetts ended the licensing of the press 24 years after
England did.

1720

John Colman was arrested in Massachusetts for his tract,
The Distressed State of the Town of Boston, because it
"reflected upon the laws of the province and other
proceedings of the government and has a tendency to disturb
the administration of the government as well as the Publick
peace." But Colman was never tried. The attorney general
and the Massachusetts Council refused to prosecute printers
for reporting a controversy between the governor and the
legislature. Samuel Mulford was dismissed from the Assembly
for a speech on unequal representation. He was tried for
publishing the speech but obtained an order from the House of
Lords that ended his prosecution.

1721

James Franklin came to Boston in 1716 with a press and
type. He became printer for the Boston Gazette under
Postmaster Brooker; but seven months later when Phillip
Musgrove became postmaster, Franklin lost his job. Franklin
started his New England Courant which contained little news
or advertising. Instead, its essays attacked the clergy, the
government, and religious writers in severe satire. Out of
resentment and at the urging of his friends who "chafed under
the rules of civil and religious authorities," the Courant,
was not "published with authority." The Courant undertook
the first colonial newspaper crusade by launching a campaign
against small pox innoculations which were being urged by the
Mathers who were the religious and civil leaders of
Massachusetts.

The Mathers attacked Franklin's Courant in the Boston
Gazette, the Boston Newsletter, pamphlets, and broadsides.
Cotton Mather wrote:

"And for a Lamentation to our amazement (notwithstanding
of God's hand against us, in His Visitation of the
Small-Pox in Boston, and the threatening Aspect of the
Wet-Weather) we find a Notorious, Scandalous Paper,
called the Courant, full-freighted with Nonsence,
Unmannerliness, Railery, Prophaneness, Immorality,
Arrogancy, Calumnies, Lyes, Contradictions, and what
noe, all tending to Quarrels and Divisions, and to
Debauch and Corrupt the Minds and Manners of New

England. And what likewise troubles us is, that it
gives Currant amoung the People, that the Practitioners
of Physics in Boston, who excot themsleves in
discovering the evil of Inoculation and its Tendencies
(several of whom we know to be Gentlemen by Birth,
Education, Probity, and Good Manners, that abhors any
ill action) are said esteemed and reputed to be the
Authors of the Flagicious and Wicked Paper; who we hope
will clear themselves of and from the Imputation, else
People will take it for granted, they are a New Club set
up in New England, like to that of Mother England."

Governor Shute asked for censorship authorization from
the General Court. The Council did pass an "Act for
Preventing of Libels and Scandalous Pamphlets and for
Punishing the Authors and Publishers Thereof." But the house
negated this act. Governor Shute dissolved the house and the
General Court, thus the press no longer was subject to any
licensing authority in Massachusetts since no law existed
authorizing licensing.

1722

A society of gentlemen called free thinkers by some, or
the Hell-Fire Club by others, supplied essays for Franklin's
Courant.

Cotton Mather, leader of the Boston establishment, wrote
in his diary that the Courant would require that: "Warnings
are to be given unto the wicked printer, and his accomplices
who every week publish a vile paper to lessen and blacken the
ministers of the town, and render their ministry ineffective.
A wickedness never parallel'd any where upon the face of the
Earth." Dr. Increase Mather said, "Whereas a wicked libel
called the New England Courant has said I support it: I (am)
extremely offended by it." The Council, however, refused at
first to stop the Courant although they did put Franklin on
"good behavior."

In making fun of an effort made by the colonial
government to catch some pirates, the Courant made a negative
reference to Governor Shute that year and James Franklin was
jailed the next day. Ben Franklin's articles began to appear
in the Courant under the name Silence Dogood.

In his eighth Silence Dogood letter, Ben wrote, "Without
Freedom of Thought, there can be no such thing as Wisdom; and
no such thing as Publick Liberty, without Freedom of Speech,
which is the right of every man, as far as by it, he does not
hurt or control the right of another; and this is the only
check it ought to suffer. And the only bounds it ought to
know."

Ben Franklin reprinted at length Cato's essay by
Trenchard and Gordon on "Freedom of Speech" in the New
England Courant. He wrote, "I am a mortal enemy to arbitrary
government and unlimited power. I am naturally very jealous
for the rights and liberties of my country; and the best
appearance of an Incroachment on those invaluable privileges,
is apt to make my blood boil exceedingly."

The Governor of Pennsylvania and his council ordered Andrew Bradford "that he must not for the future presume to publish anything relating to or concerning affairs of this Government, or the government of any of the other of His Majesty's Colonies, without the permission of the Governor or Secretary of this province."

1723

The Boston General Court ordered "That James Franklin be strictly forbidden to print or publish the New England Courant or any pamphlet or paper of the like Nature. Except that it be first supervised, by the Secretary of this Province." James produced one issue in defiance of the order, but a grand jury refused to indict him. To get around the order, Franklin substituted his brother Ben's name as editor of the paper. James Franklin later continued publishing for another three years. Benjamin Franklin deserted James since he knew James couldn't reveal his violation of the courts' orders which included falsely using Ben's name as editor. Ben went south to New York and ultimately to Philadelphia. Thus, Ben escaped his indentured status to his older brother.

Andrew Bradford, despite an earlier order by the governor of Pennsylvania, criticized Massachusetts authorities for their actions against James Franklin, calling them bigots, hypocrites, and tyrants.

1724

Passage of a Massachusetts Stamp Act made the first distinction between a newspaper and a pamphlet. This act temporarily taxed the Boston Gazette out of business.

1725

The Massachusetts Council instructed newsletters or papers no longer use the phrases "published by authority" in their publication, as the Council repudiated any official responsibility for the content of the press.

1726

Edward Elwall, a Sabbatarian, won acquittal from a blasphemy charge against his A True Testimony for God, a defense of Unitarianism.

Governor Alexander Spotswood of Virginia threatened execution or loss of an arm or leg for disseminators of seditious principles or other insinuations tending to disturb the peace.

John Checkley, a Boston bookseller, was prosecuted for publishing and selling a pamphlet, A Short and Easie Method with the Deists, which was called a false, scandalous libel. He was convicted, lost an appeal and paid fines before being released. His lawyer, John Read, presented a defense of the jury's right to decide the whole matter of such a libel, predating Fox's libel law of 1742.

1728

Andrew Bradford was jailed for wicked and seditious libel partly due to an examination by Andrew Hamilton, who was Zenger's lawyer in the famous New York trial.

American colonials read a pamphlet (reprinted in colonial publications) by William Penn titled The Peoples' Ancient and Just Liberties, Asserted, in the Trial of William Penn and William Mead at the Old Baily, 22 Charles II, 1670, Written by Themselves. The account was a somewhat jocular review of the effort of an English court to jail Penn for preaching a Quaker sermon on a London street. The pamphlet did much to convince the colonials that freedom of religion and freedom of speech were highly desirable.

By 1728, Cato's Letters by Gordon and Trenchard had fused with Locke, Coke, Pufendorf, and Grotius to produce an American treatise in defense of English liberties overseas.

1731

Ben Franklin became a significant figure in fighting for freedom of the press. In 1731, he wrote "An Apology for Printers." Franklin said that the opinions of men are quite variable and the business of printing deals chiefly with these opinions, offending some and pleasing others. He said printers realize that equal space perhaps should be provided for both sides in a dispute." Since printers tend to conform to this plan, it is not the fault of the press that some are offended. If a printer were to publish only things that would please everybody, very little would be published. When men differ in opinion, both sides ought equally to have the advantage of being heard by the publick; when truth and error have fair play, the former is always an overmatch for the latter." He remarked that unless a person is in the printer's position, he can hardly be critical of the way the printer handles his own job. He published Cato's essay on "Freedom of Speech" in his Pennsylvania Gazette.

1733

John Peter Zenger began his Journal which published articles written by several person who attacked government measures. Zenger was arrested in 1734, imprisoned for several months, and tried for libelous publications. The court set bail so high that he could not leave prison. Zenger and William Bradford were the only printers in New York and for a long time carried on a paper war against each other. Bradford condemned Zenger for publishing "pieces tending to set a province aflame, and to raise sedition and tumults" when Zenger was accused of seditious libel.

1734

In November, Andrew Bradford defined freedom of the press as "a liberty for every Man to communicate his sentiments freely to the Public, upon political or religious points." Freely in the case, meant without fear of being punished.

In April of 1734, Ben Franklin said liberty of the press does not mean being able to expose a person's private life, religion, or morality, or the conduct of political figures unless the conduct was off-color. He defined liberty to communicate to the public his sentiments, of proposing laws, or detecting "shady" politics. Franklin considered liberty of the press his greatest liberty.

James Alexander, New York attorney, said:

"It is indeed urged that the liberty of the press ought not be restrained because not only the action of evil ministers may be exposed but the character of good ones traduced. Admit it in the strongest light that calumny and lies would prevail and blast the character of a great and good minister; yet that is a less evil than the advantages we reap from the liberty of the press, as it is a curb, a bridle, a terror, a shame, and restraint to evil ministers; and it may be the only punishment, especially for a time."

1735

James Alexander, a strong Colonial disciple of the English Cato, was an editor of Zenger's New York Weekly Journal, which was one of the first politically independent newspapers in America. Much of the content was written by Alexander and Lewis Morris, New York lawyers opposed to Governor William Cosby.

Zenger was imprisoned for printing several "seditious libels" in four issues of his New York Weekly Journal. The New York House of Representatives would not concur in prosecuting Zenger, so the governor ordered the mayor's court to handle the matter; it refused. At the next term of the Supreme Court, its grand jury found the charge against Zenger invalid. The attorney-general filed an information against Zenger and a commission of judges dismissed Zenger's lawyers, James Alexander and Lewis Morris. Zenger obtained other lawyers, including Andrew Hamilton, the attorney who convinced the jury to consider the truth of the material to determine if it were libelous. This step was not allowed for in English law but the jury decided Zenger was not guilty.

The John Peter Zenger trial was based on concepts vital to the libertarian philosophy of free press. These included the rights to criticize officials and to use truth as a defense. The New York Weekly Journal claimed that libels cannot be defined and that freedom of the press should mean that every man ought to have a liberty to communicate his sentiments freely to the public on political or religious points without the fear or danger of being punished. James Alexander wrote:

"There are some things which could possibly affect the public, and these things should be made known; but, by the same token, there are those things which are better left unsaid. The exposure of public wickedness is the duty of every citizen and cannot be considered a libel because such information is in the public interest."

Lewis Timothy editorialized in his <u>South Carolina Gazette</u> that "the liberty of the press is the most unlucky scourge that can hang over the heads of the corrupt and wicked ministry; and when this essential branch of our liberties is either attacked, abridged, or taken away from us, every man may certainly predict slavery and ruin to his fellow citizens. Neither do I see how any restraint can be put upon the press in a nation that pretends to liberty, but what just sufficient to prevent men from writing either blasphemy or treason."

1736

Colonial legislative bodies were fierce oppressors of the Colonial press.

1737

A group of four essays written and published by James Alexander in Franklin's <u>Pennsylvania Gazette</u> and several of his essays published in Zenger's <u>New York Weekly Journal</u> were some of the best libertarian statements published in America in the 1700s. Alexander, called the American Cato, said, "These abuses of freedom of speech are the excresence of Liberty. They ought to be suppressed, but to whom dare we commit the doing of it? An evil magistrate, entrusted with a power to punish words, is armed with a weapon the most destructive and terrible. Under the pretense of pruning off the exuberant branches, he frequently destroys the tree." He said that "freedom of speech is a principal pillar in a free government: when this support is taken away, the constitution is dissolved, and tyranny is erected on its ruins." Alexander believed that constitutional government and freedom of the press cannot survive without each other. He said that "whoever attempts to suppress either of these (liberty of speech and liberty of press), our natural rights, ought to be regarded as an enemy to liberty and the (English) constitution." His <u>A Brief Narrative of the Case and Tryal of John Peter Zenger</u> which Zenger published in 1736 became a widely-known source of libertarian thought in the colonies and in England in the Eighteenth Century.

In 1737 two attorneys of the king produced a refutation of the concept that truth could be a defense against a libel charge; since truth multiplies the libel. William Bradford, Zenger's competitor and enemy, re-published this article but Benjamin Franklin published Alexander's rebuttal of it in his <u>Pennsylvania Gazette</u>.

1739

Charles Chauncey, a prominent clergyman of Boston and a leading liberal, wrote a strong sermon on liberty of conscience, but endorsed banning licentiousness and abuses of the press which he did not define.

1741

Thomas Fleet argued with many preachers in Boston who complained about his <u>Evening Post</u>. Fleet fought against this pressure and said, "The next strike may probably be at the Liberty of the Press, and what a fine introduction this will be to Popery we leave our Readers to judge." He published a batch of children's poems written by his mother-in-law, Mrs. Elizabeth Goose. He was jailed for fussing at the General Assembly.

1742

The Massachusetts Council ordered the attorney general to file an information against Thomas Fleet for publishing in his Boston Evening Post a scandalous and libelous paragraph reflecting on the king's administration predicting the arrest of Sir Robert Walpole. When this happened Fleet was released from prosecution.

1744

John Milton's Areopagitica became very popular throughout the colonies.

There was wide-spread reading in Northhampton, Mass., of a volume on midwifery for pornographic reasons under the guise of sex education for young people.

1747

The Virginia Gazette quoted an English journal in describing newspapers:

"Intestine Broils called young Englishmen to the abortive attempt of Charles Stuart to wrest the English Throne in 1746 from their villages to assist their king and country. The parents became anxious to know the state of their young adventurers, they caught with eagerness the publick papers and read an account of every battle, while fear forebade that their sons had fallen. It is from this era that we may date the universality of newpapers in this kingdom: they were at first the vehicles of political information only but they are now become the vehicles of general information."

Governor George Clinton of New York ordered James Parker, the colony's official printer, not to publish the assembly's remonstrance against the governor. The assembly overruled Clinton "to preserve liberty of the press." The General Assembly for years had ordered that its votes couldn't be published without prior approval, but Clinton criticized such a vote and the resulting squabble caught Parker in the middle of a fight.

1750

Jonathan Mayhew in Discourse said that submission is not required to all who bear the title of rulers, but only to those who actually perform the duties of rulers by exercising a reasonable and just authority for the good of human society. His beliefs strongly influenced James Otis, Joseph Quincy, Sam Adams, and John Adams. Thomas Hollis was effective with correspondence with Jonathan Mayhew and Andrew Eliot to continue the influence leading to the American Revolution.

William Moore was convicted of libeling the provincial constitution and the Assembly by the Bar of the Pennsylvania Assembly and jailed for his Address to the Governor. Professor William Smith, provost of the College and Academy in Philadelphia, also was convicted for publishing it in a German language newspaper.

William Parks, publisher of the Virginia Gazette at Williamsburg, was tried for printing a libel against an honorable burgess. Park begged to have official records examined; they revealed the published material was true and that the burgess had once been convicted of stealing sheep. Parks was exonerated. "It is obvious that a free press is, of all things, the best check and restraint" concluded the newspapers of that day.

Benjamin Franklin believed his newspaper was not a stagecoach for everyone who wanted to pay for publishing views. Instead, he thought they should put out pamphlets. Franklin published a cartoon of a snake cut in pieces, urging it to unite with Great Britian to fight off the Indians who were allied with the French.

1753

William Livingston, spokesman for mid-century American libertarian theory, was a proponent of freedom of the press in his Use, Abuse and Liberty of the Press. He said that the press served the greatest of purposes in spreading knowledge. Before the art of printing was discovered "the progress of Knowledge was slow because the Methods of diffusing it were laborous and expensive." He stressed that everyone could express his opinion if he so desired. Although he said the press had been abused:

> "it must be confessed that this Discovery has, like many others, been prostituted to serve the basest ends and has been the tool of arbitrary Power, Popery, Bigotry, Superstition, Profaneness, and even of Ignorance itself. To shut the press down would be violating our right to speak out. Some governments have controlled the press for this very reason. The wide influence of the Press is so dangerous to arbitrary governments that in some of these it is shut up and in others greatly restrained; it should not have to be that way."

The New York Assembly censured Hugh Gaine for publishing its proceedings in his New York Mercury. Gaine apologized and was censured, fined, jailed, and warned when released a day later.

Daniel Fowle was arrested while eating dinner by order of the Massachusetts General Assembly and its speaker, Thomas Hubbard, on suspicion of having printed a pamphlet, Monster of Monsters, which reflected upon some of the house members. After an interrogation he was jailed. Two days later Daniel

was told he could leave the jail but he refused until the
Assembly liberated him. He was released and the charges
dropped. He printed A Total Eclipse of Liberty which told
his side of the episode. He was so disgusted by the
Massachusetts government that he moved to New Hampshire and
began publication of the New Hampshire Gazette in 1756.

1754

The Massachusetts General Assembly levied a half-penny
tax on every copy of a newspaper, but it was discontinued
after a year because it was so unpopular. The press in
Massachusetts became somewhat free of legal restraints.

Benjamin Edes and John Gill began a printing house in
Boston and the Boston Gazette which became a leading pro-
Revolutionary War publication. Their paper attacked the
Stamp Act, the Boston Massacre, the Tea Tax, the closing of
the port of Boston, the letters of Governor Thomas
Hutchinson, the measures of the provincial government, and
the conduct of British soldiers.

1756

The New York Assembly levied a half-penny tax on
newspapers which simply added a charge to subscribers who did
not object to the tax.

James Parker and William Weyman were arrested for
publishing a critical essay by Hezakiah Watkins. To be
released, the two identified Watkins as the writer to the New
York Assembly. Watkins was found in contempt and was
arrested and fined, but he contritely begged his way out of
jail.

An effort was made by Governor Shively and the General
Court to control press content during the French and Indian
War and some effort was contemplated in New York. But no
restraints were authorized as a result of these efforts.

1757

William Smith, provost of the College and Academy of
Philadelphia and editor of Bradford's Magazine, was jailed
twice for attacking Pennsylvania Quakers.

1758

William Smith was arrested by the Pennsylvania Assembly
for contempt for an essay published in the Pennsylvania
Gazette. He was applauded by the gallery spectators in his
final defense before the assembly, but he was jailed and
fined. He appealed to the Privy Council in London which
exonerated him on a technicality.

1759

James Parker, in opposition to a proposed stamp tax on
newspapers in New York, said, "When Liberty truly reigns,
everyone hath a Privilege of declaring his Sentiments upon

all topics with the utmost Freedom, provided he does it with proper Decency and a just Regard to the Laws."

The Privy Council in England ruled that colonial assemblies possessed no powers of imprisonment for seditious contempt. This ruling grew out of a long prosecution of Judge William Monroe and William Smith, president of the University of Pennsylvania. They were arrested for a newspaper account critical of the upper house of the Pennsylvania Assembly. The assembly voted them guilty, then sent them through a kangaroo court to get a judicial verdict. Smith fled to England to plead his case with the Privy Council which ruled that the item was libelous but not actionable, since it had been published after the assembly adjourned.

14
Holding Hands with Repression,
1700 through 1759

In Prussia, Frederick II paid 100 ducats to have a Cologne gazette printer beaten up in 1700. In Austria, the Allegemeine Zeitung of Augsburg had to change its name and move frequently because it offended the government.

Zurich officials executed 74 writers between 1500 and 1700 for attacking authority or sneering at matrimony.

1704

Peter the Great established Russia's first newspaper, The Vedomosti. He read proof to check sensitive contributions.

1714

The first Austrian daily newspaper started as a twice-weekly publication in 1703; it became a daily in 1714, and the official government newspaper in 1724. It still exists and is now called The Wiener Zeitung.

1715

The Holy Roman Empire ordered everyone connected with the press to observe all laws against slander. These laws also pertained to newspapers and pamphlets in the Empire.

1723

The Catholic Church condemned Pietro Giannone's Napoli.

1724

Bernard Mandeville's The Fable of the Bees was denounced

as heretical and a public nuisance, and it was hanged in France.

1725

The Yung-ching emperor forbade spreading wicked ideas, rumors, or obscenity.

1730

The French Code de la librarie set up rules for copyright and for submission of books for censorship.

French censors would not allow Paul Guirand to say, "Descartes refuted all the Jesuits." Instead, he had to say, "Descartes had attacked some theologians."

1734

Voltaire's Lettres philosophiques was burned by the French Parlement.

1737

Voltaire's Traite sur la Tolerance was condemned by the Catholic Church.

1746

Denis Diderot's Pensee's philosophique was burned by the French Parlement.

1748

Tousaint's Les Moeurs was burned by the French Parlement.

Baron Charles-Louis Montesquieu believed no criminal prosecution could take place unless the thoughts a person had were accompanied by a criminal act. His major work The Spirit of the Laws added much to political theory.

1749

Denis Diderot spent three years in jail for his Lettre sur les Aveugles.

1750

Strict censorship in France created a smuggling operation using printers located just across the French borders.

The Nouvelles ecclesiastiques listed undesirable publications for condemnation.

When the French Assembly tried to condemn Montesque's L'Esprit des lois, they gave up because the book was too complicated for it to analyze.

Madame Doublet's Nouvievles a la main were filled with false news, calumnies, and allegations that circulated throughout France. She continued it despite warnings, reprimands, suppression of her bulletins, and arrests of her associates. She produced the clandestine publication for 40 years.

Voltaire, Rosseau, and Diderot began calling for freedom of the press from mid-century. The Encyclopedie, said that "any country in which a man may not think and write his thoughts must necessarily fall into stupidity, superstition, and barbarism."

Nikolai I. Novikov was imprisoned 15 years and condemned to death for his satirical retorts to Tsarina Catherine's vsyachina publication. Novikov attacked landowners and supported the peasants. He was released by Paul I, and never re-entered political publication.

The Jesuits and their University of Vienna controlled censorship in Austria until state officials governed secular publications. Maria Theresa wanted the Jesuits to control both. A government censorship commission imposed rules and surety bonds on publications in mid-century. The police banned 2,500 publications in one two-year period.

1751

Montesquieu's L'Esprit des lois was added to the Index of Prohibited Books. He said, "The tribunal (for the index) is unsupportable in all governments. In monarchies it only makes informers and traitors; in republics, it only forms dishonest men; in a despotic state, it is as destructive as the government itself."

1753

Pope Benedict IV was liberal, favored free expression, and asked for censorship reforms on the basis of his Constitution Sollicita ac provida.

1756

More than 800 authors, printers, booksellers, and print dealers were jailed in the Bastille between 1600 and 1756.

Frederick the Great of Prussia became editor-in-chief of newspapers during the Seven Years War to end criticism and use the press to manipulate public opinion.

1758

Helvetius badgered and tricked the French censor into permitting publication of De l'esprit. Officials thereafter forced Helvitius to recant in abject humiliation.

1759

The French Parlement condemned the Encyclopedie but would not burn it because it was too expensive.

15
The Patriots Lead the Way,
1760 through 1786

Benjamin Edes wrote in 1760:

"The attack made on the printers of the <u>Centinel</u> on Saturday last, by a number of well-known persons, ought to excite the serious attention of all those, who duly regard the bulwark of our liberties, THE FREEDOM OF THE PRESS. If a printer, for advertising that he intends to publish a certain book for the information, or merely the amusement or innocent diversion of his fellow citizens, is to be beset and abused by a set of club-men, because the title page does not happen to hit their taste, we may take farewell of our independence. Should the government appoint licensers of the Press, it would give just cause of offence. What right, then has any set of men to forbid the printing of a book, till it has had their imprimatur, or to punish a printer with club-law, for advertising it?

An inflamatory handbill charging the New York Assembly with a betrayal of its trust was issued for the Sons of Liberty by Alexander McDougall, who was arrested on charges of seditious libel. He served three months in jail after a widely publicized trial. The charges against him were dropped when the Assembly ended its session. He was identified by James Parker as the author of a handbill attacking the Assembly's decision to give a bill of credit to English troops. Parker felt threatened, because he was later identified as the promoter of the handbill. McDougall refused to ask for a pardon for the article, "To the Betrayed Inhabitants of New York."

1763

Most of the Colonials believed that England's

constitution was "the most perfect constitution that human powers with finite wisdom had yet contrived and reduced to practice for the preservation of liberty and the production of happiness."

The press became an important force of political agitation in opposition to colonial policies. The number of revolutionary newspapers doubled between 1763 and 1765.

1764

In a prospectus issue, The Hartford Courant said:

"Of all the Arts which have been introduced amongst mankind for the civilizing of Human-Nature, and rendering Life agreeable and happy, none appear of greater Advantage than that of Printing; for hereby the greatest genius's of all ages and Nations live and speak for the Benefit of future generations. Was it not for the Press we should be left almost entirely ignorant of all those noble Sentiments which the Antients were endowed with. By this Art, Men are brought acquainted with each other, though never so remote as to Age or Situation; it lays open to view the Manners, Genius, and Policy of all Nations and Countries and faithfully transmits them to posterity."

James Otis contended in his Rights of the British Colonies that "it is a fact as certain as history can make it that the present civil constitution of England derives its original from those Saxons who established a form of government in England similar to that they had been accustomed to live under their native country. This government was founded upon principles of the most perfect liberty."

1765

Governors and judges found their efforts to curb the growing boldness of newspapers limited by the unwillingness of grand juries to indict for critical comments. Lt. Governor Cadwallader Colden of New York said, "I agree with the Gentlemen of the Council that considering the present temper of the people, that this is not the proper time to prosecute the printers and publishers of the Seditious Papers."

Governor Francis Bernard of Massachusetts called The Boston Gazette "an infamous weekly paper which has swarmed with libells of the most atrocious kind. " He called Publishers Edes and Gill "Trumpets of Sedition." Colden of New York called John Holt a liar after Holt made the New York Gazette a propaganda publication against the crown.

John Adams urged The Boston Gazette to publish "with the utmost freedom whatever can be warranted by the laws of your country."

The Stamp Act of March 1765 was passed by Parliament, alienating two influential groups, colonial lawyers and journalists. All legal documents and intruments in writing were to use stamped paper purchased from agents of the English government; offenses against the act were to be tried in any royal, marine, or admiralty court in any part of the colonies without a jury. The Boston Gazette was the first newspaper to publish a letter attacking the Stamp Act. Newspapers were required to use stamped paper. Benjamin Franklin headed an un-succesful delegation to London which tried to get Parliament to repeal the Stamp Act. Newspapers encouraged colonial non-compliance with British law because of the stamp tax.

The Constitutional Courant was a political attack on the Stamp Act. When New York colonial members tried to find out where it had been printed, Lawrence Sweeney replied "at Peter Hassendever's iron works." Thereafter, underground publications were said to have been produced by the iron-works.

William Bradford III, publisher of the Pennsylvania Journal, reacted to the Stamp Act with, "Adieu to the liberty of the press." The Pennsylvania Journal and the Maryland Gazette announced that they would not appear again unless the Stamp Act was lifted; nevertheless, they published regular issues leaving out customary titles and substituting "Recent Occurences" or "No Stamped Paper to be Had."

Isaiah Thomas published a paragraph for the Halifax Gazette in Nova Scotia reporting the people were disgusted with the Stamp Act. He and his boss were threatened by the government if they presented such comment. Later he described an anti-stamp issue of the Pennsylvania Gazette. An effigy of the stamp master was burned.

The Pennsylvania Gazette published by Ben Franklin went into mourning with reversed column rules because of the Stamp Act. Franklin published large handbills as substitutes with the headings "Remarkable Occurences" or "No Stamped Paper to Be Had."

1766

The Stamp Act was repealed largely because of the united opposition to it by the newspapers.

John Dickinson in An Address to the Committee of Correspondence in Barbados, said, rights:

"are created in us by the decrees of Providence, which establish the laws of our nature. They are born with us! and cannot be taken away from us by any human power without taking our lives. In short, they are founded on the immutable maxims of reason and justice. The natural absolute personal rights of individuals are the very basis of all municipal laws of any great value."

Daniel Fowle won an award of 20 pounds from the Massachusetts House for his imprisonment for having published a humorous satire on the debates in the house titled The Monster of Monsters. The humorless house tried to collect a fine after he had moved to New Hampshire. He won a 31 pound, 7 shilling award in 1765 from the General Court.

William Bollan of Massachusetts and its colonial agent in London wrote The Freedom of Speech and Writing upon Public Affairs. Bollan called liberty of the press the forerunner of exercising the rest of our legal rights. His theme was that the accused in a criminal libel trial should have the right to plead truth as a defense, while the jury should have power to judge questions of falsity and malice. It contended that all things published for the purpose of informing the public or for the public welfare are worthy of being in print.

The free examination of public measures, with a proper representation by speech and writing of the sense resulting from that examination, is the right of the members of a free state, and requisite for the preservation of their rights; and that all things published by persons for the sake of giving due information to their fellow subjects, in points mediately or immediately affecting the public welfare, are worthy of commendation."

1767

With the imposition of new taxes under the Townshend Acts, on glass, painter's lead, paper, and tea, the press war in the colonies exploded with great virulence.

Chief Justice Thomas Hutchison of Massachusetts told the press not to meddle with his court. He said:

"The liberty of the Press is doubtless a very great Blessing, but the Liberty means no more than a freedom for everything to pass from the press without license. Unlicensed printing was never thought to mean a Liberty of reviling and caluminating all ranks and degrees of man with impunity, all authority with ignomity. To carry this absurd notion of the Liberty of the Press to the Length some would have it -- to print everything that is libellous and slanderous -- is truly astonishing and of the most dangerous tendency."

A Freeborn American claimed that the society whose laws least restrain the words and actions of its members is most free in an article in the Boston Gazette and Country Journal. The Gazette also declared that "man, in a state of civil society, that right is limited by the law; going beyond that law could be criminal and even destroy liberty."

1768

The Boston Gazette published an unsigned letter written by Joseph Warren that attacked Governor Francis Bernard and held him up as a hated enemy of the province. The council said this was seditious libel placing the governor in the most odious light. But the lower house would not turn Warren over to a grand jury, saying that "The liberty of the press is a great bulwark of the liberty of the people; it is, therefore, the incumbent duty of those who are constituted

the guardians the People's Rights to defend and maintain it."
Governor Francis Bernard got Hutchinson to indict for
seditious libel, saying that formerly no man could print his
thoughts without a license. When this restraint was taken
off then was the true liberty of the press. Every man who
prints, prints at his peril." But Hutchinson could never get
an indictment acted upon.

Josiah Quincy, Jr. was tried for seditious libel, but
the jury found him not guilty. Justice Hutchinson found he
could only make speeches about the dangers of libel since it
was apparent he could not punish Quincy in the courts.

1770

Sam Adams organized his committees of correspondence,
which had 80 centers in the colonies, from Boston to
Savannah. This network led to concentrated planning for
colonial resistance.

The Boston Gazette with its patriot propaganda reached a
circulation of 7,000. The governor bewailed that seven-
eighths of the people read none but this infamous newspaper.
Writers for the Gazette included Samuel Adams, John Adams,
Joseph Warren, Josiah Quincy, Thomas Cushing, Samuel Cooper,
James Otis, and John Hancock. These men met in the Gazette
office "to cook up paragraphs and heat up the political
engine."

Phillip Furneaux challenged Blackstone's law theories
including the common law restraints on expression of
religious and irreligious opinion. He believed that the
expression of opinions should be entirely free. No "bad
tendency" test of words should be applied and punishment
should only be for overt actions.

In North Carolina, the Assembly was offended by a
critical article sympathizing with the Regulators, a group of
debtor farmers. The Assembly accused a member, Herman
Husband, of writing the article. In the ensuing argument he
was expelled and jailed for two months but the grand jury
refused to indict him.

John Mein was forced to flee to England by Patriots
outraged by his attacks on their leaders in his semi-weekly
publication, the Boston Chronicle. He shot a mob member and
was hanged in effigy, assaulted on the street, and had to
have the protection of British soldiers.

"Wilkes and liberty" was a popular cry among the
colonists. The South Carolina Assembly gave John Wilkes
1,500 pounds to pay his debts and get his London publication
started again.

Benjamin Franklin said that:

"the business of printing had something to do with men's
opinions, which lead to the unhappiness of that
business, and which other callings are not liable to.
If all printers were determined not to print anything,

until it could be proven beyond a shadow of a doubt that the material printed would offend no one, then very little would be printed."

1771

An essay Isaiah Thomas wrote in The Spy caused Governor Hutchinson to summon Thomas before his Council. Thomas refused to go so the Council. Hutchison ordered the attorney general to prosecute him at common law, but the grand jury refused. An attempt to try him in a nearby county also fizzled.

1772

Joseph Greenleaf was fired as a magistrate by Governor Hutchison in Boston because of his connections with Isaiah Thomas. The Boston Gazette openly discussed an American revolution and was against British rule of the American Colonies.

1773

Ebenezer Ratcliffe believed that the majority has no right to take actions against sentiments and opinions of minority views till they had produced criminal overt acts, injurious to society.

Thomas Powell was jailed for two days for having printed the proceedings of the South Carolina legislature in his South Carolina Gazette at the request of a member of the legislature. After release he issued a special edition reporting the episode which infuriated the legislature. The Council ruled him guilty of seditious libel, but the legislature released him.

1774

Thomas Jefferson's pamphlet, A Summary View of the Rights of British America, presented resolutions for a Virginia colony convention that led to libertarian views of government and a libertarian press philosophy.

The Continental Congress passed the Quebec Declaration in an effort to enlist Canadian support. It stated:

"The last right we shall mention regards the freedom of the press. The importance of this consists, besides the advancement of truth, science, morality, and arts in general, in its diffusion of liberal sentiments on the administration of government, its ready communication of thoughts between subjects, and its consequential promotion of union among them, whereby oppressive officials are shamed or intimidated into more honorable and just modes of conducting affairs."

The Quebec Declaration rejected the English concept of speech and press control, and declared freedom of the press was a natural right. Freedom of the press was thus declared explicitly a fundamental trust of civil liberty by a group of public men for the first time in America.

1775

George Washington said: "If men are to be precluded from offering their sentiments on matters which may involve the most serious and alarming consequences that can involve the consideration of mankind, reason is of no use to us; the freedom of speech may be taken away, and dumb and silent we may be led like sheep to the slaughter."

Alexander Hamilton said that "the sacred rights of mankind are not to be rummaged for among old parchments or musty records.   They are written, as with a sunbeam, in the whole volume of human nature, by the hand of divinity itself, and can never be erased or obscured by a mortal power."

Pamphlets entitled the <u>Present Crisis with Respect to America</u> and <u>Crisis No 3</u>, were considered scandalous libels and burned by the British Government.

On November 9, 1775, the Continential Congress resolved that any member who divulged any part of its proceedings without consent was to be expelled and deemed an enemy to the liberties of America.

The Sons of Liberty, led by Alexander McDougall and Isaac Sears, destroyed James Rivington's printing shop because he published the pro-Tory <u>New York Gazette</u>. Rivington was hanged in effigy in new Brunswick when Patriots began to resent his publication of Tory arguments.   Although his newspaper was well-edited and written, he suffered further vandalism and beatings before he returned to England.

The Committee of Inspection for Newport, Rhode Island, argued freedom of the press meant diffusion of liberal sentiments but not wrong sentiments.

John Gill was imprisoned 29 days by the British for printing treason, sedition, and rebellion.

More than 400 pamphlets discussing the clash between the colonies and England appeared between 1750 and 1776 and as many as 1500 had been published by 1783.   The number of newspapers published on the seaboard grew to 48 with 23,300 subscribers.   They were crowded with arguments and counter-arguments appearing as letters, official documents, extracts of speeches, and sermons.   Other media included political broadsides, almanacs, pamphlets, and small booklets.

1776

The Virginia Bill of Rights incorporated the first specific guarantee of freedom of the press in America.   The Jefferson draft for the proposed constitution had no declaration of rights but George Mason, James Madison, and the legislature added the rights which provided "That the freedom of the press is one of the great bulwarks of liberty, and can never be restrained but by despotick governments."

Francis Hopkinson, a signer of the Declaration of Independence, said that if the channels of information were abused with a press that became an engine for sowing dissension, false alarms, or undermining the government, it should "tear from its bosom the serpent that would sting it to death." Congress urged states to prevent people from being deceived.

Daniel Fowle published an article against the trend toward American independence in January in his New Hampshire Gazette. The Provincial Assembly censured him and he promptly discontinued his paper. Benjamin Franklin favored as much discussion as possible on public measures and political opinions but recommended harsh treatment for anyone caluminating the government or affronting its reputation.

The Continental Congress declared that the colonies had five rights: representative government, trial by jury, liberty of person, easy tenure for land, and freedom of the press.

Robert Bell said:

"If new modes of government, are either in reality, or in appearance, approaching towards the inhabitants of America; it is more peculiarly necessary on those extraordinary occasions, that the liberty of the press should be freely exerted; for, if in these changes we do not fully retain all our happy privileges, but weakly suffer any restrictions or curtailing of liberty to advance upon us with new establishments, it will afterwards be next to impossible to regain the desirable possession."

Benjamin Franklin used the Virginia Declaration of Rights as the basis of the bill of rights he wrote for the Pennsylvania constitution which provided that "the people have a right to freedom of speech, and of writing, and publishing their sentiments; therefore the freedom of the press ought not be restrained." Pennsylvania accepted common law restraints on the press.

The last attempt by a royal governor to prosecute a Patriot paper bogged down in the South Carolina legislature when the House wouldn't join the Senate to punish Thomas Powell of the South Carolina Gazette. One of the objects of American Revolution was to get rid of the English common law on liberty of speech and of the press. The Declaration of Independence accepted fully the existence of natural rights as the basis for freedom.

Thomas Paine's Common Sense essay appeared in Robert Aitken's Pennsylvania Magazine; it was Common Sense that forced the American public to face the idea of separation from Great Britain and prepared the populace for the Declaration of Independence. Thomas Paine's first Crisis paper was written and published in the Pennsylvania Journal.

Samuel Loudon, editor of the New York Packet, believed all sides should be heard, so he agreed to print a loyalist pamphlet replying to Paine's Common Sense. He advertised it. When MacDougall, Scott, Sears, and John Lamb, all leaders in the Sons of Liberty, read the ad they organized vigilantes who broke into Loudon's home at night, destroyed the printing frames, and burned 1500 printed impressions and the manuscript. The vigilantes sent a communique to all printers saying, "Sir, if you print, or suffer to be printed on your press, anything against the rights and liberties of America, or in favor of our inveterate foes, the King, Ministry, and Parliament of Great Britian, death and destruction, ruin, and perdition shall be your portion. Signed, by order of the committee of tarring and feathering legion."

John Adams wanted newspapers to pass a loyalty test and take a loyalty oath for independence so the opposition press could produce no more seditious or traitorous speculations.

The North Carolina constitution said, "The freedom of the press is one of the great bulwarks of liberty, and therefore ought never be restrained."

1777

William Goddard controlled the __Maryland__ __Journal__, which displeased Baltimore Whigs because of two articles explaining both sides of a purported English offer to end the war. The Whig Legion club demanded that Goddard leave Baltimore. The legislature condemned the club and asked the governor to provide any needed protection. Goddard again infuriated the Whig club with an article written by General Charles Lee. Goddard was mobbed and cursed several times. But, by the time he was ready to move from Baltimore, he and the Whig Legion were on friendly terms.

The Georgia constitution said that freedom of the press and trial by jury were to remain inviolate forever.

George Washington encouraged the Patriot press. He aided in the establishment of the __New__ __Jersey__ __Gazette__ so that his army might have a newspaper to read in the winter of 1777.

Vermont included the Pennsylvania free press provision in its constitution.

John Adams proposed Article XVII for the Massachusetts constitution (based on a Vermont provision) which said, "The people have a right to the freedom of speaking, writing, and publishing their sentiments. The liberty of the press, therefore, is a right not to be restrained." The State convention accepted this version: "The liberty of the press is essential to the security of freedom in a State; it is a right not, therefore, to be restrained in this commonwealth." A Boston committee revised the provision to say, "The Liberty of Speech and of the press with respect to publick measures is essential to the security of freedom in a State, and shall not therefore be restrained in this commonwealth."

The Virginia Religious Liberty statute declared not only the right of liberty to profess religion and to worship God, but also the right of liberty of opinion, speech, and of the press in the subject of religion, and eliminated the English common law test of supposed bad tendency.

1778

Alexander Hamilton said, "Civil liberty is only natural liberty, modified by the sanctions of civil society." Thus natural rights become civil rights. Freedom of the press was one of the natural rights.

The South Carolina constitution provided for freedom of the press.

1780

"In establishing American independence, the pen and the press had merit equal to that of the sword. To rouse and unite the inhabitants, and to persuade them to patience for several years was effected in great measure by the tongues and pens of the well-informed citizens," William Gordon, a historian who wrote about the American Revolution , said.

1783

Thomas Jefferson proposed that "printing presses shall be subject to no other restraint than liableness to legal prosecution for false facts printed and published. Printing presses shall be free, except so far as, by commission of private injury, cause may be given for private action," as part of the Virginia constitution.

1785

The Massachusetts legislature passed a stamp act levying duties on legal documents, commercial papers, newspapers, and almanacs. Public outcry forced the legislature to rescind the action. The following year the legislature taxed advertisements. Isaiah Thomas suspended the Massachusetts Spy in protest of this improper restraint for two years. He published the Worcester Weekly Magazine instead. The Massachusetts Centenal called the stamp act, "the first stone in the fabric of tyranny. It would end freedom of the press." The act was repealed in 1788 when The Massachusetts Spy exalted: "Heaven grant that the Freedom of the Press, on which depends the freedom of the people, may in the United States be ever guarded with a watchful eye, and be defended from shackles until the trump of the celestial messenger shall announce the final dissolution of all things."

Samuel Miller of Massachusetts "Never, it may be asserted, was the number of political journals so great in proportion to the population of a country as at present in ours. Never were they, all things considered, so cheap, so universally different and so easy of access."

William Goddard received the papers of General Charles Lee and wanted to publish them. Lee was a severe critic of President Washington. Goddard wrote Washington to see if he would like to edit the attacks made by his old rival. Washington replied:

"I can only say that your own good judgement must direct you in the publication of the manuscript papers of General Lee. I can have no request to make concerning the work. I never had a difference with that man, but on public ground; and my conduct toward him upon this occasion was only such as I conceived myself indispensibly bound to adapt in the discharge of the public trust reposed in me. If this produced in him unfavorable sentiments of me, I yet can never consider the conduct I pursued with respect to his, either wrong or improper: moreover, I may regret that it may have been differently viewed by him, and that it excited his censure and animadversions. Should there appear in General Lee's writings anything injurious or unfriendly to me, the impartial and dispassionate world must decide how far I deserved it from the general tenor of my conduct. I am gliding down the main stream of life, and wish, as is natural, that my remaining days may be undisturbed and tranquil; and, conscious of my integrity, I would willingly hope that nothing will occur to give me anxiety; but should anything present itself in this or any other publication, I shall never undertake the painful task of recrimination, nor do I know that I shall even enter upon my justification."

1786

Thomas Jefferson wrote, "Our liberty depends upon the freedom of the press and that cannot be limited without being lost."

16
The King, His Ministers, and Parliament, 1760 through 1786

Chancellor Hardwicke, the king's minister, prosecuted John Wilkes for sedition in 1760 for his No. 45 issue of his newspaper. A writer said, "Let us not endeavor to enlarge the press's power of doing good. But since it is confessedly capable of producing much mischief, let it be restricted by that power of law, which make the boundaries of the prerogatives, and in all other instances, the Rights of the People."

Lord William Mansfield said that the jury was concerned only with the fact of publication, and not with other aspects of libel.

1761

John Kidgell published a stolen copy of a parody written by Wilkes intended as a private obscene joke titled <u>An Essay on Woman</u>. Kidgell published it with changes and became a witness against Wilkes.

1763

Wilkes, a member of Parliament, was arrested illegally when he criticized Parliament in his <u>North Briton</u>. The authorities couldn't get a conviction of seditious libel from an English jury, so they charged him with obscene libel for his <u>Essay on Woman</u> which was a risque parody of Pope's <u>Essay on Man</u>. Wilkes was expelled from Parliament even though the work was not published.

Wilkes in the <u>North Briton</u> attacked the favoritism and partiality and odious laws of King George III. Wilkes was jailed, but since he was a member of Parliament he was immune from prosecution until he lost his seat and had to flee the

country. He was convicted in absentia of seditious and
obscene libel and outlawry. When he returned in 1768 to
clear himself he was jailed for 22 months, even though the
outlawry charge was dismissed. He was such a popular hero
that the public contributed more than 10 times what was
needed to pay the 1,000 pound fine. Wilkes and 40 of his
associates, including 14 journeymen printers, were arrested
on a general warrant in the spring for publishing seditious
libels.

Peter Annet was sentenced to a month in jail, two
sessions in the pillory, and an additional year at hard
labor, and to post bond for good behavior for his publication
The Free Inquirer which was accused of blasphemy.

1764

The Father of Candor defended the right of the press to
criticize a bad government administration. The English jury,
not the judge, should decide the question of libel and truth
should be an absolute defense. John Almon, publisher of a
pamphlet by Father of Candor was tried in 1770 for issuing
it.

The printer and a writer for The London Evening Press
and The London Gazetteer were fined 100 pounds for libeling
the Earl of Hertford, a member of the House of Lords. The
House of Commons defeated a Whig proposal to outlaw the
general warrant to arrest authors, printers, or publishers of
seditious libel and their papers.

1765

Sir William Blackstone, jurist and legal scholar,
condemned the publication of "bad sentiments." Crown libels
he defined as:

"Where blasphemous, immoral, treasonable, schisimatical,
seditous, or scandalous libels are punished by the
English law, the liberty of the press, properly
understood, is by no means infringed or violated; the
liberty of the press is indeed essential to the nature
of a free state; but this consists of laying no previous
restraints upon publications, and not in freedom from
censure for criminal matter when published. Every
freeman has an undoubted right to lay what sentiments he
pleases before the public; to forbid this is to destroy
the freedom of the press; but if he publishes what is
improper, mischievous, or illegal, he must take the
consequences of his own temerity, but to punish (as the
law does at present) any dangerous or offensive
writings, which when published, shall on a fair and
impartial trial, be judged of a pernicious tendency, is
necessary for the preservation of peace and good order
of government and religion, the only solid foundations
of civil liberty, thus the will of individuals is still
left free; the abuse only of that free-will is the
object of equal punishment. Neither is any restraint
hereby laid upon the freedom of thought or inquiry;
liberty of private sentiment is still left, the

disseminating, or making public, of bad sentiments, destructive of the ends of society, is the crime which society corrects."

1767

Lord William Mansfield said, "The eternal principles of natural religion are part of the common law; the essential principles of revealed religion are part of the common law; so that any person reviling, subverting, or ridiculing them may be prosecuted at common law.

1768

William Bingley was sent to Newgate prison for two years for contempt without a trial, conviction, or sentence for selling No. 50 and No. 51 of John Wilkes' North Briton. He refused to answer questions from interrogators appointed by Lord Mansfield. After years of pressure and a threat of Parliamentary investigation, Mansfield released him.

A London barrister said, "The liberty of the press is one of the most valuable privileges of Englishmen; and, when employed to patriotic purposes, merits the patronage of the courts and judicature. As the interests of every member of society is concerned in the proper administration of public affairs, he has a right to publish his thoughts upon them."

John Wilkes was found guilty of obscene libel for his North Briton and fined 500 pounds and given a 10 month jail sentence. He couldn't attend an earlier trial because he was in Paris recovering from a duel wound. He became a popular hero for freedom of the press as a result of his trials. Wilkes returned from exile in 1768 and was elected to Parliament, but he was not allowed to serve because he espoused views opposed by the crown. By 1769, the Colonials believed that "the fate of Wilkes and America must stand or fall together."

1769

A series of letters written by an anonymous author appeared in Henry Woodfall's Public Advertiser. They were signed "Junius". They brought seditious libel charges, prosecutions, and convictions. Woodfall, who published the Junius Letter, was convicted only of publishing but not of sedition. Juries in two other cases brought by Lord Mansfield found those publishers not guilty. William Mansfield's rulings in these libel cases provoked a heavy debate for years about the right of the jury to determine the truth in libel cases.

John Horne Tooke had a libel conviction and a fine of 400 pounds set aside by an appeal. He had escaped an earlier sentence on a legal technicality.

Richard Steele and John Wilkes were expelled from Parliament for subversive political writings.

The British government was assessed damages of 100,000

pounds in various cases brought by printers against actions taken by Lord Halifax. The court decisions finally ended the arbitrary powers of the Regulation of Printing Act.

1770

The Letters of Junius said, "Let it be impressed upon your minds, let it be instilled into your children, that the Liberty of the Press is the Palladium of all civil, political and religious Rights of Freedom." The Letters of Junius threatened disposal of the king. Lord Mansfield tried five publishers who used the letters, but was only able to maintain one conviction.

John Almon was arrested and fined for selling a copy of the London Museum which had reprinted Junius' Letters to the King. He also published the Father of Candor letters, anti-government statements in his Political Register, and an account of the Zenger Trial.

Lord William Mansfield said, "As for the liberty of the press, I will tell you what it is: The liberty of the press is, that a man may print what he pleases without a license; as long as it remains so, the liberty of the press is not restrained."

Samuel Foote, a dramatist and comedian, condemned newspapers in a play in which a character, Sir Robert, said to an editor, "Impudent rascally printers -- those pests who point their personal arrows against the peace of mankind -- a pack of factious scoundrels and miscreants. This mongrel, squatting upon his stool, by a single line proscribes and ruins your reputation at once. The tyranny exercised by that fellow, and those of his tribe, is more galling than the absolute monarch in Asia."

1771

Commons yielded to public pressure and demonstrations to end its ban on reporting its procedures. John Wilkes engineered the strategy which saw Parliament attempt to jail John Wheble and R. Thompson for articles. The mayor and other city officials helped their cause which included an arrest and dismissal of Wheble. Parliament attempted to arrest the officials, Wilkes and others. The arresting messenger was imprisoned by the mayor. Finally a mob released two city magistrates as they were being taken to the Tower for imprisonment.

George Rous criticized Justice Mansfield's ruling that juries had no role to decide anything but publication in libel cases. Rous presented historical documentation to prove juries had the right to determine if the matter was libelous under common law jury right and that William Mansfield was wrong.

"Father of Candor" was a pen name for a person refuting a booklet written by Candor, an unidentified lawyer, which had justified Wilkes' prosecution. The reply booklet went through several editions between 1764 and 1771. The Father

of Candor believed truth should be an absolute defense
against libel.

Henry Woodfall presented a report entitled Vox Senatus.
"The Speeches at Large Which Were Made in a Great Assembly
When J.C. Phipps Made a Motion, 'For Leave to Bring in a Bill
to Amend the Act of William the Third, Which Empowers the
Attorney General to File Informations Ex Officio,' and When
Serjeant Glynn Made a Motion, 'That a Committee Should be
Appointed to Enquire into the Proceedings of the Judges in
Westminister Hall, Particularly in Cases relating to the
Liberty of the Press, and the Constitutional Power and Duty
of Juries.'"

1772

Reasons to restrict the press in England included the
contentions that freedom of the press had served its purpose
and could be discontinued, that the press was not free during
England's Glorious Elizabethan Age, that licensing would
suppress immoral and treasonable writings, that no anonymous
works would be published, and that increasing the newspaper
tax would make newspapers pay for villification.

London gave John Wilkes a silver cup to celebrate his
defense of liberty of the press.

1774

John Miller was fined 2000 pounds for libel for a letter
published in the London Evening Post. Henry Woodfall
identified John Horne Tooke as author of an article offending
the House of Commons. The author discredited Woodfall's
testimony, so the house kept Woodfall in jail for several
days and fined him 72 pounds. Printers Sealy and Hodson of
the Salisbury, England, Journal, were found guilty of
libelling Justice of the Peace William Buckler when they
published an anonymous apology to him.

1775

In England, John Horne Tooke was fined 200 pounds and a
year in jail for seditious libel for denouncing the British
killings at Lexington and Concord as murder and proposing a
public subscription fund to benefit widows and orphans.

Thomas Hayter, bishop of London, said freedom of the
press was an outgrowth of the natural and constitutional
right of free speech. Personal slander is a subordinate evil
and criticism of men in public life should not be a public
offense. A free press reveals the designs of evil men as
they can be detected and restrained. The advantages of
freedom outweigh the disadvantages.

Andrew Kippis, a non-conformist minister, said that
neither preaching or publication could be considered an overt
act justifying criminal prosecution.

1776

English law divided unlawful publications as defamatory libel; (defamation of personal or professional reputations); seditious libel (defamation of public officers, government, institutions, or laws); blasphemous libel (defamation of Christianity); or obscene and immoral libel (defamation of England's standard of public morality). The King's Bench was the criminal court having jurisdiction over these criminal prosecutions for libel. Remedy for libel was either a civil action for damages by persons, or criminal prosecution for seditious, blasphemous, or obscene libel. In civil action, the defendant had to prove the truth of his publication; in criminal libel truth or falsity was of no consequence. In libel trials, the judges determined whether material was libelous and the jury was forbidden to discuss such an issue; instead the jury only determined if the defendant had published the matter. English common law separated liberty of the press from licentiousness of the press. The King's Bench judges ruled on the tendency of publications, true or false, to excite and move people to change the existing order. The grounds of the criminal proceedings was the public mischief, which libels were calculated to create in alienating the minds of the people from religion and good morals, and the country. This summary by Sir Walter Russell depicted the law of libel in Great Britain at the beginning of the American Revolution.

1777

During the century newspapers were looked down on by many. In 1730 Monteguiere condemned London newspapers as scurrilous; Dr. Samuel Johnson attacked journalists who "sold out to one or other of the parties that divide us without a wish for truth or a thought for decency, without care of any other reputation than that of a stubborn adherence to their Abbetors." The Lincoln Inn Benchers refused membership to anyone who had ever been associated with newspapers. Reverend William Dodd, accused of forgery, was condemned for having sunk so low as to have become a newspaper editor. And Sir Walter Scott said, "nothing but a thorough-going black-guard ought to attempt the daily press unless it's some quiet country diurnal."

David Hume, an English philosopher believed England enjoyed complete press freedom. His essay for several printed editions minimized the dangers of abuse of free press and claimed it as a common right of mankind. But in 1770, this idea was omitted and by 1777 the edition condemned an unbounded liberty of the press as one of the evils of government.

1778

"Now the popular Clamour runs so high about our Disgraces in America, Our Debt at home, our Terrors of Bankruptcy, and Fear of a French War what signifies all this canting, says the Doctor? The world goes on just the same as it did, who eats the less, or who sleeps the less? Or where is all this consternation you talk of but in the Newspapers? Nobody is thinking or feeling about the matter, otherwise 'tis somewhat to talk about."

Thus Dr. Samuel Johnson complained about the bad news aspects of newspapers.

1780

Samuel Johnson, English poet and essayist, said, "The mass of every people must be barbarous where there is no printing and consequently knowledge is not generally diffused. Knowledge is diffused among our people by newspapers."

1784

The Irish House of Commons adopted a formal resolution that the Volunteer's Journal was a daring, false, scandalous, and seditious libel on its proceedings, tending to promote discontent among his majesty's subjects, to create groundless jealousies between the kingdom and Great Britain, to alienate the affection of the people from his majesty's government, and to excite an opposition to the laws of the land. The printers and publishers of the Volunteer's Journal were arrested, and the printer of Freeman's Journal also was arrested. The chancellor submitted a bill to prevent abuses in the press, precipitating the first serious clash between the Irish press and the government.

Lord William Mansfield said:

"The liberty of the press consists in printing without any previous license, subject to the consequences of law. The licentiousness of the press is Pandora's Box, the source of every evil. Miserable is the condition of individuals, dangerous is the condition of the state if there is no certain law, no certain administration of law to protect individuals or to guard the state."

William Davies Shipley, Dean of St. Asaph's, was tried for seditious libel for publishing and distributing Principles of Government, in a Dialogue between a Gentleman and a Farmer which had been written by his brother-in-law William Jones asking for reform in parliamentary representation. His attorney Thomas Erskine argued that the 12-man jury was entitled to determine if Shipley actually published the material, whether the words were actually libelous, or whether Shipley had intended to libel anyone. The court rejected this argument, however, on the grounds that "the greater the truth, the greater the libel." Erskine contended that a limited verdict would be unfair, and that court precedents clearly established all of the principles he presented. Erskine denied that the English press was truly free under the common law because people could be convicted on the mere fact of publishing. Erskine became libertarian champion of truth as a defense. The jury so confused the trial with its verdict of "guilty of publishing only" that the case was ultimately dismissed.

1786

The <u>Volunteer's</u> <u>Journal</u> in Dublin bragged that in nine months it had had two informations ex-officio filed against it, three rulings to show cause, two indictments for misdemeanors and four indictments for high treason.

17
The Reluctant Tyrants,
1760 through 1786

Local censors existed in 120 towns in the French provinces in 1760.

1761

Julie, ou La Nouvelle Heloise, by Jean-Jacques Rousseau was censored in France but became a widely-circulated book with more than 50 editions by 1789, its theme was social and political equality.

1762

The Paris Parlement condemned Jean-Jacques Rousseau's Emile and tried to arrest him. When he was found in Geneva he was expelled and both Emile and his Du Contract Social were burned.

1763

Francois de Malherbe was the French official in charge of censorship. He was lenient and used his power primarily to limit the number of copies circulated. He was fired in 1763.

1764

The Inquisitor of Boulogne reported to the Pope that banned books in his city might be being circulated. "I would not venture to assert that none are ever sold. That could happen all too easily here where various booksellers have ample privileges deemed necessary in a famous university city like this and granted either by His Holiness, the late Pope, or by the Sacred Supreme Congregation of the Holy Office. In virtue of the said privileges, they may keep and sell prohibited books of any sort on the sole condition of not putting them on view and not selling them except to those who can produce legal license to read and possess them." In 1753, the Inquisitor was afraid to approve The Oeconomy of Human Life because it had been popular in heathen countries. The cardinals approved the book. Voltaire's (Francois Arouet) Dictionaire Philosophique was burned in Berne by the public executioner.

1765

The French government permitted the Chambre syndicale to publish an edition of Charles Louis Montesquieu's works by saying, "Leave is granted to the Paris libraries on the condition they make a fine quarto edition, with fine characters and fine paper, and sell it at a reasonable price."

1766

William Bolts, a merchant from Holland, was expelled from Calcutta when he announced plans to start a newspaper.

Censorship was finally abolished in Sweden.

1768

The Serbs began an exile publication, Slaveno Serpski Magazin, to work for independence from the Turks.

1770

D'Holbach's Systeme de la Nature was burned by the French Parlement.

In Denmark, Johann Struenesse, a German physician who became the principal minister of the Danish king, granted freedom of the press. Even after he fell from grace and was executed, freedom of the press continued. Struenesse was executed in 1772 for having a love affair with Queen Caroline; Danish newspapers revealed the scandal when censorship was ended.

1771

The first Finnish language newspaper appeared. It was called The Finnish Language Weekly News.

1772

Voltaire said his oft-quoted statement "I wholly disapprove of what you say and will defend to the death your right to say it."

Denis Diderot produced his Encyclopedie, a humanistic masterpiece. The work took from 1751 to 1772. It said, "any country in which a man may not think and write his thoughts must necessarily fall into stupidity, superstition, and barbarism."

1774

The Polish Diet had a Dutch newspaper burned in Warsaw.

1775

Voltaire's <u>Dictionnaire philosophique et politique des establishments et du commerce dans les deux Indes</u>, which attacked the exploitation of the West Indes by France, was seized and condemned by French authorites.

Novels depicting the exploits and depravity of the nobility and aristrocrats as a political attack were widely circulated and read in France despite efforts to suppress them.   Censored books were agressively promoted and eagerly sought by an avid reading public.

1776

Sweden passed a law guaranteeing freedom of the press which was ineffective because the king ignored it.   Denmark abolished censorship.

1779

Dutch gazettes produced by expelled Hugenots were filled with bitter attacks on France.   French postal officials were easily bribed to circulate them.   At least nine of these clandestine journals were circulated regularly in France.

1780

Warren Hastings prosecuted Publisher James A. Hickey for criticism in the <u>Bengal Gazette</u> which was banned from the mails.

The first Hungarian language newspaper in Hungary was the <u>Magyar Himondo</u>.

1782

James A. Hickey, founder of the <u>Bengal Gazette</u>, was sued for libel, imprisoned, and stripped of his citizenship papers by the government.

Raynal's <u>Histoire philosophique et plotiquedes deux Indes</u> was burned by the French Parlement.

1784

George Vendotis started a newspaper in Greece, but the Turks had the Greek government stop it.   His brother Poulios Vendotis attempted to continue it in Vienna, but at protestations of the Turks, Chancellor Klemens Metternich had it stopped there.

18

The Triumph of Freedom and Its Destruction, 1787 through 1799

The Constitutional Convention of 1787 adopted a rule that "nothing spoken in the house be printed, published, or communicated without leave."

A motion to preface the Constitution by a Bill of Rights was defeated 10 to 0. A motion to add a statement that the liberty of the press should be preserved was defeated because Delegate Roger Sherman said it was unnecessary since the power of Congress did not extend to the press. During the week of September 12 to 17, the Constitutional Convention rejected 7 to 4 a proposal by Charles Pinckney and Elbridge Gerry that the words "The liberty of the press should be inviolably preserved" be added.

Edmund Randolph, governor of Virginia, refused to sign the proposed United States Constitution because he thought it was dangerous to liberty and a second convention was needed to eliminate its dangers. George Mason refused to sign because it had no Bill of Rights and fought for its defeat. "There is no declaration of any kind preserving the liberty of the press, or the trial by jury in civil causes." he said. As the Constitutional Convention closed, both James Madison and Richard Henry Lee attacked the proposed Constitution because it had no provision for a Bill of Rights or for freedom of the press.

Federalists maintained that nothing in the Constitution threatened freedom of the press, while anti-federalists criticized it for not protecting press freedom. On September 27, Richard Henry Lee of Virginia proposed to Congress that the Constitution be amended to include a guarantee of the right of free press. Similar amendments were proposed or adopted by seven state ratifying conventions.

Thomas Jefferson wrote to James Madison that:

"I do not like, first, the omission of a Bill of Rights, providing clearly and without the aid of sophisms for freedom of religion, freedom of the press, protection against standing armies, restriction against monopolies, the eternal and unremitting force of the habeas corpus laws, and trial by jury." Jefferson wrote Edward Carrington, "The good sense of the people is always going to be the greatest asset of American government. Sometimes they might go astray, but they have the ability to right themselves. The people should always have media to express opinions through. The basis of our government being the opinion of the people, the very first object should be to keep that right; and were it left to me to decide whether we should have a government without newspapers or newspapers without a government, I should not hesitate a moment to prefer the latter."

William Whiting, chief justice of the Court of Common Pleas of Berkshire County of Massachusetts, was convicted of seditious libel for an unpublished article critical of government actions during Shay's Rebellion. His prison term was remitted.

1788

Many newspapers would not publish anti-Federalist material unless authors submitted their names with their writings, or unless they could answer, anti-Federalist materials. Others distorted anti-Federalist views. This paper war became ferocious and bitter, but even so reflected the workings of a free press.

An angry letter contended that the Constitution gave no power to Congress not expressly granted in the Constitution, and all statements that freedom of the press was in danger were abominable falsehoods.

"American Citizen IV" said that neither the old federal constitution or the proposed one contained a Bill of Rights, nor did either notice the liberty of the press, because they were already provided for by the state constitutions.

"Brutus II" in the New York Journal pointed out that the liberty of the press should be held sacred.

Samuel Bryan in his article in the Independent Gazette said that:

"the Pennsylvania constitution provides and declares that the people have a right of freedom of speech and of writing and of publishing their sentiments. Therefore, the freedom of the press ought not to be restrained, but this belief was threatened by the new Constitution. The framers of it, actuated by the true spirit of an aristocratic government which ever abominates and suppresses all free inquiry and discussion, have made no provision for the liberty of the press, that grand palladium of freedom and scourge of tyrants, but observed a total silence on that head."

"Centinel II" in the Philadelphia _Freeman's Journal_ said:

"As long as the liberty of the press continues unviolated, and the people have the right of expressing and publishing their sentiments upon every public measure, it is next to impossible to enslave a free nation. The state of society must be very corrupt and base indeed, when the people in possession of such a monitor as the press can be endured to exchange the heavenborn blessings of liberty for galling chains and despotism. The abolition of that grand palladium of freedom, the liberty of the press, in the proposed plan of government, and the conduct of its authors, and patrons, is a striking exemplification of these observations. The reason assigned for the omission of a Bill of Rights, securing the liberty of the press, and other invaluable personal rights, is an insult on the understanding of the people."

Matthew Carey suggested this prayer for an American citizen:

"May freedom's shrine be never stormed!

May printing presses still abound, to spread blest science all around!"

Oliver Ellsworth of Connecticut insisted that the states did not give Congress the power to prohibit the liberty of the press; thus it was unnecessary to have a free press clause in the Constitution.

William Findley said, "The liberty of the press is not secured and the powers of Congress are fully adequate to its destruction, as they are to have the trial of libels, or pretended libels against the United States."

"Plain Truth" which appeared in the _Independent Gazette_ said, "The liberty of the press in each state can only be in danger from the laws of that state, and it is everywhere well secured. Besides, as the new Congress can only have the defined powers given, it was needless to say anything about liberty of the press, liberty of conscience, or any other liberty that a freeman ought never to be deprived of."

"Fair Play" wrote in the _Independent Gazette_ that, "At the glorious period of our _independence_, the newspapers were filled with publications against as well as for that solitary measure. And I am clearly of the opinion, that the liberty of the press--the great bulwark of all the liberties of the people--ought never to be restrained and that on every occasion truth and justice should have fair play."

The _Gazette of the State of Georgia_ published an essay of "A Georgian" saying, "The Liberty of the Press (that grand Palladium of our Liberties) totally suppressed, with a view to prevent a communication of sentiments throughout the

states. This restraint is designedly intended to give our
new masters an opportunity to rivet our fetters the more
effectually."

The Pennsylvania Gazette said, "The neglect of the
Convention to mention the Liberty of the Press arose from a
respect to the state constitutions, in each of which this
palladium of liberty is secured, and which is guaranteed to
them as an essential part of their republican forms of
government. But supposing this had not been done, the
liberty of the press would have been an inherent and
political right, as long as nothing was said against it."

A Federalist article in the Pennsylvania Gazette said
the First Article of the Constitution defined and limited the
power of Congress so it could not interfere with freedom of
the press since it fell within the province of the states.

"Old Whig I" in the Philadelphia Independent Gazetteer
said:

"Even the press which has so long been employed in the
cause of liberty, and to which perhaps the greatest part
of the liberty which exists in the world is owing at
this moment; the press may possibly be restrained of its
freedom, and our children may possibly not be suffered
to enjoy this most invaluable blessing of a free
communication of each other's sentiments on political
subjects. Should freedom of the press be restrained on
the subject of politics, there is no doubt it will soon
after be restrained on all other subjects, religious as
well as civil. And if the freedom of the press shall be
restrained, it will be another reason to despair of any
amendments being made in the favor of liberty, after the
proposed constitution shall be once established."

"Old Whig III" in the Philadelphia Independent Gazetteer
said:

"Suppose than an act of the continental legislature
should be passed to restrain the liberty of the press;
to appoint licensers of the press in every town in
America; to limit the number of printers; and to compel
them to give security for their good behavior, from year
to year, as the licenses are renewed: if such a law
should be once passed, what is there to prevent the
execution of it?

"The First Article of the Constitution gives unlimited
powers to Congress who may exercise their power to the total
suppression of the liberty of the press." This assessment
appeared in a petition to the Pennsylvania convention from
Cumberland County.

A Democratic Federalist wrote in the Pennsylvania Herald
that "under the enormous power of the new confederation,
which extends to the individuals as well as to the states of
America, a thousand means may be devised to destroy
effectually the liberty of the press."

M.C. in the <u>Pennsylvania Herald</u> urged that "a meeting of the citizens to be called, and a proper committee appointed to frame a Bill of Rights, for securing the liberty of the press and all other rights which the states hold sacred."

A "Republican I" article pointed out that the power for a limited time to authors to hold the exclusive right to their respective writings provides some power of the Congress to influence and control the press. "This possible avenue makes necessary and proper a stipulation for preserving inviolate the liberty of the press. The press is the scourge of tyrants and the grand palladium of liberty."

David Redick in Philadelphia feared that adoption of the Constitution would date the loss of American liberty. "Why", he asked, "was not the liberty of the press provided for?"

John Smilie, in the Pennsylvania debates said, "Suppose Congress would pass an act for the punishment of libels and restrain the liberty of the press, for they are warranted to do this. What security would a printer have, tried in one of their courts?"

William Shippen Jr. urged that a Bill of Rights be prefixed to the Constitution securing liberty of the press.

Sixteen people published a broadside called <u>An Address of the Subscriber Members of the House of Representatives of the Commonwealth of Pennsylvania to Their Constituents</u>. It urged the assemblymen to judge whether the liberty of the press may be considered a blessing or a curse in a free government and whether a declaration for the preservation of it was necessary.

Roger Sherman in his "A Countryman II" letter in the <u>New Haven Gazette</u> said freedom of the press was too important a right to trust to mere paper protection in the Constitution since legislators, executives, or monarchs could all find a means either to take them from you or to render them useless. "The Constitution of Connecticut allows that state's General Assembly to restrain the press, and patching up the national Constitution was a stipulation in favor of the press would be futile since the Constitution already gives Congress enough authority to do the greatest injury if that power is abused." George Lee Turberville believed it was absolutely necessary to stipulate liberty of the press so that violation of it could be scrupulously and jealously guarded against.

Charles Tillinghost reported that:

"Oswald (Eleazer) was the only printer who dared print the address of the Seceding Members to their constituents; some of the new Constitution Gentry told him that if he published such pieces, they would withdraw their subscriptions; He replied that they were very welcome to, if they would first discharge their arrearages. For that whatever might be his own sentiments, yet his press was free, and he would support its freedom."

James Wilson's writing concerning freedom of the press were widely read. He believed that:

> "there is given to the general government no power whatsoever concerning it; and no law, in pursuance of the Constitution, can possible be enacted to destroy that liberty."

He accepted William Blackstone's legal position allowing prosecution after publication. Wilson said liberty of the press was not secured and that Congress might license the press and declare what would be a libel. Congress' power of self-preservation could be used to destroy liberty of the press. But Wilson insisted nothing in the Constitution gave Congress such power or authority. He said,

> "It is very true that this Constitution says nothing with regard to the press, nor was it necessary, because it will be found that there is given to the general government no power whatsoever concerning it; and no law in pursuance of the Constitution can possibly be enacted to destroy that liberty. The idea of liberty of the press is not carried so far as this in any country--what is meant by the liberty of the press is, that there should be no antecedent restraint upon it, but that every author is responsible when he attacks the security or welfare of the government or the safety, character, and property of the individual. The press is undoubtedly free, but is it necessary to that freedom, that every man's tenets on government should be printed at public cost?" He said:

> "If indeed, a power similar to that which has been granted for the regulation of commerce, had been granted to regulate literary publications, it would have been necessary to stipulate that the liberty of the press should be preserved inviolate as that the impost should be general in influence whatever upon the press, and it would have been merely negatory to have introduced a formal declaration upon the subject--ney, that very declaration might have been construed to imply that some degree of power was given, since we undertook to define its extent."

Pelatiah Webster, writing as a "Citizen of Philadelphia" taunted the seceding members saying, "They object that the liberty of the press is not asserted in the constitution. I answer neither are any of the ten commandments, but I don't think that it follows that it was the design of the convention to sacrifice either the one or the other to contempt, or to leave them void of protection or effectual support."

Benjamin Workman complained that "it need not to be wondered, that the friends of this despotic scheme of government were driven to the last and only alternative from which there was any probability of success; namely the abolition of freedom of the press."

Robert Whitehill said:

"Though it is not declared that Congress have a power to destroy the liberty of the press; yet in effect they will have it. For they will have the powers of self-preservation. They have a power to secure to authors the right to their writings. Under this, they may suppress it. Article 2(1), Section 6 restrains the press because Congress members should not be questioned in any place other than Congress." He recommended that on some future date consideration as an amendment or part of a Bill of Rights, a law that the people have a right to freedom of speech, writing, and of publishing their sentiments; therefore, the freedom of the press shall not be restrained by any law of the United States.

Alexander Hamilton in the <u>Federalist</u> <u>Papers</u> belittled the need for constitutional attention to a free press. He and Madison and Jay wrote the 85 papers in an effort to convince New Yorkers to support the new constitution. Since the Constitution did not mention the free press, Hamilton dismissed the idea thus:

"On the subject of liberty of the press, as much as been said, I cannot forbear adding a remark or two. In the first place, I observe there is not a syllable concerning it in the constitution of this state (New York), and in the next, I contend that whatever has been said about it in that or any other state amounts to nothing. What is the liberty of the press? Who can give it any definition which should not leave the utmost lattitude for evasion? I hold to be impracticible; and from this in infer that its security must altogether depend on public opinion and on the general spirit of the people and of the government."

Madison's original Bill of Rights recommendation provided that:

"the people shall not be deprived or abridged of their right to speak, to write, or to publish their sentiments; and the freedom of the press, as one of the great bulwarks of liberty, shall be inviolate and that no state shall violate equal rights of conscience, or the freedom of the press, or the trial by jury in criminal cases." His first proposal for the First Amendment said, "The civil rights of none shall be abridged on account of religious belief or worship, nor shall any national religion be established, nor shall the full and equal rights of conscience be in any manner, or on any pretext, infringed. The people shall not be deprived or abridged of their right to speak, to write, or to publish their sentiments; and the freedom of the press, as one of the great bulwarks of liberty, shall be inviolate. The people shall not be restrained from peaceably assemblying and consulting for their common good; nor from applying to the legislature by petitions in remonstrances, for redress of their grievances."

Madison proposed as Amendment XIV that "No state shall infringe the right of trial by jury in criminal cases, nor the rights of conscience, nor the freedom of speech or of the press."

Richard Henry Lee wrote that "freedom of the press is a constitutional guarantee. It is a fundamental right and should not be restrained in any way. The people's and the printer's claim to freedom of the press is founded on fundamental laws and state constitutions, made by the people themselves."

Chief Justice of Pennsylvania Thomas McKean convicted Eleazer Oswald for contempt in the form of libel. Oswald contended that the common law of libel was incompatible with the consitutional guarantee of a free press, but the conviction still held. Oswald asked the Pennsylvania Assembly to impeach the judge for violating the state constitution. The Assembly ruled Oswald's charges were unsupported. This was a direct violation of freedom of the press. Oswald did have grounds and the judge should have been impeached. Freedom of the press had a long way to go. McKean accepted the English common law definition of liberty of the press wherein the editor of a newspaper was punished by the summary criminal process of contempt of court for a publication censuring his adversary and one of the judges in a pending case to which the editor was the defendant. The practice of citing publications for contempt was continued thereafter by many judges. Oswald said he was being attacked by Andrew Browne under the guise of a libel suit and that his situation as a printer and the rights of the press and the rights of the freemen were being struck at by Browne. Oswald had published anonymous articles reflecting on Browne's character. This hurt enrollment in Browne's female academy.

The Pennsylvania anti-Federalists demanded a second Constitutional Convention be called to adopt a Bill of Rights, including freedom of the press.

In the proceedings of the South Carolina convention that met to consider adoption of the Constitution, the question was asked, "The liberty of the press was the tyrant's scourge--it was the true friend and the firmest supporter of civil liberty; therefore, why pass it by in silence by not including a provision for it in the Constitution?"

Following the Carlisle Riot, the Carlisle Gazette published a polemic attack on the Constitution that included a statement that "we contend for a free press and abhor every thing that has the least tendency to shackle it."

Demosthenes Minor said:

"What control has the federal government upon that sacred palladium of national freedom? It would have been as unnecessary to stipulate that the freedom of the press should be preserved inviolate as that the impost should be general in operation; the very declaration would have been deemed nugatory, and in implication that some degree of power was given."

Thomas Jefferson wrote to James Madison that:

"it is better to establish trials by jury, the right of habeas corpus, freedom of the press, and freedom of religion, in all cases, and to abolish standing armies in time of peace, and monopolies in all cases, than not to do it in any. A declaration, that the Federal government will never restrain the presses from printing anything they please, will not take away the liability of the printers for false facts printed. In the case of religion and the press the government should not restrain the press, or make printers liable for facts printed. The licentiousness of the press produces the same effect as the restraint of the press was intended to do. Restraint keeps things from being told and licentiousness keeps things from being believed when told. Freedom of the press means freedom from prior restraint and not at all to the matter, whether good or bad."

1789

John Adams said, "The only way people can be well-informed is through the press and if truth was printed, and for the public good, no libel charges could be filed." William Cushing, Chief Justice of Massachusetts, expressed the limited liberalism present after adoption of the Constitution but prior to the Bill of Rights by saying that, while prior restraint was unacceptable, subsequent punishment was certainly in line since falsehoods and scandals against the government should be punished. He accommodated seditious libel or falsehood as a punishable offense as did John Adams.

The Georgia constitution provided that freedom of the press and trial by jury should remain inviolate.

John Allen of Connecticut asked:

"Because the Constitution guarantees the freedom of the press, am I at liberty to falsely call you a thief, a murderer, and atheist? The freedom of the press was never understood to give the right of publishing falsehoods and slanders, nor of exciting sedition, insurrection, and slaughter with impunity. A man was always answerable for the malicious publication of falsehood."

The confict about liberty of the press was between two views of government. The law of sedition was a product of the view that the government was the master; the American Revolution transformed into a working reality the second view that the government was servant, and therefore, subject to blame from its master, the people, according to Zachariah Chafee, Jr., a Twentieth Century First Amendment writer.

Judge James Iredell told questioners at the North Carolina constitution ratification convention that Congress was barred from punishing its critics by the silence of the Constitution as completely as could be done by the strongest negative clause that could be framed.

The Senate edited the House Bill of Rights proposals to

read: "Congress shall make no law establishing articles of faith, or a mode of worship, or prohibiting the free exercise of religion, or abridging the freedom of speech, or the press, or the right of people to peaceably assemble, and petition to the government for the reddress of grievances."

Madison said in debates about the proposed First Amendment that "the right of freedom of speech is secured; the liberty of the press is expressly declared to be beyond the reach of this government."

Virginia representatives insisted when they ratified the Constitution that the liberty of conscience and of the press could not be cancelled, abridged, restrained, or modified by any United States authority. This included Congress, the judiciary, and the executive branches. Madison wanted an amendment saying that "no state shall violate the equal right of conscience, or the freedom of the press because it is proper that every Government should be disarmed of powers which trench upon those particular rights." He said that "state governments are as liable to attack these invaluable privileges as the general government is, and ought to be guarded against."

Benjamin Franklin wrote a satirical article in 1789 on the abuses of the press. In defining the power of the press, he was particularly concerned with uneducated people accusing and abusing others through the press, but because of their illiteracy they had other persons write for them and therefore could not be convicted.

"Freedom of the press has been the most fought over issue of our constitutional rights and not one aspect has been neglected;" Franklin said, "Few of us, I believe, have distinct ideas of its nature and extent (of excess freedom of the press). If it means we have the liberty of affronting, caluminating, and defaming one another, I, for my part, own myself willing to part with my share of it when our legislators shall please to so alter the Law, and cheerfully consent to exchange my Liberty of abusing others for the privilege of not being abused myself." He said in irony that "my proposal then is to leave the liberty of the press untouched, to be exercised in its full extent, force and vigor; but to permit the liberty of the cudgel to go with it."

Thomas Jefferson wrote Archibald Stuart that:

"There are rights which it is useless to surrender to the government; and which governments have yet always been found to invade. These are the rights of thinking and publishing our thoughts by speaking or writing. Our citizens may be deceived for awhile, and have been deceived, but as long as the presses can be protected, we may trust to them for light."

Jefferson wrote Madison that:

"I like the declaration of rights as far as it goes, but I should have been for going further. The people shall not be deprived or abridged of their right to speak, to write, or otherwise to publish anything but false facts affecting injuriously the life, liberty, or reputation of others, or affecting the peace of the Confederacy with foreign nations.

Jefferson wrote to Francis Hopkinson that:

"I disapproved from the first moment the want of a Bill of Rights, to guard liberty against the legislative as well as the executive branches of the government; that is to say, to secure freedom in religion, freedom of the press, freedom from monopolies, freedom from unlawful imprisonment, freedom from a permanent military, and a trial by jury in all cases determinable by the laws of the land.

1790

The Pennsylvania constitution said, "The free communication of thoughts and opinions is one of the invaluable rights of man; and every citizen may freely speak, write, and print on any subject, being responsible for that abuse of that liberty." It stated the press should have no antecedent restraint, but the author would be responsible when he attacked the security or welfare of the government; however, it provided truth could be evidence in any prosecution for the publication of papers investigating the official conduct of officers or men in a public capacity. It also allowed a jury, rather than a judge, to decide whether an accused's statement was libelous as a matter of law and truth could be defense in libel prosecution.

Noah Webster criticized Jefferson for asking for a Bill of Rights to the Constitution. Jefferson replied that religious liberty was absolute and freedom of the press was a necessary fence against government wrongs.

1791

Eight states had ratified the amendments comprising the Bill of Rights. Rhode Island and Vermont did so in 1791 and final adoption of the Bill of Rights occurred December 15, 1791, when the Virginia Senate finally voted for ratification.

Edmund Freeman was prosecuted for libeling a legislator but was acquitted by the jury, but the Massachusetts judiciary accepted the William Blackstone belief that freedom of the press meant only being able to publish without a license and being liable for punishment after publication.

1792

The Delaware constitution said, "The press shall be free to every citizen who undertakes to examine the official conduct of men acting in a public capacity; and any citizens may print on any subject, being responsible for the abuse of that liberty."

The guarantees of freedom of expression in effect in ten of the fourteen states, which by 1792 had ratified the United States Constitution, gave no absolute protection for every utterance. Thirteen of the fourteen states provided for the prosecution of libel, and all of those states made either blasphemy or profanity, or both, statuatory crimes according to Supreme Court Justice William J. Brennan, Jr. in 1957.

Jefferson wrote to George Hammond that "You have seen too much of the conduct of the press in countries where it is free, to consider the gazettes as evidence of the sentiments of any part of the government; you have seen them bestow on the government itself, in all its parts, its full share of inculpation."

Jefferson wrote to President Washington that "No government ought to be without censors; and where the press is free no one ever will."

President Washington demanded Editor Freneau be dismissed from the State Department because Washington said that "that rascal" Freneau had been trying to use him as a distributing agent for Freneau's newspaper by sending him three copies every day. Thomas Jefferson in The Anas said "Freneau's paper has saved our Constitution, which was galloping fast into monarchy, and has been checked by no means so powerfully as by that paper. It is well and universally known, that is has been that paper which has checked the career of the Monocrats."

Jefferson responded to complaints of the Spanish Commissioners about press attacks on the king of Spain by writing "Considering the great importance to the public liberty of the freedom of the press, and the difficulty of submitting it to very precise rules, the laws have thought it less mischievous to give greater scope to its freedom than to the restraint of it. The President has therefore, no authority to prevent publications of the nature of those you complain of."

1794

Madison said, "that the censoral power is in the people over the government and not in the government over the people." Madison spoke in favor of emerging political societies saying that Congress shouldn't infringe on such rights of people. Congressional actions "may extend to the liberty of speech and of the press" he warned.

The Senate decided not to make public the provisions of the controversial Jay Treaty, but Senator Steven Mason gave a copy to The Aurora which published the treaty in full.

1795

James Wilson said in a lecture at the College of Philadelphia that law was divine or human, and that human law ultimately had to be based upon the divine or natural law. Justice William Patterson told a jury that the right of owning and possessing property and having it protected is one of the natural, inherent and inalienable rights of man.

1796

John Fenno's Gazette of United States, a Federalist newspaper, commented favorably on the British Sedition Act which was used later as a model for the U.S. Alien and Sedition laws of the Federalists.

Bache's Aurora said, of President Washington, "If ever a nation has been debauched by a man, the American nation has been debauched by Washington. Let his conduct be an example to future ages. Let it serve to be a warning that no man be an idol."

William Keteltas was found guilty of a "misdeameanor and contempt of the authority of this House" for publishing an article denouncing the tyranny of trial magistrates. He was jailed, and his case was widely publicized.

The Tennessee and Kentucky constitutions provided for a free press.

John Adams, supported by four-fifths of the newspapers, won the presidency with a margin of only three electorial votes. He said, "Be not intimidated, therefore, by any terrors, from publishing with the utmost freedom whatever can be warranted by the laws of your country; nor suffer yourselves to be wheedled out of your liberty by any pretense of politeness, delicacy or decency. These, as they are often used, are but three different names for hypocrisy, chicanery, and cowardice."

1797

Porcupine's Gazette and Daily Advertiser was published. Editor Cobbett spent the next two years defending himself and his paper and attacking those who were opposed to the English cause and the Federalist party. Cobbett called political opponents the refuse of the nations and frog-eating, man-eating, blood-drinking cannibals.

Chief Justice Thomas McKean of Pennsylvania applied the English common law definition of liberty of the press in his charge to the grand jury in Philadelphia that indicted William Cobbett for an alleged seditious publication in Porcupine's Gazette censuring the administration at Washington.

John Adams said the delusions and misrepresentations of the press misled many citizens at large. Jefferson warned Madison that the Federalists were preparing a sedition law to suppress the Whig presses and that Bache's Aurora was a principal target. Abigail Adams had written her sister that such a law was planned because of statements that might be prosecuted as libels upon the President and the Congress.

Rep. Samuel J. Cabell was indicted for seditious libel and for unfounded calumny against the unhappy United States government. He was formally accused of the crime of disseminating the material at a time of real public danger by sending circular letters to his constituents. This became the nation's first seditious libel case and was based on common law. Jefferson and Madison denounced the indictments as a perversion of a legal institution into a political one usurping power and infringing upon a natural right of speaking and writing freely. The Virginia House condemned the Grand Jury charge, and Cabell was never tried.

James Callender referred to Washington and Adams as poltroons and venal, and said Adams was a libeler whose hands reeked with the blood of the poor, friendless Connecticut sailor, and a liar whose office was a scene of profligacy and usury, and a heavy-handed incendiary whose purpose was to embroil this country in war with France.

The Columbian Centennial, Federalist newspaper, said "There is a liberty of the press which is very short of the liberty of burning our houses."

1798

Abijah Adams was found guilty of libel and forced to pay a fine, serve 30 days in jail, and post bond for good behavior by a Boston court. He was judged guilty of libeling the Massachusett's legislature.

Congress passed the Alien and Sedition Acts. They provided punishment with a fine of $2,000 and two years in prison for false, scandalous and malicious writing against the government. Congress authorized federal judges to bind people to good behavior in cases arising under state laws, warning them not to persist in government criticism.

The first important journalist indicted under the Sedition Law was Thomas Adams, editor of the Boston Independent Chronicle, after he pled not guilty to charges of libelous and seditious publications tending to defame the United States government; he continued to attack the Federalists. He and his brother was convicted by Massachusetts but his illness kept him from the state trial and he died.

Federalist Congressman, John Allen, said that:

"If ever there was a nation which requires a (sedition law), it is this. Let gentlemen look at certain papers printed in the city and elsewhere, and ask themselves whether an unwarrantable and dangerous combination does not exist to overturn and ruin the Government by publishing the most shameless falsehoods against the Representatives of the people of all denominations, that they are hostile to free governments and genuine liberty, and of course to the welfare of this country that they ought, therefore, to be deplored, and the people ought to raise an insurrection against the Government." He also said, "God deliver us from such liberty, the liberty of vomiting on the public, floods of falsehood and hatred to everything sacred, human, and divine."

Benjamin Franklin Bache was barred from the floor of the House of Representatives by the Federalists who disliked his anti-war views. Bache was arrested for libeling the president and the executive government in a manner tending to excite sedition, and opposition to the laws. He died of fever before his trial could occur.

John Burk, editor of the <u>New York Time Piece</u>, was arrested on charges of seditious and libelous utterances against Adams under common law. James Smith, his partner, also was arrested. Burk continued his attacks on the repression until he and Smith quarrelled and the paper was discontinued. The Federalists still wanted to punish him; he agreed to being deported, but went into hiding until the Sedition law expired.

Matthew Lyon was convicted under the Sedition Act for statements in the <u>Vermont Journal</u>. He charged President Adams with "a continual grasp for power, in an unbounded thirst for ridiculous pomp, foolish adulation, and selfish avarice." He was sentenced to four months and was brutally treated by the U.S. Marshall. He was re-elected to Congress while in jail. His vote elected Jefferson president over Aaron Burr in 1800.

James Madison argued for freedom of the press in the Virginia resolutions. He outlined principles of free government, defended the Bill of Rights, and attacked arguments in favor of the Alien and Sedition Acts. The minority report in the Virginia Resolutions, believed that:

"to contend there does not exist a power to punish writings coming within the description of the Sedition Act, would be to assert the inability of our nation to preserve its own peace, and to protect itself from the attempt of wicked citizens, who, incapable of quiet themselves, are incessantly employed in devining means to disturb the public repose. The government could punish such utterances for the judicial power of the United States extended to the punishment of libels against the government, as a common law offense. Nor does the First Amendment forbid such laws, as punishment of licentiousness is not a restriction of the freedom of the press. If by freedom of the press is meant a perfect exemption from all punishment for whatever may be published, that freedom never has, and most probably never will exist."

Congressman Harrison Otis believed every independent government has a right to preserve and defend itself against injuries and outrages which endanger its existence.

George K. Taylor said:

"In England, the laying of no previous restraints upon publications, is freedom of the press. In every one of the United States the laying of no previous restraints upon publications of false, scandalous, and malicious writing is punishable in the same manner. If freedom of the press be not therefore abridged in the government of any particular state, by the punishment of false, scandalous, and malicious writings, how could it be said to be abridged when the same punishment is inflicted on the same offence by the government of the whole people?"

Luther Baldwin saw and heard a cannon discharged accidentally near President John Adams. His smart-aleck remark that he "wished the shot had lodged in the President's posterior" caused him to be arrested and tried for sedition. The anti-Adams papers used a shorter and more basic term for posterior in their write-ups of the episode.

The English common law definition of liberty of the press was the basis of the 1798 Sedition Act and the way it was administered by Justices Samuel Chase and William Patterson of the United States Supreme Court and Judges Griffin, Hitchcock, and Peters of United States District Courts, and appears in their summing up to the juries in the prosecutions of Callender, Cooper, Haswell, and Lyon for alleged seditious publications censuring the administration of John Adams.

Charles Lee said, "The freedom of the press differs from the licentiousness of the press, and the laws which restrain the latter, will always be found to affirm and preserve the former."

The Federalists, while defending the Alien and Sedition laws as a constitutional reform, embraced the principle that truth could be used as a defense against libel and that such a plea could be presented to the jury.

Congressman Albert Gallatin in opposing the Alien and Sedition laws, said:

"the First Amendment was added to the Constitution to remove any shadow of a doubt as to whether the original charter might possibly have given Congress any power over the press. It wasn't only intended to preserve the pre-Reluntionary War victory abolishing censorship prior to publication, but to provide a new protection guaranteeing free discussion of public men and measures. It not only repudiated the English common law concept of libels against the government but also forbade Congress to add any restraint, either by previous restriction, subsequent punishment, alteration of jurisdiction, or mode of trial."

The Federalist position evaded the Constitution when it said "we claim no power to abridge the liberty of the press; that, you shall enjoy unrestrained, you may write and publish what you please, but if you publish anything against us, we will punish you for it, so long as we do not prevent, but only punish your writings, it is no abridgement of your liberty of writing and printing."

Alexander Hamilton opposed the Sedition Act, saying, "Let us not create a tyranny." John Marshall opposed it, and Madison said it was unconstitutional and a monster that would forever disgrace its parents.

Jefferson wrote the Kentucky Resolutions as an attack on the Alien and Sedition laws. They espoused libertarian theories of freedom of political expressions. Madison said that a free, republican government cannot be libeled and that freedom of speech and press guaranteed by the First Amendment was absolute as far as the federal government was concerned.

Jefferson said, in the <u>Kentucky Resolutions</u>:

"It is true as a general principle, and is also expressly declared by one of the amendments to the Constitution, 'the powers not delegated to the United States by the Constitution, nor prohibited by it to the States, are reserved to the States respectively, or the people"; no power over the freedom of religion, freedom of speech, or freedom of the press being delegated to the United States by the Constitution, nor prohibited by it to the States, all lawful powers respecting the same did of right remain, and were reserved to the States or the people. Thus was manifested their determination to retain to themselves the right of judging how far the licentiousness of speech, and of the press, may be abridged without lessening their useful freedom, and how far those abuses which cannot be separated from their use should be tolerated, rather than the use be destroyed. Libels, falsehood, and defamation, equally with heresy and false religion, are withheld from the cognizance of Federal tribunals. Therefore, the act of Congress of the United States passed on the 14th day of July, 1798, which does abridge the freedom of the press, is not law, but is altogether void, and of no force."

Only a handful of the newspapers being published supported the Jeffersonians. The Federalist press attacked incessantly with vitriolic materials. He wrote Peregrine Fitzhugh that:

"I have been for some time used as the property of the newspapers, a fair mark for every man's dirt. Some, too, have indulged themselves in this exercise who would not have done it, had they known me otherwise than through these impute and injurious channels; it is hard treatment, and for a singular kind of offence, that having obtained by the labors of a life the indulgent opinions of a part of one's fellow citizens. However, these moral evils must be submitted to, like the physical scourges of tempest, fire, &c."

1799

Anthony Haswell was sentenced to two months under the Sedition Act for criticizing Matthew Lyon's treatment.

George Hay contended there was no way a free government could be attacked criminally by opinions of its citizens. He believed that freedom of the press, like chastity, was either absolute or did not exist. Hay, an American libertarian, said, "A man may say everything which his passions suggest: he may employ all his time, and all his talents, if he is wicked enough to do so in speaking against the government matters that are false, scandalous, and malicious without being subject to prevention."

James Madison said no freedom was more deeply impressed on the public mind than the liberty of the press even though that liberty was sometimes carried to excess and even degenerated into licentiousness:

"but the remedy has not yet been discovered whereby the one could be stopped without shutting off the other. Perhaps it is an evil inseparable from the good with which it is allied; perhaps it is a shoot which cannot be stripped from the stalk without wounding vitally the plant from which it is torn. However desirable those measures might be which correct without enslaving the press, they have never yet been devised in America."

Ann Greenleaf, publisher of The New York Argus, was indicted for advocating the right to erect liberty poles to protest the Sedition law and attacks on government corruption. She was too ill to be tried, so the Federalist judge sentenced her foreman, David Frothingham, to four months in jail and fined him for reprinting an article which indicated that Hamilton was hostile to the republican form of government.

Dr. Thomas Cooper, editor of the Pennsylvania Gazette, was sentenced to six months and heavily fined for criticizing Adams. Judge Samuel Chase said the "English rule of libel on the government applied and that if a man attempts to destroy the confidence of the people in their offices, he effectually saps the foundations of government."

In debating the Sedition Act the Federalist faction contended the First Amendment did not mean that Congress could not pass laws restricting the press, especially in criminal matters such as sedition.

Madison argued that the Sedition Act was unconstitutional and that the First Amendment deprived federal courts of all jurisdiction over common law crimes and that freedom of the press must extend beyond an exemption from prior restraint to an exemption from subsequent penalties. Freedom of speech and press was absolute, admitting no exceptions, at least as far as the national government was concerned. Calumny was forbidden by state laws and libelous writing or expression could be punished by state courts, including defamation of public officials acting in public capacities.

He said:

"The Federalists, with their love of power, drew a thin line between freedom and licentiousness of the press and thus turned the First Amendment which was dictated by the most lively anxiety to preserve that freedom, into an instrument for abridging it. It is vicious in the extreme to calumniate meritorious public servants; but it both artful and vicious to arouse the public indignation against calumny in order to conceal usurpation. Calumny is forbidden by the laws; usurption by the constitution. A popular Government, without popular information, or the means of acquiring it, is but a Prologue to a Farce or a Tragedy; or perhaps both. Knowledge will forever govern ignorance: And a people who mean to be their own Governors, must arm themselves with the power which knowledge gives. To the press alone, checkered as it is with abuses, the world is indebted for all the triumphs which have been obtained by reason and humanity over error and oppression."

The Federalists became angry about insults hurled at them by Republican journalists and pamphleteers; they feared the French Jacobins when war seemed inevitable and they disliked the foreign press which exploited its freedom to the utmost in America.

Thomas Jefferson wrote that "To preserve the freedom of the human mind then and the freedom of the press, every spirit should be ready to devote itself to martyrdom; for as long as we think as we will, speak as we think, the condition of man will proceed in improvement."

Jefferson wrote to Elbridge Gerry that "I am for freedom of the press, and against all violations of the Constitution to silence by force and not by reason the complaints or criticisms, just or unjust, of our citizens against the conduct of their agents."

19
Thomas Paine Goes Home,
1787 through 1799

George IV proclaimed in 1787 the need to suppress licentious prints, books, and publications disbursing poison to the minds of the young and the unwary, and to punish the publishers and vendors thereof. William Wilberforce and his Proclamation Society suppressed Sunday newspapers and financed the prosecution of Thomas Paine's <u>Age</u> <u>of</u> <u>Reason</u>.

Lord George Gordon was sentenced to jail for a pamphlet and a libel of the judges. He escaped to France, but returned to England where he was sent to Newgate prison until his death in 1793 since he could not raise the securities for his release. Thomas Wilkins was given a two-year jail sentence for printing Lord Gordon's <u>Prisoners</u> <u>Petition</u>.

1789

John Bennett said, "Delicacy is a very general and comprehensive quality. It extends to everything where a woman is concerned. Conversation, books, pictures, attitude, gesture, pronunciation should all come under its salutary vestments. A girl should hear, she should see, nothing that can call forth a blush, or ever stain the purity of her mind."

Philip Withers wrote a pamphlet revealing that the Prince of Wales had been secretly married to Mrs. Maria Ann Fitzherbert; he called her a "Catholic whore." Mrs. Fitzherbert had the pamphlet suppressed, so Withers produced another pamphlet using his own name and the same accusations. He was arrested for libel but continued writing pamphlets about her while in jail, during the trial, and after the sentence of a year in Newgate prison because he believed his duty to church and state required that he expose Mrs. Fitzherbert. He said the English law was hostile to the discovery of truth and freedom of the press.

John Stockdale, a London bookseller, was acquitted of libel charges because Judge Kenyon instructed the jury to look at the effect of the whole pamphlet containing charges against Parliament.

John Walter, publisher of the Times in London, was fined, pilloried, and sent to Newgate for a year for stating the Duke of York and his two brothers were insincere in expressing joy for the king's recovery. While in jail, he was convicted of more libels and given additional fines and jail terms. The king pardoned him in 1791.

1790

Edmund Burke, an Eighteenth Century English statesman, coined the Fourth Estate phrase saying: "There are three estates in Parliament but in the reporters' gallery yonder sits a fourth estate more important far than they all. It is not a figure of speech or a witty saying; it is a literal fact, very momentous to us in these times." The phrase also has been attributed to Thomas Macauley in this form: "The Fourth Estate ranks in importance equally with the three estates of the realm, the Lords Spiritual, the Lords Temporal, and the Lords Common."

A writer said William Mansfield's:

"intention was simply to maintain power and to act as a soldier for the crown, and in doing this he became lost in a labyrinth of absurdity. The maxim he left is that truth is a libel. In the wide and dark and troubled ocean of what is now demonstrated to be libel, nothing can be said in private, nothing can be written of living or even dead persons but what may be liable. If History be not impeached, if Epithets be not prosecuted, and if Religious Discourses be not arraigned at the bar, it is carelessness that passes them over -- for as the law now stands -- Every human thing, that is not Panegyric, is indictable."

John Magee paid 2000 pounds damages in a libel trial after the jury decided the 8000 pounds asked was excessive. The judge, Baron Earlsfort of Dublin, kept Magee in jail with high bail requirements.

1791

William Roberts had to pay a fine of 100 pounds for libeling Thomas Walker of Manchester. Edmund Freeman, editor of the Herald of Freedom, won a verdict of not guilty of a libel charge even though the chief justice had charged the jury to apply the William Blackstone concept of libel.

A right-wing Association for Preservation of Liberty and Property Against Republicans and Levellers was organized to fight reform efforts.

Thomas Paine produced his Rights of Man in London as a

rebuttal to Edmund Burke's condemnation of the French
Revolution. Thomas Paine's work was a textbook of radical
thought and basic principles. Paine was convicted of
seditious libel in England for attacking the British monarchy
in The Second Part of the Rights of Man. He fled to France.
In his defense of Paine, Thomas Erskine contended:

> "Other liberties are held under governments, but liberty
> of opinion keeps governments themselves in due
> subjection to their duties. This has produced the
> martyrdom of truth in every age, and the world has been
> only purged from ignorance with the innocent blood of
> those who have enlightened it. The proposition I mean
> to maintain as the basis for the liberties of the press,
> and without which, it is an empty sound is this: that
> every man, not intending to mislead, but seeking to
> enlighten others with what is his own reason and
> conscience, however erroneously, have dictated to him as
> the truth, may address himself to a universal reason of
> a whole nation, either upon the subject of government in
> action, or upon that of our own particular country."

Paine said that the English government "stepped in only
when cheap copies of the Rights of Man were published.
The officials feared the common man. It is a dangerous
attempt in any government to say to a Nation, Thou Shalt
Not Read."

The Courrier de l'Europe was published in London and
Boulogne as a clandestine publication to cause English dismay
from 1776 to 1792. Francis Maseres in Dublin urged the overt
acts test to determine if a work was seditious and
occassioned the disturbance which it seemed to be intended to
create.

Lord Chief Justice Kenyon, in discussing James Perry's
Morning Chronicle, said:

> "I think this paper was published with a wicked,
> malicious intent to villify the government and to make
> the people discontented with the constitution under
> which they live. That is the matter charged in this
> information. That it was done with a view to nullify
> the constitution, the laws, and the Government of this
> country, and to infuse into the minds of his Majesty's
> subjects a belief that they are oppressed; and on this
> ground I consider it as a gross and seditious libel."

H.D. Symonds served a two year jail sentence for having
published Thomas Paine's Rights of Man while his partner
Thomas Rickman fled to France.

Fox's Libel Act of England of 1792 provided that a jury
could give "a general verdict of guilty or not guilty upon
the whole matter put in issue upon the indictment and shall
not be required to find the defendant guilty merely on the
proof of publication." The dissenting view of Justice Willes
in the Dean of St. Asaph's case and the views of Thomas
Erskine were the basis of the Fox libel act of 1792. The
common law rules of seditious libel were rendered useless by
the Act which accepted the Zenger truth principle. But there

were 200 informations filed in England for seditious libel as a reaction to the French Revolution. Penalties were heavy upon conviction.

The Friends of the Liberty of the Press was organized on December 19. Thomas Erskine presided as he did at the second meeting in January. His speeches extolling freedom of the press were enthusiastically applauded.

1793

A jury returned a verdict of guilty of publishing with no malicious intent when John Lambert, printer, and James Perry, editor of the Morning Chronicle, were tried for libeling the king. Judge Lord Kenyon refused to accept such a verdict, so the jury declared them not guilty. This was the first trial under the new Fox Libel Act.

Joseph Towers said the hypocrisy of the Association for Preserving Liberty and Property against Republicans and Levellers depriving men of the freedom of the press, and of the freedom of speech was not maintaining liberty or the English Constitution.

Thomas Fyshe Palmer, a Unitarian minister, was sentenced to fourteen years exile for publishing a seditious pamphlet for the Dundee society, and for encouraging people to read Thomas Paine. Also sentenced was William Skirving. They were exiled to Botany Bay in Australia where Skirving died. Palmer died on the way home after serving his fourteen years. George Mealmaker, author of the pamphlet, spent five years at Botany Bay.

William Frend was banished from Jesus College of Cambridge for his pamphlet Peace and Union Recommended to the Associated Bodies of Republicans and anti-Republicans. The Court of the Vice-Chancellor believed it was seditious.

John Bowles, a barrister and a member of the Association for Preserving Liberty and Property against Republicans and Levellers, said, "Those who serve the licentious excess to which the Freedom of the Press is still daily carried, will be of the opinion that it stands in no great need of the proffered protection of this new formed phalanx of defenders." He attacked the free press principles of the Friends of the Liberty of the Press, but Thomas Erskine refuted his views with legal arguments.

Thomas Muir, a pro-French revolution English writer, was sentenced to fourteen years banishment from England to Botany Bay for circulating Thomas Paine's works.

Thomas Erskine's speech on January 19, 1793, became a Declaration on Freedom of the Press and was widely distributed. Erskine believed in the unabridged liberty of utterance for which no one could be punished, so long as the mere verbal portrayal of ideas was the only factor involved.

Robert Hall, a prominent Baptist minister, worked for freedom of the press. He said, "All men should have absolute liberty to discuss every subject which can fall within the compass of the human mind." His An Apology for the Freedom of the Press separated words from actions. "The law hath amply provided against overt acts of sedition and disorder, and to suppress mere opinion by any other method than reason and argument, is the height of tyranny", he said.

1794

Thomas Hardy, secretary of the London Correspondence Society, was acquitted by a jury of high treason for circulating pro-Jacobin propaganda in England, including his Patriot publication. Eight others were arrested; two won acquittals and the charges on the other six were dismissed. Daniel Holt, however, was fined and imprisoned for four years for publishing two pamphlets asking for parliamentary reforms.

The editor and eleven proprietors of the Northern Star were arrested for having published the "Dublin United Irishman's Address to the Volunteers." They won acquittal by showing a pro-government newspaper had published the address a day earlier.

James Montgomery was sent to jail for three months for a 1789 poem with favorable references to France, because the judge believed it had become seditious in 1794 when he published it.

1795

John Horne Tooke was acquitted of sedition and charges against Jeremiah Joyce of treasonable practices for his publishing in behalf of the London Correspondence Society, the English Jacobins, and alleged sympathy for the French Revolution were dropped by the government.

Thomas Spence was arrested at least four times for selling objectionable works including Thomas Paine's Rights of Man.

Lord Eldon, attorney general, wrote the Act of 1795 which said publication which intimidated the Houses of Parliament or the king's Ministers were treasonable, and that persons could be expelled from England for causing hatred or contempt of the nation or its constitution on a second offense.

1796

James Adair, a liberal Whig lawyer, and Erskine defended William Stone against charges of publishing treasonable materials. An English jury found John Reeves not guilty of seditious charges placed against him by Parliament. The jury did say his pamphlet critical of both houses of Parliament was improper.

1797

Lord Kenyon told the jury in the prosecution of a

publisher of <u>Age</u> <u>of</u> <u>Reason</u> that "the Christian religion is part of the law of the land." Justice Ashurst said blasphemy was not only an offense against God but was against all law and government because of its tendency to dissolve all the bonds and obligations of civil society.

The Pitt government attempted to suppress radicalism and seditious pamphleteering with prosecutions of Tooke, Cobbett, the Tory warrior, Eaton, Cartwright, Thelwall, Frend, Spence, and others.

1798

James Callender and his associates (Walter Berry and James Robertson) were indicted in Edinburgh for publishing the <u>Political</u> <u>Progress</u> <u>of</u> <u>Great</u> <u>Britain</u>. Callender fled to the United States but was convicted in 1802 under the short-lived Sedition Act for material he published in the United States titled <u>The</u> <u>Prospect</u> <u>Before</u> <u>Us</u>, which was an attack upon President Adams.

Thomas Erskine became the prosecuting attorney who helped convict Thomas Williams, an impoverished printer, of sedition for publishing Paine's <u>Age</u> <u>of</u> <u>Reason</u>. Erskine did so at the request of the Society Opposed to Vice and Immorality. He believed Paine had attacked Christianity with contempt and falseness to promote civil liberties. Williams was sentenced to three years. Erskine was appalled at the refusal of the society to recommend leniency so he refused payment and talked the judge into reducing the sentence to one year.

Peter Finerty, a minor who was printer for the <u>Dublin</u> <u>Press</u>, was jailed two years for his paper's criticism of the government. British law banned material which tended to excite hatred and contempt of the person of his majesty and of the constitution and government. In England, there was only one verdict of not guilty returned under the numerous prosecutions under the sedition act. John Walter, publisher of the <u>London</u> <u>Times</u>, had to direct his paper's operation from Newgate prison for sixteen months for libeling the Duke of York.

1799

Thomas Erskine defended the Earl of Thanet and others but Thanet was fined 1,000 pounds and jailed for a year in the Tower. Robert Ferguson was fined 100 pounds and one year in the Tower.

Lord Kenyon said:

"The liberty of the press is dear to England. The licentiousness of the press is odious to England. The liberty of it can never be so well protected as by beating down this licentiousness. The liberty of the press is neither more nor less than this, that a man may publish anything which twelve of his contemporaries think is not blameable, but that he ought to be punished if he publishes that which is blameable."

The Dean of the St. Asaph's law case in which Judge Lord William Mansfield denied a motion for a new trial, redefined liberty of the press as "the liberty of the press is that man can print what he pleases without a license."

20
The French Travesties,
1787 through 1799

The Dutch press was placed under severe censorship in 1787 after the patriotic revolution.

1788

France's elite classes no longer agreed on political matters, so the power base of the government evaporated and made censorship impossible.

1789

J.P. Belin had published a book in 1913 entitled <u>Le Commerce</u> <u>des</u> <u>libres</u> <u>prohibes</u> <u>a</u> <u>Paris</u> <u>de</u> <u>1750</u> <u>a</u> <u>1789</u>. The French king subjected all printing done in France to absolute censorship. The French university had the authority to approve writing before its publication.

When the Estates General of France met to liberalize Louis XVI's government, one of its first demands was to establish freedom of speech and freedom of the press, the prime requisites of a free people. The French translation of the Virginia Declaration of Rights made in 1789 later became the basis of the French Declaration of the Rights of Man and Citizens. The Rights of Man said, "No one shall be disturbed on account of his opinions providing they do not derange public order. The free communications of ideas is one of the precious rights of man and every citizen can freely speak, write, and print, subject to responsibility for the abuse of that freedom as determined by law."

1790

Rigas Fereos and the Poulious brothers produced a weekly Greek language newspaper in Vienna which was smuggled into

Turkish ruled Greece.

Alexander Radischev of Russia said press freedom would keep rulers from departing from the way of truth, lest their policies, wickedness and fraud be exposed.

Spain forbade the importation of French books and objects, and forbade circulation of all information about the French Revolution.

1791

Louis XVI was forced to accept the new French constitution but its free press provisions had been destroyed by the revolutionaries, who controlled and censored the press very tightly.

1792

The Paris Commune defined ambigiously <u>sedition</u> and <u>libel</u>, so the press freedom promised in Article XI of the Declaration of the Rights of Man disappeared. The 1793 French Constitution indicated freedom of the press did not exist. By 1797, all French newpapers were controlled by the police.

Catherine the Great of Russia forbade all French printing and even obliterated French names. Tsar Paul I outlawed importing all literature and music. The Russian government burned 20,000 books because it was frightened by the French-Jacobin threat.

1793

The French National Council ignored the constitutional guarantee of absolute liberty of the press. It decreed the death penalty for anyone who, by writing, was convicted of instigating dissolutions of the representative assembly or working for the restoration of the monarchy. Two journalists were executed, 45 editors and publishers were exiled, 42 journals were suspended, and 11 editors were arrested and had their presses smashed.

Johann Galtieb Tichte published a short pamphlet which became the foundation of the natural law of freedom of the press: "Everything dies away, only excepting freedom of expression and thought."

1795

William Duane was escorted to the first available ship as he was deported for publishing the <u>India World</u>. (He became editor of the <u>Aurora</u> in Philadelphia.)

Francis II of the Holy Roman Empire restricted foreign publications that advocated the overthrow of existing conditions.

Hebert made his <u>Pere Duchensce</u> so slanderous that he was guillotined.

Isaac d'Isreli wrote:

"The censors of books in France were a kind of literary
inquisitors, which have long been unknown in England.
The original institution of these censors was merely
disguised as a guard of those publications which might
be injurious to society. Their laws were simple, and
their approbation at first was drawn up in this concise
manner. They declared they found nothing in the work
contrary to religion, government, or morals. They had
not even a right to judge of its intrinsic merit. It
was not long before this system was corrupted. To
gratify a faction, these censors assumed the liberty of
loading their approbations with high eulogisms and
impertinent criticisms."

1798

The Helvetic Republic of Switzerland granted press
freedom to replace the inter-cantonal censorship that had
existed from 1767.

1799

The proprietor, the printer, and the publisher of The
Courier newspaper were all sent to jail for libeling Tsar
Paul I, emperor of Russia.

Napoleon cut the number of Paris newspapers from 72 to
13. He forbade printing anything contrary to good morals or
against his government's principles.

21
The Jefferson and Madison Legacies,
1800 through 1824

Tunis Wortman wrote <u>A</u> <u>Treatise</u> <u>Concerning</u> <u>Political</u> <u>Enquiry</u>
<u>and</u> <u>the</u> <u>Liberty</u> <u>of</u> <u>the</u> <u>Press</u> in 1800. His libertarian
principles had a profound effect upon the country's attitudes
following the expiration of the Alien and Sedition Acts.
Wortman contended there was no such thing as a law of
seditious libel. That crime could never be reconciled to the
genius and constitution of a representative commonwealth. He
said:

> "The Coercion of Libel is rather a subject of domestic
> superintendence than an object that relates to the
> general interests of the Union. Wherever such Coercion
> is proper or necessary, our State legislatures and
> tribunals are possessed of sufficient authority to
> remedy the evil. It is, therefore, to be presumed to
> have been intended that the States respectively should
> soley exercise the power of controlling the conduct of
> their own citizens in such cases. It is necessary that
> every vehicle of communication, every instrument, and
> every faculty by which Mind can correspond with Mind
> should remain independent of Government, and only be
> subject to the censorial jurisdiction of society. The
> establishment of a Licensor is of all expedients, the
> most dangerous. The freedom of speech and opinion is
> not only necessary to the happiness of Man, considered
> as a Moral and Intellectual Being, but indispensibly
> requisite to the perpetuation of Civil Liberty."

Twenty-five persons were arrested, at least fifteen
indicted, eleven tried, and ten found guilty of violation of
the Sedition Act. The law expired the day before Jefferson
became president. He immediately pardoned or released all
persons arrested awaiting trial or already sentenced.
Congress later provided monetary recompense for several of

these persons.

St. George Tucker, a Virginia judge, flatly rejected William Blackstone's concept of prior restraint only, and advocated that the press should be absolutely and equally free from subsequent punishment. Tucker advocated total exemption of the press from all control, restraint, or jurisdiction of the federal government. For injuries done the reputation of any person, as an individual, the state courts were open for ample and competent reddress.

James Madison said:

"This seniority of the freedom of the press requires that it should be exempt, not only from previous restraints by the executive but from legislative restraint also; and this exemption, to be effectual must be an exemption not only from the licenser, but from the subsequent penalty of laws. It would be mockery to say that no laws shall be passed preventing publications from being made, but that laws might be passed for punishing them in case they should be made."

The Report by the Virginia House of Delegates by Madison said:

"The Sedition Act was unconstitutional. The United States possessed no jurisdiction over common law crimes. A popular free republican government cannot be libeled. The First Amendment was intended to supercede the common-law on speech and press. Freedom guaranteed by the amendment was absolute as far as the federal government was concerned because it could not be abridged by any United States authority." Madison also wrote, "It would seem scarcely possible to doubt that no power whatever over the press was supposed to be delegated by the Constitution, as it originally stood, and that the amendment was intended as a positive and absolute reservation of it."

After 1800 the rights of liberty of the press to publish truth on matters of public concern practically eliminated the old English common law of seditious libel and blasphemous libel, relegating laws about obscenity and immorality to the public nuisance level.

John Nicholas of Virginia contended there was no way to distinguish liberty from licentiousness without abridging liberty itself.

Albert Gallatin said the First Amendment meant that Congress could not pass any law punishing any real or supposed abuse by the press, that no prior restaint be imposed, nor that punishment should by law be inflicted upon it.

Benjamin Rush said, "Newspapers are the sentinels of the liberties of our country."

Thomas Jefferson told Abigail Adams that "While we deny

that Congress have a right to control the freedom of the press, we have even asserted the right of the states, and their exclusive rights, to do so."

William Duane, editor of The Aurora, was arrested after a signature drive and charged under state law with inciting a seditious riot. In July, he published an accusation of British intrigue to gain government appointments so he was arrested for seditious libel. He hid but kept writing. By the time trials could be arranged, the Sedition Act had expired.

Judge Samuel Chase sentenced Editor James Callender to nine months jail and a fine. Chase's behavior in the trial was so overbearing that the defense lawyer refused to participate. Chase wouldn't allow the jury to pass on the law of the case. It wasn't long after this trial that Chase was impeached.

Under the Sedition laws, Dr. Thomas Cooper, editor of the Reading (Pa) Weekly Advertiser, was jailed because he said President Adams was incompetent. Charles Holt was jailed three months for criticizing the army. William Durrell was jailed but pardoned for re-printing a criticism of Adams. David Brown was sent to jail for eighteen months for erecting a liberty pole to protest taxes. William Duane, editor of the Aurora, exposed a Federalist scheme to steal the 1800 election for Adams. This scandal helped win the election for Jefferson. Cooper, in his essay "On The Propriety and Expediency of Unlimited Inquiry" argued against criminal libel actions. He was one of the earliest libertarians working for complete freedom for expression.

1801

There has been no federal libel law since the Sedition Act expired in 1801.

James Sullivan, seeking a compromise between Blackstonian and libertarian press freedom, said, "A reasonable constitutional restraint, judiciously exercised, is the only way in which freedom of the press can be preserved, as an invaluable privilege to the nation."

A Review of Past Scenes, a ballad specially composed by Anthony Haswell, commemorated his release from jail where he had been sent for sedition by Vermont authorities who used the Sedition Act to punish him for articles in his Vermont Gazette. He used the time to write anti-Federalist propaganda and was a hero in Bennington.

"An Inquiry Concerning the Liberty and the Licentiousness of the Press and the Uncontroulable Nature of the Human Mind," was written by John Thomson. He supported Wortman's libertarian stand and added that citizens should have the same freedoms as their elected representatives and that expression should not be punished.

"Let the Whig and Tory, the royalist and aristocrat, the republican and democrat, or by whatever other name the

partisans of political parties are designated be allowed
to express their opinions, whether by speech or press,
with the same unconstrained freedom with which men of
science discuss their subjects of investigation.   No
more danger will result from one discussion, than arises
from the other.   Give unto all opinions the same freedom
and the same effects will follow.   It is of no
consequence to enquire who writes a paper or a pamphlet,
where principles and not individuals are the subject of
investigation.   The only reasonable enquiry is, are the
principles contended for just?   If they are, let them
have their due weight; if otherwise, they will meet with
their merited contempt.   In all cases, however, where
specific or general charges are exhibited against an
individual, or individuals; the person's name ought to
be affixed to the publication.   In this case, wilful
calumny and abuse would never dare to make their
appearance.   He who had been once convicted of
publishing a malicious falsehood, would forever after be
deprived of the means of giving currency to his
calumnies.   Let not Government interfere.   The laws of
society, as before observed, are fully sufficient to the
purpose."

Thomas Jefferson in his first inaugural address, said:

"Freedom of religion, freedom of the press, and freedom
of person under the protection of the habeas corpus, and
trial by juries impartially selected.   These principles
form the bright constellation which has gone before us
and guided our steps through the age of revolution and
reformation.   Freedom of the press I deem (one of the)
essential principles of our government and,
consequently, (one) which ought to shape its
administration.

Jefferson pointed out to Elbridge Cleaver that "The
printers can never leave us in a state of perfect rest and
union of opinion.   They would be no longer useful and would
have to go to the plow."

                    1802

Aaron Burr became involved in the burning of a libelous
book about John Adams' presidency.   The fuss started the
friction between Burr and Alexander Hamilton, which ended in
Hamilton's death.

The main speech at a Harvard commencement condemned
novel reading as indecent and morally damaging.

Joseph Dennie, a Federalist editor of the Philadelphia
Port Folio was indicted in a state court for seditious libel
for calling democracy contemptible.   He was acquitted.   J.S.
Lillie was sentenced to three months in jail for having
libeled Massachusetts Chief Justice Dana in the
Constitutional Telegraph.

St. George Tucker produced a five-volume law book set
which refuted William Blackstone's legal commentaries.

Tucker based his legal views on the United States Constitution. In a 30-page discussion of the liberty of conscience and the press, he habitually used the designation "absolute." Tucker said, that:

"liberty of speech and of discussion in all speculative matters consists in the absolute and uncontrollable right of speaking, writing, and publishing our opinions concerning any subject whether religious, philosophical, or political, and of inquiring into and examining the nature of truth, whether moral or metaphysical; the expediency or inexpediency of all public measures, with their tendency and probable effect; the conduct of public men, and generally every other subject without restraint, except as to the injury of any other individual in his person, property, or good name."

Tucker said:

"Whoever makes use of the press as a vehicle of his sentiments on any subject, ought to do it in such language as to show he has a deference for the sentiments for others; that while he asserts the rights of expressing and vindicating his own judgment, he acknowledges the obligation to submit to the judgment of those whose authority he cannot legally, or constitutionally, dispute. In his statement of facts, he is bound to adhere stoutly to the truth; for every deviation from the truth is both an imposition on the public, and injury to the individual whom it may respect. In his restrictures on the conduct of men, in public stations, he is bound to do justice to the characters, and not to criminate them without substantial reason. The right of character is a sacred and invaluable right, and is not forfeited by accepting a public employment; whoever knowingly departs from any of these maxims is guilty of a crime against the community, as well as against the person injured; and though both the letter and the spirit of our federal constitution wisely prohibit the Congress of the United States from making any law, by which the freedom of speech, or the press, may be exposed to restraint or persecution under the authority of the federal government, yet for injuries done the reputation of any person, as an individual, the state courts are always open, and may afford ample, and competent reddress."

Jefferson wrote "It is so difficult to draw a line of separation between the abuse and the wholesome use of the press, that as yet we have found it better to trust the public judgment, than the magistrate, with the discrimination between truth and falsehood."

Dr. Samuel Miller in his Brief Retrospect of the Eighteenth Century, wrote:

"Too many of our Gazettes are in the hands of persons, destitute at once of the urbanity of gentlemen, the information of scholars, and the principles of virtue. To this source, rather than to any particular depravity of national character, we may ascribe the faults of American newspapers, which have been pronounced by travelers, the most profligate and public prints in the civilized world. These considerations, it is conceived, are abundantly sufficient to account for the disagreeable character of American newspapers. In every country, the selfish principle prompts man to defame their personal and political enemies; and where the supposed provocations to this are numerous and no restraints are imposed in the indulgence of the disposition, and inundation of filth and calumny must be expected. Unhappily, too many of the conductors of our public prints have neither the discernment, the firmness, nor the virtue to reject from their pages the foul ebulations of prejudice and malice. Had they more talents, they might render their Gazettes interesting by filling them with materials of a more instructive and dignified kind."

1803

Thomas Jefferson wrote Thomas McKean that:

"The Federalists having failed in destroying the freedom of the press by their gag-law, seem to have attacked it in an opposite direction; that is by pushing its licentiousness and its lying to such a degree of prostitution as to deprive it of all credit. And the fact is that so abandoned are the Tory presses in this particular, that even the least informed of the people have learned that nothing in a newspaper is to be believed. This is a dangerous state of things, and the press ought to be restored to its credibility if possible. The restraints provided by the laws of the States are sufficient for this, if applied. And I have, therefore, long thought that a few prosecutions of the most prominent offenders would have a wholesome effect in restoring the integrity of the presses. Not a general prosecution, for that would look like persecution; but selected ones."

1804

James Kent, of the New York State Supreme Court, said, "Liberty of the press consists of the right to publish, with impunity, truth, with good motives, and for justifiable ends, whether it respects government, magistracy, or individuals."

Of the 200 newspapers, during the campaign for 1804, at least 180 supported the Federalists and only 20 supported Jefferson. This Federalist press heaped invective, falsehood, and libel in their vigorous political and personal attacks on Jefferson.

Harry Croswell, editor of the Wasp, a Federalist newspaper, was tried for criminal libel in New York under state law for an alleged libel against Jefferson. Croswell published this statement:

"(Charles) Holt says, the burden of the federal song is

that Mr. Jefferson paid Callender for writing against the late administration. This is wholly false. The charge is explicitly this: Jefferson paid Callender for calling Washington a traitor, a robber, and a perjurer; for calling Adams a hoary-headed incendiary; and for most grossly slandering the private characters of men whom he well knew were virtuous. These charges, not a democratic editor has yet dared, or ever will dare, to meet in open and manly discussion."

Croswell was indicted under New York common law for seditious libel as:

"being a malicious and seditious man, of a depraved mind and wicked and diabolical disposition, (intending with his words) to detract from, scandalize, traduce, villify, and to represent the said Thomas Jefferson as unworthy of the confidence, respect, and attachment of the people of the said United States and to alienate and withdraw from the said Thomas Jefferson, the obedience, fidelity, and allegiance of the citizens of the state of New York, and also of the said United States; and wickedly and maliciously to disturb the peace.

Alexander Hamilton defended Croswell using somewhat the same thesis Andrew Hamilton had used in the Zenger case, but the later Hamilton lost. Hamilton used the following definition of liberty of the press: The liberty of the press consists in the rights to publish, with impunity, truth, with good motives, for justifiable ends, though reflecting on government, magistracy, or individuals. Many state constitutions contain a free press clause based on this Hamilton definition.

Thomas Jefferson, wrote to Judge Tyler that:

"Our first object should therefore be, to leave open to him all the avenues to truth. The most effectual hitherto found, is the freedom of the press. It is, therefore, the first shut up by those who fear the investigation of their actions. In general, the state laws appear to have made the presses responsible for slander as far as it is consistent with its useful freedom. In those states where they do not admit even truth of allegations to protect the printer, they have gone too far. The firmness with which the people have withstood the late abuses of the press, the discernment they have manifested between truth and falsehood, show that they may safely be trusted to hear everything true and false, and to form a correct judgment between them."

The Albany **Register**, a Federalist paper, published disparaging remarks about Aaron Burr, who became so angry that the resulting arguments led to the duel in which Hamilton was mortally wounded by Aaron Burr.

1805

The New York Legislature enacted a law establishing that truth when published with good motives and for justifiable ends ought to be defense for persons accused of criminal libel, and that the jury had the right to find the law in criminal prosecutions for libel.

The Prussian minister to the United States asked Jefferson why he didn't suppress a Federalist newspaper for attacking the president when he found it in Jefferson's office. Jefferson said, "Put the paper in your pocket, Baron, and should you ever hear the reality of our liberty of the freedom of the press questioned, show them this paper -- and tell them where you found it."

Thomas Jefferson said in his second inaugural address that:

"During this course of administration (first term) and in order to disturb it, the artillery of the press has been levelled against us, charged with whatsoever its licentiousness could devise or dare. These abuses of an institution so important to freedom and science, are deeply to be regretted, inasmuch as they tend to lessen its usefulness, and to sap its safety; they might, indeed, have been corrected by the wholesome punishments reserved and provided by the laws of the several States against falsehood and defamation; but public duties more urgent press on the time of public servants, and the offenders have therefore been left to find their punishment in the public indignation. Nor was it uninteresting to the world, that an experiment should be fairly and fully made, whether freedom of discussion, unaided by power, is not sufficient for the propagation and protection of truth -- whether a government, conducting itself in the true spirit of its Constitution, with zeal and purity, and doing no act which it would be unwilling the world should witness, can be written down by falsehood and defamation. The experiment is noted, to prove that, since truth and reason have maintained their ground against false opinion in league with false facts, the press, confined to truth, needs no other legal restraint; the public judgment will correct false reasonings and opinions, on a full hearing of all parties; and no other definite line can be drawn between the inestimable liberty of the press and its demoralizing licentiousness."

1806

The Boston Ladies Visitor proclaimed that is would be "closed against politics and obscenity and against everything which might cause the crimson fluid to stain the cheek of unaffected modesty."

By 1806, seventy libel cases had been filed against William Duane whose Aurora newspaper was bellicose and reckless in promoting the political positions of Thomas Jefferson.

1807

Thomas Jefferson wrote that "Within the pale of truth,

the press is a noble institution, equally the friend of science and civil liberty."

In a letter to John Norvell, Jefferson described his frustrations with the Federalist press thus:

"To your request of my opinion of the manner in which a newspaper should be conducted, so as to be most useful, I should answer: 'By restraining it to true facts and sound principles only.' Yet I fear such a paper would find few subscribers. General facts may indeed be collected from newspapers, such as that Europe is now at war, that Bonaparte has been a successful warrior, that he has subjugated a great portion of Europe to his will, &c., but no details can be relied on. An editor (should) set his face against the demoralizing practice of feeding the public mind habitually on slander, and the depravity of taste which this nauseous ailment induces."

Jefferson wrote Thomas Seymour that:

"Conscious that there was not a truth on earth which I feared should be known, I have lent myself willingly as the subject of a great experiment, which was to prove that an administration, conducting itself with integrity and common understanding, cannot be battered down, even by the falsehoods of a licentious press, and consequently still less by the press, as restrained within the legal and wholesome limits of truth. This experiment was wanting for the world to demonstrate the falsehood of the pretext that freedom of the press is incompatible with orderly government."

1808

Judge James Kent said:

"Though the law be solicitious to protect every man in his fair fame and character, it is equally careful that the liberty of speech and of the press should be duly preserved. The liberal communication of sentiment, and entire freedom of discussion, in respect to the character and conduct of public men, and of candidates for public favor, is deemed essential to the judicious exercise of the right of suffrage, and of that control over their rulers, which resides in the free people of these United States."

A Massachusetts court said:

"When any man shall consent to be a candidate for a public office conferred by the election of the people, he must be considered as putting his character in issue, so far as it may respect his fitness and qualifications for the office. And publications of the truth on this subject, with the honest intention of informing the people, are not a libel. For it would be unreasonable to conclude that the publication of truths, which it is in the interest of the people to know, should be an offense against their laws."

William Clap was convicted of criminal libel for publishing that auctioneer Caleb Howard was a liar, a scoundrel, a cheat, and a swindler. Chief Justice Parsons agreed that truth could have been a defense, but that Clap's incitement of a breach of peace was sufficient for a two-month jail sentence.

Jefferson wrote William Short that:

"The papers have lately advanced in boldness and flagitiousness beyond even themselves. Such daring and atrocious lies as fill the third and fourth columns of the third page of the United States Gazette of August 31st were never before, I believe, published with impunity in any country. However, I have from the beginning determined to submit myself as the subject on whom may be proved the impotency of a free press in a country like ours, against those who conduct themselves honestly and enter into no intrigue. I admit at the same time that restraining the press to truth, as the present laws do, is the only way of making it useful. But I have thought necessary first to prove it can never be dangerous."

1811

H. P. Nugent said Judge F. X. Martin in Mississippi was a lecherous, treacherous, bloody, bawdy villain, notorious for libidinous amours, after the judge had called Nugent an atrocious libeler. Nugent ended up in jail for libel.

1812

Nathaniel Rounsavelt of The Alexandria (Va.) Herald refused to reveal the source of his information about secret proceedings of the House of Representatives which had him arrested. But Rounsavelt established the reporter's commitment to protect his news source.

The Revolutionary War heroes -- Richard Henry Lee and James Maccubin Lingan -- attempted to defend The Federal Republican from a mob bent on its destruction. The mayor talked the defenders into going to jail for protection, but stood aside as the mob tore open the jail to assault them. General Lingan was killed and General Lee was maimed for life.

Justice Johnson, of the Supreme Court, speaking for the majority in a decision, indicated that federal courts could not exercise common law jurisdiction in criminal cases. In 1816, he refused to change this ruling. This meant that federal courts had no jurisdiction over the common law of seditious libel. Governor Elbridge Gerry of Massachusetts asked the legislature to pass a law clarifying libel matters. He said there had been 253 libels in Boston newspapers in a nine-month period.

1814

When Thomas Jefferson gave his library to Congress, his political foes charged that it was full of books which never ought to be read and probably should be burned.

John Adams wrote:

"One party reads the newspapers and pamphlets of its own church, and interdicts all writings of the opposite complexion. The other party condemns all such as heresy, and will not read or suffer to be read, as far as its influence extends, anything but its own libels. With us the press is under a virtual imprimatur, to such a degree, that I do not believe I could get these letters to you printed in a newspaper in Boston. Have not narrow bigotry, the most envious malady, the most base, vulgar, sordid, fishwoman scurrility, and the most palpable lies, a plenary indulgence, and an inbounded licentiousness. If there is ever to be an amelioration of the conditions of mankind, philosophers, theologians, legislators, politicians, and moralists will find that regulation of the press is the most difficult, dangerous, and important problem they have to resolve".

Jefferson wrote M. Dufief that:

"I am mortified to be told that, in the United States of America, the sale of a book can become a subject of inquiry, and of criminal inquiry too, as an offense against religion; that a question like this can be carried before the civil magistrate. Is this then our freedom of religion? And are we to have a censor whose imprimatur shall say what books may be sold, and what we may buy? And who is thus to dogmatize religious opinions for our citizens? Whose foot is to be the measure to which ours are all to be cut or stretched? Is a priest to be our inquisitor, or shall a layman, simple as ourselves, set up his reason as the rule for what we are to read, and what we must believe? It is an insult to our citizens to question whether they are rational beings or not, and blasphemy against religion to suppose it cannot stand the test of truth and reason. If M. deBecourt's book be false in facts, disprove them; if false in its reasoning, refute it. But for God's sake, let us freely hear both sides, if we choose. I know little of its contents, having barely glanced over here and there a passage, and over the table of contents. From this, the Newtonian philosophy seemed the chief object of attack, the issue of which might be trusted to the strength of the two combatants; Newton certainly not needing the auxiliary arm of the government, and still less the Holy Author of our religion, as to what in it concerns Him. I thought the work would be very innocent, and one which might be confided to the reason of any man; not likely to be much read if let alone, but, if persecuted, it will generally be read. Every man in the United States will think it a duty to buy a copy, in vindication of his right to buy, and to read what he pleases."

1815

General Andrew Jackson ordered Godwin B. Cotten, editor of The Louisiana Gazette, "no publication of the nature of that herein alluded to and censured will appear in any paper of this city unless the editor shall have previously ascertained its correctness and gained permission for its insertion from the proper sources." The editor had to destroy copies of the paper which had indicated the War of 1812 was over. He was ordered to print a retraction, but accompanied it with a sarcastic introductory paragraph.

A letter in The Louisiana Courier criticized Jackson's banishment of French persons from New Orleans; Jackson attempted to have the author, Louis Louaillier, sentenced to jail, but a judge issued a writ of habeas corpus. Jackson had the judge jailed, and several additional persons were subsequently jailed. No court martial or court would convict anyone, but Jackson kept people in jail or exiled them from the city until the Treaty of Ghent was ratified.

Jefferson wrote James Monroe that:

"I hope that to preserve this weather-gauge of public opinion, and to counteract the slanders and falsehoods disseminated by the English papers, the government will make it a standing instuction to their ministers at foreign courts, to keep Europe truly informed of occurrences here, by publishing in their papers the naked truth always, whether favorable or unfavorable. For they will believe the good, if we candidly tell them the bad also.

1816

Thomas Jefferson wrote Charles Yancey that "Where the press is free, and every man is able to read, all is safe.

1817

"In America, the impertinent eagerness for news should be scolded or laughed into moderation. The country gentleman, at peace on his farm, unless for translations from the Paris Moniteur, absurdly anxious for the welfare of the Frenchmen, skipping over the carcass of their king and country. Check your impertinent curiosity. Devote not your life to hearing and telling new things. If ye have business, mind it; are you masters of familiar, stay at home. Your heads are too shallow to contain the myraid of ideas ye wish. Action, not tattle, is the business of life." Thus Joseph Dennie condemned newspaper content and readers in his comments "On News Mongers" in The Lay Preacher.

1821

The New York constitution finally provided that "every citizen may freely speak, write and publish his sentiments on all subjects, being responsible for the abuse of that right; and no law shall be passed to restrain or abridge the liberty of speech, or of the press."

Judge Isaac Parker decreed the American version of _Fanny Hill_ by John Cleland which was called _Memories of a Woman of Pleasure_, to be lewd, wicked, scandalous, infamous, and obscene even though he never saw the book. Peter Holmes was one of two booksellers convicted of selling copies. Vermont passed an anti-indecency statute.

1822

Judge Josiah Quincy allowed Joseph Buckingham of the _New England Galaxy_ to win acquittal in a libel case by admitting evidence of the truth of the alleged libel in court.

1823

Thomas Jefferson wrote to the Marquis de Lafayette that "The only security of all is in a free press. The force of public opinion cannot be resisted, when permitted freely to be expressed. The agitation it produces must be submitted to. It is necessary to keep the waters pure."

He wrote to M. Coray that:

"This formidable censor of the public functionaries, by arranging them at the tribunal of public opinion, produces reform peaceably, which must otherwise be done by revolution. It is also the best instrument for enlightening the mind of man, and improving him as a rational, moral and social being. There are certain principles in which the constitutions of our several States all agree, and which all cherish as vitally essential to the protection of the life, liberty, property, and safety of the citizen. (One is) Freedom of the Press, subject only to liability for personal injuries."

22
New Reasons for Suppression,
1800 through 1824

Benjamin Flower was sent to jail in 1800 by the House of Lords for an article in his <u>Cambridge Intelligencer</u>. English newspaper editors charged a contradiction fee so anyone could attack enemies for the price of an ad.

1801

Thomas Spence was jailed a year for seditious libel when he proposed breaking up English royal estates and distributing the land to the parishes. He had been expelled from the Newcastle Philosophical Society for such ideas in 1775. He also was sentenced to three years for his <u>Restorer of Society in Its Natural State</u>.

1802

The Society for the Suppression of Vice and for the Encouragement of Religion and Virtue throughout the United Kingdom was established. It had 800 members by 1803, and had managed 700 convictions of persons in the courts including seven obscene libel convictions. By 1825 its membership had declined to only 240 persons.

1803

Lord Ellenborough said, "Any publication which tends to degrade, revile, and defame persons in considerable situations of power and dignity in foreign countries may be taken to be treated as a libel, and particularly where it has a tendency to interrupt the amity and peace between two countries."

Sir James MacIntosh said, "Those who slowly built up the fabric of our laws, never attempted anything so absurd as to

define by any precise rule the obscure and shifting
boundaries which divide libel from history or discussion."

1805

Thomas Erskine helped convict Robert Johnson of libeling
the Irish government and officials in letters signed "Juvena"
and published in Cobbett's Register.

English Whigs frequently toasted, "The liberty of the
press -- 'tis like the air we breathe -- while we have it we
cannot die."

1808

The idea that news reports of war activities could give
information to the enemy and thus should be censored began
when Arthur Wellesley, the Duke of Wellington, was displeased
by the reports published in the London Times from an
accredited war correspondent who was covering Spain.

1809

Gabriel Richard, a French Catholic priest, started the
Essai du Michigan in 1809, the first newspaper west of the
Alleghanies. British authorities jailed him because of the
content. John Stockdale, publisher of the Annual Register in
London, was fined $200 for a statement saying "the Methodists
may be fools but their present historian is a knave."

1810

In Commons, Richard Sheridan said:

"Give me but the liberty of the press and I will give to
the minister a venal house of peers. I will give him a
corrupt and servile House of Commons, I will give him
the full serving of the patronage of office, I will give
him the whole host of ministerial influence, I will give
him all the power that place can confer upon him, to
purchase up submission and overawe resistance; and yet,
armed with liberty of the press, I will go forward to
meet him undismayed; I will attack the mighty fabric of
that mightier engine. I will shake down from its height
corruption and bury it beneath the ruins of the abuses
it was meant to shelter."

James Cheetham lost libel suits for saying that Thomas
Paine had fathered Madame Bonneville's son and for saying
that Maturin Livingston cheated at cards.

"Philagatharches" said:

"By granting the free exercise of the press, the
reasoning powers of men will be cultivated and thus the
public mind will be fortified against the insidious
attacks of sophisticated politicans. By the freedom of
the press, the publick are constituted a tribunal, to
which we may appeal, as a last resort upon the merits of
a case. Blasphemous crimes against God are not proper

subjects for a magistrate's concern; corrupt politics is best counteracted by argument in the press; only seditious libel is suppressible. Portrayal of vice is not a crime per se, unless it constituted palpably contrived obscenity. The only legitimate restraints to a free press lie in the realm of sedition, personal libel, and inculcation of vice."

Peter Finerty was sentenced to eighteen months in the court of the King's Bench for libeling Viscount Castlereagh. John and Leigh Hunt were acquitted of seditious libel in England for criticizing military flogging. There were press riots in London. The attorney general claimed there were more prosecutions for libel during 1809 and 1810 than there had been in the previous 20 years.

1811

Baron Wood said:

"It is said we have a right to discuss the acts of our legislature. That would be a large permission indeed. Is there, gentlemen, to be a power in the people to counteract the acts of Parliament? And is the libeler to come and make the people dissatisfied with the government under which he lives? This is not to be permitted to any man; it is unconstitutional and seditious."

1812

Daniel Isaac Eaton was sent to Newgate prison for 18 months for publishing Thomas Paine's <u>Age of Reason</u>. While in jail he wrote a pamphlet exposing prison conditions. This brought a second charge, but he escaped trial because of his old age. In 1793 and 1794 he won acquittals for selling Paine's <u>Rights of Man</u> and <u>Letter Addressed to the Addresser</u>.

John and Leigh Hunt were jailed two years and fined 1,000 pounds for libeling the Prince Regent by calling him an Adonis of Fifty, a libertine, and a man who had just closed a half century without one single claim on the gratitude of his country or the respect of posterity.

Thomas Starkie's libel law book refuted William Blackstone's view of libel by pointing out that the liberty of the press needed more than absence of prior restraint to achieve freedom since subsequent punishment also was a restraint.

1813

The liberty of the press did not become a legal right protected by the English courts until the rulings of Lord Ellenborough in 1808 and 1813 cases, commenced what is called the law of "fair comment on matters of public concern."

The Unitarian Toleration Act of 1813 said some doctrines were no longer punishable, but that denial of Christianity was still a common law crime.

Hugh Fitzpatrick was jailed because he wouldn't reveal the name of Denis Scully, author of a work criticizing Irish penal laws. John Magee, Jr., editor of the Dublin Mail, was jailed two years for charging the Duke of Richmond with corruption. When he published resolutions by Catholics condemning the sentence, another six months were added, and his mailing stamps denied until a brother took over the paper.

1815

Mr. Drakard, an English printer of The Stamford News, had commented on what he called the most heartrending of all exhibitions on this side of hell, an English military flogging. He was sentenced to eighteen months imprisonment, fined 200 pounds, and bonded for three years thereafter not to publish disapproved materials. In England, military floggings could not be commented on in editorials. William Cobbett was fined 1,000 pounds and jailed for two years for doing so.

Walter Cox was pilloried, jailed, and fined several times for seditious libel in his Irish Magazine. He accepted a government pension to leave Ireland after being in jail for three years.

The stamp tax on newspapers was increased greatly.

1816

The publisher of The St. James Chronicle was found guilty of publishing libel in suggesting that the Duke of Wellington and Lady Frances C. W. Webster committed adultry in Brussels following the Battle of Waterloo. Use of the pillory to punish printers was ended. Earlier the practices of ear-clipping, nose-slitting, and hand-looping had been discontinued.

1817

The home secretary authorized justices of the peace to issue arrest warrants for anyone selling libelous publications. Percy Byssche Shelley's Queen Mab was so disliked by authorities that they used it as evidence to deny him the right to rear his children after his divorce. Shelley was expelled from Oxford later for a pamphlet denying the existence of God. Thomas Wooler was judged guilty of libel for his Black Dwarf publication, which was popular among laborers. Wooler was spared a jail sentence because of faulty trial proceedings even though he had been found guilty of seditous libel and high treason. William Hone was arrested for blasphemous libel in his Reformer's Register and other printing but he was acquitted three times by juries.

Lord Sidmouth, English secretary of state, proposed that justices of the peace could jail anyone accused of blasphemous or seditous libels without bail.

Thomas Bowdler, an English doctor, and his family edited or "bowdlerized" literature to eliminate indelicate passages.

Their The Family Shakespear was a best seller with its sanitized presentation.

An English court ruled that Robert Southey's poem, "Wat Tyler", was actually libelous and thus not entitled to be his controllable property. Richard Carlile began a fight against censorship in England by hawking The Black Dwarf by Wooler and by publishing "Wat Tyler", when the poet laureate was trying to suppress his embarrassing work.

When the Society for Suppression of Vice and the Encouragement of Religion and Virtue began campaigning against blasphemy, it was heavily criticized. An anonymous English author urged that "Immoral publications must be deterred by all the rigour of existing law. And, where books evade its force, and seem to satisfy its forms, their price must be raised beyond the reach of the poorer puchasers. Books which are food for idle appetites or vain amusement should be taxed."

1818

An English jury refused to allow a judge to declare Mary Tocker guilty of libel; instead, the jury read the alleged libelous statement and declared her not guilty.

Francis Ludlow Holt, an English lawyer, considered freedom of the press to be one of the "rights of nature; that is, to say, of the free exercise of our faculties."

William Hone was tried three times for blasphemy, once for a parody on the Apostle's creed, the Lord's Prayer, and the Ten Commandments; once for a political parody of the Litany in the Book of Common Prayer and once for a parody of the "Athansian Creed." He was acquitted and sold 300,000 copies of his parodies. Richard Carlile had to serve eighteen months in jail for publishing William Hone's parodies.

Lord Eldon ruled that equity (or civil law) would not enjoin publication of a libel because such a publication is a crime and equity has no jurisdiction to prevent crimes.

1819

Lord Sidmouth, English home secretary, urged Parliament to provide measures to regulate the press which "at present is a most malignant and formidable enemy of the English constitution, to which it owes its freedom."

William Hone, satirist and parodist in England, said, "The printing press is the thing, that in spite of new Acts, and attempts to suppress it, by soldiers or tax, will poison the vermin, that plunder the House that Jack Built." When Joseph Russell was hauled into court for a political libel for selling one of William Hone's parodies, the jury became so amused and laughed so hard it refused to find him or it libelous.

W. J. Fox, in a sermon discussing the trial of Carlile

for republishing Paine's Age of Reason in England, said, "If Deists will listen to you, persuade them; if they will reason, argue with them; if they misrepresent, expose them; but in the name of Christ do not persecute them; do not abet or sanction persecution."

Jane Carlile, whose husband was in jail for libel, was indicted for selling The First Day's Proceedings upon the Mock Trial of Richard Carlile, upon the request of the Society for the Suppression of Vice. She had to buy back her furniture from the police, who confiscated almost everything in her shop, which she reopened. But she was charged with libel for publishing Sherwin's Life of Paine. Her lawyer got her indictment and sentence quashed on a technicality.

Richard Carlile was found guilty for the first time. He had published Thomas Paine's Age of Reason. He also was found guilty of publishing Palmer's Principles of Nature, but his trial for libel in Sherwin's Register was not pursued by the government. Since he couldn't make the excessive bail he was jailed. He was sentenced to three years, fined 1500 pounds, and assessed good behavoir bonds for life of 1200 pounds. His printing shops were raided and his equipment and publication stocks confiscated. He actually was never tried for anything he wrote. Carlile said:

"My whole and sole object, from first to last, from the time of putting off my leather apron to this day has been a Free Press and Free Discussion. When I first started as a hawker of pamphlets I knew nothing of political principles. I had never read a page of Paine's writings; but I had a complete conviction that there was something wrong somewhere, and that the right application of the printing press was the remedy."

The Georgian Act gave the government authority to require security bonds to control and suppress publications.

The "Peter-Loo Massacre" account claiming 400 persons had been killed, or wounded, or injured at Manchester was cause for arresting James Wroe who was jailed for a year and fined, while his wife and other family members were released on bail. These convictions bankrupted Wroe. Joseph Swann was sentenced to two years for blasphemous libel and two additional years for seditious libel for selling The Comet. This was the stiffest sentence of the times.

Thomas Wooler was jailed 15 months and George Edmonds nine months for Edmond's Weekly Register and Wooler's Black Dwarf. Bookseller Russell was convicted for selling William Hone's parodies, another person was judged guilty of libel for selling part of the Black Book and his Republican. The chairman of the Union Society was jailed a year for placards; a man was jailed for a year and a half for handling An Address to the Reformers. W. G. Lewis was jailed two years for articles in his Recorder published in Coventry.

In A Dialogue between a Methodist Preacher and a Reformer, the reformer said:

"The Two Penny Trash. And pray, is there no Sixpenny
Trash? Cannot truth and reason and sound argument be
sold for twopence? And if books become dangerous when
they are cheap, how are we to defend our cheap religious
tract Societies? Now if Cobbett, Wooler, Sherwin, and
other popular writers of political tracts, promulgate
false doctrines, the press is open, refute them. If
they publish misstatements, overwhelm them by the
production of irrefutable facts. If their laughing be
low and vulgar, expose them in a style more chaste and
eloquent. Defeat them upon their own ground. But do
not run in an affected fright to a police officer and
join associations for the purpose of arguing with swords
and batoons. Your God-fearing friends, the yeomanry,
have indeed sabred the people, but they have not thereby
convinced them of error."

Lord Sidmouth said, "But you are doubtless aware that
itinerant vendors of seditious and blasphemous libels may be
apprehended and held to bail, and by these means the
dissemination of this the worst description of poison, has
been considerably checked in many parts of the Kingdom."

William Hone created a parody of a speech made by the
Prince Regent which he called Man in the Moon, a Speech from
the Throne to the Senate of Lunataria. Another of his
parodies was called The Political House That Jack Built.
Although these parodies were clearly seditious under English
laws, the government would not prosecute for fear of popular
ridicule.

Lord Sidmouth said, "It was well-known that a conspiracy
existed for the subversion of the constitution and the right
of property. Among the means adopted for the accomplishment
of this end, the press was one of the principal." Lord
Sidmouth, Lord Castlereagh, and Lord Eldon, all government
leaders, and Parliament managed to pass six acts. Three
pertaining to the press were the act for the more effective
prevention and punishment of blasphemous and seditious libel,
the act to subject certain publications to the duties upon
newspapers, and the act to prevent delay in the
administration of justice in cases of misdeameanor.

John Hunt, a radical, was jailed for libel; this was
Hunt's fifth conviction for seditious libel. News vendors
selling Richard Carlile's publications were jailed a few
weeks each, put on good behavior for three years, and fined.

Thomas Dolby was arrested and charged for libels in both
his Pasquin and his A Political Dictionary. William Benbow,
a bookseller, was charged twice for libel. But the
government withdrew from prosecution because the actions were
based on the private association, which disintegrated in
1822. Thomas Flindell was jailed eight months for libeling
the Queen in the Western Luminary by discussing charges
against her in a trial instituted by the House of Commons.
Richard Carlile developed a book vending machine which
delivered a book for coins. This made it impossible to
arrest an identifiable bookseller and helped Carlile's shop
be a financial success despite jail sentences and

harrassment.

The Constitutional Association was founded by English Tories to suppress disloyal and seditious publications. The courts generally rejected its efforts to prosecute publications. Parliament passed an act directed at pamphlets and printed papers containing observations on public events and occurrences tending to excite hatred and contempt of the government and constitutions of these realms as by law established, and also vilifying its holy religion. John Poynder said London Sunday newspapers were an evil religious and political impiety.

1820

Between 1807 and 1821 there were 101 prosecutions for seditious libel in England. An English jury found the Rev. Blacaw guilty of criminal libel for publishing that "the queen was a Goddess of Lust who polluted the Holy Sepulchure itself, the Church at Hammersmith, by her presence."

James Mill said, "Even when it (freedom of the press) is converted to abuse, it is not for the advantage of an innocent man to seek to restrain it; he will find his advantage in continuing through life to despise its excesses."

Mrs. Susannah Wright was sentenced to jail in England for selling issues of Richard Carlile's pamphlets which he had written while serving a jail sentence.

Samuel Bailey appealed for freedom of the press in England as a factor in the natural progress of knowledge and the adaption of institutions to changes in opinion. "No power can arrest the silent march of thought made possible by a free press.

Thomas Dolby was convicted in England of libel in his newspaper and of selling A Political Dictionary. He avoided being sentenced by promising to give up book selling.

"Phoecion" contended that the press did not cause but only reflected the revolutionary spirit, as was its proper function. A writer signing as Cato had earlier said "the press must be scathed by the lightning of the law; it must be destroyed by the strong arm of power; if the existing laws be not sufficient, subsidiary laws must be created since the revolutionary press had created the rebellious spirit in England."

John Cleland's book Fanny Hill was brought into court on an obscenity charge. John Hunt was jailed for a year for publishing that House of Commons members were "venal boroughmongers, grasping placemen, greedy adventurers -- in short, containing a far greater portion of public criminals than public guardians."

Mary Anne Carlile, sister of Richard Carlile, was acquitted of seditious libel for selling her brother's pamphlets. But she was convicted of blasphemous libel and

sent to prison for two years. Jane Carlile was sentenced to
Dorchester Prison for two years to join her jailed husband
because of blasphemous libel for selling Sherwin's Life of
Paine.

John Thelwell was arrested and tried for seditious libel
for attacking the Constitutional Association in the Champion.
He was acquitted. William M'Gavin was fined 100 pounds for
statements considered libelous by a Scotland court about the
building of a Catholic chapel in Glasgow. James Mann was
declared guilty for handling Sherwin's Register even though
the jury found him guilty only of publishing. The confusion
made it impossible to sentence him. Among vendors sentenced
to jail or fined was a cripple, his sister, and a 15-year-old
child. They mayor bought and publicly burned their copies of
the Republican. An old man named Vines and his son were
jailed in Oxford for selling Sherwin's Register. Thomas
Davison said that those who said the Bible was part of the
law were bigoted old women and the Bible was derogatory of
God, destructive to morality, and opposed to the best
interests of society. For this he was heavily fined and
jailed for two years.

George Canning said the Libel Act was a dike that should
hold off the despotism of the press, but the dike was broken,
and the government ministers had to bow before the deluge.
Radical House of Commons member H. G. Bennet, angered by a
comment about him in John Bull, prevailed upon Parliament to
jail its editor and printer for two months.

In sentencing the publisher of the Manchester Observer
to jail for a year, Sir W. D. Best said:

"With the truth or falsehood of libel, the jury had
nothing to do. If this narrative were false, there
could be no manner of doubt that it was a gross and
abominable libel. If it were true, what was the duty of
the defendant as an English subject? Not to make a
paragraph of the transaction, to get a livelihood by
vending his exaggerations, but to have taken steps for
securing the offenders and bringing the affair before
the proper tribunal. By publications in his newspaper,
what did this man do? He rendered the administration of
justice impossible because he rendered a fair trial
impossible."

Mr. and Mrs. Andrew Marshall fled from England when
authorities confiscated their stocks of Richard Carlile's
Republican and Thomas Wooler's Black Dwarf before they would
be arrested. A second husband and wife team fled from
Edinburgh when accused of sedition for selling the Black
Dwarf. George Kinloch fled to the continent to avoid a
sentence for publishing his address at a reform meeting.
Gilbert McLeod was jailed four months for commenting on the
Kinloch address in his The Spirit of the Union. Two
conservative journalists had done the same thing in their
Edinburgh Correspondent. One was fined and the other jailed.
McLeod was exiled to Australia with 200 convicts.

The Constitutional Association for Opposing the Progress

of Disloyal and Seditious Principles, which was founded in 1820, said:

> "The Press, that great and invaluable blessing of civilized life -- that mighty engine for diffusing the light of Liberty and the Gospel -- has unhappily become, in the hands of evil men, a lever to shake the foundations of social and moral order. Its power, which within the last century has been multiplied an hundredfold, may now be almost said to reign paramount in the guidance of public opinion; and to those friends of their country who reflect deeply on this fact it cannot but be a matter of serious alarm to observe that a very large proportion of our periodical publications is under the direction, either of avowed enemies of the constitution, or of persons whose sole principle of action is their own private and selfish interest."

Members of the association believed that the lower orders and laborers had understanding barely enabling them to distinguish between a cabbage and a potato.

1821

More than 120 prosecutions for seditious and blasphemous libel occurred from 1819 through 1821.

James Mills prepared such a cogent explanation of liberty of the press for the fifth edition of the Encyclopedia Britannica that it was widely reprinted in pamphlet form. He said it was beneficial to allow the press to make people so unhappy with bad government that the ruling officials would find it imprudent to disregard the discontent of the many.

Sir Francis Burdett of Westminster was found guilty of writing threatening letters because the letters constituted publishing. He was sentenced to three months in a minumum security prison in which he entertained twice weekly. He was cheered by a great throng on the way to jail, but had to pay a 2,000 pound fine.

Samuel Bailey of Sheffield said:

> "Whoever has attentively meditated on the progress of the human race, cannot fail to discern that there is now a spirit of inquiry amongst men which nothing can stop or even materially control. Reproach and obloquy, threats, and persecution, will be vain. They embitter opposition and engender violence; but they cannot abate the keenness of research. There is a silent march of thought which no power can arrest; and which is not difficult to see will be marked by important events. Mankind were never before in the situation in which they now stand. The Press has been operating on them for several centuries, with an influence scarcely perceptible at its commencement, but daily becoming more palpable and acquiring accelerated force. It is rousing the intellect of nations, and happy will it be for them if there be no rash interference with the natural

progress of knowledge."

Mary Ann Carlile, sister of Richard Carlile, was convicted of libel for selling <u>Appendix to Paine's Theological Works</u>. She was fined and jailed for a year.

In the Burdett trial, Justice Best said:

"Libel is a question of law, and the judge is the judge of the law of libel as in all other cases, the jury having the power of acting agreeably to his statements of the law or not; the Liberty of the press is this: That you may communicate any information that you think proper to communicate by print; that you may point out to the government their errors, and endeavor to convince them their system of policy is wrong and attended to disadvantage to the country, and that another system of politics would be attended with benefit. It is from such writings that the religion of this country has been purified; it is by such writings that the constitution has been brought to the perfection that it now has. And God forbid I should utter a sentence to show that a man speaking with that respect which he ought to speak with of established institutions may not show that some reform may be necessary or that the military ought not to be used in the manner in which they are. But the question always is as to the manner." He told the jury that if it found a paper <u>to appeal to the passions of the lower orders of the people, and not having a tendency to inform those who can correct abuses</u>, it is a libel.

1822

John Barkley, a shop man working for Richard Carlile, was sentenced to six months in jail for operating Carlile's bookshop while Carlile was in jail. William Holmes, who voluteered to work at Richard Carlile's bookshop while Carlile was in prison, was sentenced to two years for selling seditious books. When he got out of jail he opened his own bookstore selling the same books.

For publishing an alleged blasphemous and seditious libel, Humphrey Boyle was imprisoned eighteen months, a Mr. Rhodes, who refused to give his name, was sentenced two years as a Mr. Holmes was. Mrs. Susannah Wright was sentenced to Newgate for selling the pamphlet, <u>Address to the Reformers</u>. She had to take her 6-month-old baby to jail with her. The English authorities added eighteen more months to her sentence because she believed Christianity could not be part of English law. She wasn't allowed to complete her defense in the trial.

Richard Carlile revived his <u>Republican</u> while still in prison. The Constitutional Association bankrupted itself by spending 30,000 pounds primarily to prosecute Carlile.

William Clarke was prosecuted by the Society of the Suppression of Vice for his <u>Reply to the Anti-matrimonial Hypothesis and Supposed Atheisim of Percy Byssche Shelley</u>.

But the judge said the jury was to decide "whether such a book had any other tendency than that of undermining the divine system of Christianity and substituting atheism in its room." The jury could not, and found Clarke guilty. He got four months in jail and five years good behavior.

An English jury refused to convict John Ambrose Williams of criminal libel for bringing the Church of England and its clergy into disrespect even though the judge urged conviction. Williams was publisher of the <u>Durham</u> <u>Chronicle</u>. Samuel Waddington was found guilty of blasphemy by a jury that accepted Chief Justice Abbot's view that his pamphlet saying Christ was an imposter and a murderer was a blasphemous libel.

1823

Abram Combe in Edinburgh, said much of the distress of the world is caused by ignorance and that the periodical press has a responsibility to give full and accurate information on all sides of a controversy so that truth may be perceived.

Edmund Kimball said, "The question is not whether the licentiousness of the press be an evil, but whether this evil is of equal magnitude with that which would ensue from a tyrannical restraint. An arbitrary, corrupt, or weak government cannot long resist criticism from the press. A good government will not fear it."

William Tunbridge, one of Carlile's bookshop volunteers, was imprisoned for two years as a result of prosecutions arranged by the Society for the Suppression of Vice in England. James Watson spent a year in jail for selling a copy of Palmer's <u>Principles</u> <u>of</u> <u>Nature</u> in Carlile'e bookshop. For selling materials written by Thomas Paine, Richard Carlile spent nine years in jail.

1824

In London, eleven arrests were made along Fleet Street mostly for selling Richard Carlile's publications. The sellers were fined heavily and imprisoned. The end of most prosecutions for criminal libel finally arrived in England.

John Hunt published a poem, "Vision of Judgment", ridiculing the dead king. He was indicted and Chief Justice Abbott said that a publication tending to disturb the minds of living individuals and to bring them into contempt by reflecting upon persons who were dead, was an offense against the law. Hunt was fined and required to post good behavior bonds.

Hunt said the distinction between liberty and license was a sham. He said:

"The licentiousness of the press is every disclosure by which any abuse, from practice of which they (in whose hands the supreme power of the state is vested) draw any advantage, is brought to light and exposed to shame --

whatsoever disclosure it is, or is supposed to be their interest to prevent. The liberty of the press is such disclosure, and such only from which no inconvenience is apprehended.

James Affleck, a grocer, was indicted for selling Thomas Paine's _Age of Reason_, a Chinese prayer, a book about the character of Jehovah and the prophets, a letter to the chief rabbi, the _Republican_, and Shelley's _Queen Mab_. He was jailed three months.

23
Napoleon's Destruction of Liberty, 1800 through 1824

The desire for a free press was a main principle of the revolutions in the western world for a forty-year period beginning in 1800.

The Marquess of Wellesley, as governor general of India, considered the press to be an evil of the first magnitude, useless to literature and to the public.

The Charter of Louis XVIII said that Frenchmen had the right of publishing and causing to be printed their opinions provided they conformed to the law.

Pierre Dupont de Nemours said, "A large part of the nation reads the Bible, but all of it assiduously peruses the newspapers. The fathers read them aloud to their children while the mothers are preparing breakfast."

Louis Bonald said, "A censorship of the press is thus a necessity that power may have adequate protection. Only in this way can men of evil disposition be prevented from attacking every necessary institution of society."

Napoleon said that all papers which insert articles contrary to the respect due the social part, to the sovereignty of the peoples, to the glory of the army or who publish invectives against friendly or allied governments would be suppressed immediately.

1803

The first newspaper in Australia was The Sydney Gazette and New South Wales Advertiser. During the preceding six years "pipes" or news sheets had been printed. Officials had to approve the proofs of the Gazette.

Les Nouvelles Ecclesiastiques, a printed journal from 1728 to 1803, was a clandestine publication in France. The government spent millions trying to stop it.

1805

Tsar Alexander I of Russia allowed the founding of the Magazine of Russian Letters which campaigned for press freedom until Napoleon invaded Russia. Earlier Catherine I and Paul I had censored the press and forbidden importation of literature.

Napoleon said, "I want you to suppress completely the censorship of books (in Italy). This Country already has a narrow enough mind without straitening it any more. Of course, the publication of any work contrary to the government would be stopped." Smugglers brought forbidden publications into France in plaster busts of Napoleon, or in sealed boxes off the coast of Brittainy, or in hollowed-out lumps of coal. Spain got French Revolution propaganda in hat linings and clock part wrappings. Napoleon dit, "Si je lache la bride a la presse, je ne resterai pas trois mois au pouvior."

1809

Napoleon executed Johann Polin, an Augsburg printer, for circulating an underground newspaper.

1810

Napoleon said, "A journalist is a grumbler, a censurer, a giver of advice, a regent of sovreigns, a tutor of nations. Four hostile newspapers are more to be feared than a thousand bayonets." Napoleon allowed only one newspaper in each French province and four in Paris. He said to his press bureau, "I will not judge journalists for the wrong which they have done, but for the lack of good which they have done." He imposed government control and press limitations in all the territories he conquered. He said, "Newspapers say only what I wish."

The Spanish Cortes, meeting in Cadiz, approved a free press law.

1812

Pierre Augustin Caron, in his satirical play, The Marriage of Figaro, described the French press thus, "They all tell me that if in my writings I mention neither the government, nor public worship, nor politics, nor morals, nor people in office, nor influential corporations, nor the opera, nor the other theatres, nor anyone who have aught to do with anything, I may print everything freely, subject to the approval of two or three censors."

1813

Swedish law provided that the king could suppress any newspaper for imperiling the public safety.

1814

The Norwegian constitution provided for freedom of the press.

The Catholic Church had Voltaire's remains taken from their place of honor and thrown into a pit outside Paris.

1815

The 1815 constitution of Holland indicated that liberty of the press was a useful means to promote knowledge and information.

Henri B. Constant de Rebecque broke with Napoleon and became a pamphleteer calling for civil liberties and freedom of the press.

1818

The Carlsbad Decrees set up suppression and censorship of the German press for 30 years. The resolutions said:

"So long as this decree shall remain in force, no publication which appears in the form of daily issues or as a serial not exceeding 20 pages of printed matter shall go to press in any State of the Union without the previous knowledge and approval of the State officials. The Diet shall have the right to suppress on its own authority such writings included in whatever German State they may appear, as in the opinion of a commission appointed by it are inimical to the honor of the Union, the safety of individual states, or the maintenance of peace and quiet in Germany. There shall be no appeal from such decisions, and the governments involved are bound to see that they are put into execution."

Lord Wellesley set up press censorship in India during the 1799 Revolutionary War, but Lord Hastings discontinued it in Bengal in 1818 as Lord Elphinstone did in Bombay. The press was really not free because the court still enforced controls.

In France, the printer was considered a part of the government obligated to restrain whatever was submitted to him for publication. Paris newspapers had to post a 10,000 franc good-behavior guarantee. The amount fluctuated up and down until finally the plan was abolished in 1881.

General Ramon Varvaez, Spanish dictator, said, "It is not enough to confiscate papers; to finish with bad newspapers you must kill all the journalists."

Frederich Gentz of Austria said, "As a preventive measure against the abuses of the press, absolutely nothing should be printed for years. With this as a rule, we should in a short time get back to God and the Truth."

1820

Austrian Prime Minister Klemens von Metternich said, "The greatest and consequently most urgent evil now is the press." Ludwig Franke (in his memoirs of the Austrian Metternich era written later) said, "The self-esteem of those who wrote had fallen so low that they practiced a self-censorship of their own and destroyed every inborn thought as Chronas of Greek mythology did."

1822

Viceroy Muhammed Ali edited the <u>Journal</u> <u>du</u> <u>Khedive</u> in Arabia, in French and Arabic editions. It carried official bulletins and episodes from the <u>Arabian</u> <u>Nights</u>.

When royalists again took over France, they tightened press censorship and would not allow publications to discuss religion, the monarchy, royalty, or the private lives of citizens.

Spain banned spreading rules or doctrines which referred to acts dedicated to exciting rebellion or to disturb the public peace, even though they were disguised as allegories of imaginary persons or countries, or as dreams, or fictions, or anything similar.

1823

The India Vernacular Press Act required Indian language newspapers obtain licenses. Lord Buckingham was sent home to England because British officials in India were displeased with his <u>Calcutta</u> <u>Journal</u>.

1824

Australian Governor Thomas Brisbane discontinued censorship.

The kings and tyrants of Europe should have hearkened to the words of a German student in 1821 when he said, "Man must always have an organ with which to express himself. If he is deprived of the mouth and the pen, he raises his arm, and writes, instead of on paper, on men's bodies."

24
The Great and Bitter Causes,
1825 through 1867

The English common law definition of liberty of the press in 1825 was the view expressed by Chief Justice Parker of Massachusetts in 1825 in the Blanding's case, which was a criminal prosecution for a publication in a newspaper defamatory of an inn keeper. Parker said truth or falsity was immaterial in libel law.

1827

Passage by the Massachusetts House and Senate of a law establishing truth as a libel defense finally established press freedom in that state.

1828

Editor John P. Sheldon of the <u>Detroit</u> <u>Gazette</u>, was given a huge banquet after he was released from being jailed for contempt of court. His fine was paid by sympathizers who contributed sums of no more than 12 1/2 cents each.

1829

The Southern states enacted laws punishing expression intended to incite slaves to insurrection.

William Rawle said that life is indeed of little value without freedom of speech and press. The foundation of a free government begins to be undermined when freedom of speech on political subjects is restrained; it is destroyed when freedom of speech is wholly denied. Liberty of the press did not mean an absence of punishment for abuse of that liberty.

1831

Congress provided that contempt could not be construed to extend to any cases except the misbehavoir of any person or persons in the presence of the court or so near to obstruct the administration of justice. This law resulted from actions taken by Judge James Peck in citing Luke Lawless, an attorney, for contempt in a capricious and arbitrary manner, for a letter that had appeared in The Missouri Advocate and St. Louis Enquirer in 1826. The Senate acquitted Peck of impeachment charges; Congress passed the law to forbid federal courts from fining or imprisoning editors or others for criminal contempt of court for publications censuring judges.

1832

Virginia passed a law punishing the counselling in print of insurrection or rebellion among the slaves as a result of fears generated by the Nat Turner slave revolt. In 1836, Virginia passed strict laws against abolitionist literature.

Daniel Webster said, "The open attempt to secure the aid and friendship of the public press, by bestowing emoluments of office on its active conductors, is a threat against freedom of the press, turning the palladium of liberty into an engine of party."

Phineas T. Barnum was prosecuted three times for his caustic accusations against Connecticut citizens. He was sent to jail for 60 days for calling a deacon a "canting hypocrite" and a usurer. He edited his paper from his jail cell in Danbury. A big celebration occurred when he was released from prison.

1833

The Fruits of Philosophy or The Private Companion of Adult People by Charles Knowlton did much to revolutionize the sexual habits of the English-speaking world. Knowlton was fined in Taunton, Massachusetts. While in jail, Knowlton wrote an appendix for the edition published by Abner Kneeland in 1833.

1834

Abner Kneeland republished three essays of Ben Krapac without reading them thoroughly before placing them in his Boston Investigator. He was accused of blasphemy on the bases of isolated passage exerpted from the essays. Attorney Andrew Dunlap in defending Abner Kneeland said he has "the same legal right to the enjoyment, and the maintenance of his opinions, by his voice and his pen, which we claim for ourselves, as our political birthright, guaranteed by our glorious revolution; and proclaimed in our immortal Bill of Rights."

When Noah Webster published a Bible he cleaned up its language; for example, teats became breasts, piss became secretion or excretion, and whores became harlots.

1835

Massachusetts passed an anti-obscenity statute.

Southern states asked Northern states to outlaw the printing of publications having a tendency to make slaves discontented. President Andrew Jackson asked Congress to prohibit the circulation by mail in the Southern states or any publication that would cause insurrections by slaves. Congress rejected this request, and similar measures in 1836. The number of vigilance committees to control anti-slavery expression grew rapidly.

President Jackson's seventh annual message to Congress December 7 appealed for legislation authorizing censorship of the mails. Administrative decisions by President Jackson and Postmaster General Amos Kendall made to thwart abolitionist mail and activities, started a 100-year period of postal press control. Kendall approved the refusal of Postmaster Hughes of Charleston, South Carolina, to circulate anti-slavery mail. William Leggett, editor of the New York Evening Post, attacked Kendall's position establishing censorship of the press. Elijah Lovejoy was accused of smuggling abolitionist literature with a Bible shipment.

Alexis De Tocqueville said:

"The freedom of the press and universal suffrage are two things which are irreconcilably opposed by tyrannical governments." In Democracy in America, De Tocqueville said that liberty of the press was the only cure for the evils which equality might produce in a democracy. He said, "The more I consider the independence of the press in its principal consequences, the more I am convinced that in the modern world it is the chief and, so to speak, the constitutive element of liberty. A nation that is determined to remain free is therefore right in demanding, at any price, the exercise of this independence."

In Charleston, South Carolina, a meeting concluded that abolitionist editors were "no more entitled to the protection of the laws than the ferocious monster or venomous reptile."

The mob which roughed up William Lloyd Garrison in Boston did not try to stop publication of his Liberator. Garrison said, "He who opposes the public liberty overthrows his own."

1836

By 1836 all states in the South had moved to suppress abolitionist material tending to incite insurrection. Congress passed a law forbidding the Post Office to delay circulation of mail.

Judge Luke Lawless, said he was in favor of freedom of the press but believed the law should protect society from abuses of the press such as printing sermons against slavery. Elijah Lovejoy retorted "To establish our institutions of civil and religious liberty, to obtain freedom of opinion and of the press guaranteed by constitutional law cost thousands, yea, tens of thousands of valuable lives."

A mob destroyed the press and offices of the Philanthropist, an anti-slavery newspaper produced by James Birney in Cincinnati, while officialdom gave tacit approval. Reuben Crandall wrote a pamphlet suggesting blacks had equal rights with whites and that slaves should be free. Francis Scott Key, serving as prosecuting attorney, tried him for seditious libel, but Dr. Crandall was acquitted. The American Anti-Slavery Society published more than one million pieces of anti-slavery literature in 1836.

In Newport, Kentucky, William S. Bailey's Free South plant was destroyed. Cassius M. Clay's True American was seized and he was driven from Kentucky. In Philadelphia, John Greenleaf Whittier had his shop wrecked and burned by a mob mad at his abolitionist Pennsylvania Freeman. The Utica, New York, abolitionist Standard and Democrat was sacked.

William Ellery Channing, a Unitarian minister, became identified with the abolitionists even though he deplored their extreme positions. His understanding of the importance of freedom of the press and his analysis of the censorial mind were outlined following riots in Cincinnati. The presses of A. Hugh, a printer in Cincinnati, were destroyed by anti-abolitionists.

1837

The Rev. Elijah Lovejoy was killed by a mob for his anti-slavery publication, The Observer, which he edited at Alton, Ill.

Although the Boston Courier at first considered Lovejoy's martyrdom foolish, its editor Joseph Buckingham later wrote:

"The time was, but it seems to have gone by, when a man had a right to set up a press and print a newspaper, and when that right was secured to him by laws, which were simply sufficient for that purpose. Now he runs the hazard of being murdered, if he should exercise the privilege thus guaranteed by the highest civil authority, if he should advance a sentiment, or advocate a doctrine that should not suit every ruffian or blackguard who can throw a brickbat or pull a trigger."

1838

James Fenimore Cooper, who hated American newspapers, said, "The entire nation breathes an atmosphere of falsehoods. The country cannot much longer exist in safety under the malign influence that now over-shadows it; the press as a whole owes its existence to the schemes of interested political adventurers."

1840

Daniel Webster said, "The entire and absolute freedom of the press is essential to the preservation of government on the basis of a free constitution." Webster described the function of a free press as "Given a free press, we may defy open and insidious enemies of liberty. It instructs the public mind and animates the spirit of patriotism. Its loud voice suppresses everything which would raise itself against the public liberty, and its lasting rebuke causes incipient despotism to perish in the land."

The Army and Navy Chronicle insisted that American newspapers couldn't be free institutions because they had to espouse a cause or support a political party to be financially sound.

1841

Ralph Waldo Emerson said, "Every burned book enlightens the world, every suppressed or expunged word reverberates through the earth."

Willis Hodges, a Black, went to work doing white washing in New York to earn enough money to publish two issues of his Ram's Horn newspaper. Earlier he had to pay $15 to have a watered-down version of his letter-to-the-editor of the New York Sun published.

1842

A United States Customs law provided that custom officials were to keep out undesirable foreign daguerreotypes and photographs. Custom used this law also to keep out publications it believed obscene.

1843

Charles Dickens had his character Jefferson Brick describe New York journalism thus:

"Here's this morning's New York Sewer!", cried one. "Here's this morning's New York Stabber! Here's the New York Family Spy! Here's the New York Private Listener! Here's the New York Peeper! Here's the New York Plunderer! Here's the New York Keyhole Reporter! Here's the New York Rowdy Journal! Here's all the New York papers! Here's full particulars of the patriotic locofoco movement yesterday, in which the Whigs were so chewed up; and the last Alabama Gouging Case; and the interesting Arkansas dooel with Bowie knives; and all the Political, Commerical, and Fashionable News. Here they are! Here's the papers! Here's the papers!"

1844

Suppression of the Nauvoo Expositor in Nauvoo, Illinois, led to the murder of Morman leader Joseph Smith.

1845

James Fenimore Cooper, a Democrat, was attacked repeatedly by the Whig press, including Horace Greeley's Tribune. He brought 14 libel suits between 1837 and 1845 against Whig newspapers and won most of them. The severe judgments started a move for more moderate libel laws. William H. Seward contended that American courts had widened the broad and dangerous definition of libel so much that it was impossible to justify any libel, however true. "This broad definition was an undue restraint of free expression in the public press," he said.

In December, Congress rescinded all the gag rules used to prevent abolitionist mail or discussion of slavery to enter Southern states.

1846

The National Intelligencer claimed that Americans were the most enlightened people under the sun with 1250 newspapers serving 19 million people.

1847

Small newspapers on the fighting front were suppressed during the Mexican-American war.

1849

John Banvard, an American artist, exhibited his 1,320-foot-long moving canvas of the Mississippi Panorama to Queen Victoria and her court. These moving panoramas were popular and impressive entertainment and a forerunner of the moving picture theaters 50 years later.

1850

Daniel Webster said:

"The press violent! Why, sir, the press is violent everywhere. They think that he who talks loudest reasons the best. And this we must expect when the press is free, as it is here -- and I trust always will be -- for, with all its licentiousness and all its evil, the entire and absolute freedom of the press is essential to the preservation of government on the basis of a free constitution. Wherever it exists there will be foolish paragraphs and violent paragraphs in the press, as there are, I am sorry to say, foolish speeches and violent speeches in both Houses of Congress."

1852

G. C. Lewis said, "A government, exercising a censorship over the press, may permit considerable freedom of discussion upon religion, philosophy, and the history of the past ages; but with regard to the events of the day, and its own acts, its enforcement of silence is in general inexorable."

Rev. A. C. Coxe said he was opposed to any toleration of a popular and gifted writer when he perpetrated bad morals. "Let his brokerage of lust be put down at the very beginning." This reaction was part of the outcry over Nathaniel Hawthorne's <u>Scarlet Letter</u>.

1853

Edward Beecher said, "I should feel myself called upon to protect an infidel or Mohammetan paper, if assailed; or to re-establish it, if destroyed; as much as a paper designed to advocate the truths of Christianity."

1855

Artemus Ward said, "They sed the press was the Arkymedian Leaver which moved the world."

The Supreme Court ruled that the contempt power was inherent in the courts and that legislative power was powerless to limit it, and that by immemorial usage the power extended to words outside the court room. The decision provided a rationale for punishing out-of-court writing that many courts used if they felt such writing could interfere with justice.

1857

The American Railway Literary Union was organized to improve the type of literature available on thoroughfares.

A book about slavery was suppressed but finally published in 1864 after the Civil War. "We can print, publish, read, speak, listen to exactly what we please", the editor proclaimed in 1864.

1859

William S. Bailey published his anti-slavery <u>Free South</u> in Newport, Kentucky, for nine years but finally had to give up after his shop was mobbed for the second time in 1859.

Postmaster General J. Holt agreed that Virginia's law outlawing delivery of anti-slavery mail nullified the U.S. law forbidding delay of mail delivery as the U.S. Attorney General Caleb Cushing had ruled two years earlier.

The editor of the <u>Weekly Anglo-African</u> said the purpose of the New York Black newspaper was because: "We need a press -- a press of our own. We need to know something else of ourselves. Through the press other than the every day statements made up to suit the feeling of our opponents."

1860

The editor of the Cairo, Illinois, <u>Gazette</u> dumped huge piles of written material on the floor of the military censor who demanded all copy be submitted in advance. The editor really didn't intend to publish any of it.

Founding of the government printing office ended political patronage of newspapers via printing contracts.

Scores of Northern newspapers were temporarily, or permanently, suspended during the Civil War by the United States Postmaster, and the War Department censored telegraph messages.

Irwin Beadle created the dime-novel craze by publishing Edward Ellis' rousing tale of Seth Jones. Beadle and his brother published "books for the million! A dollar book for a dime." Seth Jones sold 400,000 copies.

1861

The War Department issued a general order forbidding the printing of any news whatever of camps, troops, or military or naval movements unless approved by a commanding general. Newspapers generally disregarded this order. Several generals, including William T. Sherman and Henry Halleck ordered all newspaper men out of the war area, although later on Sherman did relent and allow in a few. General McClelland tried a partially successful gentleman's agreement for correspondents to restrain their coverage. A New York Herald reporter was sentenced to six months for an article which displeased a general.

The New York Postmaster refused to handle mailing the Daily News, a severe critic of the Lincoln administration. The government even seized papers shipped by Railway Express. The effect was to put the paper, not related to the present New York Daily News, out of business for eighteen months.

Censorship was imposed after the battle of Bull Run. General McClelland tried a voluntary restraint system but this fell apart because of cheaters and a fuss between the United States State and War departments.

At a meeting of newspaper representatives in Washington, D.C., after a consultation with General McClelland, it was agreed that editors would refrain from publishing editorials or news about anything that would furnish aid or comfort to the South. This agreement constituted a rule of action for the censor of the press. Secretary Edwin M. Stanton ordered Harper's Weekly suspended for printing sketches of Yorktown under seige.

A mob destroyed the Jeffersonian, a copperhead newspaper. Later the editor was arrested. He was exonerated and his property restored. He won a civil suit against the United States marshall for trespassing. A New York grand jury condemned the Journal of Commerce, the Daily News, the Day Book, Freeman's Journal, and the Brooklyn Eagle, but the courts refused to prosecute them. Denial of the mails put them out of business for awhile.

Civil War suppressions of the press included military, presidential, judicial, postal, and mob control of speech and press. But President Abraham Lincoln said, "Let the people know the facts, and the country will be safe."

Secretary Edwin M. Stanton required reporters to submit articles to provost marshalls who were supposed to take out only military information. But the various generals distorted this practice by insisting on a good press for them personally. Stanton said, "No news gatherer, or any other newsperson, for sordid or treasonable purposes can be suffered to intrude on national agents to procure news by threats, to spy out official acts which the safety of the nation requires not to be disclosed." Several copperhead editors were jailed with no formal charges ever being filed, and no civil court remedies provided. Postmaster Montgomery Blair denied the use of the mails to newspapers he considered subversive, and telegrams were heavily censored by the military.

The editor of The Standard in Boone County, Missouri, had his press seized, and he was ordered out of the state by a military commission for encouraging resistance to the federal laws and government.

The 150 newspapers published by editors who called themselves Peace Democrats were constantly harrassed by Union soldiers or civilian mobs who called such papers the copperhead press.

Dennis Mahoney, a Dubuque, Iowa, editor, who believed in white supremacy, was jailed for three months after an election which the Republicans won, for his anti-government editorials criticizing President Lincoln for usurping powers during the Civil War.

General Henry Halleck expelled correspondents from the Union forces in the East. General William T. Sherman disliked journalists and once said, "We don't want the truth told about things here -- that's what we don't want."

1863

Major General William Butler suspended publication of the National Advocate in New Orleans for a day until Editor Jacob Butler was able to convince him the paper had not expressed unacceptable views about foreign intervention.

The federal and the state governments tried to keep incendiary material out of the mails. During the Civil War, Postmaster Blair removed from the mails or refused delivery of anti-Union writing, or material he considered obscene.

General Ambrose Burnside issued an order that closed the Chicago Times, and the midwest circulation of the New York World, both copperhead newspapers. But President Lincoln revoked the suppression immediately.

Albert D. Boileau, editor of the Philadelphia Evening Journal, apologized for an editorial criticizing Lincoln and urging a negotiated peace, which he said was put in the paper without his knowledge. He was released from his military jail and was subsequently called a "collapsed martyr" by his former backers.

1864

The New York Journal of Commerce claimed Lincoln had so many editors arrested with no habeas corpus that the names would fill eighteen columns.

General John Dix, New York marshall, suspended The New York World and The Journal of Commerce for publishing a false and forged presidential order for drafting 400,000 men, which was a hoax created by Joseph Howard, Jr., city editor of the Brooklyn Eagle, who thought he could manipulate the stock market for huge profits by the scheme. Abraham Lincoln promptly ordered the suppression revoked.

The New York press remained relatively free of censorship during the Civil War. Northern papers elsewhere were even freer. In Chicago, the Times was closed down three days, and the copperhead Philadelphia Evening Journal was suspended and went out of business. In New York some Times staff members helped the Tribune repel a mob attack.

1865

There were at least 60 cases of threats and violence against Northern newspapers and editors from angered citizens and soldiers during the Civil War. When Lincoln was assassinated in April, mobs attacked copperhead newspapers, destroyed presses, tarred and feathered editors, and threatened to lynch them. Congress passed a law that said mailing obscene material was criminal and the sender could be fined and jailed. There were at least 46 books of an erotic nature published in the United States between 1800 and 1865.

1867

New York passed a statute to suppress obscene literature because the YMCA believed city young men had weaknesses for poker, prostitutes, vile weekly newspapers, and licentious books.

25
Stamp Taxes and Blasphemy in Great Britain, 1825 through 1867

The Society for the Suppression of Vice financed trials of fourteen blasphemous publications and twenty obscene publications between 1817 and 1825. John Walter II was imprisoned for two years for publishing seditious libels about two royal dukes in his London Times in 1825. Charles Knowlton's Fruits of Philosophy, which was a book on birth control, was ruled obscene. Annie Besant and Charles Bradlaugh were prosecuted in England for selling the Knowlton book.

An anonymous London author said, "The press is now asylum for those retiring from the public lewdness of their despicable sewers. It is open to all vice and uninfluenced by every virtue."

Jeremy Bentham said that "licentiousness of the press is charged when suppression is to the advantage of the government. Liberty of the press is the right of any expression that does not inconvenience those in power."

1827

Lord Tenterden was refuted by the London Magazine for saying that "for Christianity is part and parcel of the law of the land." When Robert Tyler was convicted of blasphemy, the magazine said it is no more part and parcel of the law of the land than it is part and parcel of Lord Tenterden's wig. It is solely a belief in the truth, subject to critical inquiry."

Samuel Cook, a Worcester merchant, was found guilty of seditious libel for a handbill in his window accusing the government ministers of contributing to hunger and recommending they be beheaded on Tower Hill.

1829

The Duke of Wellington and his political allies lost in a propaganda war when they instituted libel prosecutions which resulted in <u>Morning Journal</u> Editor Alexander being fined and jailed for a year.

1830

Richard Carlile published his <u>Prompter</u> and was soon indicted for seditious libel. The jury was tortured and intimidated into a guilty verdict so Carlile could be sentenced to eight more months in jail.

William Cobbett was able to escape libel charges for a letter published in <u>Cobbett's Weekly</u>. The jury could not reach a verdict and the case ended as a <u>nolle prosequi</u>.

The Society for Promoting Useful Knowledge was founded in England to offer good literature. It didn't survive.

1831

William Carpenter was fined and jailed for failing to pay the stamp tax for his <u>Political Letters</u> which he claimed were separate publications and thus not a periodical.

Newspapers in England cost seven pence. The stamp cost was four pence. This priced newspapers beyond the reach of most people. Many person published newspapers without paying the tax, and many suffered severe penalties for doing so. A newspaper vendor told the court in England that:

"I stands here, your worships, upon right and principle, on behalf of the poor working, unedicated classes of this country. They are called ignorant, but what is the cause of their ignorance? Why the tax which prevents them from getting information. Your worships pretty well knows the reason them in power puts on the tax; it is to keep the poor from knowing their rights; for if poor working people knowed their rights, they would soon annihiliate the corrupt institutions that oppress them."

1833

Richard Barrett was convicted of seditious libel for publishing an article by Daniel O'Connor in <u>The Pilot</u> of Dublin. Robert Barnett was convicted of libel in Dublin for letters denouncing the Irish Coercion Act. Levy Emanual Cohen, editor of the <u>Brighton Guardian</u>, was jailed six months and fined for a paragraph about magistrates.

The English tax on pamphlets was discontinued.

1834

Richard Carlile spent 10 years of his publishing life in prison for violations of press laws in England.

In opposing stamp duties, Edward Bulwar, told the House

of Commons:

> "You create two newspaper monopolies -- one a monopoly
> of dear newspapers, and another monopoly of smuggled
> newspapers; you create two publics; to the one public of
> educated men, in the upper and middle ranks, whom no
> newspaper could, on moral points, very dangerously
> mislead, you give the safe and rational papers; to the
> other public, the public of men far more easily
> influenced -- poor, ignorant, distressed -- men from
> whom all the convulsions and disorders of society arise
> (for the crimes of the poor are the punishment of the
> rich) -- to the other public whom you ought to be most
> careful to soothe, to guide, and to enlighten, you give
> the heated invectives of demagogues and fanatics."

John Wilson said, "We have never felt that liberty of
the press was so essential to our existence as the air we
breathed or that without it we should have died."

William Blackwood said, "(The press) has effected a
greater change in human affairs than either gunpowder or the
compass."

There were 74 informations for libel filed by the crown
law-officers between 1816 and 1834. There were 133
prosecutions for seditious and blasphemous libels, and libels
defaming the king or his ministers or officials. Only 24 of
207 cases of these happened after 1826.

Henry Hetherington produced his _Poor_ _Man's_ _Guardian_ for
three years and defied the stamp tax. More than 500 persons
were arrested and fined for selling it, but a jury found it
to be a legal publication and not punishable with the
decision really not based on English law. Joseph Forster, a
crippled news-vendor, was jailed three months in the House of
Correction of Cold Bath Fields, England, for selling
unstamped newspapers (_The_ _Mass,_ _Police_ _Gazette,_ _Twopenny_
Dispatch, _Pioneer_, etc.) Henry Peter Brougham pointed out
that the British stamp tax on newspapers was an evil to
society, the impolicy of the government in continuing it, and
its interference with the spread of useful knowledge.

1835

Between 500 and 750 prosecutions resulted from
violations of the British stamp tax between 1800 and 1835.
Richard Carlile was fined, imprisoned, his business closed,
and $10,000 worth of pamphlets and books confiscated. Others
were heavily fined and sentenced to long jail terms.

1836

At least 500 publications with a weekly circulation of
200,000 defied the English stamp tax from 1830 to 1836,
despite the jailing of 800 newspaper vendors and publishers.
One seller said, in 1835, "Were I to give up selling the
Unstamped, my customers declare they will get them of some
other reason; as they are determined to have an Untaxed
Newspaper, even if they subscribed among themselves to

purchase the material for printing, for cheap knowledge they would have." England conducted 728 prosecutions for selling unstamped publications between 1830 and 1836 (219 of them were in 1835). Edward Bulwar told his colleagues in the House of Commons that, instead of silencing fanaticism, they had exalted the fanantic into a martyr. There were about 150 unstamped papers being produced regularly. When the 1819 Publications Act ended between 1815 and 1836 many illegal, unstamped newspapers appeared in England fueled by reform movements and radical publishers. Through a compromise, the newspaper stamp tax was reduced. In 1836, there were 46 prosecutions for stamp tax evasions.

1837

Albany Fontblanque said:

"In considering the subject of Taxes on Information, it should never be forgotten, that the newspaper is the poor man's book of knowledge. He has no other means of becoming acquainted with the law, the opinions of society, and the facts with which his own interests are connected. In this country it is a maxim, that ignorance of the laws is no excuse for violation of them; and yet there is no attempt at promulgation, not a show or pretence of it! The laws are supposed to be made in secret, the publication of debates being a breach of privilege; and when passed, the King's Printer has the monopoly of selling the Acts of Parliament in the most expensive form, and at a price far above the means of many. The newspaper publishes the debates, and makes those who can afford to buy them acquainted with new laws and the operation of them; but the newspaper is taxed above the means of the poor, who must suffer for their ignorance. Parliament puts beyond their reach the only instrument which can warn them of its laws. It makes a darkness, digs a snare, and punishes those who fall in it."

1840

Henry Hetherington, an English newspaper editor, was tried for blasphemy for selling pamphlets in which Charles Haslam said the Bible was abominable trash. He pointed out that citing only specific passages would condemn the Bible although he declined to read his list of objectionable Bible words.

1841

Charles Southwell derided the Bible as the Jew Book in his English atheist publication, The Oracle of Reason. For this he got a year in jail for blasphemous libel. Publisher Edward Moxon was found guilty of blasphemy in England for publishing Shelley's works.

1842

George Holyoake, interim editor of the Oracle of Reason, was jailed for six months in Gloucester for blasphemy in

Cheltenham. The regular editor, Charles Southwell, was already in jail on a blasphemy conviction. Thomas Patterson, third editor of the Oracle of Reason, was sent to jail for his account of the blasphemy trial of George Holyoake.

1843

Lord Campbell's Libel Act established truth as a libel defense for private defamation if the publication was for a public benefit. However, truth could not be used for seditious or blasphemous libel.

Lord Lynhurst said, "I have never yet seen, nor have myself been able to hit upon, anything like a definition of libel, and I cannot help thinking that the difficulty is not accidental, but essentially inherent in the nature of the subject-matter."

1844

Matilda Roalfe said, "To resist bad laws is no less a duty than to respect good ones. The law which forbids the publication of heterodoxy shall never be obeyed by me. I will publish irreligious opinions, be the consequences to myself what they may."

Thomas Patterson, when he got out of jail on a blasphemy sentence, went to Edinburgh and proclaimed he would sell blasphemous books. He was arrested on eleven blasphemy charges and spent fifteen months in jail. Thomas Finlay, who owned the bookshop soon thereafter, got a 60-day sentence. Then it was Matilda Roalfe's turn to get a 60-day sentence. Next, a Mr. Baker of the United Order of Blasphemers took over the superintendency of the Atheistic Depot. They gave Sunday school classes a discount.

Daniel O'Connor, a member of Parliament, and eight others, were tried for creating disaffection of people toward the government for publishing that Ireland and England should be separated. The House of Commons jailed him, but the House of Lords freed him.

1847

Dr. Drennan was acquitted by a jury from a seditious libel charge based upon a proclamation. But Archibald Rowan, signer of the proclamation and John Robb, its printer, were found guilty. Peter Finerty, publisher of the Durbin Press, was convicted of libel for publishing a criticism of the trial and execution of William Orr.

1849

The People's Charter Union was founded and eventually became the Association for the Repeal of the Taxes on Knowledge. A ten-member Newspaper Stamp Abolition Committee was formed. Collet Dobson Collet founded the London Association for the Repeal of the Advertising Duty.

Charles Griffin was sentenced to two years for libel

against the Leigh family in his book <u>Stoneleigh</u> <u>Abbey</u> <u>Thirty-</u>
<u>Four</u> <u>Years</u> <u>Ago</u>.

1850

The House of Commons voted 190 to 89 to continue the
newspaper advertising tax. Efforts were continuing to end
stamp taxes or duties on copies of newspapers, on
advertising, and on paper.

James Grant, a British journalist, predicted that
printing would become the great ruling power.

1851

There were only fourteen prosecutions for newspaper
stamp tax evasions. The highest assessed was ten pounds.
But there had been 28 other threats of heavy penalties to
other publications during a three-year period. Charles
Dickens' <u>Household</u> <u>Narrative</u>, a sometimes series, was judged
not to be a newspaper and thus not subject to the stamp tax.
The <u>Stake</u> <u>Narrative</u> and the <u>Dimferline</u> <u>News</u> also could not be
taxed because they appeared too infrequently.

1852

<u>The</u> <u>London</u> <u>Times</u>, in replying to an attack made upon it
in the House of Lords, said that the power of the press could
not in anyway be compared with the power of government or
could newspapers be required to adopt codes as governments
must. It said:

"We cannot admit that <u>The</u> <u>Times'</u> purpose is to share the
labours of statesmanship, or that it is bound by the
same limitations, the same duties, the same liabilities
as that of the Ministers of the Crown. The purpose and
duties of the two powers are constantly separate,
generally independent, sometimes diametrically opposite.
The dignity and freedom of the press are trammelled from
the moment it accepts an ancillary position. To perform
its duties with entire independence and consequently
with the utmost public advantage, the press can enter
into no close or binding alliances with the statesmen of
the day, nor can it surrender its permanent interests to
the convenience of the ephemeral power of any
government. The first duty of the press is to obtain
the earliest and most correct intelligence of the events
of the times, and instantly, by disclosing them, to make
them the common property of the nation. The statesman
collects his information secretly and by secret means,
he keeps back even the current intelligence of the day
with ludicrous precautions, until diplomacy is beaten in
the race with publicity. The Press lives by
disclosures; whatever passes into its keeping becomes a
part of the knowledge and history of our times; it is
daily and forever appealing to the enlightened force of
public opinion -- anticipating if possible the march of
events -- standing upon the breach between the present
and the future and extending its survey to the horizon
of the world.

"The duty of the journalist is the same as that of the historian -- to seek out the truth, above all things, and to present to his readers not such things as state craft would wish them to know but the truth as near as he can attain it.

"The ends which a really patriotic and enlightened journal should have in view are, we conceive, absolutely identical with the ends of an enlightened and patriotic minister, but the means by which the journal and the minister work out these ends and the conditions under which they work are essentially and widely different. The statesmen in opposition must speak as one prepared to take office; the statesmen in office must speak as one prepared to act. A pledge or a dispatch with them is something more than an argument or an essay -- it is a measure. Undertaking not so much the investigation of political problems as the conduct of political affairs, they are necessarily not so much seekers after truth as after expediency. The Press on the other hand has no practical function; it works on the ends it has in view by argument and discussion alone, and being perfectly unconnected with administrative or executive duties may, and must, roam at free will over topics which men of political action dare not touch."

Passage of the English Common Law Procedure Act made it legally impossible for English attorney-generals to hold editors accused of libel without trial for long periods in vile prisons. Another practice had been to hang men, cut them down, disembowel them, and cut them up in four pieces for saying or writing words that were held to have been uttered to encompass the death of the king. This doctrine of constructive treason was used to punish almost any kind of political debate.

1853

The duty on advertising was repealed by the House of Commons by a vote of 200 to 169. Milner Gibson used a parliamentary trick in the House of Commons to substitute the word "naught" for the tax amount. The change sailed through and the advertising tax died.

1855

The newspaper stamp tax was ended in England.

1857

Robert Dale Owen's Moral Philosophy written in 1835 was legal in Great Britain until 1857 when new anti-obscenity laws made it obscene.

1858

England prosecuted the publisher of Tyrannicide: Is It Justifiable by W. E. Adams because they considered it a libel of Napoleon III.

The Society for Suppression of Vice and Encouragement of Religion and Virtue reported 159 prosecutions. Convictions were won 154 times.

1859

John Stuart Mill wrote in his essay On Liberty:

"The time, it is to be hoped, is gone by when any defense would be necessary of the 'liberty of the press' as one of the securities against corrupt or tyrannical government." Mill's On Liberty utilitarianism contended the greatest good of the community cannot be separated from individual liberty. He said, "We can never be sure that the opinion we are endeavoring to stifle is a false opinion; and, if we were sure, stifling it would be an evil still. The real advantage which truth has consists in this, that when an opinion is true, it may be extinguished once, twice, or many times, but in the course of ages there will generally be found persons to rediscover it, until some one of its reappearances falls in a time when from favorable circumstances it escapes persecution until it has made such a head as to withstand all subsequent attempts to suppress it. The peculiar evil of silencing the expression of an opinion is, that it is robbing the human race; posterity as well as the existing generation; those who dissent from the opinion still more than those who hold it. Wrong opinions and practices gradually yield to fact and argument: but facts and arguments, to produce any effect on the mind, must be brought before it. Very few facts are able to tell their own story without comments to bring out their meaning."

1860

William Makepeace Thackery advised journalists "Ah, ye knights of the pen! May honour be your shield, and truth tip your lances! Be gentle to all gentle people. Be modest to women. Be tender to children. As for Ogre Humbug, out sword, and have at him."

When the last warrant was served on George Holyoake for flouting the English newspaper tax, his total penalties amounted to $3,000,000. He spent six months in jail in 1860 for blasphemy. The English Stamp Duty on paper was ended in 1861.

1867

In a famous decision, Judge Alexander Cockburn proposed the Hicklin test of obscenity which was to persist for nearly 100 years. He said, "I think the test of obscenity is this, whether the tendency of the matter charged as obscenity is to deprave and corrupt those whose minds are open to such immoral influences, and into whose hands a publication of this sort may fall."

26
False Promises of Freedom,
1825 through 1867

Karl Marx, 24, wrote for the <u>Rheinische</u> <u>Zeitung</u> <u>fur</u> <u>Politick,</u>
<u>Handel,</u> <u>and</u> <u>Gewerbe</u> arguing for press freedom in 1825.
Shortly afterward, the paper was closed down, and he edited
German-language newspapers in Switzerland, Strasbourg, Paris,
and London.

1826

Francois Chateaubriand said, "Liberty of the Press is
today the entire constitution. It consoles us for disgrace;
it restrains oppressors through fear of the oppressed; it is
the guardian of manners, the protector against injustice.
Nothing is lost as long as it exists."

1827

The French monarchy issued an ordinance tightening press
censorship by setting up a bureau of six censors to examine
and authorize newspapers and periodicals in Paris. Similar
bureaus were set up in the French departments.

1829

Ion Eliade Radulescu, a Rumanian revolutionary, started
the first Rumanian newspaper, <u>The</u> <u>Rumanian</u> <u>Courier</u>.

1830

The Belgium assembly declared the press to be free; it
said, "The press is free; censorship may never be re-
established and no surety bond may be extracted from authors,
editors, or printers. In matters concerning the press,
closed hearings may be held only with unanimous consent.
Jury trial is required in all hearings of press offenses."

Whenever the Swedish king suppressed Lars Hierta's newspaper, The Aftonblatt, Herta changed the name. He did this 30 times and made the king and the law look foolish. The king finally gave up.

Zurich became the first Swiss Canton to remove press censorship as a result of a long campaign by the Neue Zurcher Zeitung.

Andrew Bent, a convict-printer, was Australia's first martyr to a free press at the hands of the governor of Tasmania.

The Belgians declared their independence from the Dutch because Louis de Poiter and other editors defied stringent press controls established by William of Nassau when he assumed the Dutch Throne.

Charles X dissolved the French assembly and abrogated press rights. The resulting defiance by the journalists led to his downfall. The French ordinance of 1830 had suspended press freedom.

1832

King Louis Phillippe jailed Honore Daumier and Charles Philipon for exciting hatred and injury to the person of the king in cartoons and caricatures they published.

1833

Even though the French constitution said censorship could never be re-established, the monarchy had prosecuted 411 newspapers, 143 of which were condemned, and journalists had been sentenced to a collective 65 years in prison and fined 350,000 francs by 1833,

1834

The first liberal Danish newspaper, Fatherland, appeared when Denmark re-established its freedom from Napoleon.

The Church condemned L'Avenir which was a liberal Catholic publication urging separation of church and state in France. Louis Veuillot was imprisoned and his L'Univers suspended for opposition to liberal Catholicism.

1835

Calcutta inhabitants considered petitioning the British governor-general for the repeal of the Press Regulation Act of 1823. India governor general Charles Metcalfe established press freedom saying that a denial of freedom of expression was to contend that the essence of good government is to cover the land with darkness.

Theodore Gautier wrote Mademoiselle de Maupin as a tribute to sensuality. The book was severely criticized in France where it was suppressed until 1887 and until 1919 in the United States. Napoleon III provided nominal freedom of the press yet prosecuted 6,000 publishers during his reign. The French outlawed any attack against government or expressing the wish, hope, or threat of the destruction of the constitutional monarchial order.

1842

Karl Marx said:

"A free press is everywhere the open eye of the national spirit, the embodied confidence of the people in itself, the verbal bond that ties the individual to the state of the world, the incorporated culture which transforms material struggles into spiritual struggles and idealizes the crude materialized form. It is the heedless confession of a people before itself, and confession, as is known, has liberating power. It is the spiritual mirror in which the people observe themselves, and self-observation is the first condition of wisdom. It is the spirit of the state which can be carried into every hut, cheaper than material gas. It is versatile, the most modern and all knowing. It is the ideal world which always originates in the real world and flows into it again, giving life, as an ever richer spirit. Bear in mind that the advantages of freedom of the press cannot be enjoyed without toleration of its inconvenience. There are no roses without thorns."

He was expelled from Prussia in 1849 after his paper there, the Newe Rheinische Zeitung, was suppressed. He lived in poverty in London for the rest of his life, writing radical political materials, including Das Kapital.

1844

Emigres from Bulgaria published 30 different newspapers between 1844 and 1876 to oppose Turkish rule.

1845

Austrian intellectuals protested that "The situation of the press with respect to the censor is, alas, one devoid of legality. The writer is judged by norms which he does not know and is condemned without being heard and without being able to defend himself."

1848

The concept of a wholly free press in France grew out of the Revolution of 1848 after the end of the Napoleonic era, and during the French Second Republic. The French constitution of 1848 said that "the press can not in any case be subjected to censorship although absolute press freedom is not guaranteed."

Press censorship was abolished in Hungary and Austria largely due to the leadership of Louis Kassuth who had opposed Klemens Metternich for years, even having been jailed for three years in defiance of Hapsburg censorship.

When liberal Thornbecke became premier of Holland, a democratic constitution guaranteeing press freedom was adopted.

The Italian constitution guaranteed freedom of the press but required police registration of newspapers and listed press offenses.

The Prussian National Assembly asked all members of the German Confederation to end press censorship. But Frederick William put a stop to that movement. In Germany nothing could be printed without previous government permission.

Pierre-Joseph Proudhon and Henri Rocheport were two persistent heroes of the French press even though they had to flee from France to save their lives. Indeed, political exiles published clandestine and exile publications throughout Europe. After the election of 1848, the French Assembly set up severe press censorship. Proudhon escaped jail because he was a French Legislator, but his newspaper Le Representat du Peuple, was suppressed.

1849

Proudhon was sent to jail for three years for articles in his newspaper, Le Peuple. While in jail he edited his La Voix du Peuple. France imposed fines from 50 to 10,000 francs plus court costs and jail sentences of fifteen days to five years on many journalists between 1814 and 1849.

1850

The Prussian constitution said, "Censorship of the press may not be introduced; and no other restriction on the freedom of the press shall be imposed except by law."

1852

Italy set up a law prohibiting editorial criticism of foreign rulers.

Louis Napoleon imposed heavy government control on the press through his Organic Decree in France which set up press licensing for the next 16 years.

1856

The Obscene Books and Pictures Act of India was that colony's first such law.

1857

France prosecuted Charles Baudelaire's Les Fleurs du Mal and Gustave Flaubert's Madame Bovary. Between 1852 and 1857, France issued 338 warnings, 27 suspensions, and 12 suppressions to 120 newspapers.

As a response to mutiny, Charles Canning, the English governor-general of India, established a gagging act to censor all Indian journalists.

The Italian newspaper <u>Crepuscolo</u> was closed down by Austrian authorities because it wouldn't publish any news about the emperor's visit to Lombardy and the Po Valley.

1858

Pierre Joseph Proudhon escaped to Belgium to avoid a three-year jail sentence for publishing <u>De La Justice Dans La Revolution et Dans L'Eglise</u> which was called "reproduction in bad faith of false news likely to disturb the public peace and excite hatred between citizens."

1860

Press controls under Louis Napoleon were characterized by a journalist thus:

"Obstacles and pitfalls on all sides beset the newspaper and those who wrote for it. Self-censorship in the first instance, re-read and corrected with meticulous care by his editor, superintended in the last resort by the printer who was responsible before the law for everything that came off his press, stifled and hamstrung, attracting the thunderbolt and yet tied to the lightning-conductor, seated on the powder-barrel and condemned to strike the tinder-box, the journalist of 1866 was truly a victim tortured by the imperial regime."

1863

Germany's crown prince scolded Bismarck's severe press ordinance for having found no other means of coming to an understanding with public opinion than by imposing silence.

1864

The Pope issued a declaration that the opinions of Catholic writers were subject to the authority of the Roman congregations. This rule caused Lord Acton of England to discontinue his <u>Review</u>, an independent Catholic publication.

1865

Pierre Joseph Proudhon, given amnesty to return to France, died and 6000 Parisians went to his grave as a public protest of the French Government.

1866

Swiss newspapers had limited freedom of the press for more than 100 years.

Henri Rochefort quit the staff of <u>Figaro</u> in 1863 because officials disliked several of his articles. He started <u>La Lanterne</u> which was seized and he was fined and imprisoned; he fled to Belgium and smuggled copies back to France in hollow busts of imperial family members.

1867

The Fundamental Law of Austria established press freedom. Act XXV for the regulation of printing press and newspapers in India became the basis of a registration and survelliance system.

27
The Fourteenth Amendment,
1868 through 1899

In South Carolina in the reconstruction period of 1868, printing fraud was extensive. Money paid for public printing in 1868 and 1876 was $1,326,589, more than the state had paid out between its establishment and 1868.

The Fourteenth Amendment was ratified.

Henry J. Raymond of the New York Times said, "The free press in all the world has but one common mission -- to elevate humanity. Journalism must be the champion of the humble, the lowly, and the poor against those who from mere position and power hold in their hands the destinies of the lowly and the poor."

The Post Office assumed broad discretion to bar from the mails whatever its officials believed obscene.

1870

Mayor Oakley Hall forbade news stand sales of Harper's Weekly in New York City because of its attacks on the William Tweed ring.

Prurient publications included the Arena and the Alligator which were called loathsome and bestial.

Whitelaw Reed said, "I rejoice in the institution of every libel suit for which there is the color of justification; and count every fair conviction for libel a gain to the cause of decent journalism."

"It is a newspaper's duty to print the news, and raise hell," according to Wilbur Storey, editor of the Chicago Times.

Dr. Simon M. Landis was given the maximum sentence of a year in jail and a $500 fine for his sex education book <u>Secrets</u> <u>of</u> <u>a</u> <u>Generation</u>. Judge Pierce refused to hear medical testimony, about the book.

1871

Thomas M. Cooley said the liberty of speech and press is a right to utter freely and to publish whatever the citizen may please. "The citizen is protected against any responsibility for so doing, except so far as such publications because of blasphemy, obscenity, or scandalous character, may be a public offence, or by falsehood and malice they may injuriously affect the standing, reputation or pecuniary interests of individuals," he said.

The Senate imposed imprisonment upon two <u>New York Tribune</u> men for refusing to reveal the name of a senator who had given them a copy of a secret treaty.

Victoria Claflin Woodhull and her sister Tennessee Claflin were jailed in New York City by Anthony Comstock for charging Rev. Henry Ward Beecher with infidelity in their <u>Woodhull</u> <u>and</u> <u>Claflin</u> <u>Weekly</u>. Comstock had as his motto "Morals, Not Art or Literature". He believed if you open the door to anything, the filth will pour in and the degradation of youth will follow.

The Supreme Court eliminated the application of the Fourteenth Amendment to the rights of the Bill of Rights in the Slaughterhouse case.

The Comstock Act, the principal American anti-obscenity legislation, was passed by Congress. It pertained to the publication of material deemed "obscene, lewd, and lascivious." Comstock's committee became the New York Society for the Suppression of Vice with a state charter and support from bankers and manufacturers. Comstock became a full-time special agent of the Post Office with police power to make arrests.

1874

In an 1874 report, the New York Society for the Suppression of Vice claimed it had seized 130,000 pounds of bound books and 60,300 articles made of rubber for immoral purposes. Anthony Comstock was assaulted and stabbed. He had traveled 23,500 miles by rail in his efforts to stamp out obscenity.

Boss William Tweed's representatives carried his traditional black bags of bribing money to 84 newspapers, some of which had to have that money to survive.

1875

Ralph Waldo Emerson said, "We have the newspaper which does its best to make every square acre of land and sea give an account of itself."

Boston set up the New England Watch and Ward Society,

and Philadelphia set up a vice suppression society as did Cincinnati, Cleveland, St. Louis, Louisville, Chicago, Rochester, Providence, Detroit, Toledo, San Francisco, and Portland.

1876

Crammond Kennedy said the press is shorn of its real power by the abuse of liberty.

1877

U.S. Postal Second Class Mail Regulations of 1878 pressured many non-commercial publications out of operation.

1879

The Senate fired its chief executive clerk James Young for revealing secret proceedings to a correspondent of the Philadelphia Star.

Postal regulations stipulated that a publication must be for the dissemination of information of public character, or devoted to literature, the science, arts, or some special inquiry, and have legitimate subscribers to enjoy low rate second class mailing privileges.

A National Defense Association was formed to fight Anthony Comstock and his New York Vice Society.

President James A. Garfield said, "Not for its own sake alone, but for the sake of society and good government, the press should be free. Publicity is the strong bond which unites the people and their government. Authority should do no act that will not bear the light."

1880

Anarchist editors were hanged in Illinois, and John Mort's New York Freiheit was suppressed because of its anarchistic propaganda. Truth, an anarchist publication, had the motto: "Truth is 5 cents a copy and dynamite is 40 cents a pound."

John Proffatt said, "Freedom of the press is no longer a blessing but operates a dangerous and unrestrained vituperation of private character in the publication of much that is vile and demoralizing, and the misrepresentation of public men and measures."

Preacher Henry Ward Beecher said, "Newspapers are the school-masters of the common people. That endless book, the newspaper, is our national glory."

1881

Walt Whitman's Leaves of Grass was charged with obscenity. Only the Library Company of Philadelphia had bought a copy; all other libraries censored it.

Cornell University students traditionally burned their textbooks in a bonfire after the semester's end. Student book burning had begun in Wittenberg, Germany, under the leadership of Martin Luther.

1882

The American Railway Literary Union produced a guide to suppress pernicious literature. Walt Whitman's <u>Leaves</u> <u>of</u> <u>Grass</u> was banned in Boston.

Ezra Heywood of Princeton, Massachusetts, was convicted of obscenity for his pamphlet <u>Cupid's Yokes</u>. He was released from jail after six months by President Hays. Soon thereafter he was re-arrested by Anthony Comstock, but the judge rejected two of Comstock's charges and the jury refused to convict Heywood of the third.

1883

The Post Office barred <u>Dr. Foote's Health Monthly</u> from the United States mails because of its discussion of sex. He tried to use Canadian post offices. A new post master, however, reversed the earlier suppression of the magazine.

1884

John Bascom complained that greater freedom of the press had eliminated legal protections of personal rights. Edward Zeus Franklin Wickes convinced a grand jury in Boston that his book, <u>Illustrated Domestic Medical Counsellor</u>, was a serious sex education book and not obscene.

1885

A trustee of the Concord Public Library said Mark Twain's <u>The Adventures of Huckleberry Finn</u> "deals with a series of adventures of a very low grade of morality; it is couched in the language of rough dialect, and all through its pages there is a systemic use of bad grammar. The book is flippant and irreverent. It is trash of the veriest sort." Twain said that the action of banning the book from the Concord Public Library would "sell 25,000 copies for us, sure."

1886

Henry Adams said, "Free discussion does not contemplate such license to press and speech as will endanger the peace and tranquility of the community."

1887

C.B. Reynolds, a free thought lecturer, was tried, convicted, and fined under state law for issuing a blasphemous work which was a satirical pamphlet circulated in Morristown, New Jersey.

Anthony Comstock seized 117 photos of French masterpieces from an art gallery because he called them lewd and a foreign foe. The courts held that the pictures were not obscene, however, when the New York World-Telegram produced sketches of them.

1888

Thomas M. Cooley said, "The freedom of the press was undoubtedly intended to be secured on public grounds, and the general purpose may be said to preclude those in authority from making use of the machinery of the law to prevent full discussion of political and other matters in which the public are concerned."

Moses Harmon was under jail sentence or bonding for ten years for having published four articles in Lucifer, the Light Bearer in Kansas about the sexual emancipation of women.

1889

Robert W. Buchanan said, "The man who says a book has power to pollute his soul ranks his soul below a book." W.S. Lilly said, "Censorship of the press is as antiquated as mail armour."

T. DeWitt Talmadge, a well-known preacher, attacked books for their influence on young people by saying:

"Cursed be the books that try to make impurity decent, and crime attractive, and hypocrisy noble. Cursed be the books that swarm with libertines and desperadoes, who make the brain of the young people whirl with villainy. Ye authors who write them, ye publishers who print them, ye booksellers who distribute them, shall be cut to pieces, if not by an aroused community, them, at last by the hail of divine vengeance, which shall sweep to the lowest pit of perdition all ye murderers of souls. If there is anything in your library that is evil, author, do not give it away, for it might spoil an immortal soul, do not sell it for the money you get would be the price of blood; but rather kindle a fire on your kitchen hearth, or in your back yard, and then drop the poison in it, and keep stirring the blaze until from preface to appendix there shall not be a single paragraph left."

1890

Criminal libel actions in state supreme courts reached their peak in the decade between 1890 and 1900, with more than 100 cases. There were 20 such cases between 1871 and 1880 and 75 between 1881 and 1890. But such cases almost disappeared by 1950.

Charles Dana said, "There is a great disposition in some quarters to say that the newspapers ought to limit the amount of news they print; that certain kinds of news ought not to be published. I have always felt that whatever the Divine Providence permitted to occur, I was not too proud to report."

J.B. Caldwell was arrested for obscenity for urging "coition for offspring only" in an article in <u>Christian Life</u>. Depictions of sex and sexuality began appearing in movies as early as 1890.

The Brooklyn Public Library barred Mark Twain's <u>Adventures</u> <u>of</u> <u>Tom</u> <u>Sawyer,</u> <u>The</u> <u>Adventures</u> <u>of</u> <u>Huckleberry</u> <u>Finn</u>, and <u>Tom</u> <u>Sawyer's</u> <u>Comrade</u>.

Frank Trigg, a Black professor, said, "Were it not for the Negro press, the country would be in comparatively total darkness as to the Negroes' real conditions."

1891

Albert Ross said:

"We do not care so much that vice exists as that it is well-dressed. The nude in literature is on trial. It is almost as sinful to write about sexual sin as it is to commit it. The professional conservators of morality in print who experience difficulties in drawing the line between the moral and the immoral have never hit upon the exellent plan of letting everybody make the decision for himself."

The Post Office attempted to keep Leo Tolstoy's <u>Kreutzer Sonata</u> out of the mails, thus boosting its circulation greatly.

Julian Hawthorne said, "It would be better to have the country flooded with genuine vicious and obscene literature than to establish the precedent of imprisoning men for publishing their honest opinions."

1893

The William Tweed ring attempted to throttle <u>The New York Times</u> by buying up a majority of its stock, indicting the paper for libeling the mayor, and taking over the <u>Times</u> building. The New York Legislature passed a law to revive libel of the government, but the governor vetoed it.

Anthony Comstock said:

"Hark! What sound is this that drowns out Niagara? It is the whirl, the united whirl, of the devil's printing press -- as it is striking off millions of pages of printed matter to infatuate our boys and girls; to defile their minds; to corrupt their thoughts; to pervert their imaginations, to sear their consciences, harden their hearts, and damn their souls."

Howard MacQueary said, "The remedy is not denunciation, but displacement of bad by good literature. Prohibition has always increased a desire for the forbidden fruit. In ignorance alone is danger; in knowledge alone is safety."

1894

The New York Supreme Court ruled that The Arabian Nights, Tom Jones, and The Decameron were not obscene, thus overturning charges made by Anthony Comstock and the New York Society for the Suppression of Vice. George A. Wilson, an Indiana bookseller, was fined for mailing Boccacio's Decameron because the postmaster believed it to be obscene. Sadakichi Hartmann was arrested in Boston for his play Christ which the authorities considered obscene.

John Biddulph Martin sought a court order to stop circulation of The Beecher-Tilton Scandal because he believed it libeled his wife Victoria Claflin Woodhull.

1895

The National Purity Congress was a forerunner of modern social hygiene movements. It criticized the press for publishing theater news and advertising the immoral stage.

1896

When cases concerning violation of the Comstock law on obscenity reached the Supreme Court, no efforts or contentions that First Amendment protection could be involved were made. The Supreme Court accepted the Hicklin test of obscenity and found a 12-page paper written by Lew Rosen called Broadway obscene.

Reporter guarantees of confidentiality of news sources have existed since 1896.

Louis Waisbrooker was arrested for mailing a pamphlet, The Lawyer's Letter, which offered free love advice. The Post Office considered it obscene.

1898

Courts acquitted the Book for Women but condemned the use of lantern slides of nude women in a lecture for ladies only. The Adult, a journal devoted to combatting sex ignorance, was suppressed.

1899

The California penal code required that articles reflecting on the personal or professional reputation of persons had to identify the author.

Walter Hunt was arrested for obscenity for his Gattling Gun publication.

United States military officials applied severe censorship at the time of the Philippine insurrection.

28
Great Britain Attacks Vice,
1868 through 1899

Lord Chief Justice Alexander Cockburn in England decided in 1868 that The Confessional Unmasked, an anti-Catholic pamphlet, was obscene. Obscenity was "whether the tendency of the matter charged as obscene is to deprave and corrupt those whose minds are open to such immoral influences and into those hands a publication of this sort may fall." This view became known as the Hicklin rule and was used in American courts until the 1950s.

Charles Bradlaugh, a British reformer, was acquitted from charges based on the English stamp act for his National Reformer. His defense helped convince Parliament to repeal the security bond system in 1869.

Alexander Sullivan, publisher of the Weekly News in Ireland was sentenced to six months for seditious libel for articles criticizing a murder trial. Richard Piggott, publisher of the Irishman, was given a year's sentence for reporting details of Finian Conspiracy activities seeking Irish independence. He was jailed in 1871 by the Dublin Commission Court for accusing the chief justice in an editorial of shameless bias and accepting perjury in a murder trial.

1873

Sir James F. Stephen said John Stuart Mill was naive to urge toleration of a variety of opinion and free discussion, for such toleration would give rise to fanatics "who, when they get to power, will not tolerate the tolerant."

1875

Benjamin Disraeli said, "The printing press is a

political element unknown to classic or feudal times. It absorbs in a great degree the duties of the sovereign, the priest, the parliament; it controls, it educates, it discusses."

English lawbooks classified indecent, obscene, and immoral publications as public nuisances rather than as libels.

1877

Charles Bradlaugh and Annie Besant were indicted for blasphemy and obscenity for publishing Dr. Charles Knowlton's The Fruits of Philosophy, an American contraceptive manual.

1879

The Society for Suppression of Vice and the Encouragement of Religion and Virtue had suppressed several cheap periodicals such as Paul Pry, Polly Pree, and Women in London. They had seized 380,569 prints and 63,486 books by 1879.

1881

In England, the government discontinued requiring cash deposits by newspapers under the Six Acts provisions, and set up a new libel law to eliminate criminal libel prosecution of publishers.

1882

Charles Bradlaugh said:

"My plea is, that modern heresy, from Spinoza to Mill, has given brain-strength and dignity to everyone it has permeated -- that the popular propagandists of this heresy, from Bruno to Carlile, have been the true redeemers, the true educators of the people. And if today we write with higher hope, it is because the right to print has been partly freed from the fetters forged through long generations of intellectual prostration and almost entirely freed from the statutory limitations, which under the pretence of checking blasphemy and sedition, have really gagged honest speech against Pope and Emperor, against church and throne."

Sir Leslie Stephen said:

"Criminal laws should not be brought into play to punish people for outrages upon good taste, but only for directly inciting to violence. The fact that an opinion is offensive to a majority is so far a reason for leaving it to public opinion which in most cases is capable of taking care of itself; and we are certainly not impartial or really tolerant till we are equally anxious to punish one of the majority for insulting the minority."

1883

The Freethinker was tried for blasphemy which was described by the chief justice as material including elements of reviling, promoting immorality, or the use of ribald language calculated to deprave public morality and to endanger the peace. George W. Foote, editor, was sentenced a year in prison for blasphemy. His printer, Mr. Kemp, got three months. W.J. Ramsey spent nine months in Holloway Jail in England for blasphemy for an article in the Freethinker. England's laws on blasphemy were repealed in 1884.

1885

Henry S. Ashbee said, "More youths have become criminals through reading of deeds real or fictitious, of murders, pirates, highwaymen, forgers, burglars, etc., than have ever developed into libertines from the perusal of obscene novels.

W.T. Stead, editor of the Pall Mall Gazette, crusaded against London prostitution in a series of articles called the Maiden Tribute of Modern Babylon.

1886

England's National Vigilance Association for Repression of Criminal Vice and Public Morality took over the campaign against pornography.

The Irish Law Times editorialized that "the newspaper as a watchdog of civilization does not believe in keeping silent because there is nothing to bark at; the law sometimes needs to let fly its bootjack to silence uneccesary howling."

1887

Henry Fox Bourne said, "Sedition, blasphemy, scurrility, and immorality, if they have not been quite kept out of newspapers, have dwindled down and have lost all their force now that enlightened public opinion has substituted a new censorship for that of the old tyranny."

1889

Henry Vizetelly was jailed in England for publishing exerpts from Nana and LaFerre, novels by Emile Zola. He was prosecuted by William A. Coote, head of England's National Vigilance Association, an anti-indecent literature group. Parliament established an Indecent Advertising Act.

1890

Oscar Wilde said, "There is no such thing as a moral or an immoral book. Books are well or badly written. That's all."

1893

M.E. Stone said, "There has never been an hour when the first aid to autocracy has not been the placing of the press in leash."

Herbert Spencer said, "so long as he does not suggest the commission of crimes, each citizen is free to say what he pleases about any or all our institutions even to the advocacy of a form of government utterly different from that which exists, or the condemnation of all governments."

1895

Thomas Hardy's novel <u>Jude</u> <u>the</u> <u>Obscure</u> was banned as immoral. Hardy was so offended that he never wrote another novel.

1898

George Bedborough was arrested in England for selling Havelook Ellis' <u>Studies</u> <u>in</u> <u>the</u> <u>Psychology</u> <u>of</u> <u>Sex</u>, his <u>The</u> <u>Adult</u> publication, and other books. He pled guilty, and later wrote a long apology to the Free Press Defence Committee entitled "George Bedborough, Coward."

1899

The National Council for the Promotion of Public Morals was founded to encourage "whatsoever things are beautiful, and honest and of good repute in literature."

29
Tentative Improvements,
1868 through 1899

The Deputies of France set up in 1870 the most liberal press law of all, but it continued a small list of forbidden press offenses. France had required printers to pay "caution" fees until 1870. Australian legislative censorship began in the six colonies. The penal code in India had provisions that added sedition prosecution and extended bureaucratic control of the press to cover class hatred and public mischief.

1871

The censor of the Czar approved Karl Marx's Das Kapital because he believed it didn't pertain to Russia which was feudalistic and not capitalistic.

1874

The German Imperial Press Law provided for a free press, but the government continued repression, including closing 42 socialist papers, and banning the Catholic Germania more than 600 times.

1875

During the 1870's, France, under command of General Begeaud, pacified Algeria with ferocity. The general said, "It may be that I shall be called a barbarian, but I consider myself as above the reproaches of the press." Benjamin Constant, a French painter, said, "With newspapers, there is sometimes disorder; without them there is always slavery."

1876

Fifty-eight Japanese editors were jailed for violations of the law by the Meiji government, which repressed editors during its entire regime. But newspapers persisted; in the 1890 elections, many journalists were elected to the National Assembly.

1878

The Vernacular Press Act placed heavy restrictions in the 170 native language newspapers of India until 1881.

Two attempts to kill the German Emperor caused Germany to repress the socialist press. During the year 127 periodicals and 278 other publications were suppressed in Germany for suspected socialistic leanings. In 1890, Bismarck had inflicted jail terms totaling 100 years on editors. He said, "Every country is held at some time to account for the windows broken by its press; the bill is presented, some day or other, in the shape of hostile sentiment in the other country."

1879

The Canadian national policy on tariffs prohibited importation of books, printed papers, drawings, paintings, prints, photographs, or representations of any kind.

1880

Austria prosecuted 2,000 newspaper post-publication cases against confiscated publications.

A house painter contracted to be the jailable editor for Germany's _Social -- Demokraton_ for 10 crowns per week, plus a bonus of five crowns per week up to thirteen weeks per jail term.

1881

France prohibited anarchy and obscenity. Obscenity was defined as an offense against public and religious morality and good taste. The French also eliminated the press caution system of deposits to cover possible fines. The French press law of 1881 replaced 42 earlier laws containing a total of 235 control provisions.

Japan had its Law of Newspaper Extermination to destroy anti-government publications. Thomas Paine's _Age of Reason_ was ruled indecent in Canada.

1883

Thomas Masaryk founded _The Athenalien_ review in which he exposed forged documents glorifying Bohemiam culture, which he believed were the wrong basis for Czech freedom.

1885

England suppressed _Bosphore Egyptian_, a newspaper critical of Great Britian, but relented to allow the Egyptian publication to resume publication. _Das Kapital's_ second volume was approved by Russian censors because it was only comprehensible to specialists.

1887

Canada declared the works of Thomas Huxely, John Tyndall, and Herbert Spencer to be immoral, irreligious, and injurious. Louis Legrand was jailed for his illustration called "Prostitution" which was published in Le Courier Francaise.

1888

The Prussian government immediately suppressed the 1848 Communist Manifesto of Karl Marx and Fredereich Engels after the Prussian revolutions.

1889

Socialist Domela Niuwenhuis was sent to jail for eight months for writing that Dutch King William III had "made little of his job."

1890

The German index expurgatorius contained the names of 13 periodicals, 83 newspapers, and 60 foreign publications. In response, socialist publications were smuggled into Germany by thousands every week from Switzerland and France. Otto Bismarck controlled the German government press; the opposition press was severely prosecuted. More than 600 "criticisms of the king" or "lese majesti" cases were prosecuted against German socialists. The German anti-socialist law was used to suppress 1,229 publications, including 104 newspapers and periodicals.

1894

Ludwig Quidde was sent to jail in Germany for remarks critical of the emperor he made at a public meeting, but actually as punishment for his Caligula: A Study in Roman Caesarean Madness. This study was a satire on the Kaiser and his megalomania and delusions of grandeur. A pamphlet of the article sold 150,000 copies. The government couldn't prosecute Quidde because that would officially identify the Kaiser as Caligula.

1895

Julius Motteler managed a socialist publication smuggling operation that brough 10,000 copies of such publications each week into Germany from Switzerland for several years.

Charilaos Tricoupis was jailed in Greece in 1874 for writing a newspaper article, "Who Is to Blame?" and pointed out the king. He was acquitted and was soon appointed Prime Minister, a position he held intermittenly until 1895. Editor Hjalmar Branting also became prime minister of Sweden, and Editor Nicholas Pasic became prime minister of Serbia after enduring government suppressions and punishments for their newspaper writings.

1896

Gustave Flaubert was charged with immorality and lasciviousness for publishing his novel <u>Madame Bovary</u> about the passions of a French woman in a provincial town. The novel became a best-seller when the court acquitted Flaubert. He refused to alter the novel for <u>La Revue de Paris</u> and said, "I'll do nothing more, not a correction, not a deletion, not a comma less, nothing, nothing. One can't whiten Negroes and one can't change the blood of a book; one can only impoverish it, that is all."

Liang Chi-Chao made three attempts to start newspapers in China. He met strong government disapproval and had to flee to Japan. He said, "The strength of a nation depends on whether the channels of communication are open or not. The freedom of thought, speech, and publication are truly the mother of civilization."

1898

Emile Zola was convicted of libel for publishing his famous <u>J'Accuse</u> letter which launched the exposure of French corruption in the Dreyfus affair. Zola fled to England to escape imprisonment.

K'ang Yu-Wei, editor of <u>Chinese Progress</u>, tried to get a Chinese law to protect the press, but had to flee the Empress Dowager's control. The Empress Dowager offered rewards for the capture of editors she hated and punished persons reading their newspapers.

1899

Among the victims of European press censorship in the Nineteenth Century were Jules Guesde and Paul Brouse, French socialists; Honore Daumier, French cartoonist; Prince Peter Kropotkin, an anarchist writer; Louis Kossuth, Hungarian nationalist; August Palm and Hjalmar Branting, Swedish socialists; Nicholas Pasic, Serbian radical leader; Victor Adler, Austrian socialist; William and Karl Lebknecht and Rosa Luxemburg, German socialists; and Michael Lemontov, Maxim Gorky, Leo Tolstoy, and Alexander Puskin, Russian authors.

30
Censorship American Style, 1900 through 1924

Justice Henry C. Brown criticized the press in 1900 for cruelty in assaulting character and invading privacy with sensationalism. He urged self-restraint, not censorship.

James R. Osgood cancelled a contract to publish an edition of Walt Whitman's Leaves of Grass when The Watch and Ward Society of Boston had a Boston district attorney complain about it.

The Iowa Supreme Court ruled that publishers did not have to print either advertisements or news items.

Stephen Crane's Maggie, a Girl of the Streets was heavily expurgated before it could be published in 1900.

The Georgia Supreme Court said, "Liberty of speech and of writing is secured by the Constitution, and incident thereto is the correlative liberty of silence, not less important nor sacred."

1901

A court ruled that performers could not collect libel damages because the public, including the news media, had the right to criticize, even severely, their public performances.

1902

The United States Post Office denied second-class mailing privileges to weekly journals edited by persons it considered to be "cranks".

Gov. Samuel W. Pennypacker signed a Pennsylvania libel law to stop criticism of state officials in a deliberate attempt to terrorize the press and stifle public comment.

Ida C. Craddock committed suicide rather than serve a second jail sentence when she was arrested a second time for her sex education book, The Wedding Night. The arrest came after a testimonial dinner honoring her after her release for serving the first sentence for obscenity. Both arrests were engineered by Anthony Comstock.

Mattie Penhallow, postmistress at Horne, Washington, was arrested for forwarding in the mails an article entitled "The Awful Fate of a Fallen Woman" published in Clothed in the Sun.

New York imposed penalties on publications about anarchy as its reaction to President McKinley's assassination. Four states had laws to punish advocacy of the violent overthrow of the government.

1903

President Theodore Roosevelt convinced Congress to pass the Immigration Act of 1903 to bar or deport anyone who advocated overthrow by force or violence of the United States government.

A Boston judge declared Boccacio's Decameron and works by Francois Rabelais to be obscene and fined booksellers for selling them. A committee of nine persons was named in Dayton, Ohio, to suppress bad books and to recommend prosecution of vile literature.

1904

President Theodore Roosevelt said:

"If there is one thing we ought to be careful about it is in regard to interfering with the liberty of the press. I think it is a great deal better to err a little bit on the side of having too much discussion and having too virulent language used by the press, rather than to err on the side of having them not say what they ought to say, especially with reference to public men and measures."

1905

Judge Joseph Story said:

"It was loose thinking to believe that freedom of the press was inviolately constitutional so that like the king of England, it could do no wrong in the United States and was free from every inquiry and provided a perfect sanctuary for every abuse, or that, in short, it implied a despotic sovereignty to do every sort of wrong without the slightest accountability to private or public justice. This freedom is an inestimable privilege in a free government; without such limitation it might become the scourge of the republic."

Bernarr McFadden was arrested for the cover design on an issue of <u>Physical Culture</u>, and for pictures in another issue on a complaint issued by Anthony Comstock of the New York Vice Society. Comstock tried to suppress George Bernard Shaw's play, <u>Mrs. Warren's Profession</u>, but failed to get "the Irish smut-dealer and foreign writer of filth" convicted. Shaw derided the effort as "Comstockery."

John S. Summer succeeded Anthony Comstock as head of the New York Society for the Suppression of Vice. He said:

"I shall go after the sellers and distributors of indecent pictures and cards and literature just as fiercely as he ever did. The Society is an agency to enforce the law where it is violated. It is not a censor. I see the need of protection for the young from the temptations of pandering enterprises which assault their eyes and ears. The judiciary should be aroused to the fact that the safeguarding of public morals is much more important than upholding alleged freedom of expression or freedom of the press. The suppression of obscene literature and pictures is an ever present necessity."

Samuel Hopkins Adams claimed that patent medicine advertisers and newspapers conspired to suppress reporting any detrimental information about the drug industry. The article helped lead to the enactment of the Food and Drug Act of 1906.

Publisher Joseph Pulitzer said, "Our Republic and its press will rise or fall together. An able, disinterested public-spirited press, with trained intelligence to know right and courage to print it, can preserve that public virtue without which popular government is sham and a mockery."

1906

U.S. Commissioner A.W. May dismissed obscenity charges against Carrie Nation for the July 1 issue of her publication <u>The Hatchett</u> for an article about little boys masturbating and for taunting President Theodore Roosevelt for not closing down 113 whore houses within six blocks of the White House.

Thaddeus B. Wakeman, a leader in the National Liberal League, believed the Comstock law was a threat to the freedom of the press, a violation of the Bill of Rights, a merging of church and state, and an offense to humanity.

M.H. Judge contended that "the freedom of the press is a jewel to be maintained at all cost, but the publication of false news is no more to be associated with freedom than theft is to be associated with free exchange."

Assistant Postmaster General Edwin C. Madden denied second-class mailing privileges to the <u>Indianapolis Union Signal</u> because it was a union publication which he believed did not disseminate information of a public character.

Theodore Schroeder intensified his efforts to champion a completely free press through writing and speaking. Natural rights and moral and social progress underlaid his insistence on unrestricted and unpunished speech and press except when it would be determined that words had inseparably accompanied some attempted or achieved violence to person or property. He believed it was anathema for government authorities to have power to decide whether words were criminal, on the basis of an ex-post facto guess about the words' psychological tendency to do damage. He wrote untiringly against punishing radical attacks on government and blasphemous attacks on religion, but he was most concerned with the law of obscenity and the activities, suppressions, attitudes, and long-term effects of the Anthony Comstock organizations and their followers.

Alexander Hill said public libraries should keep out bad books just as they would bad men and should reject books that are poisonous to the moral nature.

1907

Senator Thomas Patterson, publisher of The Rocky Mountain News in Denver, Colorado, attacked corruption of the Colorado Supreme Court for partisan decisions in a political election. The court cited him for contempt. He lost appeals in the United States Supreme Court on the basis of the First and Fourteenth Amendments. He was not able to establish press protection under the Fourteenth Amendment.

Justice Oliver Wendell Holmes, speaking for the court majority, used the English Common Law definition of liberty of the press in saying that "the main purpose of such constitutional provisions (declaring liberty of the press) is to prevent all such previous restraints upon publications as had been practiced by other governments, and they do not prevent the subsequent punishment of such as may be deemed contrary to the public welfare."

Justice John Marshall Harlan, in a minority view in the Patterson case, said:

"As the First Amendment guaranteed the rights of free speech and a free press against hostile action by the United States, it would seem clear that when the Fourteenth Amendment prohibited the States from impairing or abridging the privileges of citizens of the United States it necessarily prohibited the States from impairing or abridging the constitutional rights of such citizens to free speech and a free press. But the court announces that it leaves undecided the specific question whether there is to be found in the Fourteenth Amendment a prohibition as to the rights of free speech and a free press similar to that in the First. It yet proceeds to say that the main purpose of such constitutional provisions was to prevent all such previous restraints upon publications as had been practiced by other governments, but not to prevent the subsequent punishment of such as may be deemed contrary to the public welfare. I cannot assent to that view, if it be meant that the legislature may impair or abridge the rights of a free press and of free speech whenever it thinks that the public welfare requires that to be done. The public welfare cannot override the constitutional privilege, and if the rights of free speech and of a free press are, in their essence, attributes of national citizenship, as I think they are, then neither Congress nor any State since the adoption of the Fourteenth Amendment can, by legislative enactments or by judicial action, impair or abridge them. In my judgment the actions of the court was in violation of the rights of free speech and a free press guaranteed by the Constitution. I go further and hold that the privileges of free speech and a free press, belonging to every citizen of the United States, constitute essential parts of every man's liberty, and are protected against violation by that clause of the Fourteenth Amendment forbidding a State to deprive any person of his liberty without due process of law. It is, I think, impossible to conceive of liberty, as secured by the Constitution against hostile action, whether by the Nation or by the States, which does not embrace the right to enjoy free speech and the right to have a free press."

The court of appeals would not convict Newton Eastman of obscenity for his anti-Catholic attack of the confessional box even though his work was improper, intemperate, unjustifiable, and highly reprehensible. Clinton R. Woodruff contended that the government should protect the public against billboards which were esthetically or morally offensive. Fred T. Knowles refused to pay his $500 obscenity fine and instead served time in jail for an article about a girl who died from an abortion which was included in his Lantern publication. He attacked society for contributing to the shame of unmarried motherhood.

Minnesota had a law which prohibited newspapers from publishing the details of an execution, since, in the opinion of the legislature, it was detrimental to public morals to publish anything more than the mere fact that the execution had taken place. A court ruled that The Pioneer Press was not deprived of any constitutional right in being so limited. Chicago set up a movie censorship ordinance to determine if movies were morally acceptable. Police were the censors.

Bernarr McFadden, editor of Physical Culture, was arrested for obscenity because his magazine published pictures of scantily-clad muscle men.

1908

Arthur Bostwick, president of the American Library Association, urged that all books which had an immoral tendency be suppressed. Bram Stocker, author of Dracula, said that the lack of restraint in modern literature might require censorship. "If no other method can be found to eradicate the plague spot in fiction, even police censorship, obnoxious as it is it, may be inevitable." The editor of Outlook believed the liberty of the press did not mean liberty to villify maliciously any private citizen or public official who happened to arouse the hostility of the newspaper.

President Theodore Roosevelt attempted to prosecute the New York World and The Indianapolis News for criminal libel. He lost the Indianapolis case so convincingly that the one against Joseph Pulitzer was dropped. Roosevelt revived sedition in his displeasure about articles and editorials concerning corruption in the purchase of the Panama Canal company from France.

Fred D. Warren, Socialist editor of the Appeal to Reason, was sentenced to six months imprisonment and fined $150 for mailing 25,000 circulars with an envelope message containing threatening and scurrilous language.

Barnarr McFadden was convicted of mailing obscene matter for an article in Physical Culture appealing for enlightened sexual education. His fine was to be $2,000 and he was to serve two years in jail but the sentence was never carried out because of a technicality.

Mayor George B. McClellan closed all 500 motion picture theaters in New York City on December 24 because he thought they were unclean and immoral. A court ordered them re-opened in three days, but the mayor started New York motion picture censorship.

Newton Eastman, bishop of Gospel Workers of America, was acquitted in five libel and obscenity trials.

The Kansas Supreme Court explained that:

"If the publisher of a newspaper circulated throughout the state publishes an article reciting facts and making comments relating to the official conduct and character of a state officer, who is a candidate for re-election, for the sole purpose of giving to the people of the state what he honestly believes to be true information, and for the sole purpose of enabling the voters to cast their ballots more intelligently, and the whole thing is done in good faith; the publication is privileged, although the matters contained in the article may be untrue in fact and derogatory to the character of the candidate."

1909

A national film censorship board was formed in the United States by the People's Institute of New York City. This was a self-appointed group whose views were accepted by the movie industry.

G. Stanley Hall, president of Clark College, managed to become president of the New England Watch and Ward Society and used that old blue organization to promote sex education for a year.

1910

Court-approved press and speech restraints were carried out against militant union bodies such as the International Workers of the World, and radical organizations such as the Socialist Party and the Non-Partisan League.

George White said freedom of the press meant "freedom to write and publish anything on any conceivable subject -- not one bar, not one tiniest taboo, not one darksome cranny or corner hidden from the frankest scrutiny."

The free-love edition of The Social Democrat earned the editor jail for 60 days in Oklahoma.

1911

Pennsylvania set up a state movie censorship board. The Supreme Court affirmed Wesley Glasgow's obscenity conviction for Personal Beauty and Sexual Science. Truth Seeker magazine contended that liberty included the right to use scurrilous language. Jay Fox was jailed for two months for his article "The Nude and the Prudes" in Agitator because the court decided it created disrespect for the law.

A reporter told a Georgia court that he believed he would forfeit the respect and confidence of the community at large if he divulged the name of his informant, and that to do so would subject him to ridicule and contempt. "It would ruin me in my business; it would cause me to lose my position as a newspaper reporter for the Augusta Herald, and would prevent my ever engaging in the occupation of a newspaper reporter ever again."

The federal law code made it a crime to publish matters of a character tending to incite arson, murder, or assassination, and the Postmaster General could deny the mails to publications containing such matter. This law was designed to control and suppress anarchistic publications.

1912

The Supreme Court ruled that Post Office regulations on second-class matter were not an abridgement of First Amendment rights.

The Secretary of Commerce and Labor was authorized to license radio stations on the basis of ownership, location, purpose, hours of operation, and frequency by the Radio Act of 1912, which included 20 radio broadcasting regulations. It established the international SOS signal and required that all radio stations get a license from the Secretary of Commerce and Labor.

The National Association of Manufacturers claimed that the typographical union was planning to acquire complete newspaper control throughout the United States just as surely as it had established a stranglehold on New York City newspapers.

A judge in Idaho fined the editors of The Boise Capital
- News $500 each plus ten days in jail for printing Theodore
Roosevelt's condemnation of the Idaho Supreme Court ruling
that his Progressive Party couldn't be on the ballot.

Newspapers were apprehensive of government controls when
postal legislation required them to state their business
conditions in the semi-annual report they had to publish to
maintain second-class mailing privileges. Congress had
passed statutes which required newspapers, magazines,
periodicals, and publications to list their owners and
creditors.

Theodore Dreiser's novels, Carrie (1912), The Titan
(1914), and The Genius (1915) were withheld or removed from
book stores.

1913

A New Jersey court said that a reporter who pleaded a
privilege of withholding the name of his source asked for a
privilege which found no countenance in the law. To admit
any such privilege would be to shield the real transgressor
and permit him to go unwhipped of justice.

Judge Learned Hand, using the Hicklin test of obscenity,
found Hagar Revelly, a novel about a sensuous young woman,
obscene but said:

"I hope it is not improper for me to say that the rule
as laid down, however consonant it may be with mid-
Victorian morals, does not seem to me to answer to the
understanding and morality of the present time, as
conveyed by the words, 'obscene, lewd, or lascivious.'
I question whether in the end men will regard that as
obscene which is honestly relevant to the adequate
expression of innocent ideas, and whether they will not
believe that truth and beauty are too precious to
society at large to be mutilated in the interests of
those most likely to pervert them to base use, or that
shame will for long prevent us from adequate portrayal
of some of the most serious and beautiful sides of human
nature."

Ohio and Kansas set up state movie censorship boards.
William Lloyd Clark of Peoria, Illinois, was tried for
sending obscene matter through the mails which attacked
Catholicism. He was arrested in 1913 for obscenity for his
book Hell at Midnight in Springfield, Illinois.

The editor of Outlook said, "Freedom of speech and of
the press does not mean the right to slander, but if under
the guise of such freedom any editor claims the right to
libel a public official, he should be accused, not of
hostility to the government, but of libel, and to be made to
justify his libel or to suffer the consequences."

1914

Between the expiration of the Alien and Sedition Acts in

1801 and 1914, there were no federal sedition prosecutions in the United States.

Theodore Schroeder told the Senate Industrial Relations Committee that:

"we have less conceded and protected freedom of speech and of the press in the United States than in any country in the world at any time in the history of the world. Freedom of speech means no man should be punished for any expression of opinion on any subject so long as the consequences of that speech is nothing but the creation of a state of mind in someone else."

Margaret Sanger's The Woman Rebel was suppressed by the Post Office because it contained information about birth control. The Finnish-American humor magazine Lapatossu was convicted of publishing obscene caricatures by a Michigan court.

During World War I more than 1,900 prosecutions involving speeches, newspaper articles, pamphlets, and books were started; 800 persons were convicted; the postmaster refused mailing privileges to 100 publications, including 50 socialist newspapers. Private broadcasting during World War I was discontinued and broadcasting was reserved for the United States Navy.

Henry Schofield said, "Our own judges seem to have forgotten that the founders of the government are not distinguished for their reception of the English common law but for their adaption of the democratic leaning and tendency of the constitutional side of it." To jurists such as Blackstone, Mansfield, and Kenyon, licentiousness of the press meant the fabrication and spreading of falsehood in matters of fact, according to Schofield.

The New York Evening Post said, "That any ideal censorship could ever be worked out, we very much doubt, for it is founded on suppression, deceit, and concealment; but there are instances in which it has worked well."

In 1914, newspapers insisted that the public should be trusted with war news, but the government censors suppressed all reports of military reverses or disasters.

A North Dakota court said:

"The right of free speech and the freedom of the press are as sacred to the members of this court as they are to the defendant, and we dare say, will be longer upheld by them than by him; but such rights must not be considered unbridled license to villify and scandalize. When asked to state any reason, weak or strong, why he had even believed such an article to be true, the journalist replied that he must not tell because to do so would violate a confidential relationship. In this, he merely imitates the thief who, caught with the goods on him, insists that he has purchased them from a "tall, light-complexioned stranger."

1915

By the time Anthony Comstock died in 1915, he had destroyed 150 tons of obscene literature.

Archibald Henderson said, "No caution that human art can devise will totally exclude libels from a newspaper. The publication of the inadvertent and excusable libel is one of the unavoidable hazards connected with the production of a newspaper."

A court approved censorship of movies by the Ohio state board of censors since movies were capable of evil because of their attractiveness and manner of exhibition. Since films were commercial enterprises they did not enjoy First Amendment protection; they were not part of the press, and states could license and censor movies, the court reasoned.

Edward A. Ross said, "For organized society to allow the weapon of a free press to be wrenched from the hands of the laboring class in their struggle against oppression, constitutes connivance in one of the greatest inequities that could be committed."

John Collier said, "Censorship (of movies) is impracticable and dangerous because the means involved are indeed largely unrelated to the ends sought, and because the indirect damage of censorship infinitely exceeds the direct good which may be accomplished."

1916

Edward Bond Frate was prosecuted in the United States for distributing his <u>Borning Better Babies</u>. Margaret Sanger's articles on "What Every Girl Should Know" were seized under the Comstock Law. She was arrested for distributing obscene material about birth control.

Thomas E. Watson was the object of several unsuccessful efforts to prosecute him for his investigative book, <u>The Roman Catholic Hierarchy</u>.

Richard C. De Wolf reported that, "In the United States we have no cases reported in which copyright has been denied on the ground of the libellous, seditious, or blasphemous character of the matter involved, but we have several cases in which immorality, in the narrower sense of the term, has been held a reason for refusing to protect the work which showed it." Emma Goldman, editor of the <u>Flame</u>, was sentenced to three years for distributing birth control information.

The Post Office suppressed <u>The Worker's Voice</u> (<u>Rabochaya Rech</u>) and <u>Volne Listy</u>, a Bohemian anarchist paper.

<u>The New Statesman</u> editorialized that censorships of movies or books are defenders not of morals but of conventions. "They are almost always as unintelligent as they are useless", the magazine said.

Benjamin O. Flower won acquittal for publishing an

article saying the Catholic Church was a menace to American democracy. His book had been called an obscene criticism of the Catholic Church.

John S. Summer, head of the New York Society for the Suppression of Vice, destroyed the printing plates of Homo Sapiens because he believed it to be an obscene book.

The Nebraska Supreme Court ruled that the power of the press is the evaluation of just and efficient government. Restrictions imposed on publishers are generally indefensible. Censorship by court injunction is no less objectionable than censorship by other government departments.

Channing Pollack said, "We are a decent-minded majority, and it is normal for us to demand clean entertainment as it is clean collars. While this is true, we do not need censors and, when it ceases to be true, censors will be merely futile fools trying to sweep back the sea."

1917

Several senators attacked the Espionage Act as a system for licensing the press, since a newspaper could check with the postmaster prior to publication to get approval of its contents. In 1917 senators said the act provided heavier censorship than a Russian muzzle and prohibited content allowed in Prussia.

The Espionage Act of 1917 and its amendments of 1918 were followed by similar and farther-reaching state laws. Prosecution of almost 2,000 persons followed with almost 900 convictions; postal control was exerted on about 100 newspapers. A section of the Espionage Act forbade using false statements to willfully interfere with the military success of the United States, promoting the success of enemies, attempting to cause insubordination or refusal to serve in the military forces, or obstruction recruiting activities. The postmaster could bar letters, pamphlets, books, or newspapers containing such expression. Within a month of its passage, 15 publications were denied mailing and 75 papers were restrained by postal officials.

The National Civil Liberties Bureau, forerunner of the American Civil Liberties Association, was established under the direction of Roger Baldwin. Several people disturbed by wartime repression helped form the bureau.

Judge Learned Hand said that one could not limit free speech and free press to polite criticism. The greater the grievance the more likely people are to get excited about it, and the more urgent the need of hearing what the discontented have to say. The test for suppression of expression in a democratic government is neither the justice of its substance nor the decency and propriety of its temper, but the strong danger that it will directly incite injurious acts.

The Post Office suspended mailing privileges for Masses, a socialist publication, and its publishers were accused of espionage. Editor Max Eastman said, "The intentions of our publication is to publish a free, vigorous, satirical, humorous, and somewhat reckless magazine, from the socialist point of view." He became editor of the Liberator when Masses was suspended.

The Kissimmea Valley Gazette had to clip out an ad proposing a legal test of the Conscription Act before the Post Office would mail it. Edward E. Browne contended that freedom of the press is more important in wartime than in peacetime. The court upheld the Post Office refusal to mail The Jeffersonian because the publication opposed recruiting and Liberty Bond sales. The Supreme Court said that it would be a travesty on the constitutional privileges of free speech to allow it to be invoked to protect a person's right to discourage or interfere with enlistments by speech or writing in the Gilbert case. The postmaster in St. Louis disliked an advertisement in The American Socialist and refused to accept the publication for mailing.

George Creel, head of the U.S. Committee on Public Information, set up a system of voluntary censorship followed by the press during World War I.

The editor of Mother Earth taunted the U.S. Postmaster with knowing about dozens of United States underground newspapers discussed in Secret Service reports.

Michael Mockus, a Unitarian minister, was judged guilty of blasphemy at Waterbury, Connecticut, under a state law.

Large and powerful magazines published anti-recruiting materials freely and without interference from the Post Office or other government agencies which restrained small publications. Federal officials in Chicago had a meeting in August to list anti-draft publications to prosecute, suppress, or keep out of the mails.

The June issue of The International Socialist Review was suppressed after most copies had been mailed, so the Post Office refused to mail the July issue. Even before the Espionage Act was passed, the Post Office refused to handle its Liberty edition for the American Socialist, and a local pre-censorship postal board examined all subsequent issues. The Post Office would not mail two issues of Four Lights, a publication produced by 60 women and edited in turn by teams. Lawyers had assured the women that these publications did comply with the Espionage Act.

When the court found Raymond Halsey innocent of selling an obscene book, it considered the impact of the whole book, Madamoiselle de Maupin by Theophile Gautier, instead of isolated pages only.

The New York Post was excluded from the mails after a city election because it had supported a socialist candidate before the election. The Trading with the Enemy Act authorized censorship of all messages abroad and required any newspaper or magazine containing articles in foreign languages to file a sworn translation with the postmaster.

The Patent Office Gazette published in America could not be sent to neutral countries.

Margaret Sanger's Birth Control Review was banned because of a review of Marie Stopes's Married Love. The journal was mailable in Canada but not in the United States.

Postmaster General Albert Burleson ruled that printed materials could not say "that this government got in the war wrong, that it is in it for the wrong purposes, or anything that would impugn the motives of the government for going into the war. They cannot say that this government is the tool of Wall Street, or the munitions makers. There can be no campaign against conscription and the draft law, nothing that will interfere with enlistments or raising of an army."

William MacDonald said, "No reputable correspondent needs a censorship, no official ought to be shielded by it, no secret diplomatic intrigue ought to be fostered by it. Most of all should it find tolerance in a war which is being fought by democracies for the safeguarding of democracy.

The Kansas State Board of Review replaced the 1913 Kansas Moving Picture Censorship Appeal Commission which the Supreme Court had ruled constitutional in 1915. The board disapproved movies which it considered cruel, obscene, indecent, immoral, or such as to debase or corrupt morals.

During World War I, 90 citizens were indicted in Wisconsin under federal wartime laws such as the Espionage Act, and another 81 were indicted under the state sedition act or local disorderly conduct ordinances.

Harvey J. O'Higgins said, "In the freest of countries, in the most peaceful of times, freedom of speech and freedom of the press were never more than the limited freedom to say what you pleased and print what you pleased and take the consequence."

Seventy radical publications lost mailing privileges. A black weekly in Virginia did so because it questioned why mistreated blacks would fight for the United States. Theodore Roosevelt said, "We are convinced that today our most dangerous foe is the foreign language press." The American Defense League, the American Protective League, the Sedition Slammers, and the Terrible Threateners searched for anti-war pamphleteers. Mother Earth opposed the war and the draft so it was banned from the mails.

Harry Weinberger said, "Governmental authorities, majorities, and the newspapers do not understand that all criticism should be expressed, for expression itself is a form of relief to those who have complaints to make."

1918

Werthington C. Ford said:

"The power of the press has increased in even greater ratio, for it can make or unmake ministries, and embarrass governments by exercising its criticism as a 'knocker', one who criticizes recklessly or for some other purpose than to inform the public and to expose real dishonesty in government. Instead of circulating by the tens of thousands the leading journals count their sales by the quarter of a million and their readers by the million; and the old weekly which even in political excitement rarely attained a circulation of a hundred thousand, has been superceded by a weekly circulating many more than a million copies with readers of uncountable extent. Important as the newspaper was in 1850, as a source of information, more or less accurate, it is of far greater moment in 1918 and tends to become of greater moment each year."

E.M. Borchard said:

"Never before in history has the world been subjected to so much misinformation, carefully prepared to advance a political cause. With the skillful aid of an official censorship which surpassed all military needs in the suppression of facts, the people have been almost helpless in their effort to learn the truth. The sources of the channels of the news were polluted. Diplomacy has found the department of propaganda as essential an adjunct as the army and navy, and against its machinations the struggle is difficult. I do not condemn the press too severely, for often they are as much sinned against as sinning."

The Nation magazine pointed out that Postmaster Albert Burleson was attempting to control public opinion through his action barring the September 19 issue from the mails for criticizing the government's labor policies. For four days, the Post Office held up the September 11 issue of The Nation because postal officials believed it contained unjustified criticism of the government and its agents.

The Sedition Law specified criminal punishments for defamatory criticism of government officials. The law was repealed in 1921; 35 states passed similar sedition statutes and criminal syndicalism law. Cities had ordinances making actions or speeches calculated to interfere with the war criminal.

Chief Justice Edward White said, "It suffices that, however complete is the right of the press to state public things and discuss them, the right, as every other right enjoyed in human society, is subject to the restraints which separate right from wrong doing."

Ninety-eight American newspapers dated August 22 and 23 could not be sent out of the country because they contained reports of the Aircraft Committee on Military Affairs. The Committee also prohibited magazines being exported if they contained information about debates on those days.

Atlanta newspapers cooperated with the commanding officer of Camp Gordon who did not want it revealed that 3,000 Black troops were training there.

American military officials ordered newspapers in the occupied Rhine regions not to print anything that might inflame captured Germans against the Americans.

The New York Tribune said that censoring the addresses from casualty lists was one of the most drastic bits of censoring promulgated by the War Department, which acquiesced to French apprehensions of the Germans being able to check the effectiveness of gas attacks.

The New York Evening Post believed that six lines of news from the front with names of regiments would do more good to stir up enthusiasm than reams of synthetic write-ups from a Washington bureau.

A New York Court said prior restraints on the press would cause newspapers and other organs of information and discussion to be at the mercy of little groups of local officials here and there.

When the Post Office refused to mail A Voice in the Wilderness, the publishers changed its name to I Cannot Tell A Lie. The editor was arrested for this trick. Several issues of The Truth Seeker were denied mailing privileges because they criticized the YMCA and the Red Cross. The Post Office and the Navy would not mail the May New York Times Current History or its Mid-week Pictorial of May 23 to Manila, China, Japan, or India.

German-Americans were persecuted throughout World War I, and were afraid to be seen with a German language newspaper according to the New York Stats-Zeitung. If a German-language newspaper were delivered to an apartment building and residents saw it, there was trouble for the subscriber. The aged editor of the German-language Herold of Eau Claire, Wisconsin, was jailed for a year because he didn't have an English translation of a meaningless editorial. Another Wisconsin editor was indicted for not having a translation of his editorial saying he would not comment on the war, but this pledge of no comment was considered a war comment anyhow.

1919

Edward T. Leech, editor of the Memphis Press, was sentenced to ten days for an editorial criticizing the courts and the judges in Memphis.

The Post Office suppressed Dr. B. Liber's book on sexual life as being obscene and too radical in explaining the economics of prostitution.

President Woodrow Wilson denied that there was censorship in the American press regarding the Paris Peace Conference, but he had asked that the French censor French newspapers and dispatches sent to newspapers in other countries.

Scott Nearing was acquitted of charges of having written The Great Madness about big business and its relation to

World War I. The American Socialist Party, however, was
found guilty of publishing it. Theodora Pollock was arrested
in Sacremento for having a copy of _Solidarity_ and her own
unpublished poem, "Peace."

The American Civil Liberties Union found there had been
56 espionage cases which involved freedom of the press and
distribution of literature.

An editorial in _The_ _Tulsa_ (Okla) _Daily_ _World_ said:

"If we as free people are to retain unhampered our
prized privilege of free speech, we must heartily
encourage every reasonable effort to close the mouths of
those who habitually abuse the privilege. There have
been a number of people in our midst whose rantings have
about convinced the people that free speech is a
dangerous liberty. If the privilege is to be saved from
destruction we must see to it that its sanctity is
preserved."

William Hand attacked Postmaster General Albert
Burleson's use of power over the nation's press in the
destruction of more than 100 publications. He deplored that
a Democratic president had signed into law Congressional
action closing the mails to any abusive writing about the
form of the United States government even though President
Woodrow Wilson had once said, "If there is one thing we love
more than another in the United States, it is that every man
should have the privilege, unmolested and uncriticized, to
utter the real convictions of his mind."

Charles T. Schenck, general secretary of the Socialist
party, was indicted for causing insubordination in the armed
forces and for obstructing recruiting and enlistment.
Schenck had participated in the printing and mailing of
15,000 leaflets, many of which went to men who had been
drafted. The leaflet said the draft was unconstitutional and
that it constituted "a monstrous wrong against humanity in
the interests of Wall Street's chosen few." Although his
conviction was upheld, the Supreme Court's decision in this
case approved Justice Oliver Wendell Holmes's "clear and
present danger" test for free speech. Holmes described the
clear and present danger test thus: "The most stringent
protection of free speech would not protect a man in falsely
shouting 'fire' in a theatre and causing panic. The question
in every case is whether the words used are in such a nature
as to create a clear and present danger that they will bring
about the substantive evils that Congress had the right to
prevent."

Jacob Abrams, a Russian national, and four of his
countrymen, were convicted of violating the 1918 Sedition
Act. They opposed the sending of troops into Russia to
thwart the Russian Revolution. They tossed leaflets out a
window in the hope that munitions works might read them but
this did not happen. The Russian nationals were indicted for
publishing abusive language about the form of government, for
publishing language intended to bring the form of government
into contempt, for encouraging resistance to the United

States in the war, and for inciting curtailment of production of war materials. Justices Oliver Wendell Holmes and Louis Brandies, in the Supreme Court minority, argued that the leaflets created no clear and present danger.

1920

In the Pierce case, Justice Brandies said:

"A verdict should have been for the defendant for lack of proof of an attempt willfully to cause insubordination, disloyalty, mutiny, or refusal of duty in the military or naval forces and because the leaflet itself and the circumstances under which it was distributed were not such as to create a clear and present danger of such."

Senator William E. Borah said, "If the press is not free, if speech is not independent and untrammeled, if the mind is shackled or made impotent through fear, it makes no difference under what form of government you live, you are a subject and not a citizen."

Blasphemy as a legal prohibition became obsolete by 1920.

Booksellers Robert and Ina Wood were jailed in Oklahoma City for selling communist literature which included, in the minds of the police (who seized 10,000 items) Carl Sandburg's Abraham Lincoln, Leo Tolstoy's War and Peace, and the United States Constitution.

In a trial, that included reading the entire book to a bored jury of Maxwell Bodenheim's Replenishing Jessica, Horace Liverwright won an acquittal for having published it.

President Woodrow Wilson's criticism of Italy caused the suppression of articles from the Wall Street Journal.

Henry L. West said, "We want, and always will have a free press, but it must be a press that deserves its freedom through respecting and upholding the principles that made us a free nation."

Attorney General A. Mitchell Palmer believed that a line could be drawn easily across which man would not be permitted to go in the exercise of the right of free speech. He launched a vigorous campaign against radicals by arresting 4,000 persons and confiscating books, papers, and posters, without either arrest or search warrants. He deported hundreds of aliens and Congress considered an assortment of proposed sedition laws. But Palmer's raids found virtually no illegal radical activities.

Samuel Gompers of the American Federation of Labor said that the extension of postal mailing constraints beyond the war would prolong an aristocratic censorship over the entire American press and would destroy free speech and assembly. The extension was defeated in Congress.

Thorstein Verblen's <u>Imperial</u> <u>Germany</u> was suppressed.

Robert M. LaFollette said, "It is doubtful if the American people can ever emancipate themselves from the merciless exploitation of the colossal monopoly which control markets and prices, until they shall establish a free and independent press."

The Mississippi state legislature passed a statute making it illegal to print appeals, arguments, or suggestions favoring social equality between the white and black races.

Twenty-eight states had repudiated earlier state movie censorship agencies.

The New York Vice Society sought to suppress James B. Cabell's <u>Jurgen</u> and Gautier's <u>Mademoiselle</u> <u>de</u> <u>Maupin</u>. But a New York court ordered the vice society to pay a book clerk damages for prosecuting him maliciously for selling the Gautier book.

1921

The Sedition Act of 1917-18 was repealed.

Burgess Johnson said, "The greatest danger that lies in the recognition of the rights of censorship is that thoughtless people will grow to believe that any such real right exists."

The fourth volume of the <u>Cambridge</u> <u>History</u> <u>of</u> <u>American</u> <u>Literature</u> was withdrawn by the Putnam Company so articles could be substituted for one about Mrs. Mary Baker Eddy and <u>Science</u> and <u>Health</u> and for one on the <u>Book</u> <u>of</u> <u>Mormon</u>, because of pressure from Christian Scientists and Mormons.

Victor Berger, editor of the socialist paper, the <u>Milwaukee</u> <u>Leader</u>, was indicted for five editorials about how the war was being conducted. He was convicted in 1919, but the Supreme Court reversed the decision in 1921 because of the trial judge's severe biases. The <u>Milwaukee</u> <u>Leader</u> published material that was considered detrimental to the government during World War I. The paper charged that the war was unjustifiable and dishonorable and that great numbers of our soldiers were insane. Postmaster General Albert Burleson then revoked the paper's second-class mailing privileges. The paper attempted to regain it, but failed in lower courts and the Supreme Court.

In the Steelik case, the judge said:

"The right of free speech was guaranteed to prevent legislation which would by censorship, injunction, or other method prevent the free publication by any citizen of anything that he deemed it was necessary to say or publish, but the right of free speech does not include the right to advocate the destruction or overthrow of the government or the criminal destruction of property."

In the Pathe Exchange case, a New York Court said

freedom of speech or press did not apply to motion pictures because people who engage in show business are none too likely to confine their productions to the things which are just, pure and of good report.

A dealer sold a copy of Gautier's <u>Mademoiselle de Maupin</u> to John Summer, who was Anthony Comstock's successor at the New York Society for the Suppression of Vice. He charged that the book was obscene. Judge Andrew wrote, "No work may be judged from a selection of such paragraphs alone. Printed by themselves they might, as a matter of law, come within the prohibition of statute. So might a similar selection from Aristophanes or Chaucer or Boccaccio, or even the Bible. The book, however, must be considered broadly, as a whole."

Legislative bodies in 32 states were considering movie censorship statutes. The Motion Pictures Producers and Distributors of America was organized primarily to clean up movies. The National Association of Broadcasters was formed. It developed a code of broadcasting rules for radio and ultimately for television.

William Allen White was arrested for supporting railway workers during a strike because he placed placards in his newspaper office windows. These were considered a type of picketing. White wouldn't remove the placards and wrote a Pulitzer prize-winning editorial in his paper about the need for freedom of expression during periods of national concern.

The government squashed and suppressed a book claiming President Warren G. Harding was part Negro.

The New York Society for the Suppression of Vice seized 772 copies of the books <u>Casanova's Homecoming</u>, <u>Women in Love</u>, and <u>A Young Girl's Diary</u> from Thomas Seltzer's bookshop but he was acquitted of obscenity charges. In 1924 he was indicted for selling two of the books but managed to escape prosecution by withdrawing the books from sale.

1923

The <u>Chicago Tribune</u> won a libel suit when Chicago sought damages for critical articles published by the newspaper. The Illinois Supreme Court ruled that government agencies had no legal standing to sue persons to account for expressions of opinion. State and federal guarantees of freedom of the press preclude government suits for libel. One of the judges said, "The struggle for freedom of speech has marched hand in hand in the advance of civilization. History teaches that human liberty cannot be secured unless there is freedom to express grievances as civilization advanced and as the means for expressing grievances."

Horace B. Liverwright said, "A censorship over literature and the arts is stupid, ignorant, and impudent, and is against the fundamental social principles of all intelligent Americans."

A law was enacted in Minnesota that stated that any person who willfully furnished any paper in Minnesota with false information was guilty of a misdemeanor.

The United States Supreme Court ruled that Secretary of Commerce Herbert Hoover had to issue broadcasting licenses to all who applied and could only select wave lengths that the stations could use.

The American Newspaper Publishers Association was founded in 1887 and worked to enhance freedom of the press. In 1923 it set up a committee on federal laws to exercise utmost efforts to maintain freedom of the press whenever it was threatened.

Lucy Salmon, in her The Newspaper and Authority, said that one of the old taxes on knowledge defined the press thus:

"Every person possessing a printing press or types for printing, and every typefounder, was ordered to give notice to the clerk of the peace. Every person selling type was ordered to give an account of all persons to whom they were sold. Every person who printed anything also had to keep a copy of the matter printed, and write on it the names and abode of the person who employed him to print it. The conflict between the newspaper and authority will be settled only when the press asserts its rights to true freedom and claims it from authority. The true freedom of the press lies, and lies only, within the keeping of the press itself."

1924

The Canons of Journalism, a statement of journalistic ethics and functions, was devised by the American Society of Newspaper Editors.

The Americanism Protective League was formed to oppose a proposal for a New York Clean Books Bill. The publishers of Jurgen, a novel by Branch Cabell, were acquitted of obscenity charges. This case marked a turning point in the obscenity convictions which became more difficult to obtain.

Members of the International Workers of the World and the Worker's Party were prohibited from circulating pamphlets and books by an injunction based on a California criminal syndicalism law.

Emanuel Haldeman-Julius said that censorship robs movies of virtually every vestige of freedom save that of the indiscriminate throwing of pies.

31
Censorship European Style, 1900 through 1924

Anton Chekov, a Russian novelist, said in 1900:

> "A litterateur is not a confectioner, not a dealer in cosmetics, not an entertainer. He is just like ordinary people. What would you say if a newspaper reporter, because of his fastidiousness or from a wish to give pleasure to his readers, were to describe only honest mayors, high-minded ladies, and virtuous railroad conductors?"

Spain confiscated liberal and republican newspapers for an anti-government campaign and prohibited news reports not authorized by officials.

1901

Australia set up federal censorship with its Customs Act.

1903

Chinese <u>Pao</u> or newspaper publications as well as pamphlets propagandized for a Chinese revolution for many years despite frequent prosecutions. Officials even tried bribery to stop criticism of the government.

When Russian police found out that journalists were planning to adopt resolutions demanding press freedom, they stopped a banquet to celebrate the 200th anniversary of the first Russian newspaper.

1904

Russian Interior Minister V. K. Plehue taunted radicals

by saying, "Why do you want freedom of the press when even without it you are a master of saying between the lines all that you wish to say?"

Hungary suppressed newspapers of the Slovak and Rumanian minorities. Narodine Noviny, a Slovak paper, was prosecuted thirteen times in a 12-month period.

1905

Printing became widely available throughout India and was used to launch political movements; 1,359 newspapers had two million subscribers.

Russian censorship broke down as a result of the 1905 revolution. Nearly 1,700 newspapers and periodicals were operating as a liberalizing trend arrived in Russia. But in 1912, 317 papers were suppressed and even more in 1913; Russian censorship was extreme. The press could not use the words authorities or bureaucracy; it could not criticize the police, hospital administration, barracks sanitation, the number of schools, bribery, or use exclamation marks.

A jury found Sir Edward Russell and Alexander Jeans of the Liverpool Daily Post and Mercury not guilty of criminal libel for criticizing beerhall licensing.

1906

A special statute of the Great Ch'ing Dynasty governed publications. It was the first formal law on publications and a bureau for registering publications was established, libel could be severely punished, and the post office refused to handle seditious, libelous, or blackmailing materials if the mailer had been convicted.

Between 1876 and 1906 France averaged 50 obscenity trials each year and found almost all of the defendants guilty.

Books and newspapers hostile to the British multiplied rapidly throughout India. The press in Punjab was especially vitriolic, particularly the Panjabee, which the British attempted to prosecute for treason but could only get a racial hatred charge which created even greater anti-British antagonism. When British authorities in India prosecuted newspapers like India and Yuganter, the papers were sold to other Indians who simply changed the names. London officials wouldn't let British bureaucrats outlaw Justice, a socialist newspaper.

1907

England banned Gilbert and Sullivan's The Mikado during a visit by Prince Fushimi of Japan.

The press in Imperial Germany was the most docile, well-drilled, and the most supine press in all international questions of any in the world, according to Austin Harrison writing for The North American Review.

Chinese students in Japan published vigorously to promote a Chinese revolution. Chinese women students urged women to use assassination to carry out the revolution in their publication New Chinese Women.

1908

The editor, co-editor, printer, correspondents, and a typist served long prison terms in Hungary's Arad prison for printing only one word against the government. The Serbian newspaper was confiscated by the government. The Chinese Commerce ministry set up a new press law based on an old Japanese one. The government of India convicted staff members of twenty publications for dangerous writing.

1909

Spain set up tight press censorship because of problems with Moroccan tribesman.

Russian dissidents developed extensive underground publications. In Baku by 1910 an operation produced more than a million copies in a plant which "expanded until it covered an area underground and contained a cutting machine, type in several languages, presses, binders, even a casting machine for using stereotype mats. In this plant underneath the houses of Tartar Baku, seven printers worked and lived. The plant was without heat or ventilation; windows leading to the street were sealed with brick and mortar." At night they took turns going up for air for three hour periods, according to Bertram Wolfe.

1910

England enacted a press act to control the India press. Actions taken against Indian publications saw 1,121 items banned. There were 120 prosecutions, 15 security bond forfeitures, and 40 warnings to publications. Among Indian publications banned were The Methods of the Indian Police in the 20th Century, British Rule in India, The Infamies of Liberal Rule, Sidelight of India, Choose, Oh Indian Princess, South African Horrors, The First Indian War of Independence, and Shabash.

New Zealand legislated an Indecent Publications Act. An international conference convened in France and developed an International Agreement for the Suppression of Obscene Publications.

Between 1905 and 1910, Imperial Russia imposed 4,396 adminstrative penalities on periodicals and confiscated 1,000 newspapers. More than 400 journalists were arrested.

1911

Albert Britnell was convicted in Toronto of selling Three Weeks and The Yoke. After the Chinese Revolution, a free press existed for a brief time.

T. H. S. Escott said:

"The journalist began by stirring up against himself
Parliament's persistent jealousy and scornful hate.   He
criticized or even observed its proceedings almost with
a rope round his neck.   He knew the ascent to the
pillory as well as he did his own doorstep.   In the near
distance stood the common hangman, in one hand holding
the whip which was to flog him at the cart-tail round
the town, in the other displaying the shears that were
to crop his ears before the day's programme was
finished.   A restless, unconscionable, irrepressible
kind of being, he was, in the natural order of
providence, suffered to spit his lies, libels, venom of
all sorts abroad, and generally to infest the earth just
as a like tolerance was granted to beasts, to birds of
prey, and to other noisome creatures.   Before the
eighteenth century was out, the mightiest and most
philosophical intellect in the Parliament of his day,
Edmund Burke, had found out that this generally
distrusted, detested, but inextinguishable person had
laid the foundation of a Fourth Estate."

1912

The Chinese provisional constitution promised freedom of
writing and publication.   Dr. Sun Yat-sen and the National
Press Association ended press registration requirements.

Vigilance committees in Ireland crusaded against immoral
literature.   The British Board of Film Censors was set up by
motion picture makers and distributors.

Under the Russian Espionage Law of 1912 it was
impossible to publish any news about military or naval
affairs.   Nikolai Lenin started _Pravda_ as a revolutionary
leaflet and was its first editor.

1913

Germany sentenced more than 100 socialist journalists to
jail.

The British forced 272 security bonds from owners of
India presses and 158 deposits from newspaper editors.   Local
India governments forbade 200 publications plus 100
individual issues of newspapers.

1914

By 1914, prior censorship had been eliminated in
European countries, but World War I produced drastic new
censorship procedures.   There were no prosecutions for
sedition in England between the Reform Bill of 1832 and 1914.
The London Times said that journalists were able to discuss
the campaign in the West with far less freedom than its
Russian contemporaries.   "The Russian reports are far more
full than ours and Russian comment is far more untrammeled
and therefore illuminating."   Irish papers were suppressed,
and neither _The Irish World_ nor _The Gaelic American_ could be
distributed in England.

Austria suppressed 81 Serbian newspapers from being circulated by mail. Serbia suppressed all anti-Austrian publications at the request of the Austrian government. Georges Clemenceau, infuriated with French bungling, fought government censorship of his newspaper L'Homme Libre. When they closed him down, he started a second paper L'Homme Enchaine! When war became too severe, he eased his criticism. France reprimanded several newspapers, including the Paris edition of The New York Herald for scare headlines, interviews, and war reports. Paris journalists protested these actions; but suspensions and fines continued throughout the war.

An edition of Munchener Zeitung was confiscated when it advocated annexing Belgium, but later the censor allowed newspapers to agitate for annexations. The Bavarian Minister of War ordered Bavarian newspapers not to publish lists of war casualties.

President Yuan re-wrote the press freedom clause by adding "within the scope of laws and ordinances." His publication law containing 21 restrictions continued in force for many years.

The evening edition of Vossische Zeitung was suppressed because it quoted the chancellor as saying that the German people would have to tighten their belts. The Kaiser suspended the leading German Catholic newspaper, The Kolnische Volkszeitung, for criticizing a note he had sent to President Woodrow Wilson. Germany set up an Index Expurgatorians which contained the names of 13 periodicals, 83 newspapers, and 60 foreign publications. Within eight months officials suppressed 127 periodicals and 278 other publications.

The Chinese press could not report secret court actions, false charges against the government, or attacks on the form of government. China set up national press regulations patterned after Europe that included pre-censorship. Japan had severe censorship rules. The Peking government and European bankers censored details about conditions in China so that Europe would buy Chinese bonds.

Canada banned all seditious newspapers including the German Fatherland, four German newspapers published in Canada, and the Hearst newspapers from the United States.

The Russian Council of Ministers produced a long list of subjects which could not appear in print. Eleven months before a Press Yearbook was issued, 340 Russian journals had been administratively censored or fined. Socialist Labor and Social Democrat papers were the hardest hit. One hundred and two papers had been prosecuted in Kiev, but anti-Jewish publications carried heavy attacks on the Jews. The New York Evening Post reported that there were 1,634 cases of press repressions in Russia from 1906 through the first eleven months of 1913. One labor paper in Russia had 67 of its 137 editions confiscated; it was suspended 17 times and finally suppressed.

1915

Italy, angered by reports of naval disasters, held editors personally responsible for publishing any facts not made public by the government. The press had to present the Dutch government's attitude of what was said at an international meeting of women at the Hague.

The Austrian press was ordered not to comment on relations with Italy. Austrian censorship was even tighter than German. In Vienna, the newspaper for Czech democracy was suppressed. Despite having an edition confiscated, The Lokal Anzeiger commented on relations with the United States; when its second evening edition came out, it attacked President Woodrow Wilson.

Chinese intellectuals joined in demands for a democratic government through publications they sponsored. The war lords suppressed such thought, but not very effectively.

Mexico decreed that fines of 50 to 500 pesos or imprisonment from one to eleven months would apply to slander, libel, or false or distorted statements.

The London Globe reported Lord Kitchener had resigned despite official denials; the newspaper was suspended for more than two weeks. Austin Harrison of England said, "A democracy which does not trust itself, that is to say, its press, is a poor thing. Only the press can arouse the people to see the war as it is and take the proud steps essential to victory." Scotland Yard suppressed Jefferson Jones' The Fall of Tsingtua because it offended the Japanese government and kept it suppressed even into World War II.

The London Truth said:

"One thing which the country will have to make up its mind about very speedily is whether it is going to be governed by newspapers." British police seized every copy of The Labour Leader and The Socialist Review and hundreds of pamphlets about war-time labor problems. British officials seized the printing plant of The London Globe. The editor of The English Review said, "The British Lion is fighting the war in blinkers."

1916

A cartoon of an intoxicated soldier brought fines against the editor and the cartoonist of The Bystander in England. British officials would not allow The Manchester Labour Leader, The Cambridge Magazine, and Common Sense mailed outside England. France created a film commison de controle. Police seized a Scotland newspaper for publishing an unapproved account of a conference between Glasgow Union Officials and the British prime minister. Police seized Forwards, a Scottish Socialist newspaper. Two women were prosecuted in England for publishing a leaflet containing an article printed in an 1813 edition of the Edinborough Review, and an article written in 1902 by the home secretary of the British Cabinet. Bertrand Russell was fined 100 pounds for

violating English wartime conscription laws by circulating a
leaflet defending Ernest Everett who had been sentenced to
two years hard labor for refusing military service. The
London Times complained that the British people found
themselves waging an impersonal war of asterisks in a
chilling darkness.

The printing machinery and plant of the Nubaner, and
Kerryman, and the Liberator in Ireland were seized by
government officials. German officials banished the
editorial staff of Leipziger Volkszeitung to internment in
Switzerland and discontinued the newspaper because it was
dangerous to the state. The Berliner Tageblatt was suspended
for an editorial about food problems and war aims. German
officials closed down The Berliner Tageszeitung for reporting
Count von Reventlow's assertion that international law did
not apply to submarine war. Maximillan Harden said of German
Censorship that "right and left the foe is listening but
nowhere can he detect the voice of the German people.
Censorship attempts to show the enemy that 67 million human
beings have the same opinion as big and little matters and
contrary views must not be allowed to come to the surface."

Otto Bismarck carried "a bundle of printed forms
containing formal charges requiring merely the mention of the
name of the offender, or of the paper or papers in which the
offense had been committed." He would send several of the
completed strips each day to the states attorney.

The Berliner Post, The Lokal Amzeiger, and Vorwarts were
all suppressed for articles displeasing military and other
government officials. In Bohemia, French books were banned
because they seemingly expressed sentiments displeasing to
the Austrian monarchy. Chief Editor Marx pointed out, at the
annual meeting of the National Association of the German
Press, that press discussion of war aims could be harmful,
but that forbidding that discussion was more harmful since
the usefulness of the press is only possible with full
freedom of the press.

1917

Russian censorship eliminated all news coming out of
Russia. Nikolai Lenin said, "The capitalists define freedom
of the press as the suppression of the censor and the power
for every part to publish newspapers as they please. In
reality that is not freedom of the press but freedom for the
rich, for the burgeoisie to deceive the oppressed and
exploited masses of the people. State monopoly of newspaper
advertising is the only solution."

Maximillian Harden, editor of the Die Zukunft, was
drafted to be a military clerk, and his paper suspended for
the remainder of the war because he criticized a government
newspaper. When the war began, every newspaper in Germany
had to use all the articles provided by the Wolff News Agency
without any changes, or use none at all. Germany used its
1917 Official Censorship Book for the German Press.

Dutch journalists and professors protested strongly the
suppression of Dutch newspapers for anti-German content;

military officials punished publications for articles which displeased them.

For a little while German officials eased up on censorship, but soon stronger controls were placed on political newspapers. The Staatsburger Zeitung, an anti-Semitic paper, and The Weekly World, a radical one, were both suppressed.

J. W. Gott and J. J. Riley were convicted of blasphemy in England. Gott distributed pamphlets called Rib Ticklers and How to Prevent Conception. British postal officals would not circulate The London Nation whose editors pointed out that such censorship established a super editorship of the press so as to mold its will and intelligence into agreement with the official pattern and that 66 British publications were so super-edited.

The Goerlitzer Volkszeitung was taken over by the German government when its editors refused to publish a government article. The officials published the article and made the paper pay for the edition. The Breslau Volkswacht was suppressed for objecting to air raids which had killed women and children. A German city freed by the allies instructed its newspapers not to criticize the United States. In Bohemia all German newspapers were suspended in anticipation of May Day.

Two Athens newspapers were suspended for exposing King Constantine's pro-German intrigues. The Bull, a strident Irish publication, lost its mailing privileges for opposing wartime cooperation with the British. The French Press heaped ridicule and invective upon government censors throughout World War I. They circumvented suspension orders by renaming their newspapers. Spain imposed censorship on newspapers to resist pressures from Germany. Mexico prohibited malicious expressions to excite hatred of officials, the army, the national guard, or fundamental institutions.

1918

India's Cinematograph Act provided for motion picture censorship boards. Noel Pemberton-Billing, an ultra-conservative member of Parliament, won acquittal in a libel trial based on his Vigilante newspaper demanding vigorous prosecution of the war and a return to imperialism. He claimed 47,000 British subjects -- many in high places -- were homosexuals who had been blackmailed by the Germans into not waging a fierce war. The English Defense of the Realm Act gave great arrest powers to the government. For example, the Weekly World was fined $500 for an article about the Versailles conference based on reports in several other publications.

The Arbeiter Zeitung sarcastically observed how free the press of Austria had become with whole columns left blank by the German censors. In Germany, newspapers attacking Pan-Germans were severely punished and censorship of all content was severe.

Seven conservative Berlin newspapers were suppressed for reporting on a trial of an Independent Socialist deputy. Vorwarts and the Berliner Tageblatt were suppressed for printing news from Vienna.

Crown Prince Wilhelm telegraphed, "I beg you to forbid the circulation of the three newspapers -- Frankfurter Zeitung, Berliner Tageblatt, and Vorwarts on the western front. The damage which these three have done during the recent months to sentiment among our men is lamentable."

The commander-in-chief of the Berlin district forbade the appearance of the Berliner Neueste Nachrichten. The majority parties forming the new German government demanded modification of law to protect personal liberty, freedom of the press, and limitation of censorship about articles about foreign governments and military matters. Chancellor von Hertling's changes would see the dismantling of the German system but press regulations forbade all adverse comment on occupied area conditions. When the editors of Liberal Korrespondenz revealed that the Fatherland party was a front for the Conservative party, they were fined and threatened with jail.

Petrograd's Dien changed from being a liberal publication to a moderate socialist one, but was suppressed by Trotsky. It reappeared under a new name -- Notch (Night). Russkaye Slovo, a Russian newspaper, said, "The freedom of speech and of the press is guaranteed only for the extreme left, and the remainder of the press is exposed to the rigor of military censorship." At least 17 newspapers had been suppressed.

The Pope suspended the Roman Catholic Corriere Fuli after it printed the Pope's speech releasing Italians from serving in Italy's military forces. Swiss officials threatened to suspend the Gazette de Lausanne if it continued to print criticism of Germany. The editor of the Athens Chronos was sentenced to eight years in prison, fined $2,000, and had to suspend his paper for three months for publishing militarily prohibited articles. Thomas Masaryk had a Paris newspaper called La Nation Tcheque and in Italy he had the Czeckoslovak Samonstatnost. When he became its first president, Czechoslovakia established a free press. In Turkey, the government director of the press told Constantinople journalists that all political censorship was removed. Georges Clemenceau abolished censorship of political publications in France, but he quickly reversed this action to prevent unfavorable references being made about President Woodrow Wilson and the peace conference. When a Soviet council took over Munich, it ruled that all the contents of the newspaper would be subject to previous censorship of a press committee. In Berlin a repressive censorship existed. Chinese officials suspended the Peking Gazette when Japan complained about several of its articles.

1919

A labor union went on strike in Canadian newspapers to keep them from molding anti-union public opinion. The Cork

(Ireland) _Examiner_ was suspended and raided and its machinery dismantled without explanation. Later it and other Irish newspapers appeared, believing the fuss was based upon support for a Sinn Finn loan.

Benito Mussolini, editor of _Il Popolo d'Italio_, met with 100 followers to launch Italian fascism. One of their first acts was to burn down the Socialist paper, _Avanti_. Italian newspapers strongly opposed Mussolini and the fascists.

When the Allies took over the Rhine valley, they suppressed German newspapers in Treves and Coblenz. Robert Herrick pointed out that the curse of propaganda spread like a pestilence throughout every corner of the world because of four years of German effort, and showed no sign of abatement.

A member of the House of Lords complained the most serious thing of all was that ever since the war began the expression of honest and reasonable criticism and the publication of accurate news had been made very difficult by the stupid and ill-conceived pressure of the censorship. Facts had been suppressed or ignored, and untrue conclusions fostered in the supposed interests of the nation. Bruce Rogers was convicted of the crime of having published "to be an American patriot willing to die in defense of the trade supremacy of the British empire and her subjugation of India and Ireland." The English Rowlett Act continued the censorship of Indian newspaper following World War I.

Japan suppressed 30 newspapers for articles about the high price of rice. The Chinese government banned publications critical of the Japanese in an effort to make relations between China and Japan friendly. _The Idea Nazionale_ was seized by Italian police because an article in it was hostile to France.

1920

Nikolai Lenin said:

"Why should freedom of speech and freedom of the press be allowed? Why should a government which is doing what it believes is right allow itself to be criticized? It would not allow opposition by lethal weapons. Ideas are much more fatal things than guns. Why should any man be allowed to buy a printing press and disseminate pernicious opinion calculated to embarrass the government?"

W. L. Grant's _History of Canada_ was banned in British Columbian schools because officials believed it to be disloyal to England. The British Defense of the Realm Act prohibited distribution of leaflets and pamphlets without permission from the censor. _The Dublin Freeman's Journal_ was suppressed for six weeks because of charges it made against the government.

Adolf Hitler became owner of a weekly anti-semitic weekly, _The Voelkischer Beobachter_, by becoming chairman of the board and owner of a corporation. This business ultimately owned all the German press; Hitler was a canny publisher.

The Chinese banned literature about love because young people rebelled against traditional marriage.

1922

Mahatma Gandhi was arrested because of seditious articles which appeared in <u>Young India</u>, a newspaper he edited. He pleaded guilty and was sentenced to six years in prison, but was released in two years because of appendicitus.

1923

England ratified the International Convention for the Suppression of the Circulation of and the Traffic in Obscene Publications. Members of the League of Nations signed a convention to suppress the circulation of and the trafficking in obscene publications.

The Substantive Constitution of the Republic of China guaranteed freedom of publication which could be restricted in accordance with the law.

Italy adopted a regulation prohibiting the printing of news of a false or biased nature, with the intent of hampering the government in its relations with foreign powers, or damaging national credit at home or abroad. Police could suspend newspapers that they believed violated this regulation.

A story by Associated Press said that more than 400 papers in the Rhineland and the Ruhr had been suppressed by occupation authorities anywhere from three days to several months. Prison sentences and fines were levied against 82 editors and 31 publishers.

1924

Benito Mussolini placed all newspaper managers under the control of local prefects to end press freedom and non-fascist newspapers.

Clennell Wilkinson pointed out in <u>The Outlook</u>, a London periodical, that the notion that movies were more dangerous than the old penny dreadfuls still remained to be proved.

32
The Triumph of the Fourteenth Amendment, 1925 through 1949

The Central Conference of American Rabbis condemned in 1925 all interference, whether by private citizens or by officials, with the exercise of freedom of speech whether written or oral.

The Board of Movie Censorship maintained by the movie industry forced the makers of a silent movie of <u>The Scarlet Letter</u> to portray Hester Prynne as being married.

Frank R. Kent said that pulp magazines like <u>Hot Dog, Red Pepper</u>, and <u>Whiz Bang</u>, had made American newstands more lurid than those of France. A Clean Books League failed to get the New York legislature to pass a tougher obscenity law.

When Boston's Watch and Ward Society won a conviction of James DeLacey for selling Lawrence's <u>Lady Chatterley's Lover</u>, opponents of censorship managed to get the state law liberalized so the society and censorship became of little importance.

Benjamin Gitlow, business manager of a Socialist party paper, <u>Revolutionary Age</u>, was convicted of advocating overthrow of the government by force in pamphlets. The Supreme Court agreed that the 1902 New York criminal anarchy law did not unduly restrict Gitlow's press freedom, but accepted Gitlow's contention that Fourteenth Amendment due process guarantees should apply in First Amendment cases. This view placed The Bill of Rights under the Fourteenth Amendment, reversing an 1873 court decision. Justice Edward Sanford wrote the court's opinion upholding Gitlow's conviction. He said, "We assume that freedom of speech and of the press which are protected by the First Amendment from abridgement by Congress are among the fundamental personal rights and liberties protected by the due process clause of the Fourteenth Amendment from impairment by the states."

The significance of the Gitlow decision ultimately was the extending of constitutional protection against government regulation of First Amendment rights to all levels--state, municipal, federal, etc. -- and branches -- legislative, executive, and judicial - of government.

Margaret A. Blanchard found that state courts established a series of basic propositions involving speech and press claims, which served as a precedent for the Supreme Court entering the field. " It is possible to find state court antecedents for almost every speech and press issue placed before the high court in the 1960s and 1970s. About 250 cases were handled in the state courts. This should not be unexpected since all 50 of the state constitutions contain provisions for a free press."

1926

George R. Dale, editor of the <u>Post-Democrat</u> in Muncie, Indiana, fought against the Ku Klux Klan and political corruption and for free speech and free press. He was frequently hauled into court, assaulted, shot at, and deprived of advertising by pressures from his opponents. A judge refused to allow copies of the newspaper on city streets, but the Indiana legislature impeached the judge.

Silas Bent said that no newspaper reader would become an active champion of press feedom until "newspapers mend their ways, shovel less smut, and print more news."

The <u>Christian Science Monitor</u> editoralized, "The persistent glorification of criminals in the press, the publication of their portraits, the use of laudatory or at least striking nicknames, and the growing practice of feature writers of spreading the views and exploits of criminals all over the Sunday papers, stimulate, encourage, and increase crime."

George W. Kirschwey said:

"With the automatic gun to paralyze the victim and wayfarers, and the automobiles at the curb to ensure a quick get-away, is there any wonder that the young daredevils of the criminal profession are attracted to the game? With the newspaper reporting and dramatizing every detail of every hold-up of this character, the wonder is that more of them don't go in for it. It is certainly made it look like easy money with a minimum of risk."

On April 5, H. L. Mencken sold a copy of <u>The American Mercury</u> to Rev. J. Frank Chase of the New England Watch and Ward Society. He was arrested immediately for obscenity by the Boston police. Mencken was found not guilty for the short story entitled "Hatrack" in the magazine. The court even issued an injunction ordering the Watch and Ward Society not to harrass the magazine any more.

A special customs court assumed power and added barriers for literature at United States ports-of-entry. Works by Balzac, Boccacio, Louys, Flaubert, Georga Moor, James Joyce, Lawrence, and others were denied entry.

1927

To avoid confusion, the Customs Bureau and the Post Office made a list of 700 books that could not be imported or mailed.

Jewish groups pressured Los Angeles City Schools to discontinue using the Merchant of Venice in classes. The mayor of Chicago ordered a survey of the history books in the Chicago public library to find books tainted with British propaganda so they could be locked up.

Donald Davidson said, "Censorship gets nowhere, because nobody can decide with any sort of accuracy what really ought to be censored. I know of no person I would trust as a literary censor." Moralists attacked magazines as being obscene. A Mississippi representative proposed the formation of a National Board of Magazine Censorship. The conclusive argument against censorship according to a critic writing in The Nation is the character of the censor himself, since there never was one who was not utterly ridiculous.

In order to escape prosecution, Boston booksellers stopped selling certain books including Patrick's Rebel Birds, Newman's The Hardboiled Virgin, Pascal's Marriage Bed, and Smith's The Beadle. Boston had banned nine contemporary novels including Plastic Age by Mark, As It Was by Thomas, Elmer Gantry by Lewis, and An American Tragedy by Dreiser.

Upton Sinclair, who considered himself the prize prude of the radical movement, tormented Boston police with a fig leaf sandwich board which he wore to sell copies of his novel Oil on the streets of Boston where it had been banned. Fig leaves had been printed on some of the pages as part of the scam. He even sold a copy of the Bible wrapped in an Oil book jacket to a policeman. Sinclair was trying to be arrested and jailed for the book, but a judge only fined a book store clerk $100 for selling copies. Sinclair said that "we authors are using America as our sales territory and Boston as our advertising department."

An organizer for the Industrial Workers of the World was the first person to ask successfully the Supreme Court to apply the Fourteenth Amendment procedures in protecting his First Amendment rights.

Anita Whitney, a philanthropist and Socialist, was convicted of violating the Criminal Syndicalism Act of California, which disallowed, among other things, advocating and teaching criminal syndicalism, the revolutionary doctrine by which workers seize control of the economy and the government by general strike and other direct means. The Supreme Court upheld the conviction. In his concurring opinion Justice Brandeis elaborated on the clear and present danger test and explained why government is prohibited from restricting freedom of expression. This case reaffirmed the applicability of the Fourteenth Amendment to free speech and free press protection. Governor Young of California believed Miss Whitney should have been acquitted on the basis of the clear and present danger rule because he considered the Communist Party of little danger in the state.

Congress passed the Radio Act establishing the Federal Radio Commission. The act was requested by the broadcasting industry. It made it necessary for license holders to broadcast in the public interest, convenience, or necessity. The airwaves became a public resource for broadcasters to use but not own. The five member board was prohibited from interfering with free speech and provided equal broadcast opportunities for political candidates. Licenses could be revoked for indecency, profanity, or failure to follow license provisions. It allowed the government to take over stations in emergency situations. Commercials had to be indentified. It banned any form of censorship or prior restraint. The act was obsolete since radio technology and function both were far ahead of its provisions.

1928

The Minnesota Supreme Court upheld an injunction forbidding publication of the Saturday Press and said it did not infringe on free press rights. The court ruled that the Fourteenth Amendment did not prohibit states from operating police power in many areas and thus upheld the Minnesota gag law. In October, the district attorney of Hennepin County had charged The Saturday Press as being a malicious, scandalous, and defamatory newspaper. The judge ordered its permanent suspension. The conventional court view of freedom of the press according to the Minnesota Supreme Court in the Olson v. Guilford case, was that:

> "the liberty of the press is the right to publish with complete immunity from legal censure and punishment for the publication so long as it is not harmful in its character when tested by such standards as the law affords. The constitutional protection meant the abolition of censorship and that governmental permission or license was not to be required; and indeed the Constitution gave the individual freedom to act but to act properly or within legal rules of propriety. In Minnesota no agency can hush the sincere and honest voice of the press, but the Constitution was never intended to protect malice, scandal, and defamation when untrue or published with bad motives or without justifiable ends. It is a shield for the honest, careful, and conscientious press. There is a legal obligation on the part of all who write and publish to do so in such a manner as not to offend against public decency, public morals, and public laws."

Desmond MacCarthy said:

> "History shows that only those communities have flourished in which men were allowed to pool their experience and comment freely on life, and that the

suppression of freedom is a graver risk to civilization than the circulation of any particular book is to morality."

1929

The Federal Radio Commission set forth narrowly-defined standards for what it felt was desirable programming by broadcast licensees. In its third annual report the FRC outlined an historical basis for its broadcast fairness doctrine.

When an amendment was proposed to allow customs officials to exclude foreign literature, opponents of the plan fought it and the customs law was liberalized.

John Summer and his New York Society for Suppression of Vice failed to get a conviction of Radclyffe Hall's, The Well of Loneliness. A three judge appeals court ruled that its theme, based on lesbianism, was not sufficient to make it obscene.

Theodore Dreiser said, "Today we are faced with one of the most fanatical and dangerous forms of censorship that ever existed, because the effect is to reduce all human intelligence to one level -- and that level about that of a low-grade (not even a high-grade) moron."

Robert Herrick said, "Better to allow free pornography than to leave to any censor or board of censors the choice of what we can read or think! Less harm to public morals would be done with complete license than from the sort of censoring we suffer from at present -- haphazard, ignorant, vascillating."

George Jean Nathan said, "Why is it that censorship designed by its own admission to safeguard the young, the susceptible, and the ignorant, four times out of five desports itself not in that quarter at all but exercises itself sedulously against institutions and works whose appeal is directly and almost entirely to unsusceptible and intelligent adults."

Mary Ware Dennett won reversal of a lower court's decision that had ruled sending a pamphlet entitled The Sex Side of Life through the mails was prohibited because it was considered obscene by postal authorities. The New York Society for the Suppression of Vice burned $20,000 worth of books under orders from a district attorney.

1930

Basing its decision on the Hicklin rule of obscenity, a Massachusett's court banned in the Friede case Theodore Dreiser's An American Tragedy.

The Post Office removed second class mail privileges from Revolutionary Age, a weekly published by a Communist faction.

James A. Delacy and a clerk in the Dunster House Book Store in Cambridge, Massachusetts, were fined and given short prison terms for selling <u>Lady Chattersley's Lover</u>. <u>Married Love</u> and <u>Contraception</u>, two pamphlets about sex instruction, were ruled not to be obscene by federal courts.

Justice Louis D. Brandeis said, "The function of the press is very high. It ought to serve as a forum for the people, through which the people may know freely what is going on. To misstate or suppress the news is a breach of trust."

F. P. Dunne, an American humorist, said, "The job of the newspaper is to comfort the afflicted and afflict the comfortable."

The Motion Picture Production Code was formalized. The Hays Code of Movie Censorship was written by a trade paper publisher and a Catholic priest.

Col. Robert McCormick of <u>The Chicago Tribune</u> condemned the Minnesota gag law of 1929 as tyrannical, despotic, un-American, oppressive, and allowing the suppression of a publication exposing corruption in government. Earlier, an American Newspaper Publishers Association Committee said in 1928 that the action of the Minnesota legislature and courts would render valueless all guarantees of free speech in Minnesota. In 1930 the ANPA said the law was a violation of the First and Fourteenth Amendments and a dangerous invasion of personal liberty.

Emanual Haldeman-Julius, publisher of the Little Blue Books, said:

"The real animas of censorship lies in a dislike for art that, whether imaginatively or realistically, runs counter to notions of respectability, which the censors personally regard as sacrosanct and which they pretend have the just force of great social necessities. Censorship is foolish and the censors personally illustrate its foolishness to the last degree."

Aldous Huxley said, "The remedy against pornography is in the heads of everyone who chooses to use it. If you do not like a book, all you have to do is not read it. Let every man be his own censor."

1931

Frank Swancara said that archaic state blasphemy laws were being used to suppress radical literature which only incidentally alluded to atheism.

Lawrence Rogin said, "Political censorship of any sort in a democracy is an anomaly. To vest the power of such censorship in an official whose decisions for all practical purposes is final, is to introduce autocracy in an extreme form."

Judge John M. Woolsey lifted a 13-year ban of Customs

forbidding importation of Dr. Marie Stope's <u>Married</u> <u>Love</u>.

The United States Supreme Court declared the Minnesota gag statute unconstitutional in 1931 and said the fact that liberty of the press may be abused by miscreant purveyors of scandal does not make immunity of the press from prior restraint any less necessary in dealing with official misconduct. Censorship before publication is almost always unconstitutional, and freedom of the press even means more than restraint in advance of publication. Principal findings of the decision were that it was no longer open to doubt that the liberty of the press was within the liberty safeguarded by the due process clause of the Fourteenth Amendment from invasion by state action and that the liberty of the press precluded previous restraints in the form of licensing, prepublication censorship, or by judicial injunctions against publication of material that would not be privileged against subsequent penalities. Justice Charles E. Hughes pointed out in the Near case:

> "The administration of government has become more complex, the opportunites for malfeasance and corruption have multiplied, crime has grown to most serious proportions, and the danger of its protection by unfaithful officials and of the impairment of the fundamental security of life and property by criminal alliances and official neglect emphasizes the primary need of a vigilant and courageous press, especially in great cities."

1932

A court ruled that the continued forum use of a radio station by its owner to present personal viewpoints was not allowed by the license or by the First Amendment, and denial of a license did not abridge constitutional rights because broadcasting was really interstate commerce.

The National Council on Freedom from Censorship was founded. Holbrook Jackson said, "It is to the glory of books that ignorance and fanaticism are their enemies and that their history is disfigured with calumnities, persecutions, and neglect."

1933

Stuart H. Perry said:

> "The pattern of the press and the bar are not identical, but discrete and parallel. It is neither possible nor desirable to merge or intimately coordinate their efforts. Each should stick to his plow; but when their lines are contiguous or in the rare incident coincident, they should work together with the fullest understanding and cordiality."

Magistrate Benjamin Greenspan, in deciding Erskine Caldwell's <u>God's</u> <u>Little</u> <u>Acre</u> could not be censored, said, "The court may not require the author to put refined language in the mouths of primitive people."

Comic books were developed by imaginative publishers after kids' nickels.

In the Shuck case, the court decided that a newspaper did not have to accept or publish advertising if it decided not to.

Governor Dunnegan threatened to prosecute the Tallahassee (Ala.) Tribune for publishing editorials in opposition to the National Recovery Act. The American Newspaper Publishers Association and the American Society of Newspaper Editors compelled him to withdraw his threat. Thomas Murray had his NRA blue eagle emblem revoked for criticizing the NRA in his advertising in the Lynn (Mass.) Evening Item. By the time newspaper protests had forced restoration of the symbol, Mr. Murray had been bankrupted. American newspaper publishers reacted to the New Deal Code with this resolution: "In submitting or subscribing to this (required) Code, the publishers do not thereby agree to accept or to comply with any other requirements than those herein contained, or waive any constitutional rights, or consent to the imposition of any requirement that might retract or interfere with the constitutional guarantee of the Freedom of the Press."

The American Newspaper Guild was founded in Washington by delegates from 30 cities to preserve the vocational interest of its members, to improve the conditions under which they worked by establishing collective bargaining, and to raise the standards of journalism.

President Franklin Delano Roosevelt began his press conferences and worked with the press in an open manner. As the war began he said, in response to pressure to curb the lusty free press:

"I take it that no sensible man or woman believes that (the free press) has been curtailed or threatened or that it should be. The influence of the printed word will always depend upon its veracity; and the nation can safely rely in the wise discrimination, of a reading public which, with the increase in general education, is well able to sort out truth from fiction. Representative democracy will never tolerate the suppression of true news at the behest of the government."

The National League of Decency was set up by the Roman Catholic Church to monitor movies. The Motion Picture Producers and Directors Association set up a Production Code Administration to censor movies.

After the president of Macmillan Publishing company called to tell about the manuscript, the FBI seized and classified Japanese Diplomatic Secrets by George Bye. Tom Dewey talked the press into ignoring the event.

Customs officials would not allow many books to be

imported into the United States. Some were classics and had
already been published and distributed within the United
States. A 1930 law authorized importation of classics and
books of literary or scientific value. Custom officials in
1933 decided Ulysses by James Joyce had insufficient literary
merit to be admitted. Judge Woolsey of a Federal District
Court and later the Court of Appeals ruled the book not
obscene. The 1930 law and Woolsey's decision freed books
from censorship by custom officials. Woolsey indicated the
old Hicklin obscenity rule of England could not apply and the
work as a whole would determine its value. Woolsey said:

> "Reading Ulysses in its entirety did not tend to excite
> sexual impulses or lustful thoughts, but that its net
> effect was only that of a somewhat tragic and very
> powerful commentary on the inner lives of men and women.
> It is only with the normal person that the law is
> concerned. Such a test as I have described, therefore,
> is the only proper test of obscenity in the case of a
> book like Ulysses which is a sincere and serious attempt
> to devise a new literary method for the observation and
> description of mankind."

1934

The Federal Communications Act of 1934 established the
seven member Federal Communications Commission to control
broadcasting. It centralized government regulation of
telephone, telegraph, and broadcast activities. An effort
was made to restrict commercialism but that failed. The act
proscribed the Federal Communications Commission from acting
as a censor in the traditional sense of prior restraint;
however, the FCC could review a station's programming to see
if it had operated in the public interest.

Indiana Senator Arthur Robinson told the Senate that the
national emergency faced by the United States should not be
used as an excuse to restrict freedom of speech or of the
press.

Albert D. Lasher said, "No more vicious calumny has
every been put forth than the suspicion that the press in any
major or important way can be influenced editorially by the
advertising patrons. A free press is made possible by its
advertisers. End free advertising and you will largely end a
free press."

Columbia University banned Caldwell's books Tobacco Road
and God's Little Acre.

Robert McCormick, publisher of The Chicago Tribune,
said:

> "Freedom of the press would be abridged by any law
> passed by Congress which would license, censor,
> confiscate, enjoin, or especially tax the press; or
> introduce libel upon government; or constitute the
> judge, judge of the libel, or judge of the law; or
> prevent truth from being pleaded in defense of a libel;
> or unreasonably raise the cost of production, or

unreasonably decrease by indirect means the returns from publishing, as these would abridge its freedom as effectively as would excessive taxation; or interfere with the transmission of news by telegraph or otherwise, or interfere with the distribution of printed matter; or confine the liberty to write for publication or the liberty to publish to any fraction of the population; or prevent any citizen of the United States from printing, writing for publications, or from causing any writing to be printed; and, finally, anything that would reasonably interfere with the freedom of the press, in any way which may ever be invented."

1935

W. S. Taylor advocated <u>censureship</u> instead of <u>censorship</u> since it would not interfere with the complete freedom of publication and yet the government would have opportunity to present its opinions.

The editor of the Dothan, Ala., <u>Eagle</u> editorialized that citizens should arm themselves with shillelaghs and whale the hell out of members of the Alabama legislature for passing an anti-sedition law.

Heywood Broun said that "if labor wants to get a press which is fair to labor, it will have to organize its own newspaper. Our present press is free to do as it pleases, and it pleases to be always on the side which carries the heaviest butter."

Gilbert Montague of the New York Bar said, "In previous fights for human liberty, the bar has always taken a leading part, but in the present crisis the bar has stood aside from economic pressure and coercion while the battle is being won by newspaper writers and newspaper publishers."

1936

William T. Laprade said, "The monopolistic character of the enterprise of gathering and dispensing news and current comment and its profound influence of the material thus dispensed in shaping mass emotions certainly raises the question whether a publisher chiefly interested in earning a profit is the most suitable trustee of this undertaking?"

The Montana State Board of Higher Education banned Vardis Fisher's <u>Passions Spin the Plot</u> from university libraries.

President Franklin D. Roosevelt said, "Freedom of conscience, of education, of speech, of assembly are among the very fundamentals of democracy and all of them would be nullified should freedom of the press ever be successfully challenged."

During the 1930s, Huey Long's political machine encountered increased opposition from the larger daily newspapers in Louisiana. In retaliation, the legislature, controlled by Long and his followers, passed a special two per cent tax on the gross advertising income of papers with 20,000 or more circulation weekly. Only thirteen out of 163 newspapers in the state qualified for this tax, but twelve of the thirteen were outspoken critics of Long. It was an obvious attempt to gag press critics. The Louisiana law was overturned by the Supreme Court which ruled that the law violated freedom of the press. In this Grosjean decision, Justice George Sutherland, said such taxes are forbidden "to preserve an untrammeled press as a vital source of public information." The opinion adopted the test of Judge Thomas Cooley, the Nineteenth Century constitutional authority, that the evils to be avoided were not merely those of prior restraint or censorship but any "action of the government which might prevent such free and general discussion of public matters as seems absolutely essential to prepare the public for an intelligent exercise of their rights as citizens."

The Associated Press fired Morris Watson, an employee of its New York office. Subsequently the American Newspaper Guild filed a charge with the National Labor Relations Board claiming his discharge was in violation of Section F of the National Labor Relations Act, which allows employees to organize and bargain collectively through labor representatives. The NLRB ordered AP to restore Watson's job. The AP argued that to allow the Guild's position was contrary to the First Amendment. By a 5-to 4 decision, the Supreme Court upheld the ruling against the AP. The authority for the National Labor Relations Act was based on the commerce clause of the Constitution. The court held that the Associated Press was interstate commerce and that its business was not immune from regulation because it was an agency of the press. It further ruled that the action of the NLRB in no way restricted freedom of the press.

Paul Bellamy said, "I regard the publication of crime news as one of the primary obligations of a newspaper arising out of its mission to improve society."

1937

Dirk DeJonge was arrested when police raided a communist-sponsored meeting which was protesting police handling of a longshoreman's strike in Oregon. He was convicted of violating the state's criminal syndicalism act. The Supreme Court declared the Oregon statute unconstitutional under provisions of the Fourteenth Amendment. Chief Justice Charles E. Hughes wrote this unanimous opinion for the Supreme Court decision:

"Freedom of speech and of the press are fundamental rights which are guaranteed by the due process clause of the Fourteenth Amendment of the Federal Constitution. The right of peaceable assembly is a right cognate to those of free speech and free press and is equally fundamental. The very idea of a government, republican in form, implies a right on the part of its citizens to meet peaceably for consultation in respect to public affairs and to petition for a redress of grievances. The greater the importance of safeguarding the community from incitements to the overthrow of our institutions by force and violence, the more imperative is the need to preserve inviolate the constitutional rights of free speech, free press, and free assembly in order to maintain the opportunity for free political discussion, to the end that government may be responsive to the will of the people and that changes, if desired, may be obtained by peaceful means. Therein lies the security of the republic, the very foundation of constitutional government."

A New York art supply firm was convicted of obscenity for selling The Body Beautiful, a volume of nude photos for artists.

American book publishers refused to attend the International Publishers Congress in Leipzig as a protest of German censorship.

M. D. Kennedy contended that under freedom of the press there is a great deal of high-handed action on the part of editors and managers which is the reverse of true freedom.

Freedom of the press includes the right to write, print, and distribute and is not restricted to newspapers or periodicals but includes pamphlets, leaflets, and all sorts of publication containing information, entertainment, or opinion. The First Amendment was motivated by the desire to eliminate licensing and censorship. The Supreme Court ruled that a Griffin, Georgia, ordinance requiring permission to distribute religious pamphlets was unconstitutional as a form of licensing and censorship. The ordinance could not claim its concern with distribution excused it from First Amendment requirements. Liberty of circulation is as essential to freedom of the press as is liberty of publishing; indeed, without circulation, the publication would be of little value. Alma Lovell was sentenced to 50 days for distributing Jehovah Witness leaflets and selling tracts on street corners and door to door. The ordinance, which required obtaining written permission from the city manager, was declared unconstitutional.

A New York magistrate dismissed an obscenity complaint against James Farrell's A World I Never Made.

1938

Congress created the House Un-American Activities Committee, which led to black-listing various authors. Congress authorized greater power to the Federal Trade Commission to regulate and punish unfair or deceptive advertising.

William B. Munro said, "It is the newspaper press that has made modern democracy possible."

Life Magazine was judged not obscene for publishing an article with pictures about "The Birth of Baby". Some sellers of the magazine were arrested.

1939

William Allen White, editor of the Emporia, Kansas, Gazette, said:

"The most serious danger that menaces the freedom of the American press is the obvious anxiety of rich publishers about freedom of the press. They make so much noise about the threat to freedom of the press that they have persuaded many people that freedom of the press is merely a private snap for editors who wish to exploit the public by selling poisoned news. Whenever I read a rabid reactionary newspaper whooping it up for freedom of the press I'm scared stiff. For every boost that kind of a paper makes for freedom is a knock against it. That kind of press in Czarist Russia, in pre-war Germany and Italy or the Kindgom, must have made the public sentiment that stood by and let the freedom of the press on continental Europe go to pot. A kept press is the first sign that human liberty is being crushed."

For 19 years, the anarchist publication Man was persecuted in San Francisco.

Harold L. Ickes contended the real danger to freedom of the press came from sinister forces in the press itself rather than from the government. He accused editors of using freedom of the press as a smokescreen to suppress.

George Lang said, "A free press is at one with the Christian religion in offering the dignity and worth of the plain man. It is also obvious that a free press is at one with those who affirm the service of reason to promote human welfare."

The Studio was banned from the mails for its nudes, but protests caused the Post Office to reverse the ban.

Denys Thompson said, "The answer to the challenge to protect young people from the sinister propaganda rife in the world today is not censorship but education of children to discriminate in their reading."

The Supreme Court ruled that littering ordinances controlling distribution of handbills, leaflets, and flyers in four cities, grouped under the Schneider case were unconstitutional requirements of censorship and licensing which made impossible the free and unhampered distribution of pamphlets. The ordinances strike at the very heart of constitutional guarantees under the First and Fourteenth Amendments.

Books condemned and censored from schools and libraries included: A Farewell to Arms, Grapes of Wrath, Tobacco Road, God's Little Acre, Jack and the Beanstock, Huckleberry Finn, Tom Sawyer, Leaves of Grass, Paradise Lost, The Republic (Plato), Silas Marner, Around the World in Eighty Days, The Scarlet Letter, Macbeth, Crime and Punishment, Moby Dick, Zoo Story, To Kill a Mockingbird, Diary of a Young Girl, The Cool World, The Rabbits' Wedding, A Dictionary of American Slang,

Mickey Mouse, Three Weeks, Little Black Sambo, Five Chinese
Brothers, Doctor Dolittle, Ulysses (Joyce), Catch-22, The
Catcher in the Rye, The Grapes of Wrath, The Naked Ape, The
Encyclopedia of Witchcraft, Demonology and Their Craft,
Manchild in the Promised Land, Down These Mean Streets, Jaws,
North Dallas Forty, Go Ask Alice, Rivers of Blood-Tears of
Darkness, To Walk the Line, The Water Is Wide, Beastly Boys
and Ghastly Girls, Andersonville, Soul on Ice, The Fixer, and
Sanctuary.

1940

The Smith Act was primarily a sedition law. It made it
a crime to advocate the violent overthrow of the government
or to organize or belong knowingly to a group advocating its
overthrow. This meant it was illegal to print, publish,
edit, issue, circulate, sell, distribute, or publicly display
any written or printed matter, advocating, advising, or
teaching the duty, necessity, desirability, or propriety of
overthrowing or destroying any government in the United
States by force or violence.

Justice Felix Frankfurter said, "Without a free press
there can be no free society. That is axiomatic. However,
freedom of the press is not an end in itself but a means to
the end of a free society. The scope and nature of the
constitutional guarantee of the freedom of the press are to
be viewed and applied in that light."

Thomas Wolfe, the novelist, said, "I do not believe also
in the abolition of free inquiry, or that the ideas
represented by 'freedom of speech', 'freedom of thought',
'freedom of press', and 'free assembly' are just rhetorical
myths. I believe rather that they are among the most
valuable realities that men have gained, and that if they are
destroyed men will again fight to have them."

Justice Louis D. Brandeis said, "The function of the
press is very high. It is almost holy It ought to serve as
a forum for the people, through which the people may know
freely what is going on. To misstate or suppress the news is
a breach of trust."

Candidate Wendell Willkie said, "Freedom of the press is
the staff of life for any vital democracy."

As part of the Mayflower decision, radio station
editorials were banned. The FCC had been developing a
doctrine of fairness for presenting various views and this
decision was influenced by that prohibition.

The idea of using community standards in judging
obscenity was added by an appeals court in the Parmelee case.
Judge Learned Hand in a case 25 years earlier suggested
community standards could serve as a limiting factor in
calling a work obscene.

1941

The Post Office kept Father Charles Coughlin's Social

Justice and the Trotskyite *Militant* from the mails.

Three men and a woman were sent to jail for ten years under an Oklahoma syndicalism law for displaying their 10,000 books which were seized and burned. Ida Wood was sent to prison for possessing Communist books in Oklahoma.

With organization of the country for war, newspaper men recalled that the Espionage Acts of 1917 were still on the statute books. The use of these acts kept publications from the mails and suppressed free speech more sharply than in World War I.

Senator Millard Tydings fought Robert Jackson's confirmation as a Supreme Court Justice after Jackson as United States attorney general would not file criminal charges against Columnist Jack Anderson in 1939.

W. G. Vorpe, a newspaper editor, defined freedom of the press as the right of any editor, writer, or publisher of any newspaper, magazine, or pamphlet to express an opinion whether it be endorsement, denunciation, praise, criticism, or suggestion, so long as these expressions are not treasonable.

Walter D. Fuller, president of the National Association of Manufacturers, urged preservation of the free press to guard American democracy.

Harry Bridges, long-shoreman labor leader, sent a telegram to the United States Secretary of Labor severly criticizing a judge's decision in a labor case seeking a new trial as being outrageous. He threatened a major strike and shipping tie-up because of the decision. Bridges was found guilty of contempt of court for commenting on pending litigation. The United States Supreme Court upheld the contempt citation because the telegram posed a clear and present danger to the fairness of the upcoming trial. The Supreme Court said that courts could not hold editors in contempt to punish them for what they write except in the presence of clear and present danger to the court's authority. Justice Black pointed out that one of the objects of the American Revolution was to get rid of the English common law on liberty of speech and the press. The court pointed out that freedom of the press does not bear an inverse ratio to the timeliness and importance of the ideas being expressed. The First Amendment cannot be understood as approving practices in England at the time of its adoption; the unqualified prohibitions laid down by the framers of the amendment were intended to give to liberty of the press the broadest scope that could be countenanced in an orderly society. The Bridges case began a period of applying the clear and present danger test by most judges who would no longer cite writers for contempt unless the danger to the administration of justice was imminent and serious.

The Supreme Court ruled in the Nye case that judges could not cite newspapers for contempt unless the actionable behavior occurred in the physical proximity of the court room. Publishing criticism could not be punished by contempt of court citations.

1942

Boston banned an issue of <u>Life</u> because it reprinted six nude pictures on display in a Dallas Art Museum. The Georgia Board of Education banned <u>A Man Named Grant</u> by Helen Todd. When the Japanese citizens of the West Coast were interned by the United States, their Japanese language newspapers were discontinued. Records indicate that as many as 2,000 persons were arrested under provisions of the 1917 Espionage Act and more than a hundred publications kept out of the mails by the law. President Franklin D. Roosevelt established a Coordinator of Information to find information, not give it.

Roosevelt said:

"I have always been firmly persuaded that our newspapers cannot be edited in the interests of the general public from the counting room. Freedom of the news instead of freedom of the press should be the chief concern. All Americans abhor censorship, just as they abhor war, but the experience of this and all other nations has demonstrated that some degree of censorship is essenital in wartime and we are at war."

Alfred G. Stephens said, "Indecency, or even obscenity, simply cannot enter into the artistic question. A picture of a saint has no more artistic merit than a vile Pompeian fresco, and it may have less." He believed a community could control who could see indecent works.

Peadar O'Donnell said, "Censorship is the screen the dying order sets up to hide its weakness and shame." Governor Herman Talmadge of Georgia urged books dealing with better race relations be burned.

E. R. Stevenson, a newspaper editor, exhorted people to fight for freedom of the press against the government if need be and to fight for it against any newspaper, if need be. George Seldes said that the nation's "press is corrupt and that it has usually perverted the war news as well as labor news of social and economic importance."

Franklin D. Roosevelt said, "We all know that books burn; yet we have the greater knowledge that books cannot be killed by fire." The <u>Medical Library Association Bulletin</u> said, "Today, suppression of books in general and of medical books in particular is still a lawful procedure in many countries, democratic and totalitarian."

The Supreme Court upheld a New Hampshire law forbidding the use of any offensive, derisive, or annoying word to a person who is lawfully in a public place or of calling him by an offensive or derisive name. Walter Chaplinsky, a Jehovah's Witness, scolded a police chief and called him a God-damned marketeer, and a Facist. The Supreme Court agreed that Chaplinsky's words were <u>epithets</u> likely to provoke the average person to breach of the peace by physical retaliation. This decision established the doctrine that fighting words are not protected by the First Amendment. Publications beyond constitutional protections are the lewd and obscene, the profane, the libelous, and the insulting or fighting words, those which by their very utterance inflict injury or tend to invite an immediate breech of peace. They are not an essential part of any exposition of ideas, and are of such slight social value as a step to truth that any benefit that may be derived from them is clearly outweighed by the social interest in order and morality.

The Supreme Court ruled in the Valentine case that commerical advertising on city streets could be regulated by provisions in the New York Sanitary Code which prohibited such advertising. Commercial leaflets could not escape this restraint even though they had moral platitudes.

The court pointed out in the Douglass case that freedom of speech and freedom of the press are not the subjects of a direct constitutional grant, but they are constitutionally recognized and confirmed as attributes of liberty incident to all persons under the Constitution and the law of the United States regardless of their citizenship, and they are secured by the First Amendment against abridgement by Congress and by the Fourteenth Amendment against deprivation by a state without due process of law.

The Supreme Court decided that the city of Opelika, Ala., could not require the purchase of a license from the City Council before a person could sell books in the city. Mr. Jones, a Jehovah's Witness, had been convicted of breaking this city ordinance. In 1942, the Supreme Court ruled against Jones because it didn't consider the license charge an unconstitutional tax on freedom of the press. But in 1943, the court reconsidered and reversed itself on the basis of Chief Justice Harlan F. Stone's assessment which said "The First Amendment is not confined to safeguarding freedom of speech against discriminatory attempts to wipe them out. On the contrary, the Constitution by virtue of the First and Fourteenth Amendment has put those freedoms in a preferred position."

1943

The Federal Trade Commission had the authority to prohibit false advertising since the courts had ruled that commercial speech in advertising was not protected by the First Amendment.

George F. Booth, publisher of the Worcester, Mass., Telegram and Gazette, said:

"The freedom of the press is not primarily for the protection of newspapers and other publications; it is for the protection of the right of the whole people. With the right of free speech, free press is the greatest protection against tyranny that we as a people possess. A free press is the organ through which democracy breathes."

Robert E. Cushman wrote in The Boston University Law

Review that the ultimate responsibility for the protection of freedom of speech and press rests upon people like ourselves, the ordinary citizens whose ideas and feelings taken together constitute what we call American public opinion. Within the legal barriers set up by the Constitution and the courts to protect free speech and free press, there remains ample room for the play of legislative and executive intolerance and repression when supported or instigated by an excited and brutal opinion. Freedom of speech and freedom of press will be effectively preserved in this country only if people themselves value these vital civil liberties and demand that they be protected.

Thelma Martin, a Jehovah's Witness, was fined $10 in Struthers, Ohio, for distributing handbills. The Supreme Court reversed her conviction because the city ordinance violated both her freedom of the press and of religion. Justice Hugo Black said the city could not decide for its citizens who could not ring their doorbells. The city could not make a person a criminal for carrying information. A householder could place a note on the door asking persons not to knock if they were distributing literature.

The Supreme Court ruled that denial of a radio station broadcasting license does not deny freedom of the speech when that denial is based upon consideration of the public interest. Although the 1934 Communications Act forbids the FCC from censoring broadcast materials, the agency does exercise broad powers over program content. The court said that if the denial was not based on the applicant's political, social, or economic views it would not be a denial of free speech. Justice Frankfurter explained:

"Freedom of utterance is abridged to many who wish to use the limited facilities of radio. Unlike other modes of expression, it is subject to governmental regulation. Because it cannot be used by all, some who wish to use it must be denied." The National Broadcasting Company brought the suit in an effort to set aside anti-network provisions in the FCC's Chain Broadcasting Regulations.

The court in the Winters case said freedom of the press like freedom of speech is a fundamental public right which state statutes cannot abridge because the due process provisions of the Fourteenth Amendment safeguards against encroachment by Congress, but the Constitution does not deprive the states authority to enact laws in the legitimate exercise of police powers.

1944

Arthur B. Tourtellot said, "The free press vindicates the special right guaranteed it in direct proportion to the truth of its news and the honesty of its opinions."

Herman Ould told the tercentenary celebration symposium for Milton's Areopagitica that "books are the lines of communications between free men, and it is not merely out of caprice but for more sinister reasons that dictators burn, ban, and mutilate books."

Democrat and Republican parties both supported world freedom of information and unrestricted communication for news throughout the world at the urging of the American Society of Newspaper Editors. The House and the Senate noted its belief in the world wide right of the interchange of news by news gathering and distributing agencies, whether individual or associations, by any means, without discrimination as to sources, distribution, rates or charges; and that this right should be protected by international compact.

David Lawrence said:

"I do not believe the First Amendment to the Constitution of the United States is today an adequate protection for the freedom of the press in America. Judicial interpretation has nullified the original purpose. I believe there must be an additional amendment to safeguard the freedom of the press. The most essential problem in the making of a durable peace is in the dissolution of any partnership that may exist in any country between government and the press."

Norman Cousins, editor of The Saturday Review, made the post office back down on its threat not to mail copies of his magazine containing ads about Strange Fruit. Cousins said, "We not only protest your order; we refuse to follow it without due process of law."

Michael Bradshaw said that if the people can trust the press they will come to its rescue. Freedom of the press can be endangered by the slanting of local news.

The Court pointed out in the Kerner case that each liberty specified in the First Amendment is a liberty secured by the due process clause of the Fifth Amendment to all persons without regard to citizenship.

In the Thomas case, Justice Jackson said:

"But it cannot be the duty, because it is not the right of the state to protect the public against false doctrine. The very purpose of the First Amendment is to foreclose public authority from assuming a guardianship of the mind through regulating the press, speech, and religion. In this field every person must be his own watchman for truth, because the forefathers did not trust any government to separate the true from the false from us."

1945

One Hundred or more publications were suppressed during World War II. The House UnAmerican Activities Committee investigated seven radio news commentators to determine how far the nation could go with free speech. The FCC ruled that broadcasters should provide or sell time under the fairness rule to interest groups wishing to present viewpoints.

The American Society of Newspaper Editors Committee on

World Freedom of Information proposed that World War II treaties provide that there would be no censorship, no use of the press as an instrument of government, and to allow the free flow of information.

Earl L. Vance asked, "Is freedom of the press to be conceived as a personal right appertaining to all citizens, as undoubtedly the Founding Fathers conceived it; or as a property right appertaining to the ownership of newspapers and other publications, as we have come to think of it largely today?"

The duty imposed on publications to contribute to the public good did not confer on the postmaster general the power to censor if his standards were not met, according to The Georgetown Law Journal.

Arthur Sulzberger, publisher of the New York Times, appealed to an audience of publishers to teach that freedom of the press is the right of the people and not of publishers.

The Associated Press was charged under the Sherman Act with being a combination and conspiracy in restraint of trade and commerce in news among the states, and with attempting to monopolize a part of that trade. The charges cited the AP bylaws allowing members to prohibit the sale of its news to non-AP members and to block the admission of new members. For the Court, Justice Black said:

> "Surely the command that the government itself shall not impede the free flow of ideas does not afford a non-governmental combination a refuge if they impose restraints upon that constitutionally guaranteed freedom. Freedom to publish means freedom for all and not just for some. Freedom to publish is guaranteed by the Constitution but freedom to combine to keep others from publishing is not. Freedom of the press from governmental interference under the First Amendment does not sanction repression of that freedom by private interests."

Harlan Stone said in the Isenstadt case:

> "Lillian Smith's Strange Fruit had a strong tendency to maintain a salacious interest in the reader's mind and to whet his appetite for the next major episode. Even in this post-Victorian era, the book would tend to promote lascivious thoughts and arouse lustful desire in the minds of substantial numbers of that public into whose hands this book, obviously intended for general sale, is likely to fall."

1946

The Administrative Procedures Act loosened the government's willingness to make records available, but still authorized officials to limit that access, for good cause or for the public interest.

The FCC ruled that its Fairness doctrine applied to broadcast advertisements, but how it applied to institutional or editorial advertising versus product advertising was confusing.

Rep. Karl Mundt said that the extreme privilege of free press and free speech would not stop the House UnAmerican Activities Committee from exposing persons in unAmerican activities, even though those activities were legal.

Nine Nieman Fellows concluded that the press must assume responsibility for public service or face government control. The readers in the final analysis determine what kind of press the nation is to have.

Theodore Schroeder argued that obscenity exists only in wishful or fearful thinking, wholly in the feelings of the accusing person, and can never be transmitted by mail, express, freight, or by interstate commerce, with any book, picture, or play. It was said that finding a yardstick for proving a serious book indecent is as difficult as weighing a pound of waltzing mice because of the actions taken against Wilson's Memoirs of Hecate County.

Kenneth Stewart considered the threat to a free newspaper is from monopoly newspaper ownership and profit making.

Palmer Hoyt said:

"I believe entirely that the world cannot stand another war. But I believe as completely that the world is headed for such a war and destruction unless immediate steps are taken to insure the beginning at least of freedom of news, American style, between the people of the earth. A civilization that is not informed cannot be free and a world that is not free cannot endure."

John Knight said:

"Had not the Nazi and Facist forces in Germany and Italy seized and dominated the press and all communication facilities at the start, the growth of these poisonous dictatorships might well have been prevented and the indoctrination of national thought in the direction of hatred and mistrust might have been impossible.

William Benton said:

"The State Department plans to do everything within its power along political or diplomatic lines to help break down the artificial barriers to the expansion of private American news agencies, magazines, motion pictures, and other media of communications throughout the world. Freedom of the press, and freedom of the exchange of information generally, is an integral part of our society.

The second-class mailing privilege of Esquire magazine was revoked under the Classification Act which established the requirements for the second-class privilege. Postmaster General Frank C. Walker had originally brought the suit but he was substituted for later by his successor, Robert E. Hannegan. _Esquire_ was charged with failure to meet the act's fourth condition, which said a publication must be originated and published for the dissemination of information of a public character, or be devoted to literature, the sciences, arts, or some special industry and have a legitimate list of subscribers. The Supreme Court affirmed the lower court ruling that the postal action against _Esquire_ should be reversed. The decision greatly restricted the Postmaster General's powers as a censor.

Motion pictures, like newspapers and radio, are included as part of the press, whose freedom is guaranteed by the First Amendment according to the Paramount Pictures case.

1947

A committee for the First Amendment was formed to protest the attempts of the House Committee on Un-American Activities to smear movies and the press.

The American Association of Schools and Departments of Journalism, opposed censorship of undergraduate student publications in any form whatsoever.

A Commission of Freedom of the Press issued a general report on mass communication, newspapers, radio, motion pictures, magazines, and books entitled "A Free and Responsible Press." The Commission itself and its report were generally condemned by the media. Nevertheless, it provided the basis for the social responsibility theory of the press which frequently appears in discussions about the role of the press in contemporary society. Among its recommendations were expanded self-regulation of the mass media and repeal of the existing prohibitions of "expressions in favor of revolutionary changes in our institutions" where there is no clear and present danger that violence will result from these expressions.

The Commission on Freedom of the Press in its formal report said:

"Nor is there anything in the First Amendment or in our political tradition to prevent the government from participation in mass communications; to state its own case, to supplement private sources of information and to propose standards for private emulation. Such participation by government is not dangerous to the freedom of the press. Valuable ideas may be put forth first in forms that are crude, indefensible, or even dangerous. They need the chance to develop free criticisms as well as the chance to survive on the basis of their ultimate worth. Hence the man who publishes ideas requires special protection. To protect the freedom of the issuer is to protect the interest of the consumer and in general that of the community also. Freedom of the press means freedom from and freedom for. The press must be free from the menace of external compulsions from whatever source. To demand that it be free from pressures which might warp its utterance would be to demand that society should be empty of contending forces and beliefs. But persisting and distorting pressures -- financial, popular, clerical, institutional -- must be known and counterbalanced. The press must, if it is to be wholly free, know and overcome any biases incident to its own economic position, its concentration, and its pyramidal organization. The press must be free for the development of its own conceptions of service and achievements. It must be free for making its contribution to the maintenance and development of a free society. This implies that the press must also be accountable. It must be accountable to society for meeting the public need and for maintaining the rights of citizens and the almost forgotten rights of speakers who have no press. It must know that its faults and errors have ceased to be private vagaries and have become public dangers. The voice of the press, as far as a drift toward monopoly tends to become exclusive in its wisdom and observation, deprives other voices of a hearing and the public of their contribution. Freedom of the press for the coming period can only continue as an accountable freedom. Its moral right will be conditioned on its acceptance of this accountability. Its legal right will stand unaltered as its moral duty is performed."

This view is the basis of the "social responsibility" concept of the press, which demands an enforcement mechanism to force its musts and imperatives on the press.

Arthur Hays Sulzberger, publisher of the New York Times, said:

"I have a profound and deep faith in democracy, and that unless the spirit of man is free I find no point in existence. Man finds his noblest expression in his desire for knowledge and in supplying that knowledge. Ours is a sacred and special mission. The manner in which we perform our duties may well determine the destiny of the world. We can give strength to liberty or selfishly destroy it and ourselves. Let us fight for a free press. Let us make it a reasonable one."

Arleigh B. Williamson argued that safeguards of communication channels should develop codes of social responsibility, improve standards of accuracy, enlarge the group who could discriminate between fact and opinion, and expand the consciousness of the general public that welfare of the individual or the group is inseparable from the welfare of the whole.

William E. Hocking said, "With the rights of editors and publishers to express themselves there must be associated a right to the public to be served with a substantial and honest basis of fact for its judgments of public affairs."

The court indicated in the Josephson case that whenever speech or propaganda presents an immediate danger to national

security, First Amendment protection ends. Congress may
legislate to protect national security and may investigate
circumstances and facts to determine the need for such
legislation.

1948

The House Un-American Activities Committee accused ten
Hollywood writers and directors of being agents of un-
American propaganda in motion pictures. The movie industry
blacklisted them for refusing to testify, and the House held
them in contempt.

Philadelphia police seized 2,000 copies of 18 books they
considered obscene. The Pennsylvania law didn't require a
warrant.

The American Library Association adopted a Bill of
Rights which said that no book should be excluded because of
the race or nationality, or the political or religious views
of the world. Censorship of books must be challenged by
librarians in maintenance of their responsibility to provide
public information and enlightenment through the printed
word.

Joseph C. Williams said, "Freedom of expression is the
right of every citizen; it is a right because such expression
is of benefit to the community. Obviously, then, the
community through the government may at any time limit this
right for its own protection. This protection is called
censorship, and such censorship is vital to democracy."

The Society of Professional Journalists, Sigma Delta
Chi, began issuing annual freedom of information reports
because "the whole structure of human rights in a world of
free men with governments of their own choosing rests upon
one basic right--the right to know."

William H. Stringer said, "There is genuine danger today
that the world's international sparring match is leading to
increased censorship, less news, and more blocking of the
usual avenues of journalistic information along the western
diplomatic front. It can perilously restrict a nation's
knowledge of what its own diplomats are up to.

Robert D. Leigh, director of the staff for the Hutchins
Commission on Freedom of the Press, said:

"The focus changes from free individual expression as a
right, to the primary need of the citizen everywhere, to have
regular access to reliable information, and also, ready
access to the existent diversity of ideas, opinions,
insights, and arguments regarding public affairs. This does
not deny freedom, but it joins freedom with a positive
responsibility that freedom shall serve truth and
understanding. The concept of responsibility, carried to its
logical conclusion, may even imply defining a clearly harmful
class of public communications which falls outside the
protection of freedom itself."

Arthur Brown said, "The democratic philosophy is based upon a man's ability to reason, to decide for himself his own best interest, on man's educability, and his conscience. Censorship denies all these premises. Regardless of the issues of truth and falsehood, danger or obscenity, free expression is invaluable for progress. Censorship cannot be justified in a democracy."

Dorothy Thompson said, "A free press is indeed a press which appeals to reason in the light of facts, and one in which ownership and direction respect truth and reason. In our country it seeks to pay its bill by pleasing its readers. And if readers also respect the truth, they will keep it free, and make it more so."

The freedoms of speech, press, petition, and assembly, guaranteed by the First Amendment do not include a right to use any force, directly or indirectly, such as bodily harm, threats of bodily harm, or hunger, loss of work, starvation to any other human being or to those persons dependent upon him, according to the Le Baron case.   The scope of the First Amendment extends to all voluntary associations, both public and private, who must conform with First Amendment requirements in matters of freedom of expression. Judicial enforcement of restricted covenants are state actions according to the Shelley v. Kraemer case.

The court ruled in the Winters case a New York statute invalid because it did not specify a sufficiently definite standard of conduct in saying that pictures of lust and bloodshed would invite violent and depraved crimes.

1949

The New York City Board of Education banned The Nation magazine from city high schools.

The Report on Editorializing by Broadcast Licensees issued by the FCC presented comprehensive statements establishing a new doctrine. The Commission believed that the fairness doctrine was justified by the public interest part of the law, because of the scarcity of available licenses, because such a plan would enhance First Amendment opportunities for all, and because it would keep one agency from monopolizing content. Part one required affirmative presentation of news of public interest or issues. This meant the broadcaster had to actively provide for the presentations of various viewpoints. Part two specified that the presentation of news and comment in the public interest required the licensee to operate on a basis of overall fairness making facilities available for the expression of contrasting views of all responsible elements in the community as various issues arise. The third part removed the ban on station editorials.

The first general order of the Public Information Office of the Department of Defense applied military censorship to military personnel in time of peace.

The Library of Congress awarded Ezra Pound the Ballinger

prize for poetry even though he was in jail for treason. Pound was sentenced in 1945 to 13 years for making broadcasts on Italian radio.

Leonard V. Irwin pointed out that the inevitable effect of attempts at private censorship would not only endanger the right of a free speech for everyone, but also bring about within minorities the very kind of attitude the restrictions we're seeking to avoid.

Elmer Rice said that the supreme freedom is the freedom to think, talk, and write with independence and without threat.

Judges of the Massachusetts Supreme Court said that sexual episodes abound to the point of tedium in Kathleen Windsor's Forever Amber but since the book had historical interest it was not obscene.

A court ruled in the Kobli case that the public and the press have the right to attend a public trial in criminal prosecutions and that the Sixth Amendment does not permit exclusion of the public from such a trial.

33
Laggards and Totalitarians,
1925 through 1949

Benito Mussolini closed down many Italian newspapers in 1925 and re-opened them after he had replaced the staffs with fascists. He created a Ministry of the Press and Propaganda and said, "I consider Facist journalism as my orchestra."

1926

Austria set up a Film Censorship Board.

The Index of the Soviet Inquisition required that the religious section of libraries could contain only anti-religious books.

French police prosecuted Frank Harris, author of My Life and Loves, which revealed his bed hopping amongst English society circles but within two years, France cleared the book of all obscenity charges.

Shao P'iao-p'ing, Kung Te-pai, and Lin Pai-Shui, editors in Peking, were executed for criticism of the government and other offenses. Other editors who displeased authorities elsewhere in China were executed. Despite these executions and suppression, there were constant demands for freedom of the press.

An Inter-American Press Association was organized by 550 western hemisphere publications and people to guard freedom of the press.

1927

The League of Nations passed resolutions to improve international telecommunications, facilitate the distribution of newspapers between countries, limit censorship, and provide international freedom for journalists.

A Japanese delegation to the League of Nations Conference of Journalists demanded the prevention of news reports harmful to world peace. This was a reflection of the press struggle within Japan.

Shane's The Contab, a novel about religious and sexual questions of English undergraduate students, was tried for obscenity in London.

1928

Ireland enacted a Censorship of Publications law. Poet William Butler Yeats vigorously opposed an Irish censorship bill while serving as a senator in the Dail Eiream. He said it would create "an instrument of tyranny and place control over the substance of our thoughts in the hands of one man, the Minister of Justice."

England banned the movie Dawn to appease the Germans.

1929

The Chinese KMT Central Political Committee set up publication laws to safeguard freedom of the press and to prevent circulation of improper publications such as those propagating reactionary ideas.

Illustrations by D. H. Lawrence, and Geog Grosz's Ecce Homo were forced out of a gallery exhibition in London because they contained pictures of female genitals and pubic hair.

Yugoslavia banned the works of George Bernard Shaw.

1930

The League of Left-Wing Writers and Communist Writers inundated China with calls for revolution. The government harrassed, kidnapped, and prosecuted these propagandists through the 1930s.

A press ordinance was established in India designed to control newspapers and presses with security bonds. More than 175 persons were assessed.

During the decades of the 1920s and 1930s Latin American governments boycotted United States films which they believed belittled them and Latin American people.

Shakespeare's Venus and Adonis and Erich Maria Remarque's All Quiet on the Western Front caused convictions of booksellers in Australia. The Australian Customs Department banned Defoe's Moll Flanders, Huxley's Brave New World, and Orwell's Down and Out in Paris and London.

Voltaire's Dictionnaire philosophique was banned in Russia. The London County Council censored several Russian films including Mother, Ten Days That Shook the World, The

Fall of St. Petersburg, and The General Line.

1931

The word censorship was censored out of Russian regulations, but publications had to indicate government approval to be distributed.

1932

Count Potocki de Montalk was jailed six months for obscene libel involving translations of Francois Rabelais and Verlione.

1933

Under the German editors law devised by Paul Joseph Goebbels, all journalists had to negotiate with the state. The chief editors became state officials publishing only Goebbels approved materials. By 1936 the Nazis owned more than 100 newspapers and Goebbels banned criticism by newspapers.

The Cambridge public library banned George Bernard Shaw's Adventures of the Black Girl in Her Search for God.

The Book Censorship Abolition League of Australia sought to ban British political works.

The Nazi's in Germany and later in Czechoslovakia burned Franz Kafka's works because he was a Jew. The Nazi's burned books by Maxim Gorki, Stefan Zweig, Karl Marx, Sigmund Freud, Helen Keller, Jack London, Ernest Hemingway, John Dos Passos, Leon Trotsky, Josef Stalin, Felix Mendelssolin-Bartholdy, Rosa Luxemburg, Upton Sinclair, and Arnold Zweig.

1934

The Censorship Commission for Books and Periodicals was established in Shanghai. The government prepared lists of nearly 2,000 forbidden publications and books; some editors were executed; some beheaded, and others were imprisoned by government officers.

Jerusalem banned The Brown Book of the Hitler Terror so that Adolf Hitler would be somewhat mollified.

Waldo Sabine was fined 500 pounds for his Guide and the Girls which said the president of the board of education was a religious maniac.

1935

John A. Spender said in The Spectator:

"The really important freedom is not that of dancing on the edge of Campbell's Act, but freedom to write fearlessly on matters of public importance, freedom, above all, to express unpopular opinions -- opinions which the established authorities may think dangerous. A free and courageous press is needed to prevent conservatism from slipping into fascism and radicalism into revolution."

Wallace Smith was fined 100 pounds for his novel about a Chicago prostitute, Bessie Cotter. The court also ordered that Edward Charles' An Introduction to the Study of the Psychology and Physiology and Biochemistry of the Sexual Impulse be destroyed.

The Soviet Union banned the works of Voltaire.

1937

Britain censored a March of Time film.

Stephan Brown contended that "some sort of censorship over the printed word is not only the right but the duty of Governments such as Ireland; in the case of pornography few would question that right."

The London Economist reported that:

"some of his Majesty's judges, taking an increasingly serious view of the wickedness of criticism and the sordid motives of the press, had employed on the bench of the art of advocacy which they learned at the bar to stimulate jurymen to award swinging damages. Comments, which less judicial minds would regard as harmless and unjustifiable have been treated by the judges as gross defamation; and plaintiffs, encouraged by the prevailing fashion, have brought actions that in earlier generations would have been laughed out of court."

Jawaharlal Nehru founded the National Herald in Luchnow when he was released from prison in an effort to promote the cause of Indian freedom.

The Newspaper Asahi had its presses and editorial offices wrecked. From then on, no one dared oppose the military.

1939

Geoffrey Dennis' Coronation Commentary was taken to court because it libeled the Duke of Windsor.

The Chinese National Congress in its Program of Armed Resistance and National Reconstruction, promised to protect freedom of the press but then set up strong and comprehensive war-time censorship provisions, which were revised and made stronger each year thereafter.

The Canadian Supreme Court invalidated the Alberta press act which gave the government complete control over the press so it could suppress communist doctrines.

Paul Joseph Goebbels said, "News policy is a weapon of war. Its purpose is to wage war and not to give out information."

1940

Harold J. Laski, a British socialist, said, "A people without a reliable newspaper is, sooner or later, a people without the basis of freedom."

Sir Hugh Walpole said:

"For many centuries now the Englishman has enjoyed perfect freedom in the reading of any kind of literature. So the freedom of books is indestructable and the men and women of our country, with all their faults and lacks, are made of this freedom. No government is tolerable to them for a moment that tries to prevent their right to think for themselves, often studying all the evidence, past and present. That trust in their independence is their right, owned through years of conflict, and never again to any power on this earth will they surrender it."

Adolph Hitler said:

"The organization of our press has truly been a success. Our law concerning the press is such that divergencies of opinion between members of the government are no longer an occasion for public exhibitions, which are not the newspapers' business. We've eliminated that conception of political freedom which holds that everybody has the right to say whatever comes into his head."

1942

England suspended 96 Indian newspapers and jailed 25,000 people including Mahatma Ghandi and Nehru.

Hundreds of underground publications were circulated throughout Denmark during the Nazi occupation.

1944

More than 80 per cent of German newspapers were controlled by the Nazi Press Trust. The Reich Propaganda Minister directed the content of all newspapers.

The London Times said that freedom of the press is not a privilege of the newspaper but a fundamental liberty of the subject. Various British agencies had about 4400 "public relations" employees to promote understanding of the war, plus their overseas employees.

1945

Throughout the war Chinese officials censored and suppressed publications as did the Japanese in occupied territory.

Propaganda against Adolf Hitler was smuggled into Germany disguised as pudding packages, cook books, games, tea packets, and other items.

George Orwell said:

"The controversy over freedom of speech and of the press
is at the bottom of a controversy over the desirability,
or otherwise, of telling lies. What is really at issue
is the right to report contemporary events truthfully.
Intellectual freedom is under attack on the one hand by
apologists of totalitarianism and, on the other, by the
drift toward monopoly and bureaucracy."

The American Society of Newspaper editors sent a
delegation to 22 cities and eleven nations to carry the
message of an international free press into every friendly
capital of the world.

The Mexico City Inter-American Conference on Problems of
War and Peace accepted the United States proposal for free
access to information. A free flow of information was a
paramount consideration in forming the constitution of
UNESCO.

Three anarchists were jailed for nine months for
articles appearing in War Commentary because the English jury
considered them guilty of the crime of conspiring to cause
disaffection.

1946

The UN Charter, The UNESCO Constitution, and the
Universal Declaration of Human Rights all said, "Everyone has
the right to freedom of opinion and expression; this right
includes freedom to hold opinions; and to seek, receive, and
impart information and ideas through any media and regardless
of frontiers." The Mass Communications Division of UNESCO
set up a section on the free flow of information and, at the
request of the American delegation, a subcommission on
freedom of information and of the press. The General
Assembly of the United Nations resolved that "freedom of
information is a fundamental human right, and is a touchstone
of all the freedoms to which the United Nations is
consecrated."

The Economist of London carried an article complaining
that personalism not monopoly, was the chief threat to
freedom of the press in England. "The practice of certin
publishers to use their newspapers merely as giant megaphones
for their own whims and prejudices in a menace to a free
press."

Ireland had the Irish Censorship of Publications Act and
used a Register of Prohibited Publications to suppress
literature.

The British Prosecution of Offenses Regulations required
that police send offensive books and publications to the
Director of Public Prosecutions.

1947

The Constitution of the Republic of China again promised

freedom of the press but provided the press could be
controlled. There were nearly 4,000 works banned for India,
or for the British Museum, or for the India Office Library.

1948

The Conference on Freedom of Information adopted the
United States view of the free flow of information but
weakened the impact by having only two signatures appear on
the document. UNESCO sent the document to the United Nations
General Assembly where no action was taken.

Part of the Klement Gottwold coup d'etat in
Czechoslovakia was the purging of journalists and newspapers
so those remaining were completely controlled by the
communist government.

1949

The German Basic Law provided freedom of the press for
West Germany, and licensing of the press ended in the United
States occupation zone.

A Royal Commission on the English Press, formed in
response to a request from the National Union of Journalists
who were fearful of newspaper monopoly, recommended that a
General Council of the Press be established to admonish the
press for its sins.

The United Nations Economic and Social Council passed
sixteen resolutions pertaining to freedom of information and
freedom of the press based upon a 1948 conference on freedom
of information. The United Nations also updated and adopted
the old 1910 agreement for suppressing obscene publications.

France had a law prohibiting children's comics wherein
banditry, lying, sloth, cowardice, hate, or depravity were
shown favorably.

Publications in areas of China controlled by the
Communists were totally regulated. The KMT government
engaged in heavy press repressions with arrests, kidnapping,
killing, and bribery. Nevertheless, constant demands for a
free press occurred daily on a widespread basis.

34
Concepts from the U.S. Supreme Court, 1950 through 1959

President Harry S. Truman vetoed the Internal Security Act of 1950 which required Communists to register. He referred to it as the greatest danger to freedom of speech, press, and assembly since the Alien and Sedition laws of 1798. Congress over-rode his veto, and the Supreme Court deemed it constitutional in 1961.

Oklahoma's American Legion forced a librarian out of her job because she subscribed to the <u>Nation</u> for the library.

Publisher Bernard Kilgore said, "Whenever you start nibbling away at freedom of the press, it's hard to know when to stop. We've got to have a free press, whether it's responsible or not." He also said, "The fish market wraps fish in paper. We wrap news in paper. The content is what counts, not the paper."

Herbert Bayard Swope said, "The first duty of a newspaper is to be accurate. If it be accurate, it follows that it is fair."

Broadcasting propaganda from an enemy country against the war was action and not merely expression and could be considered treason.

The Supreme Court rejected the clear and present danger test in the Douds case and a new balancing test was described by Chief Justice Fred Vinson as, "When particular conduct is regulated in the interest of public order, and the regulations result in an indirect, conditional, or partial abridgment of speech, the duty of the Courts is to determine which of these two conflicting interests demands the greater protection under the particular circumstances presented."

Judge Curtis Bok's decision in the Gordon case concerned sex expression in modern literature. He said, "I believe in the censorship of the open market place rather than the police station. No publisher who prints a lot of smut because a ban has been lifted will make much money; actually it is the ban that keeps the price up; when the market is open the demand seals itself off; the pickings are scarce." He ruled that books by James T. Farrell, William Faulkner, Erskine Caldwell, Calder Willingham, and Harold Robbins were not obscene.

The essence of constitutional freedom of the press and of speech is to allow more liberty than the good citizen will take, according to the Williamson case.

1951

The Federal Security Administrator ordered Charlotte Towle's book Common Human Needs destroyed because the American Medical Association said it was viciously anti-American and advocated state socialism.

The New York Board of Regents closed the showing of the Italian film, The Miracle. Leo Pfeffer asked, "Shall American democracy continue the Jeffersonian tradition of freedom in religion, or shall we return to the Augustinian dogma of the duty of the state to extirpate heresy."

Alexander Trachtenberg and fifteen others were indicted under the Smith Act for teaching Marxism, Leninism, and publishing more than 40 books through the International Publishing Company.

The Chicago Police Bureau of Censorship attempted to ban Maude Hutchin's A Diary of Love. A proclamation by the president committed the United States to abide by provisions of the 1949 international agreement to suppress the circulation of obscene publications. Police Inspector Herbert Case made up a list of books that publishers couldn't offer for sale in Detroit. This Detroit list was thereafter used in several cities.

Justice Henry C. Greenberg recommended that reporting be categorized, and exposed to those who have a legitimate need to know the event. "The court and the press by working out an agreement to safeguard the freedom that both are dedicated to protect, can do so without denying to the people its right to see the processes of justice at work, or infringing upon the liberties of the press," he said.

Justice Hugo Black said, "The First Amendment does not speak equivocally. It prohibits any law 'abridging freedom of speech or of the press.' It must be taken as a command of the broadest scope that explicit language, read in the context of a liberty-loving society, will allow."

Col. Robert McCormick, publisher of The Chicago Tribune, said that the newspaper furnishes that check upon government which no constitution has ever been able to provide."

Maryland radio stations broadcast news reports about a person in custody on a murder charge. The trial court sought to punish the broadcasting companies for a report that the man arrested for a brutal murder had confessed, had a long criminal record, and upon being taken to the scene of the crime, had re-enacted the crime. The Court of Appeals of Maryland reversed their contempt citation and the Supreme Court denied certiorari in the Pennekamp case.

The Supreme Court decided that an Alexander city ordinance making the selling of subscriptions illegal was constitutional since it did not interfere with freedom of the press or of interstate commerce. But in the Kunz case of New York, the Supreme Court said that its decisions have made clear that a person faced with an unconstitutional law requiring a license before communication is to take place, may ignore it and engage with impunity in the exercise of the right of free expression for which the law purports to require a license.

1952

Latuko, a film made by the Museum of Natural History and which had pictures of nude people, was banned in New York City. Ohio state censorship was abolished for films by the Department of Education which had inherited that chore in 1921. The Television Code of Good Practices was enacted by the Television Board of the National Association of Broadcasters.

B.K. Sandwell pointed out that since channels of communications are limited, every citizen cannot have an absolute right to speak over the radio. "Somebody has to determine who shall speak over the radio and who shall not. Other media are available to citizens."

Leo Strauss argued that threats of persecutions had caused writers to write the truth between the lines so only trustworthy and intelligent readers, not all the readers, could discern that truth.

W.D. Patterson said, "The answer to censorship in a democracy is the progressive education of the public taste to reject the bad and demand the good, without recourse to official censors or to the extremism of many private pressure groups.

Joseph Beauharnais was found guilty and fined $200 for violating a 1949 Illinois group libel law by distributing anti-Negro leaflets on the streets of Chicago. The Supreme Court upheld the Illinois criminal group libel law 5 to 4. Freedom of the press does not protect a person when he makes statements about another person that are libelous. While truth is a complete defense in civil libel, in criminal libel some states require truth plus good motives for justifiable ends.

The Supreme Court held that a state may not deny a license to show a motion picture on the grounds that it is a sacreligious, as the New York Board of Regents had found

Rosellini's The Miracle to be. The court stated that motion pictures are a significant medium for the communication of ideas and brought them under the protection of the First Amendment. Justice Tom Clark said, "It is not the business of the government to suppress real or imagined attacks upon a particular religious doctrine whether they appear in publications, speeches, or motion pictures." The court indicated that motion pictures do have First Amendment protection even though commercial enterprises.

George Turnbull was vindicated by the Oregon Supreme Court of charges of criminal libel after his newspaper, The Medford, Ore., Tribune, crusaded against actions taken by local government officials.

1953

The Gathing Committee Report on Pornographic Books recommended that the House of Representatives give strong powers to the Post Office to impound obscene mailed materials. Faculty and students of St. Cloud Teachers College successfully pressured the city council to suspend a board of review which had banned books by James T. Farrell, Richard Wright, and Somerset Maugham.

The greatest menace to free journalism according to Mary T. McCarthy, is "the conceptualized picture of the reader that governs our present day journalism like some unseen autocrat. The reader, in this view, is a person stupider than the editor, whom the editor both fears and patronizes."

The American Bar Association resolved that the freedom to read is a corollary of the constitutional guarantee of the freedom of the press and American lawyers should oppose efforts to restrict it.

James R. Wiggins said, "Man must have the right to discover the truth. They must have the right to print it without the prior restraint of pre-censorship of government. They must have the right to put printed material into the hands of readers without obstruction by government under cover of law, or obstruction by citizens acting in defiance of the law."

Judge Curtis Bok said, "Above the bare legal right to speak or to read is the courage to use these rights well; to speak clearly, bravely, and accurately, and to read with understanding. On the other side is the right to maintain silence, and this right must be fought for."

President Dwight Eisenhower said, "Don't join the burners. Don't be afraid to go to your library and read every book, as long as any document does not offend your own ideas of decency; that should be your only censorship."

Julius O. Adler said, "Democracy will survive as a system of government only where the individual citizen has access to all information that is necessary for sound judgment."

The community standards test of obscenity had emerged from several lower court decisions, but the court ruled in a Bantam Books case that the dominant theme of the material taken as a whole must appeal to prurient interests. Isolated passages and the effect of the material on persons usually susceptable to a pernicious effect were rejected as obscenity tests.

A House of Representatives committee, investigating lobbyists, called Edward A. Rumely, secretary of the Committee for Constitutional Government, to testify. He refused to name persons who made bulk purchases of his group's political books for further distribution. The Supreme Court set aside his conviction of contempt. Justice Douglas detailed conflicts that can arise between the investigative powers of Congress and the right of press freedom. The Supreme Court said that expression by radio, television, and movies are speech and press freedoms protected by the First Amendment.

1954

Post Office officials seized a copy of the 1926 translations of <u>Lysistrata</u>. When challenged, the Post Office delivered the book, but only because it was not for general distribution. Alabama had a law requiring that every book used in schools or colleges have a label indicating whether or not its author was an advocate of socialism.

President Dwight Eisenhower issued an executive order forbidding military persons to provide information to a subcommittee investigating a controversy between Senator McCarthy and the Army. The order soon became the basis for all government agencies to withhold information from the press.

A writer in <u>Justice of the Peace</u>, said, "The practical harm to young people from the exhibiting of the great mass of vulgar post cards, is almost negligible."

An Ohio court banned an American film on the ground it was "tending to promote crime." On appeal the Supreme Court reversed the Ohio courts, citing the <u>Miracle</u> case as precedent. Justice Black and Douglas said that any censorship of motion pictures is repugnant to the First Amendment.

According to the Arnold case, freedom of the press is not absolute but it must be measured by public welfare and limited by it. Freedom of the press implies the right to publish whatever is desired with immunity from legal censure so long as it is not harmful according to the standards of the law. The guarantee of free press does not carry with it freedom of responsibility for any abuse of that right. Freedom of the press is a fundamental liberty guaranteed by the First Amendment; the states are restrained by the due process clause of the Fourteenth Amendment.

1955

The trade association of book publishers, through its council, began publication of a <u>Censorship</u> <u>Bulletin</u>.

American film distributors cut 22 minutes from the French film, <u>Wages of Fear</u>, because they showed friction between an American company located on foreign soil and the local population.

The National Organization for Decent Literature was set up in Chicago to ban literature that was lascivious and threatened moral, social, and national life. Its list of banned books included ones by Hemingway, Faulkner, Dos Passos, Orwell, O'Hara, and Zola.

Judge Learned Hand said, the First Amendment "presupposes that right conclusions are more likely to be gathered out of a multitude of tongues, than through any kind of authoritative selection. To many this is, and always will be, folly; but we have staked upon it our all."

George Sokolsky said the policy of the Post Office of increasing ignorance by refusing to allow Russian publications to pass through the mails was wrong. "I cannot know what I'm talking about in opposing communism unless I have the freedom to read what the other side publishes."

George Seldes said, "For the first time in American history, the press, which Jefferson described as playing a greater role in a democracy than government itself, is under sustained attack from the right -- the reactionary or potentially fascist element in the United States."

Columnist Walter Lippman said:

"A free press is not a privilege but an organic necessity in a great society. Without criticism and reliable and intelligent reporting, the government cannot govern. For there is no adequate way in which it can keep itself informed about what the people of the country are thinking and doing and wanting. The theory of free press is that the truth will emerge from free reporting and free discussion, not that it will be presented perfectly and instantly in any one account."

Jehovah's Witnesses were involved in at least 46 cases in the United States Supreme Court concerning their rights of free speech, free press, and free worship.

The use of telecasting equipment in the courtrooms was considered to be a violation of due process and was prohibited in all but two states.

A state cannot abridge freedom of the press to alleviate a slight annoyance or inconvenience to the public, or to forbid conduct which does not pose a clear danger of violating a valid public policy statute, according to the Starr case.

1956

The Citizens for Decent Literature had 300 chapters. There was a Churchman's Committee for Decent Publications. There also was a Catholic National Office for Decent Literature. California had its CLEAN project. The Motion Pictures Production Code was liberalized so movies could deal with several topics previously taboo. The movie censorship laws of Ohio and Pennsylvania were declared unconstitutional.

Simon E. Sobeloff said, "The editor and the judge are set apart from other citizens; only they may act as guardians of other men's liberties."

The Supreme Court declared the Congressional resolution that created the Un-American Activities Committee did not meet constitutional standards since it enroached upon an individual's right of privacy, and abridged liberty of the press, speech, and assembly.

The courts ruled in the Drew case that commercial speech or advertising is not protected by the First Amendment.

1957

Between 1947 and 1957 at least 24 novels were banned or blacklisted in the United States. Lolita was approved by Customs Officials for importation into the United States, but France would not allow it to be exported.

Laurence Lipton wrote in "50 Million Censors Can't Be Wrong" in Frontier, the Voice of the New West that:

"No matter how you may try to hedge it about with safeguards, legal censorship is the imposition of force, police force, on thought, art, judgment, and conscience; in such matters 50 million censors, or more, acting for themselves alone, are better than any one censor with legal police power. At the newstand or in the bookstore, as in the polling booth, the people have a right to make their own mistakes."

Author Albert Camus said, "A free press can of course be good or bad, but most certainly without freedom the press will never be anything but bad. Freedom is nothing else but a chance to be better, whereas enslavement is certainty of the worse."

The American Society of Newspaper Editors declared that people have an inherent right to know, to gather information, to publish, and to distribute without censorship or prior restraint or punishment without due process.

A Detroit bookseller won acquittal by appealing to the Supreme Court for selling Griffin's The Devil Rides Outside.

The Supreme Court ruled in the Butler case that a Michigan penal provision about obscenities unconstitutional. The Michigan statute defined obscenity as material having a deleterious effect on youth, and it made the circulation of books that tended to incite minors to violent or depraved or immoral acts a crime. The law was unreasonable, violated the Fourteenth Amendment, and it wasn't restricted to the evil it sought to control. The use of the Hicklin test for obscenity reduced the adult population of Michigan to reading only what was fit for children.

The court ruled Allen Ginsberg's <u>Howl</u> <u>and</u> <u>Other</u> <u>Poems</u> was not obscene, when Police Captain William Hanrahan brought booksellers to trial over the book.

The Supreme Court ruled in the Kingsley Books case that a New York law against the sale or distribution of any indecent written or printed matter was constitutional since it did not provide prior restraint and pertained to materials already published and then only if they were obscene.

To inhibit the freedom of thought and association of newspapermen is to infringe upon the freedom of the press, according to the Peck case.

The Supreme Court combined the Roth and Alberts case. David F. Roth worked in New York selling books, magazines, and photos. He was convicted of mailing an obscene book. Alberts was a Los Angeles business man charged with keeping and selling obscene books. In the majority opinion, Justice William J. Brennan said that while obscenity is not within the area of constitutional protection, it is vital that any standards for judging obscenity safeguard freedom of the press for material which does not appeal to prurient interests. The publication must be judged as a whole, and the effects of the publication on a normal person should be considered.

Freedom of the press according to the Sunshine Banks case is wholly immune from prior restraint or abridgement. Any censorship of material prior to publication is an unconstitutional and illegal prior restraint. Liberty of the press means principally, but not exclusively, immunity from previous restraints or censorship.

Freedom of the press is not absolute or unlimited under the First and Fourteenth Amendments, according to the <u>Tribune</u> <u>- Review</u> case. The rights in these amendments in some situations are secondary to the need for order without which any guarantee of civil rights would become a mockery.

1958

Massachusetts established an Obscene Literature Advisory Commission. Washington state had a law giving a state supervisor regulating control over comic books. The law was declared unconstitutional in 1958 by the Supreme Court.

1959

The editors of the <u>Seattle</u> <u>Union</u> <u>Record</u> were arrested for espionage as was the editor of the <u>Business</u> <u>Chronicle</u> after there had been some Armistice Day killings.

Congress passed an amendment to the 1934 Communications
Act which gave statutory status to the fairness doctrine but
that exempted news presentations from its requirements. The
equal access requirement for political candidates was
established by the FCC for radio and television broadcasts.
It did allow some exceptions, one of which was denial to Lar
Daly, a fringe presidential candidate, who wanted to reply to
a major candidate.

Justice Black said:

"Certainly the First Amendment language leaves no room
for inference that abridgement of speech and press can
be made just because they are slighted. The First
Amendment, which is the supreme law of the land, has
thus fixed its own value on freedom of speech and press
by putting there freedoms wholly beyond the reach of
federal power to abridge. I do not believe that any
federal agencies, including Congress and the Supreme
Court, have power or authority to subordinate speech and
press to what they think are more important interests."

A Florida state librarian urged libraries to withdraw
such books as Uncle Wiggly, Tom Swift, Tarzan, and The Wizard
of Oz because they "were poorly written, untrue to life,
sensational, foolishly sentimental, and consequently
unwholesome for children."

Justice Black in the Barenblatt case insisted that the
First Amendment means what it says. "The First Amendment
says in no equivocal language the Congress shall pass no law
abridging freedom of speech, press, assembly, or petition."

The Supreme Court decided in the WDAY case that
broadcast stations could not be required to excise libelous
material from speakers' remarks because doing so would hamper
discussion of political issues by legally qualified
candidates.

The court ruled in the Katzen case that an ordinance
forbidding dissemination of crime comic books to children was
unconstitutional.

The court ruled in the Kingsley Pictures case that a New
York law banning the showing of "Lady Chatterley's Lover" was
a violation of the First Amendment right to advocate ideas.
Even adultry can be advocated, and ideas expressed need not
be ordinary or shared by a majority. Discussing what has
been called "ideological obscenity," Justice Potter Stewart
outlined how such censorship strikes at the heart of the
First Amendment which encompasses the right to advocate
ideas, however unpopular or even immoral they can be.

35
Press Suppression in Asia and Latin America, 1950 through 1959

The Indian Constitution guaranteed freedom of the press in 1950. In 1951 the government controlled newsprint supply and punished the publication of material which was likely to undermine the government, interfere with necessary services, or seduce military persons from completing their duties.

Winston Churchill said:

"A free press is the unsleeping guardian of every other right that freemen prize; it is the most dangerous foe of tyranny. Under dictatorship the press is bound to languish, and the loudspeaker and the film to become more important. But when free institutions are indigenous to the soil, and men have the habit of liberty, the press will continue to be the Fourth Estate, the vigilant guardian of the rights of the ordinary citizen."

Mao-Tse-Tung stated that "the role of the press in China would be to organize, to stimulate or encourage, to agitate, to criticize, and to propel. The press must be a collective propagandist, collective agitator, and a collective organizer." All published and broadcast material had to be channeled through a high party bureau.

Juan Peron took over La Prensa and made that newspaper a government mouthpiece. But Peron was finally driven from power in 1955, and La Prensa was again edited by Gainza Paz.

Ilya Ehrenburg's The Thaw and Boris Pasternak's Dr. Zhivago opened a new phase of Russian literary courage despite heavy government controls.

Stanley Kauffmann's The Philanderer was judged not

guilty of obscene libel in England.

The state of Queensland in Australia had an Objectionable Literature Act. The most banned book in Quebec was entitled the <u>Awful Disclosures of Maria Monk; As Exhibited in a Narrative of Her Sufferrings During a Residence of Five Years as a Novice, and Two Years as a Black Nun, in the Hotel Dieu Nunnery at Montreal</u>.

Fulgencio Batista imposed strict censorship in Cuba.

The British Obscene Publications Act authorized the government to be more strict than even the old Lord Campbell's act of 1857 and Judge Alexander Cockburn's Hicklin Rule of 1868.

K.R. Srinvasa Iyengar of India said:

"Literature can present sex or vice or perversion, and yet remain literature, so long as these are imaginatively seized and fully consumed in the whole design. Literature that boldly and purposefully describes those aspects of human experience over which polite society feels compelled to throw a blanket of silence is a kind of strong meat which may conceivably injure weak or diseased stomaches, but these risks of indigestion are the necessary concomitants of all good things."

France prosecuted Henry Miller's <u>Sexus</u> and Boris Vian's <u>I'll Spit on Your Grave</u>. South Africa's Suppression of Communism Act and Sabotage Act forbade publications by listed authors considered communistic.

American occupation administrators fired hundreds of Japanese journalists who had supported the Japanese war, but they soon returned to their jobs. The Americans fired 700 pro-Communist journalists. American restrictions on the Japanese press did not end until the San Francisco Peace Treaty.

Milovan Djilas, had his works banned in Yugoslavia after he denounced the Communist regime.

1952

The Cinematography Act insured that all motion pictures would be censored. Britain's Customs and Excise Act had provisions against importing obscene and indecent imports.

1953

British publishers set up a voluntary press council. The Ministry of Cinematography was the Chief Directorate of the Cinema as part of the Russian Ministry of Culture. Soviet citizens were instructed to cut out the pages about Lavrenti Beria in the <u>Large Soviet Encyclopedia</u> after he had been executed.

William Nathan Oates, an Associated Press correspondent,

was jailed in Czechoslovakia for activities hostile to the state. He was sentenced to ten years after being held incommunicado for 72 days. In 1953 he was released, but not cleared of guilt until eighteen years later after a Czechoslovakian action which admitted the whole thing was rigged.

1954

The Directors of Public Prosecutions prosecuted a series of books published by reputable as well as disreputable publishers. The only conviction was for a guilty plea of Werner Laurie for Margot Bland's <u>Julia</u> who didn't want to waste time and money defending against the charge.

1955

A Hornsey bookseller was jailed for two months for stocking <u>Lady Chattersley's Lover</u>.

1956

Russian pre-censorship eased during the Kruschev leadership.

1957

Russian officials rejected Boris Pasternak's <u>Dr. Zhivago</u> and said:

"We were both alarmed and distressed. The thing that disturbs us about your novel is something that neither the editors nor the author can alter by cuts or revisions. We mean the spirit of the novel, its general tenor, the author's view of life, the real one or not, but whose collective opinion you have no reason to regard as biased, so that it would be reasonable, at least, to hear it out. The spirit of your novel is that of non-acceptance of the socialist revolution. The general tenor of your novel is that the October Revolution, the Civil War, and the social transformation involved brought the people nothing but suffering, and destroyed the Russian Intelligentsia, physically or morally."

He was expelled from the Soviet Union of Writers and future publishing; he was pressured into not accepting the Nobel Prize for literature.

1958

The Central Board of Film Censors in India completed the Cinematography censorship rules which by 1970 applied to Indian films but not to imported films.

The Administrative Tribunal of Paris ruled that the government couldn't ban 25 books published by the Olympic Press.

Bertrand Russell, philosopher, said:

"The invention of printing is a doubtful blessing if it is not accompanied by the safeguarding of freedom of discussion. For falsehood is printed just as easily as truth, and just as easily spread. It avails a man precious little to be able to read if the material put in front of him must be accepted without question. Only when there is freedom of speech and criticism does the wide circulation of the printed word enhance inquiry. Without this freedom it would be better if we were illiterate. In our time this problem has become more acute, because printing is no longer the only powerful medium for mass communication. Since the invention of wireless telegraphy and television it has become even more important to exercise that eternal vigilance without which freedom in general begins to languish."

36
Postwar Adjustments,
1960 through 1969

The China Lobby pressured Macmillan in 1960 to stop distribution of Ross Y. Koen's <u>The China Lobby in American Politics</u>. Four-thousand copies were destroyed. Right-wing groups stole many of the remaining 800 copies from libraries, even placing copies of <u>The Red China Lobby</u> in their place. The few remaining copies are locked up as rare books by librarians.

When Congress suspended the equal access rule for presidential candidates, the major networks gave 39 free hours of television broadcast time to major candidates.

Publisher Arthur Hays Sulzberger said:

"The publisher is not granted the privilege of independence simply to provide him with a more favored position in the community than is accorded to other citizens. He enjoys an explicitly defined independence because it is the only condition under which he can fulfill his role, which is to inform fully, fairly, and comprehensively. The crux is not the publisher's freedom to print; it is rather the citizen's right to know."

President John F. Kennedy said:

"It is never pleasant to read things that are not agreeable news, but I would say that it is an invaluable arm of the Presidency to check on what really is going on in the administration. And more things come to my attention that cause me a terrific advantage to have the abrasive quality of the press applied to you daily, to an administration, even though we never like it, and even though we wish they didn't write it, and even though we disapprove, there isn't any doubt that we could not do the job at all in a free society without a very, very active press."

Broadcaster Edward R. Murrow said, "It is well to remember that freedom through the press is the thing that comes first. Most of us probably feel that the real reason we want the newspaper is to be free."

Isidor R. Rabi said that "to live at peace with the atom we must find our way back to the fundamental principles on which this republic was founded. We must again become a nation of free men informed by a free press."

Eric Johnson, president of the Motion Pictures Association of America, urged a crusade for freedom of choice instead of censorship. "The freedom to accept or reject, to approve or disapprove of movies, or of radio and television programs, books, or newspapers belongs to the people."

Justice Felix Frankfurter said, "Without a free press there can be no free society. That is axiomatic. However, freedom of the press is not an end in itself but a means to the end of a free society. The scope and nature of the constitutional guarantee of the freedom of the press are to be viewed and applied in that light."

Alexander Meiklejohn pointed out that the fairness doctrine was a bitter disappointment.

"The radio as it now operates among us is not free. Nor is it entitled to the protection of the First Amendment. It is not engaged in the task of enlarging and enriching human communication. It is engaged in making money. And the First Amendment does not intend to guarantee men freedom to say what some private interest pays them to say for its own advantage. It intends only to make men free to say what, as citizens, they think, what they believe, about the general welfare."

Columnist Marquis E. Childs said, "Whatever else one may say about the newspaper business, self-examination is one of its virtues. Searching questions about right conduct or wrong conduct are put wherever journalists gather."

The court said a Georgia ruling forbidding photography, television, and radio on streets and sidewalks surrounding a courthouse was constitutional.

When Grove Press published an unexpurgated copy of <u>Lady Chattersley's Lover</u>, the postmaster barred it from the mails. An appeals court ruled that the earthy language used by novelist D. H. Lawrence was an appropriate and effective literary device in a significant novel, and did not appeal to prurient interest so it could not be considered obscene.

The Supreme Court ruled in the Talley case that a Los Angeles city ordinance forbidding distribution of anonymous handbills was unconstitutional. Justice Black said anonymous publications have been important in human progress throughout history. "In many cases persecuted groups have only been able to criticize authority anonymously. Indeed, the Federalist papers were published under fictitious names. Anonymous pamphlets, leaflets, brochures, and books have played an important role in the progress of mankind."

1961

After the Bay of Pigs fiasco, President Kennedy told Turner Catledge, editor of the New York Times, that "if you had printed more about the operation you would have saved us from a colossal mistake." He also blasted the press and demanded more cooperation from the American Newspaper Publishers Association, saying, "Every newspaper now asks itself in regard to every story - Is it news? All I suggest is that you add the question - Is it in the interest of national security?"

Robert McNamara asked the New York Times not to publish a report about seven persons held hostage on a plane loaded with Tibetan rebels being flown to Tibet by the CIA for a coup. McNamara said National Security would be damaged. The Times complied.

Marjorie Holmes, a mother asking for control of sexual material in media and movies, said, "Movies glorifying prostitution, books that smile at adultry, even songs about infidelity -- that is what we have tolerated until smut has finally taken over. What's the next step -- the acceptance by society of complete sexual freedom with all its consequences?"

The First Amendment assumes that the widest dissemination of information is essential to the welfare of the public and that a free press is a condition of a free society. One of the principal purposes of freedom of the press is to preserve the right of the American people to free information concerning the doings or the misdoings of public officials. This knowledge guards against maladministrations in government, according to the Goodfader case.

In the Konigsberg case, Justice Black said, "I believe that the First Amendment's unequivocal command that there shall be no abridgement of the rights of free speech and assembly, shows that the men who drafted our Bill of Rights did all the balancing that was to be done in this field." He and Justice Douglas frequently espoused the contention that the First Amendment was absolute in guaranteeing free speech and free press.

Police in Missouri confiscated 11,000 copies of 289 magazines at six news stands on the basis of a search warrant authorizing them to seize obscene material. The Supreme Court ruled in the Marcus case that the procedure was unconstitutional and otherwise faulty because it did not provide for non-seizure of protected, non-obscene material.

A film distributor sued to restrain Chicago officials from interfering with the showing of the motion picture Don Juan. Times Film Corporation refused to submit the picture for previewing to obtain a license, and was thus prohibited from showing it. The content of the film itself, which was considered innocuous, was never an issue. The Supreme Court held that in the Times Film case there is no complete and absolute freedom to exhibit any and every kind of motion picture. It held that the Chicago ordinance, requiring submission of films for examination by city officials as a prerequisite to granting a permit for public exhibition, was not a prior restraint in First and Fourteenth Amendment terms.

1962

Communist political propaganda could be withheld by the Post Office until the addressee asked for it in writing under provisions in the Postal Service and Federal Employees Salary Act.

Thirty-four states had laws permitting the press to inspect public records and 28 had open meeting laws.

Pentagon officials and employees were ordered to report the substance of each interview and telephone conversation with a media representative before the close of business on the day such contacts occurred.

Senator Robert F. Kennedy said, "In my opinion, the newspapers are equal to the courts--sometimes ahead of the courts in our system--in protecting the people's fundamental rights."

At least 50 criminal trials had occurred in the United States for selling Henry Miller's Tropic of Cancer. Finally the court ruled that the book was not obscene despite its discussion and graphic description of sexual encounters since it was not prurient in its approach.

The court ruled in the Henry case that the FCC could require a radio broadcast license applicant to demonstrate an earnest commitment to serve a community by demonstrating knowledge of that community and its needs with program content and origination.

The Postmaster refused mail service to a series of magazines of nude male models, including advertisements offering to sell nude photos. The Supreme Court ruled in the Manual Enterprises case that the material was not patently offensive to the group for whom the magazines were intended. The uncouth and tawdry pictures were not obscene. The Post Office had no proof that the publisher knew that the photos advertised were or would be obscene, so the court ruled the magazine could use the mails.

1963

William Landau, a neurologist, accepted a stormy appointment on the St. Louis County Council Decent Literature Commission in an effort to keep that council from censoring literature.

John Henry Faulk won a libel judgment for $3,500,000 from Aware, a private anti-Communist organization publication, for blacklisting him as a Communist, which kept him from working on CBS, or in any communications media.

The California State Board of Education returned the American Dictionary of Slang to use at Carlsbad High School even though the State Superintendent of Public Instruction opposed the book.

Walter Strauss said that obscenity is that which goes counter to accepted standards of propriety at a given time and place; an erotic work is one which gives serious consideration to physical love; a pornographic work is the degradation and distortion of the erotic. In a healthy society, obscenity should be met with laughter, pornography with a yawn."

Freedom of the press is not absolute but is subject to the paramount right of the government to regulate with reasonable and non-discriminatory exercise of police power to restrict the press whenever necessary for the public safety, health, morals, or general welfare, according to the Andress case.

The Rhode Island legislature created a commission to "educate the public about obscene literature and material manifestly tending to corrupt youth." By an 8-to-1 decision, the Supreme Court held in the Bantam Books case that the commission's methods constituted informal censorship which violated the First Amendment.

An appeals court ruled in the Carter Transmission case that the FCC could deny a CATV-cable project because its success would bankrupt a local broadcast television station. Thus the FCC took cable under its jurisdiction.

1964

The Republican platform promised enforcement of legislation to curb the flow through the mails of obscene material which has flourished into a multi-million dollar obscenity business.

The book Candy was banned in Chicago. Chicago launched an extensive program of book banning which became the most repressive in the nation.

Between 1960 and 1964, the FCC revoked licenses or denied license renewals to 26 radio and television stations for violations of FCC rules.

A Nassau County vice squad seized 21,000 copies of the April-May issue of Evergreen Review because it contained portfolios of nude photos taken by Emil J. Cadoo.

The FCC declined to be an arbitrator of radio programming standards and indicated the stations should have wide latitude in program content and selection. The equal access rule for political candidates for president was applied in such a way that only 4 1/2 hours of free time for campaigning was provided in 1964 in contrast to the 39 free hours in 1960.

Former President Dwight Eisenhower told delegates to the Republican National Convention that they should not let themselves "be divided by those outside our family, including sensational-seeking columnists and commentators."

James R. Wiggins said:

"It is doubtful that anyone can devise a set of rules or a code of ethics that would free the press from this burden of life. The best for which we can hope is a press with a sense of values that will inspire them to resolve conflicts of interest in favor of their larger public responsibility as opposed to their narrow individual interests."

John P. Sullivan said the FCC Fairness Doctrine was unconstitutional, and did not ensure fairness, or respect for a democratic country.

Irvin S. Cobb said, "If the depth of the dirt exceeds the breadth of the wit, then in my opinion the book is obscene."

J. David Stern, a monopolist publisher himself, believed monopoly ownership of the press had made its voice a chorus of castrati.

Arthur J. Goldberg told the 1964 Convention of the American Society of Newspaper Editors that the first and primary responsibility of the press is as protector and promoter of all the rights and liberties of Americans. The entire Bill of Rights is in the press's charge -- not only the free speech clause of the First Amendment. Our Constitution has made the press free. It is for you to demonstrate that press freedom and responsibility are viable and indivisable concepts.

A Kansas law was declared unconstitutional because it allowed confiscation of supposedly obscene materials without providing an adversary hearing prior to the seizure. The law did not protect non-obscene material which might be seized; for example, the sheriff in Junction City was told to destroy 1,715 copies of novels he had seized with no determination of their obscene nature.

According to the 18 Packages of Magazines case, the rights of readers cannot be curtailed because printed materials they wish to read come from certain geographical areas. The First Amendment protects the rights of readers and distributors of publications as much as it protects the rights of writers and printers. The essence of freedom of the press is really not as much the right to print as it is the right to read.

The United States Supreme Court questioned whether state courts used proper standards to decide that the motion picture, <u>The Lovers</u>, was obscene and therefore not entitled to the free expression guarantees of the First and Fourteenth Amendments. The Court concluded the film was not obscene and reversed the Ohio conviction of Nico Jacobellis.

The Supreme Court held that constitutional guarantees of free press prohibit a public official from recovering damages for defamation -- even a defamatory falsehood -- concerning official conduct unless that official could prove that the defamatory statement was made with actual malice and with the knowledge that it was false or made with reckless disregard of the truth. This decision established a federal First Amendment defense against libel cases against the media by public officials. L.B. Sullivan who was not actually named in an ad published in The New York Times, claimed he had been defamed. The ad had been placed by a Committee to Defend Martin Luther King and the Struggle for Freedom in the South. It described an episode in which Montgomery police "armed with shotguns and tear gas ringed the Alabama State College campus after students sang "My Country Tis of Thee" on the state capital steps. In the ruling written by Justice William J. Brennan, Jr., the Court said:

> "It is uncontroverted that some of the statements about the alleged Montgomery incident were not accurate descriptions of events which occurred in Montgomery," But "we considered this case against the background of a profound national commitment to the principle that wide-open debate on public issues should be uninhibited, robust, and some times contain unpleasantly sharp attacks on government and public officials."

This decision led to a theory that freedom of expression serves as a safety valve for minority groups. Anything which might touch upon an official's fitness for his office is relevant in a discussion of his performance or qualifications. The Supreme Court ruled that the rule also limited state power to impose criminal sanctions for criticism of the official conduct of public officials. The Court said the Times-Sullivan rule extended at the very best to those employees who have or appear to the public to have substantial responsibility for or control over the conduct of government affairs.

1965

President Lyndon Johnson ordered the FBI to investigate news leaks to the <u>Washington Evening Star</u>. The FBI said a book about the Rosenbergs should be kept off television and forced out the public eye.

The American Bar Association's Canon 35 was adopted by all states but Texas and Colorado. Press and broadcasting groups objected on the grounds that a newsman with a camera is as much a reporter as a newsman with pencil and paper and has just as much right to be in the courtroom. A California legislative committee gave a tryout of the ability of the press to use cameras and recording devices in reporting proceedings of sessions of the California State Legislative Assembly Interim Committee of the Judiciary.

Congress passed a national Freedom of Information Act, which was broadened to make access to federal materials easier in the amendments of 1974 and 1976.

The Motion Picture Producers Association set up a new code of self-regulation that included labeling films as being suggested for mature audiences only.

The Reardon report of the American Bar Association was established to give fair-trial free-press guidelines acceptable to the legal profession as a rebuff to the American Newspaper Publishers Association which refused to set up newspaper codes, which the 1964 Warren Commission thought might be a good idea.

Police arrested a clerk in the City Lights bookstore for selling Lenore Kandel's poem, The Love Book. Oliver LaFarge was saddened to hear his novel Laughing Boy was banned from public school libraries in Amarillo, Texas. Censorship in school English classes and libraries was widely continued long after the National Council of English Teachers had issued their call for the "Students' Right to Read."

Mayor Robert Wagner of New York City appointed 21 persons to a Citizen Anti-Pornography Commission. He served as chairman. The Commission condemned Tropic of Cancer, Fanny Hill, Candy, and Touch Magazine as obscene. It recommended new laws and vigorous enforcement to protect the morals of children, and the establishment of federal, state and city commissions to identify salacious literature.

Marcus Steven said:

"The literary genre that pornographic fantasies -- particularly when they appear in the shape of pornographic fiction -- tend most to resemble is the utopian fantasy. For our present purposes I call this fantasy pornotopia. Pornography is not literature because of its endless repetition; it exists less in its language than any other kind of creative writing; unlike literature it is not interested in persons but in organs, in sex without human emotion. The open publication of pornography is inevitable, necessary and benign."

Clare Boothe Luce said, "Censorship, like charity, should begin at home but, unlike charity, it should end there."

George Steiner said, "The present danger to literature is not censorship or verbal reticence. The danger lies in the facile contempt which the erotic novelist exhibits for his readers, for his personages, and for the language. It is not a new freedom that they bring, but a new service."

Zachariah Chafee had said, "The First Amendment was written by men who intended to wipe out the common law of sedition, and make further prosecutions for criticisms of the government, without any incitement to lawbreaking, forever impossible in the United States." Others say the framers were consciously lying when they extolled freedom of the press. But William O. Douglas believed history would prove Chafee's view. Douglas also said, "The press is free in this country; and it has acquired vast business interests under the First Amendment. No censor sits at the editorial or news desk. Government places not a hand on the publisher's shoulder for expressing views on any subject." Douglas was concerned, however, about the one-sidedness, the blandness, and the support of the orthodox, and the condemnation of the unorthodox by the press and the broadcast media.

Walter Lippman said:

"A free press exists only where newspaper readers have access to other newspapers which are competitors and rivals, so that editorial comment and news reports can regularly and promptly be compared, verified and validated. A press monopoly is incompatible with a free press; if there is a monopoly of the means of communication, of radio, television, magazines, books, public meetings, it follows that this society is by definition and in fact deprived of its freedom."

Between 1916 and 1965, there were 31 criminal libel cases brought because of criticism of public officals which ended up in state supreme courts or in United States federal courts.

The Supreme Court reversed the ban on <u>Fanny</u> <u>Hill</u>, ruling that a book could not be suppressed unless it met three obscenity criteria: "appeal to prurient interests,""patent offensiveness," and "lack of redeeming social value." It was not obscene because it was not unqualifiedly worthless despite its continuous depiction of sexual activities in London brothels.

In the Ashton case the Supreme Court reversed a conviction concerning a pamphlet containing strong words about a labor strike. The publisher was accused of criminal libel. The court said "a function of free speech under our system is to invite dispute. Speech is often provocative and challenging, but that is never grounds for restraining or punishing it." The Supreme Court banned the French film <u>Chant</u> <u>d'</u> <u>Amour</u> which dealt with homosexuality. Lower courts generally ruled that obscenity had to be determined on the basis of a national standard.

The American system of government must not allow suppression or censorship of expression, even though the expression is hateful or offensive to those in power, or strongly opposed by the public, according to the Cox case.

Ronald L. Freedman, a Baltimore theater operator, was convicted in Baltimore Criminal Court of publicly exhibiting a film before submitting it to the board of censors. The Supreme Court reversed because the procedures of Maryland's movie censorship law didn't contain adequate safeguards against undue restrictions on protected expression.

A New York Court issued an injunction against showing

the movie John Goldfarb, Please Come Home.

The Supreme Court ruled in the Griswold case that the First Amendment protects the right to speak and print and also the right to distribute, receive, read, teach, assume, think, and imagine. The First Amendment has a penumbra where privacy is protected from governmental intrusion. Connecticut law restricting contraceptive information was overturned.

The standard followed by the courts for banning expression is the so-called hard-core pornography rule for media other than radio or television, according to the Klaus case.

In the Lamont case the Supreme Court struck down an act of Congress which was meant to slow down the flow of millions of communist tracts in the United States. President Kennedy had ruled that such interceptions had to stop, but Congress had in effect overruled him by passing the law which the court struck down.

In the Mills case an editorial was published in Alabama which severely criticized a political candidate on election day. Justice Black said, "Suppression of the press to praise or criticize governmental agents and to clamor and contend for or against change, which is all this editorial did, muzzles one of the very agencies the framers of our constitution thoughtfully and deliberately selected to improve our society and keep it free." A state acting under its powers to regulate elections and to prevent corrupt practices may not require a newspaper to be silent on election day or any other day.

A Boston Judge found William Burroughs' book, Naked Lunch, to be obscene, but in another trial, a United States Federal District Court judged it not obscene.

Freedom of the press gives a publisher or a writer the right to print, publish, disseminate, circulate, and distribute publications without any prior restraint. Such activity is subject to libel laws and to some criminal laws. The government does not have to assist in circulating any publication, according to the Overseas Media case.

All ideas having even the slightest redeeming social importance, unorthodox ideas, controversial ideas, even ideas hateful to prevailing opinion have full protection of the constitutional guarantee of a free press, unless they encroach on more important interests limited severely in scope by the courts, according to the Vollmar case.

In the Walker case, the Court said, "Denying public officials the right to recover for libel relating to their public acts except where they can prove actual malice, applies also to public figures who are not public officials."

The right to speak and publish does not carry with it the unrestrained right to gather information, according to the Zemel case.

1966

The Chicago office of the FBI approved a break-in of the offices of the Chicago Committee to Defend the Bill of Rights to find out who its financial backers were.

The Supreme Court set aside the conviction of Dr. Sam Sheppard because of newspaper and other media publicity surrounding the case making an impartial trial impossible. The court scolded court and public officials more severely than it did the press for using the publicity to gain prestige. The court said, "Trial judges have the authority and must use it to prevent law enforcement officials from prejudicing trials through dissemination of information or opinions which affect the outcome of a case. Courts may not require the press to remain silent about events in open court."

1967

Fifty-six participants in an underground publication workshop were arrested by customs agents on the basis of a raid and testimony of two undercover agents. Most charges were dropped. Author John Sinclair was convicted of possessing two joints of marijuana and sentenced to ten years, the longest term ever given in Michigan for such an offense.

On July 4, the new federal Freedom of Information Act went into effect. It provided that the government had to prove it had a legitimate reason to withhold certain information to protect national security or individuals.

Congress passed and President Johnson signed legislation to create a national commission on obscenity and pornography. The commission was charged with the task of analyzing existing laws pertaining to obscenity and pornography, studying the effect of pornography on the public and particularly on minors, and to recommend legislation or administrative action.

The United States Justice Department Community Relations Service gathered news executives and local officials in more than a dozen cities and tried to get them to agree to a series of guidelines for covering civil disorders. The plan included: waiting 30 minutes before reporting anything about a disorder, clearing information through the police, and holding the news until the uprising was under control. This effort failed.

The FCC issued specific rules covering the right to reply for personal attacks which indicated the right could only apply when an issue of public controvesy was involved and an attack on the honesty, character, integrity, or similar characteristics of an identifiable person or group was made. It did not apply to foreign persons, or to attacks made by political candidates or their agents. If the broadcaster attacked the candidate, the broadcaster had to provide time for a prompt reply.

Over several years, the FBI and other federal, state, and local government agencies maintained a vigorous program to harass and destroy underground publications.

In a Pennsylvania case, Helen Caly Frick, daughter of the Nineteenth Century industrialist Henry Caly Frick, was unsuccessful in her effort to halt distribution of a state history of Pennsylvania -- Birthplace of a Nation -- by Slyvester Stevens. She objected to several of his statements about her late father.

The American Newspaper Publishers Association concluded a two-year study of the "people's right to know." It opposed suppression of the news concerned with law enforcement and judicial proceedings; the press must be vigilant to anything that threatens freedom of the press. A committee of the Association concluded no conflict exists between the First and the Sixth Amendments.

Details of 53 separate episodes of government censorship of Stars and Stripes, the military newspaper, were published in the Congressional Record.

Jacqueline Kennedy attempted to censor William Manchester's book, The Death of a President, by court order. But she and the author reached an out-of-court agreement. She had asked him to write the book.

A.H. Raskin said, "The real long-range menace to America's daily newspapers in my judgment lies in the unshatterable smugness of their publishers and editors, myself included."

The New Jersey Committee for the Right to Read surveyed psychiatrists and psychologists of the state to determine their assessment of forbidding sexually oriented publications from persons under eighteen years of age. They indicated that reasons to forbid distribution of obscene matter to children under 18-years-of-age were invalid in the eyes of most psychiatrists and psychologists.

Ervin J. Gaines said:

"The crucial error in censorship whether by government or by volunteer groups, is that it presumes that there is an inferior segment of society that requires protection. Censorship is undemocratic because it runs counter to the fundamental assumption that all men have a right to be heard and that, in the market place of ideas, all thoughts are permissible."

John S. Knight said, "The American press, despite recent threats and blandishments of government has performed well. It has exposed public graft, demanded that public business be transacted in the open, fought extravagance and waste in government, laid bare land frauds, and insisted on justice through the courts."

Felix Morley said, "Books have often been burned by tyrants who did not agree with the views expressed. A more efficient censorship plan is to eliminate profit from publishing and then bring that business under political control."

A United States District Court upheld the right of high school publications to print advertisements and editorials dealing with the Vietnam controversy because the newspaper is a "forum for the dissemination of ideas."

The Supreme Court indicated that it did not believe that Lust Pond or Shame Agent or girlie magazines were obscene and there was no assault upon privacy by the publications to make it impossible for an unwilling person to avoid exposure to them.

Ralph Ginzburg was sentenced to five years in Pennsylvania of using the mail to pander in advertising publications which were not obscene themselves. The Supreme Court said in upholding the case that he was engaged in the sordid business of purveying textual or graphic matter openly advertised to appeal to the erotic interest of his customers.

If a person was to be prosecuted for mailing obscene material, a federal offense, he could be tried in the courts of the community wherein the material was mailed, or wherein it was delivered, or through which it passed. Those courts would use their community standards to judge obscenity since a national or federal standard no longer existed even though federal law was at issue, according to the Reed Enterprises case.

Courts accept a very broad definition of newsworthy material published in the press, including the fact that a person may be newsworthy on either a voluntary or involuntary basis, and that material that entertains readers also can be a matter of public interest. The Supreme Court held that former baseball pitcher Warren Spahn was not damaged by being the subject of a fictionalized biography for children.

The First Amendment protects the right of persons to distribute printed materials on the streets. Persons can be punished for littering only after they have actually littered the street, but prior restraint of distribution cannot be imposed simply because of the possibility of littering, according to the United Steelworkers case.

The Supreme Court ruled that a former Army officer could not recover damages from the Associated Press for an inaccurate report that he had taken charge of a group of students physically opposing federal marshall's seeking to uphold the admittance of Black students into the University of Mississippi. The hurried report might have been negligent but it was not a matter of malice. The case arose out of the distribution of a news dispatch giving an eyewitness account of events on the campus of the University of Mississippi on the night of Sept. 30, 1962, when a massive riot erupted because of federal efforts to force a court decree ordering the enrollment of a Negro, James Meredith, as a student in the university. The dispatch stated that Walker, who was present on the campus, had taken command of the violent crowd and had personally led a charge against federal marshalls.

Eugene H. Wirges, editor of The Weekly Democrat in Morrilton, Arkansas, was freed of all charges by the Arkansas Supreme Court which dismissed a three-year perjury sentence because he had charged county political bosses with corruption. He had been convicted of conspiracy, lost libel cases, lost his job, became bankrupt, jailed, victimized by arson, his home and office damaged, shot at, and beaten up by a county official.

1968

J. Edgar Hoover told all FBI offices to institute a detailed survey of New Left-type publications and to report names, staff members, printers, and funding sources.

The American Civil Liberties Association made a strong stand at its conference in an effort to resist government interference with the press. O.R. Strackbein asked that a public review board be created to consider cases of abuse of the freedom of the press.

The Motion Picture Association of America set up a motion picture classification system of General, Mature, Restricted, and X categories.

There was a decrease of 41 per cent of television stations carrying political editorials and a 42 per cent decline for AM radio stations in the 1968 campaigns because of the chilling effect the 1967 equal access rules had upon broadcast media. In 1964, seventeen television stations used political editorials but only ten did so in 1968. There were 140 radio stations using political editorials in 1964 but only 80 did in 1968.

The Warren Commission criticized Dallas police severely in their handling of the Kennedy assassination, and not the press.

Richard Szilagyi contended that the courts were so zealous in protecting freedom of the press that they overlooked the need to protect the individual's right against carte blanche defamation.

Kyle Haselden said, "Control and censorship of knowledge, ideas, and feelings -- though required under certain circumstances -- must be viewed generally as hostile to that human freedom that is indispensable to authentic morality."

Wes Gallagher said, "The newspaperman had never had a halo. Every emotional news era in our history has brought out distrust and criticism of the press. Attacks on the news media will rise in direct proportion to the intensity of public frustration in meeting the problems of the day."

Neither state constitutions nor the federal Constitution guarantees that persons have an unqualified right to distribute their writings in any manner or at any time or place without consequences to others, according to the Lyons case.

The Supreme Court ruled in the Fortknightly case that cable TV stations may pick up distant broadcasts and deliver them to their subscribers without violating the copyright of the original performer.

In the Ginsberg case, the concept of "variable obscenity" emerged. Sam Ginsberg, whose diner had a newstand that sold "girlie" magazines, was convicted for allowing a 16-year-old boy to purchase some of the magazines. The court noted that although such material might not be obscene for adults, the state had greater authority over minors and greater responsibility for their well-being.

The right of a free press is not absolute, to be exercised independently of other rights guaranteed by the Constitution. Any attempt to restrict the liberty of the press must be justified by clear and public interest, threatened not doubtfully or remotely, but by a true clear and present danger, according to the Brodhurst case.   The Supreme Court ruled in the Interstate Circuit case that a Dallas law was unconstitutionally vague when it indicated scenes of sexual promiscuity by young people were not suitable for viewing by persons under sixteen, since it did not indicate what sexual promiscuity was.

The Federal Communications Commission does have jurisdiction over cable television operations and can establish local programming requirements, but its regulations must relate to the commission's performance of its duties. Its control over cable television is thus limited, according to the Southwestern Cable case.

1969

The San Diego Free Press published a report about a corrupt businessman. At least two of the underground newspaper's street sellers were arrested each week thereafter on loitering charges which were subsequently dismissed by the courts. The editors of Spokane National were arrested on vagrancy charges while trying to sell their paper. In New Orleans, a seller of the NOLA Express was arrested for carrying an umbrella which police called a dangerous weapon. Other Express sellers were frequently arrested, but obtained an injunction prohibiting such arrests. College administrators in many universities forbade the distribution of underground publications on campus but a three-judge federal panel found that the ban was unconstitutional, ruling that First Amendment freedoms are not dependent upon the will of an administrator.

Howard Godfrey led this Secret Army Organization on a raid of the San Diego Free Press and Street Journal offices to take business and subscription records and to destroy equipment. Police did not investigate the incident. The windows of the San Diego Free Press and Street Journal were shot out but police ignored the incident. Police searched the offices twice without search warrants; when the office doors were smashed and 250 copies of the paper stolen, the police did nothing. The paper was evicted by a landlord who had been threatened by phone calls. A new landlord evicted the San Diego Free Press and Street Journal after he had a murder charge dropped.

There were at least 500 "underground" publications being produced and distributed by high school students in their schools. Student newspapers meet the general definition of being a newspaper since they are printed, distributed at stated intervals, convey news, advocate opinions and usually contain advertisements and other matters of public interest.

Four-hundred and forty-four motion pictures had been rated. 32 per cent were were considered "G", 39 per cent "M", 23 per cent "R", and 6 per cent "X". The MPA's code applied only to member companies and to those independent producers and distributors who voluntarily submitted their pictures for classification.

The National Commission on Violence reported it believed that television was contributing to violence in America.

In September, while in Des Moines, Iowa, Agnew gave a 30-minute speech over national television that attacked commentators and producers of television news who control the flow of information to viewers. Seven days after Agnew's telecast in Des Moines, he attacked the print media, specifically the New York Times and the Washington Post. Agnew attacked the press as being, "A small number of media men, not elected by anybody, who are determining the news."

Herb Klein of the Nixon White House staff scolded CBS for a "60 minutes" program. Klein and J. Edgar Hoover wire-tapped Hedrick Smith, a New York Times reporter. President Nixon said he might give some contaminated moon rocks to journalists. The Nixon White House asked the FBI to put a wire-tap on Marvin Kalb, a television journalist. Spiro Agnew called the press an effete corps of impudent snobs. Herb Klein asked CBS for advance content of editorials about a Nixon speech. Spiro Agnew attacked "a small band of network commentators and self-appointed analysts who provided only instant analysis." President Nixon assailed the networks for their immediate analysis of his press conferences and speeches.

G.N. Acharya said, "All talk of freedom of the press is unreal, as newspaper ownership rights are governed by the same old musty outmoded laws, principles and modes of thought, that apply to other species of property. It can be made free only by freeing it from the power of property and profit."

Zechariah Chafee Jr. said:

"There were practically no satisfactory judicial discussions before 1917 about the meaning of free speech clauses. The pre-war courts in construing such clauses did little more than place obvious cases on this side or that side of the line; when we asked where the line actually ran and how they knew on which side of it a given utterance belonged, we found little answer in their opinions." He said that state courts "told us, for instance, that libel and slander were actionable, or even punishable, that indecent books were criminal, that it was contempt to interfere with pending judicial proceedings, and that a permit could be required for street meetings; and on the other hand, that some criticism of the government must be allowed, that a temperate examination of a judge's opinion was not contempt, and that honest discussion of the merits of a printing caused no liability for damages."

A task force report to the National Commission on the Causes and Prevention of Violence recommended that journalists should re-examine judgments about violence, write calm investigative articles, give minorities access, interact with the community, upgrade professionalism, set up codes, and provide for balanced treatment.

William H. Orchard, a psychiatrist said, "Censorship is an institutional form of childlike denial designed to preserve equanimity at the expense of reality."

Jerome A. Barron contended that the First Amendment should be interpreted as giving the public the right of access to the media no matter who the owners might be.

Narcotics agents took the Los Angeles Free Press to court for publishing agents' names and phone numbers. They charged the paper had invaded their privacy. They lost.

A federal court approved importation of the Swedish film I Am Curious (yellow).

A Chicago bookseller was arrested for selling Chicago Seed, an underground newspaper with a two-page obscene illustration. The case was dismissed.

The Supreme Court declared an Ohio statute unconstitutional because it punished mere advocacy. Clarence Brandenburg, speaking at a national Ku Klux Klan rally, had used such statements as "Bury the niggers," and "Send the Jews back to Israel." The Ohio court had convicted him for "advocating the duty, necessity, or propriety of crime, sabotage, violence or unlawful methods of terrorism, and for assembling a group to advocate such doctrines." But the Court said if published material does not incite violence or lawlessness it is constitutionally protected.

Leiferman was a UPI reporter who wanted to examine the situation in Memphis one year after the Martin Luther King assassination in an article for Nation. UPI's policy was to clear manuscripts of its reporters for other publications. Leiferman knew this policy and correspondingly mentioned his planned article to UPI executives. The executives said the article would not be approved if it criticized Memphis newspapers. Leiferman wrote the article and reported that the Memphis newspapers were part of the establishment and that they were discriminatory on racial matters. He was suspended without pay for five days. He resigned. The Wire Services Guild supported his claim that he was exercising his rights. The court disagreed.

Individual states are entitled to provide by whatever means they choose to give wider freedom for expression than either the First or Fourteenth Amendments requires, according to the Milky Way Production case.

Rules established by the Federal Communications Commission for controling pay television broadcasting were held to be constitutionally valid.

Students distributed literature on the campus of East Tennessee State University calling its administrators despots who should be disciplined by students. The court ruled in the Norton case that suspension of the students was constitutionally proper since the literature was designed to disrupt university activities.

Open City, an underground newspaper in Los Angeles, was bankrupted by lawyer's fees because of a lower court conviction of obscenity and $1,000 fine. A higher court vindicated the publication.

The decision in the Red Lion Broadcasting case declared the interest of free speech by broadcasting is the public's, not the broadcaster's. The Supreme Court held that the equal access rule did not abridge freedom of speech and press. The court stated, "It is the purpose of the First Amendment to preserve an uninhibited marketplace of ideas in which truth will ultimately prevail, rather than to countenance monopolization of that market, whether it be by the government or a private license. The FCC imposed upon licensed broadcasters a rule, known as the Fairness Doctrine, which, among other things, obliged licensees to provide time for reply to candidates in political controversy who have been attacked in a broadcast. The rule, which journalists say effectively deprived them of control of their work, nevertheless was upheld 7 to 0 by the members of the court voting at that time. The Supreme Court decision upholding the Fairness Doctrine was a statement of "the First Amendment rights of the audience as the paramount right of viewers and listeners, not the right of the broadcasters. It is the right of the public to receive suitable access to social, political, aesthetic, moral and other ideas and experience which is crucial here."

The Supreme Court in the Stanley case ruled that a state had no business telling a man, sitting alone in his own home, what books he could read or what films he could watch even though such material might be considered obscene. It was not the concern of the state of Georgia that a person spent time watching pornographic films at home. The Supreme Court held that the Georgia statute, in so far as it made mere private possession of obscene matter a crime, was unconstitutional.

37
The World-Wide Struggle Continues,
1960 through 1969

The Danes abolished all legal sanctions against pornography for adults in 1960.

Statesman Jawaharlal Nehru said, "Never do anything in secret or anything that you wish to hide. For the desire to hide anything means that you are afraid, and fear is a bad thing, and unworthy of you. Privacy, of course, we may have and should have, but that is a very different thing from secrecy."

Maurice Girodias said, "I accept the title of pornographer with joy and pride. I enjoy annoying people I dislike deeply, the bourgeois class which is in power everywhere. I think it is very healthy to shock them. Censorship is absurd, inefficient, and without justifiable function in a society which claims to be an adult and civilized democracy."

The Public Bodies Act of England which concerned public admission to government meetings allowed public agencies to keep the public and the press out in the public interest.

An English Court ruled that Lady Chattersley's Lover was not obscene. The publisher susequently dedicated the next three editions to the trial jury.

                          1961

New Zealand set up film censorship with the Cinemaograph Films Act.

Frederick Show's conviction for distributing a magazine with call girl ads was dismissed by the House of Lords. Penguin books spent 13,000 pounds of legal costs to prove D.

H. Lawrence's works were not obscene.

1962

The Australian government ignored its Literature Censorship Board and suppressed Lady Chattersley's Lover as it did Peyrefitte's The Keys Of St. Peter in 1958.

Valery Tarsis was sent to a mental institution for smuggling his Ward 7 out of Russia for publication.

France banned the movie Octobre in Paris because it discussed the killing of 200 Algerians.

Milovan Djilas was sentenced to eight years imprisonment in Yugoslavia for his Conversation With Stalin, which criticized Stalin.

Olympia, an English language publication printed in France, had its number two issue banned in France, Italy, and Lebanon for immorality.

Helen Joseph was sentenced to house arrest in South Africa but managed to forward an article to an Australian publication, The Nation, in which she predicted a new censorship law would suppress all opinion in politics and the arts which might be displeasing to the South African government.

1963

South Africa controlled the press through laws on registration, licensing, court reporting, defamation, indecency, obscenity, sedition, and race relations.

That Was The Week That Was and BBC kitchen-sink plays aroused heavy public criticism, including the Women of Britain Clean-Up TV campaign. The programs were soon dropped.

Nikita Kruschev personally banned Manlen Khutsiev's film Ilyich's Gate. Gerald Brooke was sentenced to five years in jail in Russia for smuggling anti-Soviet printing plates into Russia.

1964

Maurice Girodias was arrested and convicted in France for the publication of six English language books by his Olympia Press of Paris. In 1962 he said, "To corrupt and deprave is my business. It is my business to publish those forbidden books, those outrageous obscenities." Girodias, as a result of French government raids and actions, acquired 100 banned books, orders not to publish anything for 80 years, six years of jail sentences, and 29,000 pounds in fines. But he only was in jail for two days.

New Zealand's Indecent Publications Tribunal declared James Baldwin's Another Country was not indecent.

The subcommittee of science and technology of the United Nations Committee on the Peaceful Uses of Outer Space pointed out that "direct broadcast satellites able to transmit programs direct to television sets is likely to take place by 1974 or so."

Yugoslavia censored Mihajlo Mihajlov's Moscow Summer.

300 French persons had been prosecuted for insulting President Charles DeGaulle. Mrs. DeGaulle was active in seeking the repression of literature.

Fanny Hill was judged obscene by an English Court. The Obscene Publications Act made it illegal to have an obscene article for publication or gain. The National Viewers and Listeners Association proposed a program to promote moral and religious welfare, to influence broadcasting, to arouse public opinion, to set up local groups, to maintain standards of public service and responsibility in broadcasting in England. Cain's Book was among 49 novels and 906 magazines confiscated by English police in raids on Sheffield bookstores. It was judged to be obscene.

1965

President Van Thieu closed down 36 Vietnamese newspapers near Saigon when he came to power. He allowed 23 to resume publication on sufferance.

The English Race Relations Act of 1965 forbade publishing words likely to stir up hatred on the grounds of color, race, or ethnic or national origin.

David Holbrook's The Quest For Love was banned by Australian Customs. Pressures from advertisers were exercised against television programs.

An English court decided that Cunliffe's magazine, Poetmeat/Golden convulvus was not obscene.

1966

The Vatican announced the abolition of the Index of Prohibited Books which started in the year 405 A.D. More than 40 indexes of prohibited books had been issued by the Catholic Church since the Renaissance. The latest one was produced in 1948 with a supplement in 1961. It had 510 pages and listed more than 6,000 titles.

Scotland Yard had a 14-member obscene publications squad to seize filth literature. It accumulated 75 tons of obscene material. Its storage problem was so great that it simply sold materials back to the market, and extorted as much as 2,000 pounds each month for each squad member from obscenity sales. Several agencies lobbied and worked for freedom in British broadcasting and television.

The Soviet Supreme Court sentenced Adrei Sinyavsky for On Socialist Realism to seven years and Yuli Daniel for Moscow Calling to five years. The books were published outside Russia. Censorship was officially ended in Russia, but the prosecution of journalists continued with cruel regularity under various sections of the penal code.

Anthony Grey, a Reuters man, was imprisoned 26 months in Peking in retaliation for England's imprisonment of several Chinese journalists after the Hong Kong Communists riots.

Dr. W.A. Dering won one halfpenny damages for libel, but had to pay $5,000 court costs in England when he sued Leon Uris, author of Exodus for accusing him of experiments in human sterilization in Auschwitz prison. Peter Fryer poked fun at the British Museum for its shielding practices that kept its 5,000 cupboard books of erotica away from both mutilators and serious scholars.

1967

Last Exit to Brooklyn by Hubert Selby, Jr., was tried for obscenity in London under provisions of the British Obscene Publications Act of 1959.

Aleksander Solzhenitsyn told the Russian Union of Writers that the "Now intolerable oppression, in the form of censorship, which our literature has endured for decades, the Union of Writers can no longer accept."

Finland tried a plan giving government subsidies to political parties for their newspapers. Sweden and Norway tried similar plans, but none of these really insured continuation of the newspapers.

The Irish 1967 Censorship Bill removed bans on 110 books, some of them twentieth century masterpieces. But thousands more were still banned.

South Africa listed 11,000 titles of literature censored in a ten year period, and had a system of suppressing the writers.

1968

Costa Silva declared a dictatorship in Brazil and imposed censorship on the press. He said, "The entire nation understands that the military does not accept criticism and abuse covered by cowardly immunity."

Czechs used a scheme of underground replicas of regular newspapers and clandestine radio and even television broadcasts. When Alexander Dubcek announced new controls on the press, the Czechs no longer accepted his leadership. In summing up, a journalist said:

"The Czeckoslovakian people learned during that time that freedom of the press is the groundstone of all our liberties. The Soviets were so afraid of that freedom that they sent soldiers with guns and tanks to suppress it. The muzzling of the free press and the re-introduction of censorship was a result of their criminal adventure. The world is not going to forget that."

1969

The 24 lawyers in the English Customs Solicitors Office found 1,500,000 books and magazines showing those parts of the human body which ought not to be shown in an artistic photograph.

The Ryazan unit of the Soviet Writers Union expelled Aleksander Solzhenitsyn. Dr. Tricis Menders was sentenced to five years for libeling Russia when he submitted a manuscript to an American historian about the Latvian revolution.

38
The White House Offensive, 1970 through 1974

Newsstands and bookstores discontinued selling The East Village Other in New York City in 1970 after one newsstand was fined for selling it because of obscenity. The editor of The Daily Planet, an underground newspaper, was arrested 29 times for selling obscene literature on the streets of Miami. He was acquitted 28 times, but had to pay $93,000 in bail bonds. Federal courts ordered city officials to provide the city auditorium to The Daily Planet so Allen Ginsburg could read "Pentagon Exorcism."

The New York Times reported that over half of those questioned in a poll would not give everyone the right to criticize the government if the criticism were thought to be damaging to the national interest, and 55 per cent added that newspapers, radio, and television should not be permitted to report stories considered by the government to be harmful to the national interest.

Dan Hicks, editor of The Monroe County Democrat in Madisonville, Kentucky, was assaulted, shot at, threatened, robbed, and burned out for his investigative reporting.

The National News Council was formed to serve as a conscience for news media, as an ombudsman for readers and viewers, and as a protector of the First Amendment.

The motion picture classification code was changed to G for audiences including children, PG for audience wherein parents should exercise parental guidance as to whether children should attend, R for restricted to adults or children accompanied by adults, or X for adults only.

Street vendors of Kaleidoscope, an underground publication, in Madison, Wisconsin, were repeatedly arrested

for selling obscenity to minors. The publisher was arrested
for obscenity and for refusing to reveal sources. The
offices of the paper and the car of an editor were fire-
bombed. A Jackson, Miss., underground newspaper called the
Kudzu received harrassment from Jackson police and the FBI.
Searches of homes and newspaper offices lead to arrests and
subsequent releases with no charges being filed.

The only state movie censorship board still in operation
was in Maryland.

William F. Schanen, Jr., of The Ozaukee Press in Port
Washington, Wisc., printed dozens of underground newspapers,
because other printers refused to do so under pressure of
local persons, police, and even the FBI.

The Reporters Committee for Freedom of the Press was
formed at Georgetown University in response to a threat posed
by the Justice Department's subpoena policies. It maintains
a legal defense and research fund, and publishes newsletters
and other materials.

The FBI thought spraying newspapers with foul-smelling
Skatole could ruin thousands of copies in seconds. The
Legion of Justice destroyed the Guild Bookstore in Chicago.
The Legion worked with and was supported by such agencies as
the Chicago Police Red Squad, the CIA, and the Army's 113th
M1 Team.

Persons selling the San Diego Free Press and Street
Journal were arrested and charged for breaking laws that did
not exist.

The Report of the Commission on Obscenity and
Pornography said that evidence indicated no damage to society
occurred from such matter; indeed society benefited from it.
The Hill-Link minority report disagreed. The Senate voted 60
to 5 to reject the Commission report. At least 150 bills
seeking to toughen obscenity controls were introduced in
Congress.

Television and newspapers were subpoenaed for materials
about the Black Panthers and the SDS Weatherman. They
cooperated fully with grand juries until they realized the
process was a threat to freedom of the press. Army
Specialist Robert Laurence, serving in Vietnam, broke off
from his usual voice-over commentary of film clips to charge
that he and other enlisted men who worked for American Forces
in Vietnam were not free to tell the truth.

At one time, President Nixon spoke thus of the press:

"Communication is the life blood of a community. And it
is most appropriate that America set aside a special
week to honor the nation's newspapers and the men and
women who produce them. The printed word is a powerful
instrument of progress. As we celebrate National
Newspaper Week, we take stock of the benefits a strong
newspaper tradition brings to the nation, to its
individual communities, and to each one of us as a

citizen -- and also of the continuing importance of journalistic integrity. We reaffirm our belief in the fundamental freedom of the press as well as in the awesome responsibility it carries. A potent force in the history of our nation since the very beginning, newspapers continue to grow with our society."

Editor Vermont Royster said, "A journalist owes nothing to those who govern his country. He owes everything to his country."

Spiro T. Agnew aimed an attack at what he called "the columns and editorials of the liberal news media of this country -- those really illiberal, self-appointed guardians of our destiny who would like to run the country without ever submitting to the elective process as we in public office must do." He criticized television for overplaying controversy and presenting contrived action.

Thomas I. Emerson suggested a broadcast regulatory plan to promote the system of freedom of expression through encouraging wider participation by those who wish to communicate and greater diversity by those who wish to hear as affirmative concepts of the First Amendment.

Roger B. Fransecky said, "The freedom to read is a freedom that is shared by all -- by teacher and pupil -- and it can never be a right we label 'For Adults Only'."

William F. Buckley, conservative writer and editor, said that the opinion-making community misunderstands the usefulness of repression.

Herbert Brucker said, "Editors should be left on a long leash free to examine each interest and issue before determining which side to take."

San Francisco District Judge Alfonso J. Zirpoli ruled that a reporter must appear before a grand jury if subpoenaed, although the reporter cannot be compelled to reveal confidential information unless the government can prove the information is a matter of "national interest" and there is no other way to obtain the information.

The president of Fitchburg State College censored an article and ordered that all future editorial material for the student newspaper be approved by an editorial board made up of faculty members. The Antonelli case decision said that college officials have been forbidden to censor expression which they dislike and have been reminded that they are not the unrestrained masters of what they create. They have no power to tell a student what thoughts to communicate. The college setting of college-age students being exposed to a wide range of intellectual experiences creates a relatively mature market place for the interchange of ideas. Massachusetts law does not make the president responsible for what is printed in the student newspaper. It would be inconsistent with First Amendment freedoms to permit a campus newspaper to be simply a vehicle for ideas the state or the college administration deems appropriate.

The mere threat of prosecution can become a stifling prior restraint on free expression, according to the Hanby case.

Maine sought to restrain an educational TV station from broadcasting political content in programs, but the court ruled such a practice violated both FCC rules and the First Amendment.

Rights guaranteed by the First Amendment are not so much private rights as they are the rights of the general public. The guarantee of free expression under the First Amendment is a fundamental one that protects that expression from the vagaries of local censorship and political opportunism, according to the Meyer case.

The Supreme Court upheld in the Rowan case a federal law which included the prohibition of pandering mail advertisements in which a person may notify the post office to order a sender to stop sending advertisements that offended the receiver because of possible obscene nature.

Scanlan's Monthly editors decided to print exerpts of extreme right and left propaganda, but the printer refused to print the magazine.

Principals in Des Moines, Iowa, schools told students not to wear black arm bands to school as part of a protest. Two days later children from Tinker family wore arm bands to their schools as did Christopher Eckhardt. They were sent home and did not return to school until January. The Supreme Court ruled that wearing arm bands to express opinions is symbolic speech clearly protected by the First Amendment. The schools did not exclude other symbols, some of which were equally controversial. The students did not disrupt school or bother other students. The Supreme Court in its landmark Tinker decision held that political communication and expression could not be barred from the school as long as they did not cause a substantial disruption of the school. It said that people of the United States:

"May not be regarded as closed circuit recipients of only that which the state chooses to communicate. They may not be confined to the expression of those sentiments that are officially approved. It can hardly be argued that either students or teachers shed their constitutional rights to freedom of speech or expression at the school house gate. Employees of the school such as administrators, staff, or faculty are agents of the state when participating in an action involving censorship. They are for all times and purposes the state.

Since the FCC does not or cannot preempt local regulations, local regulations of Cable TV subject to constitutional constraints are permitted, according to the TV Pix case.

1971

The Columbia Broadcasting System was attacked by the United States government for its showing of the "Selling of the Pentagon." The film was originally shown in the spring of 1971, and the government contended that certain parts of the program were out of context and therefore gave false ideas to the viewer.

The Federal Communications Commission adopted the "prime time access rule" -- a move aimed at drastically curtailing the role of the three major networks in controlling television programming. The Federal Election Campaign Act of 1971 required that broadcasters allow reasonable time for a legally qualified candidate for federal office, and required the station to charge its lowest time fees for such broadcasts.

The Fairness rule was not found applicable for army recruiting materials, or for Chevron product claims of reducing pollution, but found ads supporting the Alaskan pipeline were discussion of only one side of a controversial issue of public importance.

The FBI denied that it had used wiretaps on journalists or government officials. The Army General Counsel emphasized a policy of the Executive Branch of the government which said that all files, records, and information in the possession of the Executive Branch were privileged and not releaseable to any part of the Legislative Branch of the Government without specific direction of the President. Press freedom to report the Vietnam War was almost complete despite efforts to muffle reports critical of military operations.

The press rather than the President should be investigated according to Presidential Press Secretary Ron Zeigler. Walter Cronkite was severely criticized by Spiro Agnew, who said the media was paranoid and coverage of the Vietnam War was slanted. Walter Cronkite in charging that the harrassment of the media was a conspiracy, said he did not regret use of that word.

Reuven Frank said that concentrated ownership of the media was less a danger to freedom of the press than leaving to a few government officials the power to decide what can be discussed and what cannot. The role of the press is to inform society about problems, not to solve them.

Elmer W. Lower said, "In 38 years as a professional journalist, I have never encountered such a wave of criticism of mass media as we have today."

Charles H. Sandage said that mass media should be considered as common carriers and adhere to the principles that apply to other transportation agencies.

Morris Peterson argued that while the editor has the right to determine the content of the paper, the public has the right to demand complete and accurate details plus the full disclosure of the sources supplying those facts and the opinions related to those facts.

Horace M. Kallen said, "Neither obscenity nor libel can be said in any sense to present a clear and present danger of anything, yet there remains a strong momentum for subjecting them both to some degree of control.

Thomas I. Emerson said, "The basic theory underlying the legal framework (of free press) has remained substantially unchanged since its development in the seventeenth and eighteenth centuries."

Erich Segal said:

"Obscenity is a poor excuse for art, a kind of book juggling to hide artistic bankruptcy. Shakespeare, fortunately, was neither curious nor yellow, because Shakespeare had the courage, and it takes courage, to attempt to say the ineffable instead of showing the indelicate. Far more glorious than the human groin, and far more interesting, is the human heart. Legalized freedom, rather than censorship, is the greatest blow to pornography."

J. Edgar Hoover said NBC broadcasts about the FBI, were venomous and malicious and the liberal communications media had certainly tried to represent the FBI for some time as an American Gestapo.

The Court of Appeals noted in the Associates and Aldrich case that publication of a newspaper is not a government conferred privilege and nothing in the constitution compelled a private newspaper to publish advertisments without editorial control of their content merely because the advertisments are not legally obscene or unlawful.

Truthful publication is privileged if it is newsworthy and does not reveal facts so offensive as to shock the community's notions of decency. Newsworthy considers the social value of the facts published, the depth of the article's intrusion into ostensibly private affairs, and the extent to which the party voluntarily acceded to a position of notoriety, according to the Briscoe case.

The First Amendment prohibits censorial discrimination among ideas. One function of free speech is to invite dispute. It may induce a condition of unrest, create dissatisfaction with conditions, and even stir people to anger. The central purpose of the First Amendment is to protect and promote controversy, uninhibited, robust, and wide open on public issues, according to the Business Executives' Move for Vietnam Peace case.

One of the principal functions of the First Amendment is the invitation of dispute and the exchange of provocative ideas. That the language is annoying or inconvenient is not the test. Agreement with the content or the manner of expression is irrelevant. First Amendment freedoms are not confined to views that are conventional or thoughts that are endorsed by the majority. Student publications have equal protection of First Amendment rights to those of other publications, according to the Channing Club case.

William Farr, a reporter for the Los Angeles Herald-Examiner, obtained copies of statements implicating persons in the Charles Manson crime by promising the sources he would keep their names confidential. Farr refused to tell the court the names of his sources and wrote articles based on the data. He was held in contempt and jailed. He had quit his reporting job by the time the court interrogated him. The appeals court upheld the contempt citation since it believed the shield law would interfere with the court's duty to compell information about these statements.

Disappearance of a national standard for obscenity made federal prosecution confused after cases were brought under community standards in various jurisdiction.

Generally, the government had the right to regulate public displays, bill boards, and signs in the interest of public safety, health, traffic control, public welfare, and morality, according to the Lou Bern Broadway case.

Any exercise of congressional power that permissibly affects freedom of the press can only be an exercise of some power directed to an end other than restricting the press. the fact that the First Amendment is in the Bill of Rights rather than in the main body of the Constitution does not imply that it is only a modal restriction on the limitation of Congress' power, according to the Mandel case.

Daniel Ellsberg was arrested for giving "confidential" information concerning the Vietnam War and the pre-Vietnam War period to the New York Times, The Washington Post, and other newspapers. Ellsberg, once a Pentagon aide, felt the information "was for the public good" but the government contended the information release would be dangerous to United States Security. The court ruled that the Justice Department did not prove that the national interest in suppressing publication of the Pentagon Papers was more important than preserving the rights of the First Amendment. President Nixon's efforts to restrain publication of the Pentagon papers was the first such government effort since the Sedition Act expired in 1801. When the United States sought to keep the History of U.S. Decision-Making Process on Vietnam Policy from being published by the New York Times, the Supreme Court ruled that publication would not interfere with national security even though it would embarass some officials.

The Supreme Court reversed the decision handed down by a state court in Rosenbloom v. Metromedia. A Philadelphia radio station, WIP, had accused the distributor of a nudist magazine of being a smut peddler. He was awarded a substantial sum, but the Supreme Court, in reversing the decision, ruled that private individuals who are involved in matters of public interest have no more protection from libel than public figures and cannot collect without a showing of malice. Justice Brennan in delivering the majority opinion, said that Rosenbloom was neither a public official or a public figure but "We think the the time has come forthrightly to announce that the determinant whether the First Amendment applies to state libel actions is whether the utterance involved concerns an issue of public or general concern."

The courts believed that publications could report public controversies and not be held responsible for accusations made by the agencies in the controversy since the publication was presenting neutral reportage of the controversy so its readers could know about the issue on the behalf of two Time cases.

In the Trujillo case the Court re-instated the student newspaper editor who was fired because she sought to publish a cartoon critical of the college president and an editorial critical of a local judge. The requirement that controversial material had to be submitted for approval abridged the editor's right of free expression. Once a State University or College has established a student newspaper, it may not then place limits upon the use of that forum which interfere with constitutionally protected speech.

1972

The Great Speckled Bird, an underground publication in Atlanta, was seized by the U.S. Postal Service for printing abortion referral service information. This was identical to advertising which had appeared in The New York Times.

300,000 copies of the preview issue of Ms. magazine hit the newsstands in January. They sold out in eight days. The preview issue of Ms., a magazine "owned by and honest about women" was financed by the Washington Post publisher Katherine Graham and New York Magazine editor Clay Felker. The creators of Ms. hoped to support the Women's Liberation movement by producing a full-fledged national magazine, created and controlled by women, "that could be as serious, outrageous, satisfying, practical, sad, funky, intimate, global, compassionate, and full of change as women's lives really are."

The IRS kept an index of political activists for special investigations of their tax returns. The FBI took the manuscript of The Politics of Heroin in Southeast Asia by Alfred Cook from the publisher before it could be printed, despite Cook's protests.

Pat Buchanan, speech writer for President Nixon, threatened to launch anti-trust legal action against the networks if they continued to freeze out Nixon's opposing viewpoints.

Spiro Agnew attacked television networks for lack of objectivity in reporting the news about the Nixon Administration. The media called the attack demagoguery and a censorship threat. Agnew attacked The New York Times and The Washington Post with scathing criticism.

The White House asked for a study of how to install

special FM radios so the government could turn them on automatically and be able to communicate to 100 per cent of the population at any time.

Clay T. Whitehead, Director of Telecommunications for Nixon, told networks they'd have license renewal problems for the television stations they owned if they failed to correct imbalance or consistent bias in newscasts and programming.

Justice Byron R. White said, "We cannot accept the argument that the public interest in possible future news about crime from undisclosed, unverified sources must take precedence over the public interest in pursuing and prosecuting those crimes reported to the press."

Greg Cornell contended that the only real freedom of the press is the freedom to distort, twist, and suppress information for profit making. "It is only when we have a mass circulation, socialist press of the workers, the Blacks, the Chicanos, women, and students that we will have a press that can tell the truth and be heard."

The report of the Twentieth Century Fund Task Force entitled "A Free and Responsive Press" said:

"A free society cannot endure without a free press, and the freedom of the press ultimately rests on public understanding of, and trust in its work. The public as well as the press has a vital interest in enhancing the credibility of the media and in protecting their freedom of expression. One barrier to credibility is the absence of any established national and independent mechanism for hearing complaints about the media and for examining issues concerning freedom of the press."

The Pennsylvania Supreme Court in the Armao case ruled the state's libel law unconstitutional and said that criminal libel laws are obsolete and nugatory in modern society.

In the Branzburg case, the Supreme Court rejected arguments that ability to preserve the secrecy of news sources is essential to a free press and held that a reporter must testify for a grand jury. Branzburg had witnessed illegal preparation of marijuana in Kentucky. Paul Pappas, a TV newsman, attended a Black Panthers' meeting and agreed not to report anything but an anticipated police raid which did not occur. The Supreme Court said he had to answer a grand jury subpoena since it did not indicate he would be querried on any confidential matters. Earl Caldwell refused to tell a grand jury about Black Panthers activities. The Supreme Court said there was no First Amendment protection to keep a reporter from testifying or appearing before a grand jury.

The First Amendment affords the right for each adult to read in his home what he chooses, according to the Collins case.

It took staff members of The Columbus Free Press a year to win acquittal from charges that they had caused a riot which they were covering for the publication.

No distinction can be made between a political editorial and a paid political advertisement under the First Amendment, according to the Committee for Impeachment case.

Justice Douglas pointed out that the First Amendment would protect the <u>Beacon Press</u> from prosecution in publishing the Pentagon Papers because Senator Mike Gravel had placed them in an official committee record of Congress.

The First Amendment protects not only the right of a person to publish, expose, and disclose, but also the right to the public to see and to know, according to the Lubie case.

Although the First Amendment protects criticism of the government, nothing in the Constitution requires the government to divulge information. The government's needs for secrecy of intelligence source and methods justify a system of prior restraint against disclosures by employees and former employees of the CIA of classified information, according to the Marchetti case.

In the Papish case, the Supreme Court ruled that a Missouri University graduate student could not be expelled for distributing an underground newspaper containing four letter words and containing a cartoon of the Goddess of Justice and the Statue of Liberty being raped by policemen. "The mere dissemination of ideas -- no matter how offensive to good taste -- on a state university campus may not be shut off in the name alone of conventions of decency.

The Supreme Court ruled that government has no power to restrict expression because of its message, ideas, its subject matter, or its content. The essence of forbidden censorship is content control; any restriction on expressive activity because of its content would completely undercut the profound national commitment to the principle that debate on public issues should be uninhibited, robust, and wide open, according to the Mosely case.

One of the reasons for the First Amendment as well as the Freedom of Information Act is to promote honesty of government by seeing to it that public business functions under the hard light of full scrutiny, according to the Tennessean Newspapers case.

Protection by the First Amendment does not depend upon the truth, popularity, or social value of the ideas and beliefs which are expressed, according to the Visual Educators case.

1973

The Society of Professional Journalists, Sigma Delta Chi adopted a code of ethics saying that freedom of the press must be guarded as an inalienable right of the people.

The FCC proposed a rule requiring newspapers owning television stations, or 236 newspaper-radio combines, to sell either the newspaper or the broadcast station within five years. But the rule was not adopted.

The FBI edited a local radio reporter's teletype reports about the Wounded Knee story so that slanted and partial articles appeared without his knowledge.

The CIA intercepted 28,322,796 pieces of mail between 1953 and 1973. A 25-year mail interception project of the FBI failed to find even one illegal agent.

The AFL-CIO claimed that Richard M. Nixon had committed an impeachable offense by interfering with the constitutionally guaranteed freedom of the press by means of wiretaps, FBI investigations, and threats of punitive action. Buried in the Nixon proposed federal crime statute was a provision to deal with disseminating obscene materials, which would have set up federal repression of the film and publishing businesses. Government threats to freedom of the press during Nixon's administration included Spiro Agnew's speeches, Clay Whitehead's schemes to politicize broadcasting, Congressional investigations of the "Selling of the Pentagon", White House efforts to censor a Watergate documentary, attacks on individual reporters, challenging licenses of television stations, failure of both media owners and the public to support journalists, Attorney-general Mitchell's guidelines to subpoena newsmen, the Supreme Court's ruling against a reporter's privilege in testimony, and threats to public television.

Richard Nixon, in his first major speech about Watergate, said:

"It was the system that brought the facts to light and that will bring those guilty to justice--a system that in this case included a determined grand jury, honest prosecutors, a courageous judge, and a vigorous free press." Later, in the White House press room, he said to the journalists, "We've had our differences in the past, and just continue to give me hell when you think I'm wrong. I hope I'm worthy of your trust."

Hodding Carter III questioned "whether the men who own and run American journalism today give enough of a damn to mobilize that powerful mechanism and restore the First Amendment to the Bill of Rights."

In analyzing the Media and the First Amendment, The Georgetown Law Journal Association pointed out that legal precedents in broadcast regulation were becoming inadequate, largely due to technological advances in cable TV and satellites. "Before a new regulatory scheme can be shaped by the courts, a new rationale for regulation must emerge." Jerome Barron of the George Washington University Law School said traditional regulations were based on the concept of scarcity of frequencies, public ownership of broadcast frequencies, and the legitimate claims of those unable to gain access to those frequencies to express their views.

Thomas Eagleton said, "If the Constitution prohibits Congress from making any law abridging freedom of the press, then I submit that is is also our duty to prohibit any other institution from violating that same freedom."

Ricky D. Pullen reported, "The idea that the press is an any way reponsible to the government or society is in direct contrast to the libertarian idea incorporated in the First Amendment that government and society should have no control or power to manipulate the press."

Katherine Graham said, "The founding fathers gave the press the mission to inform the people and promote the free flow of facts and ideas, however untimely or challenging or disagreeable those facts and ideas may be.

Ben Bagdikian said, "The future of journalism is not in the hands of the technologists and the social scientists and the city planners. It is in the hands of the political leaders and the courts. And how the public, leaders, and the courts emerge depends to a great degree on the determination of every journalist to remain free at any cost."

The Supreme Court ruled in an ACLU case that provisions of the Federal Elections Campaign Act of 1931 established impermissible prior restraints, discouraged discussion of public concerns, and chilled the right to associate freely because of its public disclosure rules. The result of the ruling allowed publication of political advertising that had been restrained because publications feared criminal prosecution.

In the Bazaar case, the court upheld the right of a student literary magazine staff to publish four letter words and two tasteless stories. But the court allowed the University to stamp a disclaimer on the magazine which said that it was not an official publication of the University.

The Appeals Court ruled that a shield law did not protect a reporter from testifying before a grand jury about a bribe attempt since he had already revealed the sources of such information. Peter Bridge spent 20 days in jail for refusing to answer the grand jury questions after claiming First Amendment protection.

The Court decided the Fairness Doctrine would not be applicable to editorial advertising, and broadcasters could be free to reject such advertising. This case blunted the Red Lion view. Chief Justice Burger concluded that in the area of discussion of public issues, Congress chose to leave broad journalistic discretion with the licensee. Only when the interests of the public are found to outweigh the private journalistic interests of the broadcasters will government power be asserted. For better or worse, editing is what editors are for, including the editing and selection of materials. This ruling in effect discarded the Red Lion notion of the audience's First Amendment right, and returned to the traditional First Amendment right of the broadcaster.

The Supreme Court ruled in the Mink case that reports to the President concerning underground nuclear tests were executive exemptions authorized under the Freedom of

Information Act and did not have to be released.

A shield law may protect the reporter's source of information but not the information itself. The reporter's personal observations are thus not privileged, according to the Forest Hill Utility Company case.

The Supreme Court ruled in the Heller case that a single copy of a motion picture film could be seized as evidence in an obscenity trial providing that a judge issued a search warrant authorizing the seizure after he had viewed the film and determined an obscenity trial was justified. The theater owner could make a copy of the film or obtain another copy for continued showing until the trial decision was made.

State colleges are not enclaves immune from the sweep of the First Amendment, according to the Joyner case. A college as an instrumentality of the state may not restrict speech simply because it finds views expressed by any group to be abhorrent. If a college has a student newspaper, its publication cannot be suppressed because college officials dislike its editorial comment. That colleges cannot withdraw financial support from a student publication because of its editorial stance is sustained by well-charted legal waters. Freedom of the press enjoyed by students is not absolute or unfettered; students, like all other citizens, are forbidden advocacy which is directed to inciting or producing imminent lawless action.

The Supreme Court ruled in the Kaplan case that a book, Suite 69, which contained no illustration, was obscene because of its descriptions of sexual activities.

A Maryland statute forbidding the advertisement of prescription drug prices was ruled unconstitutional.

The right to publish is firmly embedded in the First Amendment and is central to the constitutional guarantee of a free press, according to the McMillan case.

In the Miller case, the Supreme Court re-defined obscenity to occur when the average person applying contemporary community standards would find the work, taken as a whole, to appeal to prurient interests. If the work depicted or described in a patently offensive way sexual conduct specifically defined in an applicable state law such as representations of normal or perverted, actual or simulated sex acts, or descriptions of masturbation, excretory functions, and lewd exhibition of genitals or if the work, taken as a whole, lacked serious literary, artistic, political, or scientific value, it could be considered obscene.

When student newspapers are established by state college authorities as a forum of free expression of the ideas and opinions of students, the authorities may not then place limitations upon their use which infringe upon the rights of students to free expression as protected by the First Amendment. The imposition by college authorities of restrictions upon the operations of the campus newspapers, prohibiting attacks against religion from being published in such newspapers was an unconstitutional infringement of the rights of free expression of students attending the colleges where there was no showing that publication of the matter constituted a threat to the orderly functioning of the colleges, according to the Panarella case.

The Supreme Court upheld in the Paris Adult Theatre case a Georgia Supreme Court ruling that the showing of pornographic movies was not protected by the First Amendment even though viewing was restricted to persons over 21.

The Supreme Court ruled that a Pittsburgh Human Relations Commission order prohibiting male-female classified ads was permissible since it pertained only to commercial speech and not to viewpoints.

The FCC stopped "topless" radio programming which was based on discussion of fellatio by women calling in to a talk host type program. This meant the FCC could ban both obscene material as defined in the Miller case standard and indecent speech not legally obscene, according to the Sanderling Broadcasting Corporation case.

The Appeals court upheld an FCC order requiring that radio stations have knowledge that the content of their programs and music are in the public interest, convenience, and necessity. Drug related music doesn't qualify and lost a license for a station in the Yale Broadcasting Company case.

1974

A Security Assistance Symposium proposed using the media to convince people that a number of harsh control measures were for their own good.

The Federal Communications Commission reaffirmed its Fairness Doctrine with these guidelines: Opposing views are not required on an individual broadcast basis, or on a formula, but over a reasonable period of time and as an aspect of overall programming. An issue is not controversial merely because of media coverage. The broadcaster must play a conscious and positive role in encouraging opposing viewpoints. Genuine partisans must be selected to present particular viewpoints. There is no right of access as such. The Commission attempted to untangle the confusing fairness requirements for commercial messages, which meant that the Fairness Doctrine would not apply to product commercials but it would apply to commercials discussing issues.

Robert Criley contended the Criminal Code Reform Act proposed by the Nixon Administration included provisions for press censorship.

Movie industry censors changed, or tried to, scenes in these movies: <u>Battleground, The Outlaw, From Here to Eternity, Gone with the Wind, A Street Car Named Desire, Spartacus, The Caine Mutiny, Francis Goes to West Point, The Defiant Ones, The Longest Day, Deep Throat, Carnal Knowledge,</u> and <u>The Lottery.</u> Harry Snyder, who was blind, was a member of the movie censorship board in Clarkstown, New York. He relied on his feelings rather than his sight to discover pornography.

By 1974 the following books had been censored in various cities and states: Zoo Story by Albee, Looking Backward by Bellamy, West Side Story by Bernstein, The Good Earth by Buck, Tremor of Intent by Burgess, God's Little Acre by Caldwell, The Stranger by Camus, Canterbury Tales by Geoffrey Chaucer, The Ox Bow Incident by Clarke, Sand on Ice by Cleaver, 50 Great American Short Stories by Crane, poems by Cumings, Crime and Punishment by Dostoevsky, Invisible Man by Ellison, Silas Marner by Elliot, Manchild in the Promised Land by Fast, The Great Gatsby by Fitzgerald, Diary of a Young Girl by Frank, Point of Departure by Gold, Lord of the Flies by Golding, the western books written by Zane Grey, Black Like Me by Griffen, Scarlet Letter by Hawthorne, Mr. and Mrs. Bo Jones by Head, Catch 22 by Heller, A Farewell to Arms by Hemingway, The Sun Also Rises by Hemingway, I'm Really Dragged But Nothing Gets Me Down by Nat Hentoff, Hiroshima by Hersey, The Outsiders by Hinton, Brave New World by Huxley, The Toilet by Jones, A Patch of Blue by Kata, Flowers for Algernon by Keyes, A Separate Peace by Knowles, Home of the Brave by Laurents, Inherit the Wind by Lawrence, To Kill a Mocking Bird by Lee, Rosemary's Baby by Levin, The Contender by Lipsyte, Raintree County by Lockridge, Poems by McKuen, Moby Dick by Melville, Hawaii by Michener, Cool World by Miller, Death of a Salesman by Miller, The Crucible by Miller, A Canticle for Leibowitz by Miller, The Naked Ape by Morris, McTeague by Norris, The Scarlet Pimpernel by Orczy, Animal Farm by Orwell, 1984 by Orwell, Good Morning, Miss Dove by Patton, The Republic by Plato, The King Must Die by Renault, Catcher in the Rye by Salinger, Beulah Land by Settle, Macbeth by William Shakespeare, East of Eden by Steinbeck, Grapes of Wrath by Steinbeck, Portable Steinbeck of Steinbeck's writings, A Love, or a Season by Stolz, Lust for Life by Stone, The Hobbit by Tolkien, Huckleberry Finn by Twain, Tom Sawyer by Twain, Slaughterhouse Five by Vonnegut, Around the World in 80 Days by Verne, The Dictionary of American Slang by Wentworth and Flexnor, The Mentor Book of Major American Poets by Williams and Honig, and The World's Great Religions, by Smith.

Periodicals which have been censored included Mad Magazine, Harper's, Life, Read Magazine, National Geographic, National Observer, Scholastic Magazine, Time, Newsweek, and Glamour. The New York Times was also censored as were such films as Birth of a Nation, Of Black America, and Portland Express. Recordings have been censored including those by Bob Dylan, the Beatles, Rod McKuen, and Bill Cosby.

The school board in Drake, North Dakota, had Kurt Vonnegut's Slaughterhouse Five, James Dickey's Deliverance, and the anthology Short Story Masterpieces burned.

Some Parents wanted Ms magazine removed from the school library. Some church members burned Playboy and The Exorcist in Junction City, Kansas. A teacher was arrested in South Carolina for recommending Slaughterhouse Five to minors. In Prince William County, Virginia, 500 persons condemned The

Dynamics of Language textbooks. David Dalton's Janis was considered obscene by some parents in Hillsborough, New Hampshire. The school board in St. Francis, Wisconsin, banned Ralph Ellison's Invisible Man. Some parents couldn't stand the curse words in John Steinbeck's Of Mice and Men.

Television programs receiving severe criticism were Kojak, Soap, Maude, and Welcome Back, Kotter. In Battle Creek, Michigan, a fundamentalist group burned eleven television sets worth $1,400. In state legislatures, at least 350 bills were submitted to control motion picture obscenity.

Erica Jong, author of Fear of Flying, accused the Smithsonian Institute of trying to censor her planned lecture there.

Claude Brown, author of Manchild in the Promised Land, said, "It's a cruel thing to tell people not to read. It's not only a violation of people's constitutional rights; it's cruel. It's a waste of time telling students what not to read. They're going to get access to it anyway."

Dwight G. Deay contended that newspapers could publish deliberate falsehoods and recklessly disregard the truth in at least seven ways and that, except for gossip mongering and invasion of a person's sex life, a reporter's right to report news of public interest is almost unlimited.

George E. Reedy contended the American press arouses such heated controversy because of its high quality and because it is not dominated by consistent ideological viewpoints.

Senator Sam Ervin said, "A press which is not free to gather news without threat of ultimate incarceration cannot play its role meaningfully. The people as a whole must suffer. If the sources of that information are limited to official spokesman, the people have no means of evaluating the worth of promises and assurances. The search for truth among competing ideas, which the First Amendment contemplates, would become a matter of reading official new releases. It is the responsibility of the press to insure that competing views are presented, and it is our responsibility as citizens to object to actions of the government which prevent the press from fulfilling this constitutional role."

Ben Bagdikian said:

"The country has passed through more than a decade of radical change, in race relations, in the assassinations of three national leaders, in a disastrous war, in lifestyles, in international strategy, all of it inevitably creating turbulence and confusion under the best of conditions. All of it was transmitted to the public by the news media. The news was real. The events would have occurred without the media. But they have made the media, the bearer of bad and disturbing news, a perfect scapegoat. The most powerful leaders of the country have done precisely this, turning public confusion and uneasiness about events against the press."

Vermont Royster said, "Among the many revolutionary ideas to emerge from the American Revolution, none proved more revolutionary than freedom of the press. None has proved more durable, for it has withstood two centuries of assault. Freedom of the press, once proclaimed, admits to no logical limit."

Chief Justice Earl Warren said:

"When secrecy surrounds government and the activities of public servants, corruption has a breeding place. Secrecy prevents the citizenry from inspecting its government through the news media. The minimum amount of secrecy needed for the proper operation of the government should be fixed by law, and no secrecy beyond that point should be countenanced."

Katherine Graham said, "The press should be considered not as a fourth branch of government, but as an essential counterweight to government, the basic check against abuse of official power."

Floyd Abrams said, "With respect to press coverage of the courts, it seems to me that the press and the entire publishing industry must be unremitting in telling the courts that the press alone decides what is fit to print."

P.M. Schenkkan said that the belief that the power of the broadcast media presents a clear and present danger of oligarchy in the market place of ideas and that this constitutes a substantial evil that Congress had a right to prevent by content regulations is suspect. The most suspect consequence of this belief is that the Fairness Doctrine is applied to television. On examination neither the power rationale nor its fairness doctrine corollary can withstand First Amendment scrutiny.

Michael M. Sasser said, "The question of a journalistic privilege necessitates the balancing of two competing interests -- enhancing the administration of justice through compulsory testimony of all citizens versus promoting the free flow of news, and hence the people's right to know. To be sure, both interests are basic to American philosophy."

Bessie Stagg, editor of the Baronville, Illinois, _News_, quit after seventeen years of harrassment, boycotts, bomb threats, and threats to kidnap her children.

Lazlo Toth, a tantalizer created the write spurious letters for Don Novello, a comedian, taunted Roland L. Elliott, a special assistant to President Nixon, with the comment: "Chocolate is good, but too much of it makes you sick. The same goes for freedom of the press."

The right to distritbute pamphlets and leaflets is accorded full constitutional protection, according to the

Concerned Consumers' League case.

A prominent Chicago attorney, Elmer Gertz, sued Robert Welch, Inc., for calling him a communist in a John Birch Society publication and for making other accusations. The Supreme Court ruled in Gertz's favor, saying he was neither a public figure nor a public official and therefore had the normal protections against libel. Continued legal procedures extended settlement until late 1982 when Gertz received a $400,000 damage payment. The Court found that Gertz had made no effort to thrust himself into the vortex of any public issue and therefore must be considered a private individual. A private citizen may be required to show only negligence on the part of a publication rather than actual malice with reckless disregard of the truth to obtain damage awards for defamatory publications.

Constitutional safeguards which shield and protect the communicator perhaps more importantly also assure the public of the right to receive information in an open society, according to the Fritz case.

William Hambling and five other defendants were judged guilty of mailing obscene materials in the form of 55,000 advertising leaflets for an illustrated report of the President's Commission on Obscenity and Pornography. One side of the mailer had scenes of hetereosexual and homosexual intercourse. The court ruled the California community standards were adequate to convict since the Miller rule had eliminated national standards.

The Supreme Court found in the Jenkins case that the movie Carnal Knowledge was not obscene even though some nudity and a sex theme existed.

The First Amendment protects the right to receive ideas no less than it protects the right to disseminate them, according to the Johnson case.

The Supreme Court refused to hear an appeal of a ruling from a Court of Appeals which had upheld the CIA's prior restraint of 168 passages in a book written by John Marks based on remarks by former CIA agent Victor Marchetti, who had contracted to allow CIA review when he joined that agency. Alfred Knopf publishers contended such an arrangement constituted illegal government prior restraint forbidden by the First Amendment.

In the Tornillo case, the Supreme Court declared unconstitutional a Florida statute that gave a candidate for political office the right to equal free space for reply to a newspaper criticism of his character or official record. There is no right of access to reply to a political endorsement run in a newspaper. The choice of material to go into a newspaper, and the decisions made as to the limitations on the size of the paper, and the content and treatment of public issues and public officials -- whether fair or unfair -- constitutes the exercise of editorial control and judgment.

A New York court said in the Rosemont Enterprises case prior restraint of speech is illegal censorship. Prior restraint may not be used even against a publication alleged to be false or scandalous.

Freedom from prior restraint of the press applies to false as well as to true statements. Prior restraint cannot be justified because there might be some abuse of freedom of the press, according to the Pelczynski case.

A system of prior restraints on the press is not necessarily invalid, but comes to court with a heavy presumption against its constitutional validity, according to a United Artists Corporation case.

The Supreme Court has consistently ruled that the Federal Trade Commission can forbid deceptive advertising practices.

39
International Agreements and Repressions, 1970 through 1974

Gore Vidal's <u>Myra Breckinridge</u> was banned in Australia in 1970.

President Eduardo Montalvo of Chile prohibited the publication of alarmist news when reports about his government were published.

An underground typewritten press called Samizdat circulated a newspaper predicting the collapse of the Soviet Union in the 1980s after a war with China.

Rhodesia and South Africa expelled foreign correspondents and disciplined the foreign press.

Panama installed government editors to be sure no criticism of the government was printed.

President Milton Obote of Uganda would not allow the press "to interfere with the government. We cannot have a government and a press enjoying the same responsibility." He jailed magazine editor Neogy for five months without a trial.

Argentine President Juan Carlos Ongania suspended civil liberties and gagged the press.

The government of Kenya declared that the local press is expected to identify itself with the aspirations of the country.

The InterAmerican Press Association reported that press freedom had declined greatly in Latin America.

The International Press Institute reported "newspapers in Africa are at best tolerated and generally endure harrassment or suppression and at worst are propaganda organs aimed at telling the people what the government wishes them to know."

Dictator Juan Alvardo of Peru decreed fines and jail for any journalist he decided had insulted his government.

The Student, a French campus newspaper, was fined for circulating a leaflet mentioning venereal disease and was forced to stop its distribution.

The editor of France's L'Idiot International was arrested for publishing political subversion. The police banned L'Hebdo Hara-Kiri because it published a cartoon showing police being chased by a herd of pigs.

Publishers, booksellers, and college students defied the Australian ban on Portnoy's Complaint to print and sell 125,000 copies of the book.

Pyotr Grigorenko was sent to a Russian prison hospital for smuggling his diary to Norway for publication. Juares Medvedev got out of a Russian jail in a month because of protests after he had exposed Lysenko's nonsensical biology theories. The Russian central censorship office required a proof copy for approval as "signed for printing."

Something of a crisis in international news occurred in the 1970s between industrialized nations and developing nations. This crisis led to combining a New International Order and a New International Communications Order. UNESCO turned its attention on the content of news and the role of the media in society.

The Council of Europe issued a Declaration on Mass Communications Media and Human Rights urging the end to censorship, the independence of the press and other mass media, the reponsibility of such agencies, and the protection of individual rights to privacy.

1971

Christopher Kypreos operated The Running Man Press in England and published sexual magazines. He was acquitted of obscenity charges for his promotions of Paul Abelman's The Mouth and Oral Sex. Richard Handyman was fined 50 pounds plus 115 1/2 pounds in court costs when judged guilty of obscenity for his The Little Red Schoolhouse. Mary Whitehouse crusaded for many years against obscene literature in England. The Pope praised her for such efforts. An English appeals court dismissed obscenity charges against OZ 28, an English magazine dealing with sexual literature. The Greater London Council issued a license to Tropic of Cancer although the British Bureau of Film Censorship would not license it.

1972

Germaine Greer was fined $40 for saying shit in Aukland, N.Z., but was acquitted of obscenity for saying bullshit.

Bukovsky, a Russian citizen, was jailed eight years for slander in reports to the west and for trying to smuggle a printing press into Russia. Byelorussia proposed a "Declaration on the Media" to bring United Nations pressure on foreign broadcasts to Eastern Europe and Soviet Russia.

The United Nations General Assembly voted that it was necessary that states, taking into account the principle of freedom of information, reach arrangements concerning direct satellite broadcasting to the population of countries other than the country of origin of the transmission. The United States cast the only vote against the idea. Frank Stanton said it ignored "the rights which form the frame work of our constitution, the principles asserted in the Universal Declaration of Human Rights, and the basic principles of the free movement of ideas."

Aleksander Solhenitzen said, "Woe to that nation whose literature is disturbed by the intervention of power. Because that is not just a violation against (Freedom of Print). It is the closing down of the heart of the nation, a slashing to pieces of its memory."

Japan conducted a study for a plan for an information society with a national goal for the year 2000.

The Report of the InterAmerican Press Association said, "At this moment there is hardly a country where the press is not subject either to a frontal onslaught of its many enemies or to severe tensions and threats even if practically every one of our constitutional guarantees of freedom of speech , written as well as oral, secrecy, and news management, and sometimes even prior restraints as well as open censorship are the order of the day."

1973

Nasty Tales, an English comic magazine, was acquitted of all obscenity charges by an English jury. Raids to confiscate pornography saw the London West End porno team pick up 40 tons of material and arrest the nine principal pornographers.

The Algiers non-aligned Summit Meeting issued a statement on communications issues to increase communications and communications media. The meeting in Algiers said national media had to be strengthened to eliminate the harmful consequences of the colonial era."

Finland's President Urho Kekkonen told the Helsinki Conference of Security and Cooperation in Europe that "a mere liberalistic freedom of communications is not in everyday reality a neutral idea, but a way in which an enterprise with many resources at its disposal has greater opportunities than weaker brethren to make its own hegemony accepted."

South Africa's Censorship Act listed 97 definitions of what is considered undesirable to literature, not to mention the apartheid blinders placed on writers.

1974

In Ireland, John Kell said that freedom of the press which was permissible including forming ideas, expressing opinions in the abstract, arguing for abstract ideas, and temperate discussion of men and measures. Areas which could bring criminal or civil libel prosecutions included imputing criminal acts, inciting evasions of the law, reducing respect for the law, and advocating resistance to the law.

The French law of 1974 said that French broadcasting assigned information, education, entertainment, culture, and the values of civilizations as radio's goals.

George Orwell said, "In this country intellectual cowardice is the worst enemy a writer or a journalist has to face. Anyone who challenges the prevailing orthodoxy finds himself silenced with suprising effectiveness."

Police seized 10,000 copies of 238 different magazines in a raid on Johnson's Central News Agency in Bath, England; 146 were ruled obscene. Customs officials seized 324,000 copies of Men Only, a Dutch magazine specializing in female masturbation photos. 2000 policemen arrested 40 pornographers in the Soho District of London. Officials also picked up 100,000 copies of books and magazines at Cobham farm, including soft pornography as well as hard pornography in the eighteen ton lot.

40
Individual, Corporate, or Penumbral Right, 1975 through 1979

Thomas E. Gish suffered boycotts, threats of violence, social isolation, and arson for in 1975 being the crusading editor of The Mountain Eagle in Whitesburg, Kentucky.

The broadcast access rule for political candidates was declared not to apply to debates or press conferences because they were not controlled by the candidates.

The Student Press Law Center was established in Washington, D.C., as an outgrowth of the project producing Captive Voices and with the encouragement of the Reporters' Committee for Freedom of the Press. Its reports and magazine are highly effective as are its other activities related to laws affecting both college and high school publications. The SPLC is the only national agency devoted exclusively to protecting the First Amendment rights of the nation's high school and college journalists.

Ben Bagdikian said that a voluntary press council would be the best guarantee against government suppression.

J.F. Terhorst said, "The press is constitutionally required to live in a kind of no man's land, subject to constant criticism of both government and public and loved by neither."

Eli M. Oboler said, "Censorship -- any censorship -- cannot be justified in a democracy if we really believe in man's freedom to choose for himself, in man's God-given right to motivation by his own conscience, and finally in the ability of man to learn only when he is given an opportunity to learn by receiving all knowledge spread out before him."

Judge Irving R. Kaufman said, "We value freedom of

thought, freedom of speech, freedom of the press because they furnish vehicles for the new and provocative, and serve as barriers to tyranny."

A statement of principles was adopted by the Society of Newspaper Editors strongly defending freedom of the press as a right of the people. The National Council of Editorial Writers adopted a similar basic statement of principles.

William J. Fullbright said the inquisitorial style of the press tended to be vindicative and less concerned with uncovering and correcting mistakes in public affairs than in embarrassing and punishing those who make them. The media have acquired an unwholesome fascination with the singer to the neglect of the song. There is no one to restrain the press except the press itself--nor should there be."

Justice Potter Stewart, in an address at the Yale Law School sesquicentennial, said:

"The Free Press guarantee is, in essence, a structural provision of the constitution; most of the other provisions in the Bill of Rights protect specific liberties or specific rights of individuals: freedom of speech, freedom of worship, the right to counsel, the privilege against compulsory self-incrimination, to name a few. In contrast, the free press clause extends protection to an institution. The publishing business is, in short, the only organized business that is given explicit constitutional protection. This basic understanding is essential, I think, to avoid an elementary error of constitutional law. It is tempting to suggest that freedom of the press means only that newspaper publishers are guaranteed freedom of expression. They are guaranteed that freedom, to be sure, but so are we all because of the free speech clause. If the free press guarantee meant no more than freedom of expression, it would be a constitutional redundancy, the primary purpose of the constitutional guarantee of a free press was to create a fourth institution outside the government as an additional check on the three official branches. The relevant metaphor, I think, is the metaphor of the Fourth Estate. If freedom of the press means simply freedom of speech for reporters, this question of a reporter's asserted right to withhold information would have answered itself. None of us--as individuals--has a 'free speech' right to refuse to tell a grand jury the identity of someone who has given us information relevant to the grand jury's legitimate inquiry. Only if a reporter is a representative of a protected institution, does the question become a different one."

Chief Justice Warren Burger and the Supreme Court rejected the concept of institutional press freedom rather than individual press freedom by pointing out that the First Amendment does not belong to any indentifiable category of persons or entities. It belongs to all who exercise it.

The First Amendment tolerates absolutely no prior

restraint predicated on a surmise or conjecture that some untoward consequences will occur, according to the Bertot case.

Courts have held in a number of cases that publications do not lose their First Amendment rights because they are commercial in nature. The relationship of speech to the marketplace of products or of services does not make it valueless in the marketplace of ideas, according to the Bigelow case.

One of the purposes of the First Amendment is to protect the press from harrassment, not merely from liability, according to the Buchanan case.

The Supreme Court ruled in the Cox Broadcasting Corporation case that states could not forbid broadcasters and media from identifying rape victims as long as the names were available from public records or from testimony in open court.

An individual's right of privacy must yield to the greater public interest in the dissemination of newsworthy material. It makes no difference whether the person involved is a public official, a public figure, or a private individual. The subject matter does not have to be of political, public, or private concern, according to the McNutt case.

Freedom of the press is not, and has never been, a private property right granted to those who own the news media. It is a cherished and almost sacred right of each citizen to be informed about current events on a timely basis so each citizen can exercise discretion in determining the destiny and security of himself, other people, and the nation, according to a Miami Herald Publishing Company case.

Among the evils prevented by the press guarantee of the First Amendment are not merely the censorship of the press, but of any action of the government which might prevent free or general discussion of public matters. Such discussions seem absolutely essential to prepare the people for an intelligent exercise of their rights as citizens. First Amendment rights are protected not only against heavy-handed frontal attacks but also from being stifled by more subtle governmental interference, according to the P.A.M. News Corporation case.

In the _Schiff_ case, the court ordered three college student editors re-instated after they were fired by the University president because he used as grounds for such action "poor grammar, poor spelling, and poor language expression" in the paper which he considered to be a discredit and embarrassment to the University and because the paper's editorial policy emphasized "villification and rumor-mongering, instead of accurately reporting items likely to be of interest to the University community."

The concept that a statement on a public issue may be suppressed because it is believed by the Court to be untrue is entirely inconsistent with constitutional guarantees and raises the spectre of censorship in its most pernicious form, according to the Wilson case.

1976

A revision of the copyright law relaxed controls somewhat in light of contemporary technology and practices, particularly if the uses do not involve financial benefits to the user.

The Buckley Amendment was not intended to punish or restrict publication by newspapers. It restricts public college and school agencies from releasing personnel and personal records without the permission or knowledge of the students.

The Government in the Sunshine Act was passed. It required 50 federal agencies to conduct their activities in meetings open to the public.

James C. Goodale said:

"If the courts recognize the right to know, however, they will begin to perform the function of gathering information. They will also act as editors. Editing will require judgments about what information to release to the public and what to withhold. The right to communicate will thus be affected, since one cannot communicate what has been withheld."

The increasing dependence of the electorate on television, radio, and other mass media for news and information has made such modes of communications indispensable instruments of effective political speech. Protection of the First Amendment against governmental abridgement of free expression cannot be made to depend upon a person's financial ability to engage in public discussion, according to the Buckley case.

The courts have held that the context in which a trial is held could justify a rule of inherent prejudice because the community has been so saturated with prejudicial news reports that it is improbable that the judge would be able to rely on a prospective juror's statement that he is impartial, according to the Calley case.

The Court ruled in a Consumers Union case that an American Bar Association rule concerning advertising by attorneys was constitutionally overbroad because it kept the plaintiff from receiving or gathering information in a legal directory for consumers.

Adviser Paula Endress was dismissed because she had helped prepare an article exposing conflict of interest on the college's board of trustees. In a resulting suit the lower Court re-instated her, granted her tenure, gave her back pay, and fined the president and each of the six board members $10,000 in punitive damages for violation of her First Amendment rights. The lower court judge said he believed the courts should teach a lesson to wrong-headed administrators who abused persons through illegal acts. Subsequently, an appeals court eliminated the punitive damages assessed board members, but required the college president to pay Endress $2,500.

Just as the First Amendment forbids the making of any law which would abridge freedom of the press or speech, it also protects against any law or activity which would interfere with or reduce the concomitant rights to receive those thoughts disseminated under protection of the First Amendment, according to the Gaspor case.

In the Hanneman case, the Court ruled that the First Amendment not only protects the individual's interest in speaking out, but also the public's interest in being informed. In relation to government employees the Court ruled that an employee, by accepting employment with the Central Intelligence Agency and by signing a secrecy agreement, did not surrender his right of free speech.

The Court ruled in a KQED case that the First Amendment mandated a maximum amount of public access to radio broadcasts. In the Nebraska Press Association case, the Supreme Court ruled that an order of the Nebraska judge banning publication of information obtained in open court or by other sources constituted prior restraint and violated the constitutional guarantee of freedom of the press.

Since restricting access to the courts by the press or the public implicates the guarantees of the First Amendment, only a compelling state interest will permit an infringement of that right, according to the Thompson case.

The Court overturned a state statute forbidding the advertising of the price for any prescription drug in a Virginia case. Truthful statements made for a commercial purpose, if neither misleading nor offensive, are protected by the First Amendment.

Although broadcasters have the right to form a trade association to lobby on behalf of the industry and to share ideas about programs and to promote high standards by adopting a code, any such association of broadcasters has no constitutional right to set up a network board to censor and regulate American television, according to the Writers Guild of America West case.

1977

The Protection of Children Against Sexual Exploitation Act made it illegal to use children in the production of pornographic materials.

Mrs. I. Toguri D'Aquino was pardoned from treason, which had resulted from her role as Tokyo Rose in Japanese wartime propaganda broadcasts.

A Chicago school of theorists proposed that the rise of mass democratic politics was made possible by communications media that intricately linked local communities to larger society as a whole. A Frankfurt School of Critical Theorists believed that media have caused the decline of mass politics and discourse because economic constraints have eroded media used to create a truly democratic society. The democratic socialist theory of the press believes that the press should not be an instrument for private owners; instead, the press should be instruments of the people, operating as public utilities through which the people's aspirations, ideas, and criticism of the state and society would be disseminated since people would have positive access to place their views in the press, which would be considerably subsidized by the government.

Leonard R. Sussman, executive director of Freedom House, said:

"The free journalist does not have to display a social responsibility in order to earn his freedom. He must be responsible to the craft of journalism; the craft, at its best, is understood to demand high standards of truth, personal integrity, a sense of inquiry, and commitment to the commonwealth. That standard need not be spelled out in a code such as UNESCO will now try to create. Sooner or later some government is likely to insist on enforcing that code. Then even the best code becomes another noise of government, appropriate only for authoritarian societies. The primary question is not press performance; it is press freedom. A free but badly performing press serves its peoples far better than an efficient, government-controlled press."

The fundamental purpose of the First Amendment is to protect from state infringement free expression of controversial and unpopular ideas, according to the Aumiller case.

The Supreme Court ruled that the Arizona Bar Association could not prevent lawyers in Arizona from advertising fees and services. The Business and Professions Code of California was declared unconstitutional for prohibiting price advertising by opticians.

The Supreme Court ruled that the First Amendment protected the advertising of contraceptives even though such ads might be offensive to some people.

The Supreme Court ruled in the Edwards case that the First Amendment protects the right to report accurately and disinterestedly serious charges made against an individual by an agency, regardless of the reporter's private view of the truth of the charges. The fact they were made is newsworthy.

The Supreme Court ruled that corporations enjoy a free speech right in the First National Bank of Boston case when Massachusetts had sought to stop the bank from advertising its views on a state referendum. A commercial advertisement is constitutionally protected not so much because it pertains to the seller's business as because it furthers the societal interest in the free flow of commercial information.

There is no conflict between the First Amendment and copy right laws, according to the Schnapper v. Foley case.

A film-maker was ruled to be a journalist in the Silkwood case, by the Court and thus eligible for First Amendment protection.

When the right of freedom of the press weighs in the balance, the scales must necessarily tip in favor of this fundamental freedom, according to the Penthouse v. Putka case.

The Supreme Court decided that in the Smith case legislative bodies were not capable of defining community standards of obscenity, and that the only agency thus able to identify those standards were the jurors in a specific obscenity trial.

Ordinances restricting billboards can be constitutional rules of time, place, and manner of expression, according to the Suffolk Advertising case.

1978

The International Communications Agency was formed by combining the United States Information Agency, the Voice of America, and the Bureau of Educational and Cultural Affairs to develop a national policy on international communications and the free flow of information.

Florida Governor Rubin Askew vetoed a bill that would have established committees on each University of Florida campus to censor films and other educational resources for pornography because he believed the University must be free to examine ideas in an atmosphere of freedom.

In 1971, there were more than 400 so-called underground publications in the United States. By 1978, the number had declined to 78, according to the Underground Press Syndicate.

Steven J. Simmons characterized the FCC Fairness Doctrine as being an unfairness rule as it was administered. The broadcast industry began a campaign to have it changed or dropped as being archaic, unnecessary, and unadministrable.

The CIA went to Court to stop publication of <u>Decent Interval</u>, a book criticizing CIA activities in Vietnam.

Chief Justice Warren Burger used a Massachusetts case to say that no special protection exists for the press and that there is no basis for such a conclusion. He said the process of defining who might be entitled to any special protection is perilous and reminiscent of Tudor and Stuart England -- a system the First Amendment was intended to ban from this country. Robert Klaus objected to the Potter Stewart position by saying that it is a "claim that a distinct class of people called <u>the press</u> have rights not enjoyed by the general populace. It is a corporate vision, in the sense that it views society as a single organism in which different citizens play different roles and have different legal needs.

Academics would be the brains of this social corpus, and reporters the eyes and ears, leaving the rest of us to fight for the positions below the neck."

A newsman's privilege is a fundamental personal right well-founded in the First Amendment, according to the Anderson case.

The Supreme Court upheld FCC orders that 16 television companies divest themselves of newspaper ownership connections before operation licenses could be renewed. This was an effort to diversify viewpoints and break up economic concentrations. The Court said the FCC had authority to make such rulings in the public interest and they were not arbitrary or capricious.

In the Pacifica Foundation case, the Court ruled that the Federal Communication Commission could restrict the repeated broadcast of "seven dirty words" to the time of day when children are likely not to be in the audience. The occasional use of such words at such times would be permissible. In ruling that the George Carlin monologue over station WBAI was patently offensive, the Court noted that broadcasting is not entitled to the same First Amendment protection as print media because broadcasting had established a uniquely pervasive presence in the lives of all Americans and is uniquely accessible to children, even those too young to read. When the FCC finds a pig has entered the parlor, it does not have to prove the pig is obscene.

In the Gambino case, the Court ruled that school officials could not prohibit the student staff of the high school newspaper from publishing information about birth control despite a valid school rule prohibiting teaching about contraception in sex education classes. A school-funded newspaper is not a part of the school's curriculum.

The press cannot be required to justify or defend what it prints until after the expression has taken place, according to the Goldblum case.

The Court held in a Home Box Office case that the FCC exceeded its authority with rules about program content since the ends to be thus achieved were not ends for which broadcast television could be regulated.

Cable TV operators, like operators of other media, are entitled to First Amendment protection, according to the Midwest Video Corporation case.

The Supreme Court refused to release the Nixon tapes for commercial publications because the First Amendment generally grants the press no right to information about a trial superior to that of the general public. Content of the tapes had already been made available to and through the media.

The Supreme Court ruled in the Pinkus case that children were not to be considered as part of the community in determining community standards for obscenity.

The Court ruled that journalists have no right to
maintain the secrecy of their sources, including records of
long distance telephone billings subpoened from the telephone
company, against a valid criminal investigation. Any
incidental burden placed on journalists by government
inspection of such records does not abridge First Amendment
rights, according to a Reporters Committee for Freedom of the
Press case.

Corporate activities can clearly come within First
Amendment protection, according to the Universal Amusement
case.

1979

The Federal Communications Commission confused the
fairness doctrine applicability to commercial messages by
ruling that a station had violated the rule in pro-nuclear
energy commercials. The Federal Communications Commission
dismissed a complaint about an NBC broadcast on truck safety,
indicating stations did not violate the Fairness Doctrine.
The Fairness Doctrine and the Equal Access for Political
Candidates are mutually exclusive. A political candidate
cannot complain under the Fairness rule, nor can non-
politicians ask for access time.

Arkansas college and high school student journalists won
police press accreditation when the Arkansas State Police,
faced with the threat of a lawsuit from several students and
scholastic press organizations, reversed its position and
issued press passes to student reporters.

David Broder said:

"We, in the press, are troubled by the definition of our
responsibility. Journalists, for the most part, crave
the comfortable position of neutrality so long as the
story comes out, as long as we get to cover it every
step of the way. By the same token, we hate to become
part of the story we are covering. But Iran has robbed
us that luxury. We are not neutrals in this stuggle and
we find our values being turned inside out on us."

Prior restraint on publications and speech is the most
serious and least tolerable infringement on rights under the
First Amendment. A court must use the rigorous test of clear
and present danger rather then the balancing test if the
state is seeking to avert a danger, according to the Aryan
case.

In the Gannett case, the Court ruled that the right of a
public trial belongs to the defendant and his right
supercedes the right of the public or the press to insist on
a public trial. Reporters thus may be barred from court
proceedings. (This ruling was reversed in the Richmond
newspapers case, subsequently.)

James Howe won a $100 judgment from the University of
Florida which also had to pay his $1,560 attorney's fees in
his suit based on threatened arrest and denial of his First

Amendment right to sell or give away publications of a socialist party.

The International Society for Krishna Consciousness won a case in a Wisconsin District Court when it complained about a Milwaukee ordinance preventing it from distributing literature at the Milwaukee airport. The Court ruled that the policy requiring permission of the airport director was unconstitutionally vague.

The freedom of communication encompasses the right to receive as well as to disseminate ideas, according to the Medrano case.

The clear and present danger test was never intended to express a technical legal doctrine or convey a formula for adjudicating cases under the First Amendment. Properly applied, the test requires a court to make its own inquiry into the magnitude of the danger from a particular utterance. The court must then balance the character of the evil as well as its likelihood against the need for free and unfettered expression. The Court held in the Landmark Communications case that the media could not be criminally punished for publishing truthful reports of confidential judicial proceedings concerning actions of government officials. If the constitutional protection of a free press means anything, it means the government cannot decide what a newspaper may or may not publish, according to Justice Potter Stewart. The Supreme Court said that free discussion of governmental affairs is a major purpose of the First Amendment.

The First Amendment rests on the principle that the wide dissemination of information from diverse and antagonistic sources is vital to the public welfare according to the Naked City case.

The Florida Supreme Court invalidated a canon of the Code of Judicial Conduct so television and photography could be used in Florida court rooms.

Removal of MS. Magazine from the school library because of objections to its content was unconstitutional. The First Amendment generally prohibits the government from cleansing public debate to the point where it is grammatically palatable to the most squeamish among us, according to the Salvail case.

The state may legitimately prohibit speech of a harmful sexual nature to minors even if that speech is protected by the First Amendment for adults, according to the Schimmelpfennig case.

Above all else, the First Amendment means that government has no power to restrict expression because of its message, ideas, subject matter, or content. The First Amendment's protection extends to the circulation and distribution of newspapers, according to the Rockwell case.

41
An International Debate,
1975 through 1979

South Vietnam president Van Thieu censored the press in 1975, that of his opponents and that of constructive criticism as well.

A regional conference on information imbalance in Asia was held in Kandy, Sri Lanka, under the auspices of the Asian Mass Communication Research and Information Center. The Information Act of the Helsinki Conference on Security and Cooperation in Europe urged greater access, circulation, and exchange of information between governments, and improved working conditions for journalists. Participants in the Dag Hammarskjold Seminar for Third World Journalists stated that their national governments should share information media experiences.

The House of Commons reported that 250,000 obscene articles were confiscated in London; this grew to 375,000 in 1978-79 and to one million in 1979-80. Police confiscated 16,000 gay magazines in London.

The Danish Film Institute withrew its guarantee of a 42,800 pound loan which film maker Thorsen wanted to use to make a movie called "The Love Affairs of Jesus Christ." The Vatican had protested such a film.

1976

The Declaration of San Jose issued by the UNESCO intergovernmental conference in Costa Rica urged that communications policies contribute to greater knowledge and understanding of peoples. Twenty-one Latin American nations demanded balanced North-South reporting.

Inside Linda Lovelace was acquitted of obscenity charges

by English Courts. <u>Gay News</u> was fined 1,000 pounds plus court costs, and Denis Lemon, its editor, was fined 500 pounds for blasphemous libel in England.

Soviet Russia sponsored a draft resolution at the Nairobi UNESCO conference which said, "States are responsible for the activities in the international sphere of all mass media under their jurisdiction." UNESCO adopted it. The United States contended that the Soviet proposed draft on mass media would reduce freedom of the press.

Ferninand Marcos told the Philippine Broadcasters Association that freedom of the press was based on a policy that required that the media wholly participate in the government as committed agents of the government for development."

Dictator Soekarno said journalists must follow the slower Indonesian ways of reporting issues or his government would ban foreign journalists.

Ministers from 58 non-aligned nations meeting in New Delhi planned a Third World news pool.

Harvey Stockwin said the Western press told Third World leaders what they didn't want to know.

Indira Gandhi said, "We want to hear Africans on events in Africa. You should similarly be able to get an Indian explanation of events in India. It is astonishing that we know so little about leading poets, novelists, historians, and editors of various Asian, African, and Latin American countries while we are familiar with minor authors and columnists of Europe and America."

UNESCO in its Nineteenth General Assembly in Nairobi formed the International Commission for the Study of Communication Problems.

At a summit meeting of 84 non-aligned countries, the participating heads of state said that a new international order in the fields of information and mass communications was vital to a new international economic order.

The Council of Europe called a conference to draft an international treaty for data protection.

1977

The World Administrative Radio Conference for broadcasting satellites set up an <u>a priori</u> plan for all areas of the World except the Western Hemisphere.

Dr. Arabella Melville and Colin Johnson won acquittal from obscenity charges for the English magazine <u>Libertine</u> specializing in historical erotica. Chief Constable James Anderton ordered 286 raids, confiscated 160,000 obscene articles, and won convictions in all his cases designed to rid Greater Manchester of pornography. Private actions against obscenity had to have the approval of the English attorney-general to proceed. English courts refused to accept any therapeutic value for pornography. Margaret Thatcher, prime minister, and Mary Whitehouse joined forces in England to urge Parliament to outlaw kiddie porn.

A huge scandal broke out concerning the Scotland Yard "Dirty Squad" which had staged many raids. Officers were fired, retired, and arrested. Many top offices and lower echelon officials ended up in prison for corruption and bribery. When the function was reorganized it no longer fought pornography.

1978

The Declaration on the Mass Media was adopted by consensus at the 20th UNESCO General Conference in Paris in 1978. The Organization for Economic Cooperation and Development set up a group of experts to provide guidelines for trans-border data flow. A world wide conference on trans-border data flow was planned for 1980. The UNESCO declaration emphasized human rights, diversity of news, free flow of information, and the journalist's right of access to news.

Sean Mac Bride said:

"It is obvious that communication in the world today, in all forms and at all levels, is vital to building a more humane, more just, and more prosperous world tomorrow. Hence I firmly believe the news agencies and media bear a heavy responsibility to inform the peoples of the world about the urgency and magnitude of the problems facing humanity."

The Williams Committee report on obscenity, nudity, and violence in England said "The printed word should be neither restricted nor prohibited since its nature makes it neither immediately offensive nor capable of involving the harms we identify and because of its importance in conveying ideas."

42
Events in America, 1980 and Beyond

Supreme Court Chief Justice Warren Burger knocked a camera from the shoulder of a TV cameraman in 1980. The CBS crew had asked him questions at an elevator concerning an anti-busing conversation he and former President Nixon were said to have had.

The Society of Professional Journalists and the Reporters Committee on Freedom of the Press formed a joint legal research and defense program for freedom of the press litigations.

A First Amendment Congress was convened in Philadelphia in January when 300 persons representing media and other agencies met to discuss the basic nature of the free press concept. A second "working" session met in Williamsburg, Virginia, in March. Subsequently, state, regional, and local First Amendment Congresses were held throughout the nation.

The Gallup Poll reported that 40 per cent of the people thought there should be stricter curbs on the press.

Margaret A. Blanchard told an Association for Education in Journalism convention that it was possible to find earlier state court antecedent decisions for almost every speech and press issue decided recently by the Supreme Court.

The Supreme Court, to determine which commercial speech could be regulated, said:

"At the outset we must determine whether the expression is protected by the First Amendment. For commercial speech to come within that provision, it must at least concern lawful activity, and must not be misleading. Next, we ask whether the asserted governmental interest is substantial. If both inquiries yield positive answers, we must determine whether the regulation directly advances the governmental interest asserted, and whether it is more extensive than is necessary to serve that interest."

The guarantee of free speech is a restriction on governmental action and not on the action of individuals, according to the Aclin case.

In entering an adult bookstore, a member of the public exercises his or her own right under the First Amendment to see, read, and observe on film sexually explicit, even sordid, activities. This is what the store purports to offer its customers. But to attribute to each customer a concurrent expectation that he or she will be solicited to perform sexual acts would have a chilling effect upon the right of privacy and the right to receive information, according to the Adult World Bookstore case.

The use of vulgar language is not without at least some protection under the First Amendment, according to the Aiello case.

Any restraint of freedom of the press even though narrow in scope and duration is subject to the closest scrutiny and will be upheld only upon a clear and imminent threat to the fair administration of justice, according to the Arkansas Gazette case.

The Supreme Court ruled in a CBS case that legally qualified political candidates had a limited right of access to broadcasting to advance their candidacies once a campaign had begun.

The Supreme Court ruled in the Chandler case that state courts may allow television coverage of criminal trials even if the defendant objects and unless the defendant can show that such coverage would affect the fairness of the trial. During the 1980 presidential campaign, third party candidates were denied low third class postage rates granted candidates of the two major parties. A United States District Court ruled this denial was unconstitutional because "the protection of unpopular ideas is the very essence of the First Amendment, according to the Greenberg case.

Chuck Reineke, high school student, won a suit alleging the evisceration of his First Amendment rights and requesting injunctive relief against McEachern High School in Cobb County, Georgia. The Court said that censorship of constitutionally protected expression in student publications in a public school cannot be imposed. The school cannot suspend the editor, suppress circulation, require an imprimatur of controversial articles, excise repugnant materials, withdraw financial support, or assert any form of censorial oversight based on the institution's power of the purse.

The United States Supreme Court ruled in the Richmond Newspaper case that trials must be open to the public and the press unless a compelling reason can be established to do otherwise. Journalism organizations consider the case a breakthrough in establishing a general newsgathering and access right.

1981

The FCC reduced its regulations of the content of radio programming.

Andrea Dworkin in her <u>Pornography: Men Possessing Women</u> and Susan Griffin in <u>Pornography and Silence</u> postulated that male dominance and violence in sexual actions was the basis of pornography. This concept led to a proposed city ordinance in Minneapolis, but which was vetoed by the mayor twice in 1983 as being unconstitutional. The mayor of Indianapolis approved a similar city ordinance in 1984. A United States Federal District Court ruled that one unconstitutional, as did the Seventh Circuit Court of Appeals in 1985.

Thousands of copies of Cuban newspapers and periodicals enroute to United States citizens were seized by agents operating under the International Economic Powers Act and the Trading with the Enemy Act.

Vincent Blasi observed that in the realm of civil liberties it is not always the case that the force of public opinion aids the cause of freedom. He said:

"The label 'prior restraint' could plausibly be applied to a variety of regulatory procedures. Consider, for example: registration requirements; withdrawals of postal privileges; film classifications systems; police surveillance practices; taxes and other cost impositions on publishing enterprises; <u>in choate</u> crimes; systematic threats to enforce the criminal law; probation conditions; allocation judgments regarding public resources such as parade routes, meeting rooms, or even lecture fees; administrative cease and desist orders; loyalty oaths and job disqualifications based on past or present beliefs; insurance requirements for demonstrators; restrictions on the use of certain equipment by media organizations; book seizures; arrest and bail; procedures relating to prosecutions for advocacy; and denial of press access to newsworthy events and records.

A city ordinance which prohibited the distribution of handbills, notices, or advertising devices of any kind unless the distributor had obtained a permit from the chief of police was unconstitutional because it required a standardless rule of prior approval for distributing political leaflets according to the Supreme Court of New Hampshire in the Chong case.

The loss of freedoms under the First Amendment, even for minimal periods of time, constitutes an irreparable injury which justifies granting a preliminary injunction ordering the cause of the loss to cease. Once an infringement has occurred, it cannot be undone by monetary relief alone, according to the Deerfield Medical Center case.

1982

The Defense Department blocked the presentations of 100 technical papers scheduled for a San Diego symposium of the Society of Photo-Optical Instrumentation Engineers.

The Office for Intellectual Freedom of the American Library Association found that one-third of 860 high school librarians had experienced efforts to remove books from the library's shelves. Between 1970 and 1982 there had been at least 1300 such efforts.

President Reagan's order 12356 was the most restrictive provision yet to deny access to governmental information by expanding the classification of documents.

Floyd Abrams said, "The American Press has never been more free, never been more uninhibited, and -- most important -- never been better protected by law."

Rev. Donald E. Wildmon, who served as head of the Coalition for Better Television, contended that television networks discriminated against Christian views and values.

A magazine article is not constitutionally protected in defamation suits merely because it is parody, satire, or humor, according to the Miss America Pageant case.

The Court said in the Schreiber case that commerical speech is a constitutionally protected form of communication but it does not receive the same staunch protection under the First Amendment as noncommercial speech does. Commercial speech occupies a subordinate position in the scale of values of the First Amendment; but if the commercial speech is connected with ancillary notions such as political, idelogical expressions, or associational rights, the cloak of the First Amendment is heavier.

The mere conclusion of a police officer on where the line between obscenity and constitutionally-protected speech has been drawn does not suffice as grounds for the seizure of allegedly obscene materials, and the state's impoundment of such evidence ordinarily must be preceded by some form of judicial procedure, according to the Furuyama case.

The Court said in the Gilbert case that dissemination of non-newsworthy private facts is not protected by the First Amendment; however; the privilege does immunize reporting of the private facts when discussed in connection with matters customarily regarded as "news". Any information disseminated for the purpose of education, amusement, enlightenment, or when the public may reasonably be expected to have a legitimate interest in what is published is protected by the First Amendment.

The state's substantial interest in child welfare is reason enough to justify regulations against procedures or dealers of kiddie porn irrespective of any First Amendment consideration, according to the Griffen case.

The Court said in the Jurkowski case that a deliberate factual lie has no protection under the First Amendment and proof of the knowledge of the falsity of material prior to its publication eliminates any protection under the First Amendment. To recover from defamation, however, a public official must show an actual awareness of the probable falsity of the material by the defendant prior to publication, even when the publication can be considered reckless. Failure to investigate by the defendant does not establish the actual malice required to hold the publisher liable for defaming the public official.

The United States Court of Appeals for the sixth circuit ruled that secret police documents of the 1970 shootings of Vietnam war protestors at Kent State University had to be made public because of First Amendment interests and the historic nature of the events portrayed.

The Court said in the Tribune-Republican case that when a reporter fails to contact and question obvious sources of corroboration, fabricates specific facts appearing in a story, and writes the story in a manner calculated to incite a factual inference that the newspaper had uncovered governmental corruption and bribery, he only risks the likelihood that the statements and inferences are false and do not have the protection of the First Amendment. The actual malice standard holds that a public official must show with clear and convincing evidence that the defamatory publication was made with actual malice.

The Kentucky Supreme Court in the McCall case rejected the theory of neutral reportage to protect from libel liability.

The Readers' Digest failed to convince the Supreme Court to review a case wherein it had been fined $1.75 million for using false checks as a promotional gimmick in 1973 and 1974.

The court said in the Miscellaneous Pornography case that material published by a newspaper as bonafide news is not per se nonobscene under a theory that obscenity is to be determined for all purposes by reference to the newspaper's use of the materials, or under the theory that obscenity is to be determined under one standard for the press and another for the public.

1983 and 1984

The American Civil Liberties Union changed its attitude toward libel in 1983 by endorsing the concept that the existence of the right of action for defamations is violative of the First Amendment when speech relates to a subject of public concern, which can be deemed to be related to anything having an impact on the social or political system or climate.

The government, including the FBI, could not keep secret

information about punishing high officials by claiming the information was in a personnel file.

People for the American Way, an organization which defends the First Amendment, reported there had been attempts to censor books, literature, school courses, and counseling programs in 48 states. Maine and Hawaii had no censorship episodes.

The National Commission on Free and Responsible Media was founded. It had no official standing and was not interested in laws or regulations governing the press, nor did it want to tell the media how to operate. The commission's goal was to inspire the public to think about and analyze the many issues surrounding the media's expanding role in American society.

Late in 1983 the United States notified UNESCO that antagonism to freedom of the press and continuous efforts to license and control journalists was a reason to withdraw from the international organization.

The National Newspaper Association found that about only four per cent of smaller newspapers had softened coverage because of the spectre of large libel awards.

By the end of 1983 nearly 14,000 motion pictures had been classified by the MPA Code. Many unclassified films were also exhibited in theaters.

The FTC issued an order making advertisements by dentists permissible and prohibited the American Dental Association from restraining its members from advertising.

The National Endowment for the Humanities awarded a million dollar grant to develop a national newspaper bank. This United States Newspaper Program will ultimately contain the contents of 300,000 newspapers published in America.

Newsweek was taken from a tenth grade world history curriculum because a school board member thought it was scutzy and too liberal.

After Ed Asner, star of Lou Grant, criticized United States actions in El Salvador, the popular television show was cancelled.

School officials took the Merriam Webster Dictionary out of the Carlsbad, New Mexico, classrooms because they believed it contained obscene words.

Actress Jane Fonda complained about the irresponsibility of the press when a false report of her physical condition was published as an incidental story. Jane had to stop her lawyer from filing a suit to stop publication of a book about her. Jane had presented a dramatic reading of the First Amendment on an "I Love Liberty" program on ABC. It turned out that the book was very laudatory of Jane.

Mark S. Fowler, chairman of the Federal Communications

Commission, urged the government to get out of the content control business so broadcast journalists would have the same rights as print journalists.

Atlanta television stations WAGA-TV and WANX-TV discontinued broadcasts by Assembly of God evangelist Jimmy Swaggart because the Roman Catholic archdiocese complained about his anti-Catholic statements. Swaggart also criticized Presbyterians and Baptists and asked for contributions.

The Federal Election Commission ruled that broadcasters could offer free time to political parties.

Charleston, South Carolina, police arrested four television journalists for broadcasting the picture of a suspect charged with killing two persons. The police hand-cuffed the general manager, the news-director, the anchor man, and a reporter. A rival TV station took pictures of the arrest. Ninth Circuit Solicitor Charles Cordon said, "This is not freedom of the press, but pure profit motive to make a buck and build ratings." John Rivers, president of WCSC-TV, said the solicitor's remarks were offensive and demeaning to the public's right to know. "If the police and the solicitor have the right to determine what the viewing and reading public can know and hear, then we are doomed to terminating our free society."

Martin Mary said television programs, especially sit-coms, should use a good dose of religious content to improve television even if doing so would cause some problems.

President Ronald Reagan ordered an expansion of government authority to withhold defense and foreign affairs information from the public. The White House complained about CBS early election returns and coverage. President Reagan called on news media to report only good news for a week instead of all the bad news. The Society of Professional Journalists gave President Reagan a failing performance grade on fourteen free press issues and a passing grade on only two during 1983. The only favorable marks were given for the State Department's resistance of UNESCO efforts to regulate journalists, and FCC chairman Mark Fowler's efforts to repeal regulation of broadcasters.

A 1983, order issued by President Reagan required that all persons having access to classified information had to sign a non-disclosure agreement as a condition of that access: anyone with a clearance for the higher "sensitive compartmented information" had to sign a non-disclosure agreement and to agree to pre-publication review, government agencies had to devise policies for regulating contacts with the news media to discourage leaks, and the development of investigative procedures to trace leaks including the forced use of polygraph tests on employees.

The Reagan Administration continued its campaign to weaken the Freedom of Information Act by proposing amendments to Congress and by cutting back fee waivers authorized journalists. The administration authorized heavy use of the secrecy stamp. Denial of access to the Grenada invasions for the news media was the first occasion of governmental denial to the media to a war zone in the history of the United States.

The Agents Identities Protection Act made it a crime to publish any information that identified an individual as a covert agent of the CIA or FBI even if the information was unclassified, or a public record, or obtained from public sources.

More than 160,000 federal employees signed contracts agreeing not to write or speak about intelligence related subjects without preclearance. This compliance was forced despite a congressional prohibition of such a procedure. The Reagan Administration's use of lie-detector tests to find government employees leaking information to the press met solid opposition in Congress, among employees, and the media.

The Reagan Administration imposed in contracts a policy on 100,000 employees who were forced to agree not to provide information unless cleared by administrative officials. The contract extended beyond the term of government employment until death. The Defense Department scrutinized 10,000 articles and books which it considered security-related. It also conducted 10,502 polygraph examinations of federal workers.

Alan Stanifield Turner had the tables turned on him by the CIA and had to fight censorship of his book. Earlier while he was CIA director he had prosecuted a former agent for failure to clear a manuscript.

The Foreign Agents Registration Act allowed the Justice Department to require labels on material coming from foreign nations. If the Department decided the material was political propaganda, a disclaimer had to be attached to it. Three Canadian films on acid rain and anti-nuclear war were so designated, but a court issued a temporary restraining order denying use of the labels.

The Central Intelligence Agency reaffirmed its ban on using journalists in agency activities.

Rep. Timothy Wirth and 130 co-sponsors asked the House to designate March 16 as Freedom of Information Day. The First Amendment Congress urged the action, based on the birthdate of James Madison. Several states quickly designated the date for state recognition.

The Society of Professional Journalists urged Congress in 1984 to repeal the Fairness Doctrine applied to radio and television broadcasting.

The FCC eliminated rules requiring television stations to broadcast public affairs programs, to limit commercial air time, and to maintain records of program broadcasting.

The Judicial Conference of the United States rejected a request from 28 news organizations to permit television or photo coverage of federal trials. The Conference was made up of 25 federal judges and Chief Justice Warren Burger. A few weeks later Burger asserted that no television or camera coverage would occur in the Supreme Court as long as he was Chief Justice.

The FCC ruled that political ads which were obscene or indecent could be rejected by broadcasters. Political Action Committees could not force broadcasters to accept advertising under the equal access rule for political candidates since PACs are not candidates.

Pornography became an eight billion dollar business. A federal law set penalties for procedures and distributors of kiddie pornography at a $100,000 fine plus ten years imprisonment for the first offense. The Justice Department established a commission to study the effects of pornography on society, and provided seminars to aid prosecutors to attack pornography. In the United States there were more than 20,000 adult book stores and 900 X-rated movie theaters. Department of Defense personnel spent $300,000 on dial-a-porn calls from the Pentagon.

Censorship: 500 Years of Conflict was a major exhibit presented in the Samuel and Jeanne H. Gottesman Exhibition Hall of the New York Public Library on 42nd street.

The National Coalition Against Censorship reported these books had recently been embroiled in litigation because of censorship efforts.

> Alexander, Rae Pace, and Julius Lester, eds., Young and Black in America
>
> Allen, Donald, Ed., The New American Poetry
>
> Anonymous, Go Ask Alice
>
> Archer, Jerome W., and A. Schwartz, eds., A Reader for Writers
>
> Blatty, William P., The Exorcist
>
> Blume, Judy, Are You There, God? It's Me, Margaret; Deenie; Then Again; Maybe I Won't
>
> Boston Women's Health Book Collective, Our Bodies, Ourselves
>
> Brautigan, Richard, The Abortion: An Historical Romance; The Pill Versus the Springhill Mine Disaster; A Confederate General from Big Sur; Rommel Drives on Deep into Egypt; Trout Fishing in America
>
> Burgess, Anthony, A Clockwork Orange
>
> Burroughs, William, and Allen Ginsberg, The Yage Letters
>
> Childress, Alice, A Hero Ain't Nothing But a Sandwich

Cleaver, Eldridge, Soul on Ice

Ferlinghetti, Lawrence, Coney Island of the Mind;
   Starting from San Francisco

Ginsberg, Allen, Kaddish and Other Poems

Heller, Joseph, Catch-22

Hughes, Langston, ed., The Best Short Stories by Negro
   Writers

Kesey, Ken., One Flew Over the Cuckoo's Nest

Larrick, Nancy, and Eve Merriam, eds., Male & Female
   Under 18

Levin, Ira, Rosemary's Baby; The Stepford Wives

Malamud, Bernard, The Fixer

Mann, Patrick, Dog Day Afternoon

Morris, Desmond, The Naked Ape

O'Hara, Frank, Lunch Poems

Plath, Sylvia, The Bell Jar

Price, Richard, The Wanderers

Simon, Sidney, Values Clarification

Thomas, Piri, Down These Mean Streets

Vonnegut, Kurt, Cat's Cradle; God Bless You, Mr.
   Rosewater; Slaughterhouse Five

Waxman, Stephanie, What Is a Girl? What Is a Boy?

Wright, Richard, Black Boy

Materials often censored in 1983 included The American
Heritage Dictionary, Newsweek, Of Mice and Men, The Diary of
Anne Frank, Doris Day: Her Own Story, Huckleberry Finn, and
Let's Talk About Health.

The United States Information Agency refused educational
certificates to a number of American documentary films which
impeded their use in other countries. The USIA said these
films presented a point of view, yet the agency certified
similar films having an opposite point of view.

National Security Decision Directive 84 was signed by
President Reagan in 1983. When it was instituted, heavy
objections caused the administration to rescind two sections,
but it retained thirteen others. Employees of the CIA and of
the National Security Agency have long been subjected to
censorship. For example, Charles E. Wilson, deputy director
of public affairs for the CIA, reported that between 1977 and

late 1984 the agency's Publication Review Board had reviewed 501 articles, 146 books, 60 book reviews, 29 speeches, 6 letters to editors, 21 outlines, and 6 scripts -- all written by CIA agents. The CIA stopped the publications of 15 items, forced changes in 212, but approved the remaining 274 in their original form.

Congress passed the Central Intelligence Agency Information Act which exempted CIA operational files from the federal Freedom of Information Act review and search provisions; however, CIA decisions are subject to review.

1985

The Federal Communications Commission planned to change its ownership restrictions for radio and television stations. The plan would allow ownership of as many as fourteen television stations. The first twelve would have to control no more than 25 per cent the "reach" of the nation's TV households. The owner could also buy into two additional stations which were owned primarily by minority persons controling more than 50 per cent of the shares of the additional stations, and could then increase the total audience "reach" to 30 per cent.

A Gallup poll indicated that 59 per cent of Americans believed that media should not be restricted in covering military operations.

Sen. Robert Packwood was awarded the 1985 Society of Professional Journalists First Amendment Award for his efforts to end federal content control regulations of broadcast media.

R. E. Carter Wrenn, director of the National Congressional Club, headed up Fairness in Media, Inc., in an effort to have conservatives allied with the Jesse Helms faction, buy stock in CBS to gain ownership or control of the network news operation. Ted Turner, owner of Cable News Network Television, also made efforts to purchase CBS. Both efforts failed.

People in Yuba City, California, staged a good-natured protest of being rated as the worst place to live in the United States by the Rand-McNally Company. As part of the spoof, they gathered all the maps and books produced by the company and tossed them in a bonfire.

The New York Times-Sullivan federal defense for libel demonstrated its strength in American courts by providing favorable court actions for defendants despite emotional rhetoric by the plaintiffs. General Ariel Sharon of Israel lost his $50 million suit against Time because he could not prove the magazine had exhibited malice. General William Westmoreland withrew his $100 million case from court because it became clear that he could neither prove falsity or malice on the part of CBS. Melvin Blasi lost his $85 million class action libel suit against two California banks because Blasi had thrust himself into a public controversy and had thus become a public figure required to prove malice.

The Office for Intellectual Freedom of the American Library Association reported that an increase of 300 per cent in reported censorships occurred between 1979 and 1985. Main battlegrounds for the more than 1,000 recent censorship efforts were the libraries of elementary and secondary schools. People for the American Way, a group that keeps records of attempts to challenge school programs and curricula, said that efforts to censor materials used in public schools had increased 66 per cent between 1982 and 1985. The California Board of Education rejected a series of science textbooks because publishers had catered to pressures to eliminate evolution study. The publishers agreed to revise the books to be scientifically accurate and comprehensive. The completed revisions, however, were so limited that science instructors criticized them heavily.

The House of Representatives voted 216 to 193 to stop the Library of Congress from printing a braille edition of **Playboy** magazine. Daniel Boorstin, librarian of Congress, called the action censorship.

August 4, 1985, was proclaimed as Freedom of the Press Day by President Reagan, commemorating August 4, 1935, the date John Peter Zenger won his colonial court case against seditious libel charges.

A President Commission on Obscenity was appointed to prepare a 1986 report for the United States Justice Department for use in recommending new control laws.

The National Conservative Federation planned a $1 million campaign to convince the public that the media had a liberal bias.

The Federal Communications Commission recommended that Congress discontinue the Fairness rule because the FCC believes it inhibited free speech and coverage of major issues.

X rated movies were widely available on video-tapes and became so popular for home viewing on VCR's that many X movie theaters went out of business.

1990

AT&T agreed not to engage in any electronic publishing activities until the end of seven years, or until about 1990. Its ownership of facilities would create an unsurmountable monopoly.

1991

December 15, 1991, marks the bicentennial of the date when the Bill of Rights, including the First Amendment's free press clause, went into effect as part of the constitutional law of the United States.

On September 24, 1789, the First Congress meeting in New York City submitted amendments to the Constitution to the states for ratification, which became the first ten amendments of the Constitution. They went into effect December 15, 1791; thus December 15, 1991, is a bicentennial date of great significance. The Committee on the Judiciary of the United States Senate introduced in 1982 legislation to establish a national commission to arrange for and encourage a bicentennial observance of the United States Constitution. Congress authorized the Commission in 1984 but it did not function until late 1985, and did so in secret meetings under the Chairmanship of Warren Burger, Chief Justice of the Supreme Court.

1994

The video-text market might be worth $500 million by 1994, with up to 80 per cent of its income from advertising, according to a 1984 *Videoprint* magazine.

1995

Telephone companies began installation of fiber optic cables in selected large cities in 1985 with the objective of having this multi-dimensional communications system in operation throughout the nation in the late 1990s.

43
Viewpoints and the Courts, 1983 to 1985

Gene Jankowski, president of the CBS Broadcast Group, said, in 1983, "If you believe -- as I do -- that a major cause of the world's problems today is prejudice, and if you also believe that ignorance is a root cause of prejudice, then you recognize the paramount importance of better communications. Through better communications we can have better understanding among the peoples of the world. Ignorance is one social ailment that we can do something about."

The First Amendment Congress, a coalition of media groups dedicated to the public's right to know, strongly objected to restraints placed on journalists attempting to cover the Grenada invasion. It said, "The First Amendment guarantees the American public more than a spoon-feeding of information by military and government spokesmen. Such methods of controlling the news defy tradition and deny the public access to information it needs and expects. The administration's Grenada press policy amounts to news censorship. We recognize and accept the need to keep military actions secret prior to execution. But, once troops are in combat, we cannot tolerate government policy that excludes or severely limits reporters and photographers."

Bob Schieffer, CBS news reporter, characterized the Reagan Administration National Security Directive 84 as a system of peacetime censorship that has no precedent in the nation's history. "It will dry up the reservoir of information, the pool of facts and opinions, upon which Americans draw to govern themselves."

Mike Wilkins, writing in The Observer student newspaper at the University of Notre Dame asked, "With such lofty goals as Father Hesburgh has expressed in his own book, why has the administration dealings with two student publications appeared so hardline? Are we really learning in an environment of freedom, or are we only free to learn as long as we do not offend those who teach us to be free?"

Burt Neuborne, national legal director of The American Civil Liberties Union, said:

> "But in the past few years, the government has gone beyond the attempt to control its own secrets, legitimate or otherwise. Now it is trying to restrict and control information and ideas that are <u>not</u> classified or that are <u>already circulating publicly outside the government</u>. If these attempts succeed, the government will be well on the way to establishing a system of offical censorship."

Joseph Costa, one of America's most noted photo-journalists, spent several years combatting an erroneous description of the role of photo-journalists covering the Hauptman trial for the kidnapping and murder of the Lindbergh baby, conducted in a small New York city court room. Local officials created and exploited the circus atmosphere around the court house and in its corridors. The judge would not allow picture taking in the court room except for one newsreel camera whose sound was muffled by an enclosing box. A substitute still camera photographer took pictures one day in violation of the judge's order because he did not know of those orders. At one point, the newsreel persons turned on their camera in violation of the judge's rules. It was only supposed to be used when the court was not in session to depict persons entering or leaving the room. The still photographer did not disturb the court and the newsreel camera was so silent no one knew it was operating. Costa took pictures of the news reel in a New York theater for use in his newspaper on Sunday. Since the principals in the trial were not available in the courtroom for pictures, the photographers tagged the word journalists around outside the court house. This caused a considerable hullabaloo outside the court at times, but the trial itself was decorous and dignified. Unfortunately, a person who had not been at the trial reported incorrectly several years later that the trial had been made a shambles by loud, aggressive photographers who invaded the court room with shouts and noise, even jumping on tables and thrusting cameras in the faces of witnesses and others. No such thing happened; this false report was used by the American Bar Association to set up its Canon 35 which kept cameras from American court rooms for many years.

Ann Kahn, member of the Fairfax County, Virginia, school board, told a forum on censorship and book selections, that "One sentence does not a bad book make, and a dictionary shouldn't be thrown out just because of four entries."

Mark Fowler, chairman of the Federal Communications Commission, said, "I take an absolutionist approach to all attempts to control the content of broadcasting. They're simply censorship."

Floyd Abrams, a constitutional lawyer in New York City, wrote in the <u>New York Times</u> that "in the two and a half years it has been in power, the Reagan Administration has:

"Consistently sought to limit the scope of the Freedom of Information Act.

"Inhibited the flow of films into and even out of our borders; neither Canada's academy award-winning "If You Love This Planet" nor the acclaimed ABC documentary about toxic waste, "The Killing Ground," escaped Administration disapproval.

"Rewritten the classification system to assure that more rather than less information will be classified.

"Subjected governmental officials to an unprecedented system of lifetime censorship.

"Flooded universities with a torrent of threats relating to their right to publish and discuss unclassified information -- usually of a scientific or technological nature -- on campus."

"The effect of the new guidelines is to permit the government itself to decide what information about its conduct is "meaningful," Abrams said.

Herbert Schmertz, vice president for public affairs for Mobil Oil Corporation, led a strong attack on the press stemming from the corporation's efforts to place editorial advertising and oppose articles the corporation considered unfair and unfavorable. He told USA Today that:

"It's our view that its performance in terms of responding to the needs of society could be improved. We think the press, to some extent, follows a code of conduct for itself which the public does not accept and which the public has become increasingly cynical and disenchanted about. The increasing, widespread use of unnamed sources, the increasing use of tactics to get material -- receiving stolen documents from sources, and very poor editing of reporters' activities. Editors, in our view, increasingly fail to ask tough questions of their reporters. The press has placed a premium on reporting things that tend to undermine the public confidence in our institutions. They have distorted what the world is all about in this country." In one of the Corporation's "advertorials", Mobil said, "At any given time, the pubic can withdraw the privileges it has accorded the media if they are no longer serving the public interest. All the free institutions in our society are constantly subjected to this test, and the media do themselves no good in seeking special immunity through fostering the myth of the threatened First Amendment."

Senator Bob Packwood, in an editorial supporting the proposed Freedom of Expression Act of 1983, said:

"Despite the intent of our founders, freedom of expression is abridged in this country. Despite the fact that there are 9,000 radio stations, over 1,000 televisions stations, and a huge diversity of programming available to the consumer through cable television, broadcasters are shackled while the press remains free. Based on law that was written in the age of the crystal set, we have created two classes of media; the press, with full freedom to express its opinion, and radio and television, which cannot. The subordinate status of the electronic media should trouble the print media. Communications technology is merging the two. This convergence may soon undercut pleas for First Amendment protections from publishers."

Harker Collins, testifying before the Citizen's Choice National Commission on a Free and Responsible Media Dialogue on the Media, Business, and Economy said:

"Businesses must also recognize that just as with their own products, there is an art to selling news. The media cannot be faulted for practicing that art. Though, I must say, that it is not unreasonable for business to expect that, in the practice of that art, the media adopt a responsible posture consistent with the professionalism required of such an important community service. The media continually demonstrates an expectation for this type of responsibility on the part of other businesses. The media should exercise as much responsibility as it expects of others."

As part of its 75th Anniversary in 1984, the Society of Professional Journalists, Sigma Delta Chi published 224 letters and statements made or written by leading American media personalities discussing their perceptions of the values of a free press in American Society.

President Ronald Reagan said, on the occassion of National Newspaper Week for 1984, that:

"The theme of the 1984 observance of National Newspaper Week, 'Newspapers Lighting Freedom's Way,' provides us with an opportunity to reflect on the importance of this institution to our way of life. As Herbert Hoover once said, 'Freedom of the press is a foundation stone of American liberty.' The Statue of Liberty stands as a beacon guide our great Republic through these troubled times just as a strong, independent, and free press illuminates our country's journey with the light of freedom's way."

Pope John Paul II said, "Pray so the social world of communications carries out with fidelity its function to serve the truth, liberty, the promotion of man." He called upon media to present a positive picture of man and not concentrate on bad news.

Edward M. Joyce, president of CBS News, said: "This is not the first time in recent history when we in journalism have been under attack from a group which wants its narrow ideological bias to control the press and ultimately the country."

Sen. Jesse Helms of North Carolina told members of the Conservative Political Action Conference that "the real threat to freedom of speech and the real threat to our constitutional system is on our TV screens every evening and on the front pages of our newspapers everyday."

George Keyworth, science adviser to President Reagan, told the Scientists' Institute for Public Information that:

"we're trying to build up America, and the press is trying to tear down America. There are several reasons. Number one, for some reasons that I just do not understand, much of the press seems to be drawn from a relatively narrow fringe element on the far left of our society. Number two, there's an arrogance that has to do with the power of the press. It's easier to achieve power by being negative and tearing at foundations." Secretary of State George P. Shultz said, after the Grenada invasion, that American reporters were not on our side but always against us. They are against our side militarily -- in other words, all of America."

Upon being informed that 42 per cent of the high school graduates of the Land of Id were illiterate, the King quipped, "It won't be long now before we can do away with censorship."

The Supreme Court ruled in the Ferber case that pictures or depictions of children engaging in sexual activities were so odious that the state had a sufficiently compelling interest to regulate such material even if it did not meet the tripartite rules of the Miller test of obscenity. Such material is not protected by the First Amendment.

The Supreme Court ruled that broadcasters could present public issue commercials that did not identify the true sponsor.

The Supreme Court let stand a Court of Appeals ruling in the Ad World case, that shopper and free distribution newspapers are more than mere commercial speech and are entitled to First Amendment protection; ordinances restricting distribution were unconstitutional.

A known false statement and false statements made with reckless disregard of the truth do not have constitutional protection, according to the Apple Tree case.

The Supreme Court in a 5 to 4 decision decided students could challenge in court a school board's decision to remove books from school libraries. The case began in 1975 after the Island Trees Union Free School District Board of Education on Long Island removed nine books they had been told were objectionable by a pressure group.

In the Bose case, the Supreme Court reaffirmed the principles it enunciated in the New York Times-Sullivan case requiring public officials to prove actual malice or reckless disregard of the truth to prevail in libel cases as a necessary role of the higher courts, which have reversed three-fourths of the adverse libel judgments made against the press by lower courts.

A court cannot find motion picture producers liable for the actions of persons seeing the movie because such an imposition would be too chilling of the selection of subjects suitable for filming. This would be a First Amendment violation, according to the Bill case.

Video game entertainment is not protected expression under the First Amendment, according to the Caswell case.

A United States Court of Appeals upheld the FCC's deregulation of radio actions. A Court of Appeals ruled that the FCC policy on children's programming was not a flat requirement forcing broadcasters to provide regularly scheduled weekday children's programs.

Freelance Photographer Ronald Galella, after being threatened with a heavy fine, ended ten years of photographing Jacqueline Kennedy Onassis and her children. She obtained an injunction against him in 1972, and he was ordered in 1975 by the court to stay 25 feet away from her and 30 feet away from her children. Gallela had violated these rules twelve times.

The right of the press to observe criminal trials does not extend to televising, recording and broadcasting trials. Court rules about the time, place, and manner of access of the press to observe criminal trials are constitutional if they are reasonable, promote significant government interest, and do not abridge communication of thought, according to the Hastings case.

A federal judge in Los Angeles ruled the Public Broadcasting System television stations and National Public Radio stations could broadcast editorials and also declared an FCC regulation against editorializing was unconstitutional.

The Supreme Court ruled in a Metromedia case that billboards containing non-commercial speech could not be banned; however, regulations of commercial messages could be established.   In the Milliner v. Turner case, the Court said, the choice of content of the material to go into a state college student newspaper is an exercise of editorial control and judgment, and regulation of this editoral process by the college administration would be inconsistent with the guarantees of a free press of the First Amendment. The government is denied the power to exercise prior restraint on expression with regard to public areas, including state college campuses, because of the message, ideas, subject matter, or content. The relationship between a university and its student newspaper is anomalous and cannot be compared with a publisher and its newspaper, since the publisher may exercise censorship to the fullest as it deems commercially proper to do so, while the state university is almost completely barred from censoring its student newspaper.

Minnesota's tax on paper and ink used for publications

could not replace a sales tax since it would single out the press for a special tax burden and would be a threat to First Amendment rights.

Public broadcasting stations may decide what programs they will broadcast, and listeners disagreeing with such decisions do not have any First Amendment rights violated. KUHT-TV decided not to broadcast <u>Death of a Princess</u>, as did the Alabama ETV network. The Fifth Circuit Court of Appeals ruled in the Muir case the broadcasters had operated within their First Amendment rights.

The Supreme Court refused to block public access to the tapes covering the Nixon presidency. It ruled that the use of a 1974 legislative veto law was unconstitutional, but allowed the General Service Administration to establish regulations for releasing 1,500,000 documents about the Nixon situation.

Courts ruled ordinances in Ohio and Maryland that restricted the rights of commercial speech on billboards to be unconstitutional.

A Court in Philadelphia ruled that a township could not restrict the distribution of shopper newspapers.

Princeton University could not convince the Supreme Court to hear its appeal of a Circuit Court of Appeals ruling in favor of Chris Schmid. The university had denied him the right to distribute socialist newspapers, even though other publications were freely distributed. The Court said that changes in the Princeton rules made the legal issues moot. The Circuit Court of Appeals thus set something of a precedent indicating that private colleges cannot infringe upon First Amendment rights.

The Securities and Exchange Commission had no authority to review, censor, or in any way restrain investment advisory material prior to publication.

Programs broadcast over the air by television stations may be recorded on video cassettes since such an act is fair use of copyrighted materials and does not require the payment of royalties, according to a Sony case.

In the Stanley case, the editors of the <u>Minnesota Daily</u> sued the president and the board of regents for changing the newspaper's financial base. The Court ruled that a public university cannot unconstitutionally take adverse action against a student newspaper, such as withdrawing or reducing funds, because the university disapproves of the content. The action resulted in a loss of revenues to the newspaper and had a chilling effect on the newspaper's future content. The university's motive, in reducing the funding, was a response to public outcry against the offensive contents of one edition of the newspaper. Newspapers in other branches of the university did not suffer similar funding changes. The university did not like the ruling of the state's Appellate Court and appealed to the United States Circuit Court of Appeals of the Eighth Circuit. A three-judge panel upheld the judgment of the lower court. The university, still unsatisfied, moved to have the full panel of the Court rule on the case, but the United States Court of Appeals for the Eighth Circuit voted 4 to 4 not to grant a rehearing in 1984. The settlement of the case caused the University to pay the student newspaper $183,000 for legal fees and restitution of funds withheld.

The motion picture rating of X cannot be used to establish that a film is legally pornographic in place of a judicial hearing, according to the Swope case.

Five persons were arrested for defiant trespass while distributing leaflets at Muhlenberg College, a private institution. The Pennsylvania Supreme Court reversed a guilty verdict because the state constitution protected the right to use public areas of the campus which had been used by others as a place of public forum. Although the private college could protect its property, its vague rules about the distribution of publications were completely unreasonable, according to the Tate case.

The First Amendment did not immunize a reporter from testifying before a grand jury as to what he saw, heard, felt, and experienced personally when two crime figures were involved in an assault outside the courtroom and in his presence, according to the Ziegler case.

The Ninth Circuit Court of Appeals ruled that more than one franchised cable television company could serve an area because an exclusive license would create an impermissible risk of covert discrimination based on the content of the views expressed in the operator's proposed programming. The ruling was headed to the Supreme Court for a final decision.

The Supreme Court ruled that material's arousing lustful thoughts was constitutionally protected expression because feelings of lust were healthy reactions.

44
Press Control and New Dictators, 1980 and Beyond

UNESCO issued its 1980 report of its International Commission for the Study of Communications Problems, otherwise known as the MacBride Commission, in a book entitled <u>Many Voices, One World: Communication and Society Today and Tomorrow</u>; it said:

> "Such values as truthfulness, accuracy, respect for human rights are not universally applied at present. Higher professional standards and responsibility cannot be imposed by decree, nor do they depend solely on the goodwill of individual journalists, who are employed by institutions which can improve or handicap their professional performance. Voluntary measures can do much to influence media performance. Nevertheless it appears necessary to develop further effective ways by which the right to assess mass media performance can be exercised by the public. All those working in the mass media should contribute to the fulfillment of human rights. The media could contribute to promoting the just cause of peoples struggling for freedom and independence and their right to live in peace and equality without foreign interference. Censorship or arbitrary control of information should be abolished."

The conference set up a formal International Program for the Development of Communication.

Sean MacBride said, "Surely it is time to draw up national and international standards on journalistic practices, not only to protect journalists on perilous assignments, but to guarantee their freedom in carrying out professional tasks."

England decided video-cassettes were covered by its 1959 Obscenity Act. Pornography was accepted as part of London life.

1981

Timothy Sainsbury got his Private Members Bill through Parliament to control pornography and indecency with heavy fines and stiff jail sentences.   But the English pornographers made a shambles of it as enhancement for their wares, which they labeled with the law's admonitions.

Primary areas of concern of world wide communications covered news flow, mass culture, technology transfer, national sovereignity, and communications rights.

Jozef Cardinal Glemp, Roman Catholic Primate of Poland, said, "The mass media often gives a distorted view of life, so that often man does not know how to deal with that which is written.   The world of political journalism, of speculation, again showed itself to be superficial."

All of the recommendations of the study groups of the Conference Toward an American Agenda for a New World Order of Communication reflected historical values that have permeated American communication practices.

Russian journalists claimed and believed that they had a free press.

Chad's rulers, established by a coup in early 1983, set up censorship of foreign journalists.

A sex shop clause of the Local Government Miscellaneous Provisions Bill and The Indecent Display Bill of 1981 were mild English controls of pornography.

The National Guard of Panama occupied the offices of La Prensa and caused considerable damage for which it refused to pay.

1983

The French Minister of the Rights of Women had to tone down her speech seeking a law in the National Assembly because in its original form it violated existing obscenity laws.

A crowd of several hundred persons attacked eight foreign journalists in Karachi.

The channels of dissent employed by individuals and groups include underground samizdat or self-published literature circulated in the Soviet Union and smuggled to the West.   An English language newscaster for Radio Moscow no longer was heard after broadcasting for two days that Soviet troops entering Afghanistan were "invaders".

Canada set up its first Freedom of Information law.

The annual general assembly of the International Press Institute passed resolutions condemning harrassment and

persecution of the press in South Africa. It criticized
Argentina, Brazil, Uruguay, and Nicaragua. Committee on
Freedom of the Press and Information of the Inter American
Press Association said, "Governments continue to close and
harrass newspapers, censor news, imprison journalists, and
conspire to restrict the flow of news." Garcia Lavin of
Mexico reported that the Inter American Press Association,
sent 36 protests about press violations to 23 countries in
his year as president of the organization.

Horacio Aguirre, publisher of _Novedades de Yucatan_,
said, "One of the most serious threats against freedom of
expression in the world is the increasing use of licensing
for journalists."

Terrorists kidnapped Pedro Julio, editor of _Prensa Libre_
and held him for two weeks. The Sandanista government
harrassed, closed, censored, and intimidated _La Prensa_ of
Managua, but eased restrictions on the paper's efforts to
obtain newsprint. News media in El Salvador were threatened
and vandalized by both left and right extremists. Chilean
authorities arrested the editor of _Analisis_ magazine.
Chile's constitution gives the president power to restrict
new publications. Columbia required a license of
journalists. During the year three newsmen were murdered.
Newspaper, radio, and magazine personnel were arrested and
intimidated in Paraguay.

Senegal and Cuba defended UNESCO proposals for
restraints on information under the New World Order of
Information and Communication.

Fernando Belaunde Terry, president of Peru, said,
"Freedom of expression is so fundamental an ingredient of
democracy that it must be preserved even at the cost of
enduring excesses and abuses." His election in 1980 returned
democratic government and freedom of the press after the
nation had been under military dictatorship for several
years. He said the free flow of information including that
critical of his administration must be protected because he
believed freedom of expression cannot be hampered with
restraints of any kind. He said excesses of the press
resulting in a climate of free expression are eclipsed in the
truthful, guiding, and respectable light of a free press.
Even so, Peru has a Collegium of Journalists paid for by an
assessment on newspapers.

Uraguay suspended _El Dia_ for an article about Wilson
Aldunate, an exiled politician. Gonzalez Delvalle, a
Paraquayan editor, was jailed, and held incommunicado without
charges. He was turned lose after 76 days. The government
of the Cayman Islands dropped its efforts to discontinue the
principle of qualified privilege for reporting public
meetings. Haiti, Cuba, Guyana, and Grenada (prior to the
United States invasion) had no freedom of the press of any
kind. Efforts to re-establish a free press in Grenada began
after the invasion. For at least eight years, journalists in
Argentina were jailed, threatened and put under survellience.
Brazil's national security law and press law ominously hung
over the press. The Jamaican government owned all television

and radio broadcasting facilities in that nation.

Each year the International Press Institute of London and Zurich took inventory throughout the world. The conclusion for 1983 indicated journalists generally were living in an age of severe repression which had become worse world-wide year by year. The institute estimated that only 24 of 86 covered nations, mostly in the West had a press free enough to criticize governments or publish opposition views. In 1983 it made sixty-five formal protests to governments for press repression. Turkey had the worst record with its fining and jailing of editors and reporters. South Africa had convicted or threatened 15 editors and 24 newspapers for failure to support the government's pro-white racist view. Reporters had been threatened with death in Eastern bloc nations, Asia, Latin America, and Africa.

Costa Rica sentenced an American journalist to three months in jail for practicing journalism illegally. Raids by Canadian officials on several Thompson newspapers violated the Canadian Constitution. Zimbabwe, Zambia, Mozambique, Angola, Tanzania, and Botswana banned foreign correspondents.

A seminar on the Future for Books in the Electronics Era speculated that the future would see:

1. A book would be a bubble-wrapped package containing a dust jacket and a computer chip from which the text is printed out at home.

2. Publishers will print out books when ordered and not stock them.

3. Information will be in computerized data books, but literature and poetry may still be in books.

4. Language usage may change to staccato TV-talk.

5. Electronic technology may create an isolated living room culture.

The conference report was prepared by J. Robert Maskin, senior editor for the Aspen Institute which co-sponsored the Jerusalem seminar with the Jerusalem International Book Fair.

12,000 feet of film shot by ABC for a news documentary on Black labor unions was sabotaged before it left South Africa.

The Sandanista government of Nicaragua continued to harrass La Prensa and freedom of the press. The Panama National Guard inflicted heavy damages upon the newspaper La Prensa and confiscated newspapers belonging to the Panama America publishing company, and Radio Impacto. Cuba imprisoned Luis Rodriguez of El Pais and Fernando Rivas of Bohemia for more than twenty years. Paraquay expelled several journalists, restricted materials needed by independent newspapers, and imprisoned journalists. Peru increased taxes on newsprint to weaken newspaper financial positions. Eight journalists were massacred in Uchuraccay,

Peru. Uraguay prohibited information about political activities, closed at least six newspapers, harrassed journalists with police interrogations, and devised other publishing restrictions.

Polish police held briefly American and West German television networks in Gdansk when they tried to cover a demonstration supporting the Rev. Henryk Jankowski whose sermons on religious freedom had been called slanderous by the government.

1984

Jacobo Timmerman, an Argentine journalist exiled for four years, returned to his country after civilian rule was re-established following the ouster of the military dictatorship. He became a chief witness in the prosecution of the officers who jailed and tortured him for 30 months, stripped him of his citizenship, and exiled him to Israel.

Nigeria created a law giving the government authority to shut down newspapers and radio stations and to jail reporters for stories that ridicule the government.

Ranka Cicak, a Yugoslav journalist, was convicted of damaging that nation's reputation by criticizing former President Tito.

In Chile, six opposition newspapers were shut down, and very tight censorship for all other media was enforced. Only opposition publication permitted to continue was Hoy, the Christian Democratic weekly, which had to submit copy for a 48-hour review.

Turkey stopped efforts to circulate a petition protesting press censorship.

India banned journalists from the Sikh riot areas.

Paraquay closed down ABC Color, that nation's independent newspaper. The majority of Latin American nations continued heavy press repression and control.

Scott Lind was sent to Mexico by the McAllen Monitor to cover a hunger strike by workers at the Zenith Electronics plant in Reynosa. He was arrested, booked, handcuffed, blindfolded, beaten, and shocked by electronic cattle prods to force a confession that he had come to Reynosa to stir up labor troubles and to rape homsexually a laborer.

Juvencio Mazzarallo, a magazine editor, was convicted in Brazil of violating national security for articles about the government's treatment of persons living near a hydro-electric project. Stephen Schmidt was convicted of practicing journalism without a license by the Costa Rican Supreme Court.

In its 1984 report of a Comparative Survey of Freedom created by Freedom House for its January Map of Freedom, fifty-two nations were depicted as maintaining freedom for the press.   There were fifty-six nations providing partial freedom of the press.   All other nations practiced severe press repression and control.   Repression appeared mostly in Asia, eastern Europe, Arabian areas, and in Africa.

Polish government newspapers began publishing explicit sex articles and other entertaining contents in efforts to regain circulation that had been lost to the 700 underground newspapers produced by Polish journalists who began such publications in defiance of the 1981 Polish martial law order which suppressed hundreds of regular publications.

1985

Even after the United States withdrew from UNESCO in 1985, press organizations in the United States continued efforts to keep UNESCO from approving press control by government regulation.

News personnel of the British Broadcasting Company went on a 24-hour strike to protect a refusal by management to broadcast an interview with an Irish terrorist at the request of the government.   Many commercial newscasters joined in the strike in an effort to convince the government to refrain from censorship efforts in the future.

Chinese officals dropped charges against a reporter they had detained for several months after they had searched his office without a warrant.   Newspapers reported three additional government press harrassment episodes.

Adam Michnik and Maciej Polewski, were two of the leading underground and opposition writers and publishers in Poland.   Police seized Polewski, bloodied his head, but couldn't keep him from shouting his name and pseudonym and publishing agency to bystanders as he was led from an apartment where he had been visiting his children.

The Inter American Press Association reported that in El Salvador, staff members of El Diario were intimidated by the government which also used placement of advertising and foreign exchange allocation needed to purchase newsprint to pressure newspapers and taxes to do the same for radio and television.

Complete government control of the press existed in Nicaragua, Chile, Cuba, Guyana, Suriname, and Paraguay. Journalists in Costa Rica, the Dominican Republic, Colombia, Venzuela, Honduras, Panama, Ecudor, and Peru could only work if authorized by a journalists' collegium or by government license.   Freedom of the press possibilities were improved in Argentina, Brazil, Uraguay, and Guatemala, where journalists timidly practiced self-censorship.   Mexican terrorists killed three journalists and a news photographer.

South Africa imposed severe press censorship as rioting and unrest esculated because of the government's aparthied policies.   South African journalists were jailed, and American and other television news coverage was virtually eliminated.   But the restraints actually proved to be ineffective.

Under the strict provisions of its Official Secrets Act, inherited from the British, Malaya arrested one reporter for disclosing that the government planned to buy United States AWACS planes. Earlier a reporter was jailed for articles about Malaysian-Chinese relations.

All newspapers in Israel are licensed by the government. Alef Yad, a West Bank settlers newspaper was shut down because the government believed it was initiating rebellion.

The Uganda military government imposed strict press controls.

At the end of 1985, the United Kingdom withdrew from UNESCO in protest of its new information order of press control.

1989

At least 19 major international conferences were planned between 1980 and 1989 to study and decide how the electromagnetic spectrum, the basic building blocks of communication, would be allocated among the nations.

1991

The world probably would have 523 million main telephone stations in operation by 1991 according to a telecommunications study by Arthur D. Little.

45
The Promise of the Twenty-First Century

Between the bicentennial of the Bill of Rights in 1991 and
the end of the Twentieth Century only nine years remained.
In the 1980's, media watchers predicted tremendous
technological changes that would alter completely the media
mix in place in 2000. Much of the change seemed to indicate
that electronic media utilizing broadcast, cable, satellite,
and telephonic transmission using computers and readers would
be everywhere.

Predicting the future of communication, Business Week,
in its Fiftieth Anniversary issue, confidently stated, "By
2029, the communications and information-processing
technology available to business people and consumers will be
infinitely more powerful than today's. Individuals on
opposite sides of the globe will be able to see each other in
living color as they talk. Robots will do most of the
production jobs in the manufacturing plants that remain.
Problems with products or machines -- even health problems --
will be diagnosed electronically from remote locations.
Broadcasting in its present form will give way to the
superior transmission and individual programming will be made
possible in digital, wired networks."

The first efforts to develop such communications marvels
as teletext and video-text met with little financial success.
The cost to the new owners was prohibitive. Simpler units
just didn't deliver much. Some of the description of the new
devices read suprisingly like the description of facsimile
newspapers transmitted to living rooms prior to and following
World War II. These wondrous and attractive but far too
limited publications lost their financial hope when
commercial television arrived fully by 1950. The arrival of
video cassettes, available at low purchase or rental prices,
delayed the commercial development of the exotic
transmitters.

Computers were hyped throughout society as a panacea for education, data storage, marketing, and computation. Less important were graphics creation capabilities and word processing, both great conveniences.

Actually the true value of the computer was its ability to access huge data banks where unlimited information and entertainment could be stored. The other computer uses were of limited, and perhaps even trivial consequence. And the expense could be horrendous when purchasing copyright data transmitted via common carrier or via scrambled cable or satellite signal. Sixty-five million subscribers could purchase their newspapers and supplementary books and magazines for a total annual investment of about $250 per year in the United States during the 1980s. Data bank charges would eat this amount up in a month. And the additional electronic equipment needed by the individual user would cost at least $1,000 and probably three times as much. Persons working in the areas of developing electronic media were enthusiastic about the future of such devices. They predicted fortunes in the Twenty-first Century, and proclaimed the end of print media. Actually, neither the mechanical or electronic means of transmitting expression in and by themselves can determine the significance of expression. They may enhance its pleasurability or its misery, but the substance the expression produces is its lasting effect on comprehension and understanding. Effective communication can be achieved through many approaches and media. Rather than being a threat, improved media could presage an era of improved communications if they were to be affordable and cost-accountable as profit driven agencies.

Can the media of the future be afforded by sufficient numbers of viewers or users? Can the media be corporately organized to be continuing economic enterprises? Can the media live long enough because of rapid obseleting caused by new media even more promising? Generations of electronic media high tech and computers last only a few years, far too short a period to realize a return on heavy investment.

Can the media charge enough and obtain enough commercial message utilization to make enough money to rely upon adequate income from that source? The fractionalization of the audience which would occur by too many units, too much program selectivity, and too few viewers would make advertising too expensive for an advertiser. Smaller audiences and lower rates would be disastrous to profit motivated operations.

The question is not whether advertising messages can be made effective. The question hinges upon the ability of a media to deliver the advertising message efficiently to an audience of a sufficient number of potential customers at a low and reasonable cost per customer.

Two restraining agencies could restrict the content allowable in electronic media. The first would be the prejudices and selections of corporate ownership. Such a problem has existed since the invention of the printing press, but a new corporate establishment could be more repressive than the old press lords. Even with such worries of the print era, almost anyone for little money could buy handbills, or publish a newspaper, and go to the public prints, with messages and viewpoints. The other problem is the Federal Communications Commission, a government agency created to control radio broadcasting, largely at the insistence of the radio industry of the 1920s. The FCC subsequently became a government control agency regulating television regardless of its transmission system (including cable and/or fiber optics), radio of all types, and common carriers such as telephone systems. Although efforts to relax regulations occurred from time to time, the FCC would have to respond to possible legislation requiring a stiffening of those regulations. Since the managers of FCC controlled media voluntarily agree to those regulatory powers and rules when applying for licensing, the First Amendment protection becomes very cloudy. If virtually all mass communication would be via government regulated media, dissent would become a marshmallow. Efforts were frequently made to eliminate or weaken the FCC, but the Congress was reluctant to give up the politican's equal access notion, and the fine sounding fairness phrase for others.

Because of a sustained, comprehensive, and bitter campaign conducted by conservative political and religious organizations, the press -- meaning newspapers and network news programming -- lost credibility among readers and viewers. About the time this public criticism seemed to be devastating, however, the anti-press elements became involved in stupid if not corrupt gaffs which restored the press to a more favored role.

Supreme Court judges have a record of paying less attention to political bias and pressure and of giving more attention to constitutional and statuatory law after their appointments to the high courts. By 2000 the composition of the Supreme Court would be a matter of conjecture only.

If a constitutional convention where to occur, freedom of the press and the First Amendment could become victims of a repressive agenda manipulated by elements in society which really do not want or believe in free expression. Call for a constitutional convention was pushed by school prayer advocates, anti-abortion groups, anti-feminists, and balanced budget demanders. A convention could ultimately re-write the entire Bill of Rights.

The Twenty-First Century is fraught with dangers for a free press, including the awesome possibility that not many persons would really care about a guarantee of freedom of the press or expression or speech for themselves, or anyone else, let alone the protection of the First Amendment.

An atmosphere similar to the philosophy and societal controls during the Tory dominations of England and its American colonies seemed to permeate the United States in many aspects of contemporary life. National and international developments could swing the pendulum away from Toryism back toward libertarianism, or back and forth several times.

In society, as well as in physics, the phenomenon of the rise of equal forces to oppose forces initiated in the universe exists. This means that just as anti-press feelings or threats have or may arise, pro-press beliefs and attitude tend to arise and ultimately equalize the threats of adverse actions.

Media, both print and electronic, either singly or in organized efforts, have presented pro-freedom of the press and First Amendment materials in an increasing amount. The First Amendment Congress could become a very effective avenue for raising the levels of understanding of First Amendment values and provisions.

Perhaps Congress can put the Federal Communications Commission in its proper place.

It is doubtful that the new electronic media will shove print and other electronic media into oblivion. Print media began an updating of content and appearance that made them more readable and appearance-wise competitive with the electronic media. The cost of frequent or occasional print media communication and its facility for thorough distribution for a geographic area will make such efforts ever effective. Commercial newspapers may even give up subscriptions income, which is not very revenue producing anyhow, to achieve 100 per cent coverage of a population.

Americans have a rather fierce tradition of independence and freedom of thought that guides them individually. In the face of an overwhelming or opposing majority opinion, individuals take the stump, make pronouncements, distribute leaflets, and raise all sorts of political hell to present a different view. Surprisingly such views with persistence, manage to prevail form time to time.

If government regulation can be limited, if the courts continue reading the Constitution, if that Constitution can remain intact, if programs of education about First Amendment values can be presented in and out of schools, and if the media can improve performance, the Twenty-First century is not a fearsome era for freedom of the press, even though challenges to that freedom will continue to surface almost every day in the United States. The century will be a challenging and exciting opportunity to strengthen and expand freedom of the press for all Americans.

The Twenty-First century will need its Thomas Jefferson, James Madison, and Justice Douglas to remind us all, in the great rhetoric of three centuries, that freedom of the press, that great palladium of liberty, is the basis of all our rights and liberties.

Selected Bibliography
and Index

Selected Bibliography

The Adversary Press. St. Petersburg, FL: Modern Media Institute, 1983.

Alexander, James (S.N. Katz, editor). A Brief Narrative of the Case and Trial of John Peter Zenger. Cambridge, MA: Harvard University Press, 1963.

Ambler, Effie. Russian Journalism and Politics 1861-1881. Detroit: Wayne State University Press, 1972.

American Enterprise Institute. Freedom of the Press. Washington DC: American Enterprise Institute, 1976.

American Library Association. Censorship, Litigation and the Schools. Chicago, IL: American Library Association, 1983.

Bailyn, Bernard, and John B. Hench. The Press and the American Revolution. Boston: Northeastern University Press, 1981.

Bailyn, Bernard. The Idealogical Origins of the American Revolution. Cambridge, MA: The Belknap Press of Harvard University Press, 1973.

Barron, Jerome A. Public Rights and the Private Press. Toronto, Canada: Butterworths, 1981.

Barron, Jerome A., and C. Thomas Dienes. Handbook of Free Speech and Free Press. Boston: Little, Brown and Company, 1979.

Bennett, H. S. English Books and Readers (1475-1640). Cambridge: Cambridge University Press, 1965-1970. (Three Volumes)

Berger, Fred R. Freedom of Expression. Belmont, CA:

Wadsworth Publishing Company, 1980.

Berger, Melvin. Censorship. New York, NY: Franklin Watts, 1982.

Berns, Walter F. The First Amendment and the Future of American Democracy. New York: Basic Books, Inc., 1976.

Bleyer, Willard Grosvenor. Main Currents in the History of American Journalism. Boston: Houghton-Mifflin, 1927.

Bohun, Edmund. Freedom of the Press, 1664-1693. New York: Garland (Reprinting), 1975.

Bosmajian, Haig A. Censorship, Libraries, and the Law. New York, NY: Neal-Schuman, 1983.

Bosmajian, Haig A. Obscenity and Freedom of Expression. New York, NY: Burt Franklin, 1976.

Boyce, G., et at, editors. Newspaper History. Beverley Hills, CA: Sage Publications, 1978.

Boyer, Paul S. Purity in Print. New York: Charles Scribner's Sons, 1965.

Brant, Irving. The Bill of Rights. New York: The New American Library, 1965.

Brenner, David L., and William L. Rivers. Free But Regulated: Conflicting Traditions in Media Law. Ames, IA: Iowa State University Press, 1982.

Brigham, Clarence S. History and Biliography of American Newspapers, 1690-1820. Worcester, MA: American Antiquarian Society, 1947.

Busha, Charles H. Freedom v. Suppression and Censorship. Littleton, CO: Libraries Unlimited, 1972.

Calvocoressi, Peter. Freedom to Publish. New Jersey: Humanities Press, 1980.

Carter, T.B., M.A. Franklin, and J.B. Wright. The First Amendment and The Fourth Estate. Mineola, NY: Foundation Press, 1985.

Carter, T.B., M.A. Franklin, and J.B. Wright. The First Amendment and The Fifth Estate. Mineola, NY: The Foundation Press, 1986.

Cavennah, Frances. Freedom Encyclopedia. Chicago: Rand McNally, 1968.

Chafee, Zechariah, Jr. The Blessing of Liberty. Philadelphia: Lippincott, 1956.

Chafee, Zechariah, Jr. Government and Mass Communications. Chicago: University of Chicago, 1947.

Chafee, Zechariah, Jr. *Free Speech in the United States*. Cambridge, MA: Harvard University Press, 1941.

Chamberlain, Bill F., and Charlene J. Brown, editors. *The First Amendment Reconsidered*. New York and London: Longman, 1982.

Chenery, William Ludlow. *Freedom of the Press*. New York: Harcourt Brace, 1955.

Clor, Harry M. *Obscenity and Public Morality: Censorship in a Liberal Society*. Chicago: University of Chicago Press, 1969.

Clyde, William M. *The Struggle for the Freedom of the Press from Caxton to Cromwell*. New York: Burt Franklin Reprinting, 1974.

Collins, Keith S., ed. *Responsibility and Freedom in the Press*. Washington, DC: Citizens Choice, 1985.

Commission on Freedom of the Press. *A Free and Responsible Press*. Chicago: University of Chicago Press, 1947.

Comstock, Anthony. *Traps for the Young*. New York: Funk and Wagnalls, 1883.

Comstock, G. *Television in America*. Beverley Hills, CA: Sage Publications, 1980.

Countryman, Vern, editor. *The Douglas Opinions*. New York: Berkley Publishing Company, 1977.

Cox, Archibald. *Freedom of Expression*. Cambridge, MA: Harvard University Press, 1981.

Cranfield, G.A. *The Press and Society: From Caxton to Northcliffe*. London: Longman, 1978.

Dahl, Svend. *History of the Book*. Metuchen, NJ: Scarecrow Press, 1968.

De Grazia, Edward, and Roger Newman. *Banned Films*. New York, NY: Bowker, 1982.

Dennis, Everette E. and William L. Rivers. *Other Voices: The New Journalism in America*. San Francisco: Canfield Press, 1974.

Dennis, Everette; Gillmor, Don; and Richard Grey. *Justice Black and the First Amendment*. Ames, IA: Iowa State University Press, 1978.

Devol, Kenneth S., editor. *Mass Media and the Supreme Court: The Legacy of the Warren Years*. New York: Hastings House, 1971.

Dilliard, Irving. *The Spirit of Liberty: Papers and Addresses of Learned Hand*. New York: Knopf, 1963.

Douglas, William O. _Justice Douglas and Freedom of Speech_.
Metuchen, NJ: Scarecrow Press, 1980.

Downs, Robert B., editor. _The First Freedom: Liberty and_
Justice in the World of Books and Reading. Chicago:
American Library Association, 1960.

Emerson, Thomas I. _Toward a General Theory of the First_
Amendment. New York: Random House, 1966.

Emerson, Thomas I. _The System of Freedom of Expression_. New
York: Random House, 1970.

Emerson, Thomas, I. and David Haber. _Political and Civil_
Rights in the United States. Volume I. Chapter 3.
Buffalo: Dennis, 1952.

Emery, Edwin and Michael Emery. _The Press and America_.
Englewood, NJ: Prentice Hall, 1984.

Ernst, Morris. _The First Freedom_. New York: Macmillan,
1946.

L'Estrange, Roger. _Freedom of the Press_, 1660-1681. New
York: Garland (Reprinting), 1974.

Febvre, Lucien, and Henri-Jean Martin. _The Coming of the_
Book: The Impact of Printing 1450-1800. London: NLB,
1976.

Fisher, Desmond. _The Rights to Communicate_. Paris: UNESCO,
1982.

Fliess, Peter J. _Freedom of the Press in the German Republic_
_1918-1933_. Baton Rouge, LA: Louisiana State University
Press, 1955.

Ford, Edwin H. _History of Journalism in the United States:_
A Bibliography of Books and Annotated Articles.
Minneapolis: Burgess Publishing Company, 1938.

Ford, Edwin H., and Edwin Emery, editors. _Highlights in the_
History of the American Press. Minneapolis: University
of Minnesota Press, 1958.

Fowler, Dorothy Canfield. _Unmailable_. Athens, GA: Georgia,
1977.

Francois, William E. _Mass Media Law and Regulation_.
Columbus, OH: Grid Publishing Company, Inc., 1982.

Frank, Joseph. _The Beginnings of the English Newspaper_.
Cambridge, MA: Harvard University Press, 1961.

Franklin, Marc A., assisted by Robert L. Trager. _The First_
Amendment and the Fourth Estate: Communications Law for
Undergraduates. Meneola, NY: Foundation Press, 1981.

Friendly, Fred. _The Good Guys, the Bad Guys, and the First_
Amendment. New York: Random House, 1975.

Friendly, Fred. The Constitution: That Delicate Balance.
New York, NY: Random House, 1984.

Gerald, James Edward. The Press and the Constitution.
Minneapolis: University of Minnesota Press, 1948.

Gillett, Charles R. Burned Books, Westport, CT: Greenwood
Press, 1932.

Gillmor, Donald M., and Jerome A. Barron. Mass
Communications Law. St. Paul, MN: West Publishing
Company, 1984.

Glessing, R. The Underground Press in America. Bloomington,
IN: Indiana University Press, 1970.

Gordon, David. Problems in Law of Mass Communications.
Mineola, NY: Foundations Press, 1982.

Grant, I. The Newspaper Press. London: Tinsley Brothers,
1871.

Graham, F. P. Press Freedoms Under Pressure. New York:
Twentieth Century Fund, 1972.

Greenfield, Jeff. Television: The First Fifty Years. New
York: Abrams, 1977.

Gregory, Winifred, editor. American Newspapers, 1821-1936.
New York: Wilson, 1937.

Hachten, William A. Muffled Drums: The News Media in
Africa. Ames, IA: Iowa State University Press, 1971.

Hachten, William A. The Supreme Court on Freedom of the
Press. Ames, IA: Iowa State University Press, 1968.

Haight, Anne Lyon. Banned Books, 387 B.C. to 1978. New
York, NY: Bowker, 1978.

Halperin, Morton H., and Daniel N. Hoffman. Top Secret:
National Security and the Right to Know. Washington,
DC: New Republic Books, 1977.

Hamilton, Alexander, James Madison, and John Jay. The
Federalist Papers. New York: New American Library,
1961.

Hand, Learned. The Spirit of Liberty. New York: Knopf,
1953.

Hand, Learned. The Bill of Rights. Cambridge, MA: Harvard
University Press, 1958.

Hansen, Laurence William. Government and the Press, 1695-
1763. Oxford, England: Clarendon Press, 1936.

Hart, Harold H., editor. Censorship, For and Against. New
York: Hart Publishing Company, 1971.

Hartshorn, Merrill F., editor. *Freedom of the Press*.
    Washington, DC: National Education Association, 1980.

Hemmer, Joseph J., Jr. *Communications Under Law, Volumes I
    and II*. Metuchen, NJ: Scarecrow Press, Inc., 1979,
    1980.

Hentoff, Nat. *The First Freedom*. New York: Delacorte
    Press, 1980.

Herd, Harold. *The March of Journalism: The Story of the
    British Press from 1622 to the Present Day*. London:
    Allen and Unwin, 1952.

Higman, Francis M. *Censorship and the Sorbonne*. Geneva:
    Librarie Droz, S.A., 1979.

Hasking, William E. *Freedom of the Press: A Framework of
    Principle*. Chicago: University of Chicago Press, 1947.

Hohenberg, John. *Free Press, Free People: The Best Cause*.
    New York: The Free Press, 1973.

Hoyt, Olga G. and Edwin P. *Censorship in America*. New York:
    The Seabury Press, 1970.

Hoyt, Olga G. and Edwin P. *Freedom of the News Media*. New
    York: Seabury Press, 1973.

Hudon, Edward Gerard. *Freedom of Speech and Press in
    America*. Washington, DC: Public Affairs Press, 1963.

Hudson, Frederic. *Journalism in the United States from 1690
    to 1872*. New York: Harper and Brothers, 1873.

Hurwitz, Leon. *Historical Dictionary of Censorship in the
    United States*. Westport, CT: Greenwood Press, 1985.

Ingelhart, Louis Edward. *Press Law and Freedom for High
    School Student Publications*. Westport, CT: Greenwood
    Press, 1986.

Ingelhart, Louis Edward. *Freedom for the College Student
    Press*. Westport, CT: Greenwood Press, 1985.

Inglis, Brian. *Freedom of the Press in Ireland, 1784-1841*.
    Westport, CT: Greenwood Press, 1985.

Jenkinson, Edward B. *Censors in the Classroom*. Carbondale,
    IL: University of Southern Illinois Press, 1979.

Jones, Robert W. *Journalism in the United States*. New York:
    E.P. Dutton and Company, 1947.

Kaminski, John P., and Gaspare J. Sladino. *Documentary
    History of the Ratification of the Constitution*.
    Madison, WI: State Historical Society of Wisconsin.
    1976-1991. (17 volumes)

Kessler, Lauren. *The Dissident Press*. Beverly Hills, CA:

Sage Publications, 1984.

Kesterton, Wilfred H. A History of Journalism in Canada.
Toronto: McClelland and Stewart, 1967.

Kobre, Sidney. The Development of the Colonial Newspaper.
Gloucester, MA: Peter Smith, 1960.

Konvitz, Milton R. First Amendment Freedoms. Ithaca, NY:
Cornell University Press, 1963.

Lacy, Dan Mabry. Freedom and Communications. Urbana, IL:
University of Illinois Press, 1965.

Ladenson, Robert F. A Philosophy of Free Expression and Its
Constitutional Applications. Totowa, NJ: Rowman and
Littlefield, 1983.

Lee, Alfred McClung. The Daily Newspaper in America. New
York: Macmillan, 1937.

Levy, Leonard W. Constitutional Opinions. New York, NY:
Oxford University Press, 1986.

Levy, Leonard W. Emergence of a Free Press. New York, NY:
Oxford University Press, 1985.

Levy, Leonard W., editor. Freedom of the Press from Zenger
to Hamilton. Indianapolis, IN: Bobbs-Merrill, 1966.

Lewis, Felice Flanery. Literature, Obscenity, and Law.
Carbondale, IL: University of Southern Illinois Press,
1976.

Lippman, Walter. Liberty and the News. New York: Harcourt,
Brace, and Howe, 1920.

Locke, John. Two Treatises on Government. Bibliography
Distributors, 1975.

Locke, John. The Workes of John Locke. London: C. and J.
Rivington, 1824. (Nine Volumes)

Lofton, John. The Press as Guardian of the First Amendment.
Columbia, SC: University of South Carolina Press, 1980.

Madison, James. Notes of the Debates in the Federal
Convention of 1787. Athens, OH: Republished by the
Ohio University Press, 1966.

McCormick, Robert R. The Freedom of the Press. New York:
Arno and the New York Times, 1970.

McCoy, Ralph Edward. Freedom of the Press: A
Bibliocyclopedia. Carbondale, IL: Southern Illinois
University Press, 1979.

McCoy, Ralph Edward. Freedom of the Press: An Annotated
Bibliography. Carbondale, IL: Southern Illinois
University Press, 1968

Meiklejohn, Alexander. Political Freedom: The
    Constitutional Power of the People. New York: Oxford
    University Press, 1965

Meiklejohn, Donald. Freedom and the Public. Syracuse, New
    York: Syracuse University Press, 1965.

Merrill, John C. The Imperative of Freedom. New York:
    Hastings House, 1974.

Miller, John C. Crisis in Freedom: The Alien and Sedition
    Acts. New York: Little Brown, 1964.

Mill, John Stuart. On Liberty. New York: Norton, 1975.

Milton, John. Areopagitica and Of Education. Oxford,
    England. Clarendon Press, 1973.

Morison, Samuel Eliot, editor. Sources and Documents
    Illustrating the American Revolution and the Formation
    of the Federal Constitution. New York: Oxford
    University Press, 1965.

Morris, Robert. Framing of the Constitution. Washington,
    DC: National Park Service, 1976.

Mott, Frank Luther. American Journalism. New York, NY: the
    Macmillan Company, 1949.

Mott, Frank Luther. History of American Magazines. New
    York: Macmillan, 1930 to 1968. (Five Volumes)

Myers, Robin. The British Book Trade from Caxton to the
    Present Day. London: National Book League, 1973.

Natarajan, Swaminath. A History of the Press in India. New
    York: Asia Publishing House, 1962.

National Commission on Obscenity and Pornography. Final
    Report. New York: Random House, 1970.

National News Council. In the Public Interest. New York:
    National News Council, 1979.

Nelson, Harold L., editor. Freedom of the Press from
    Hamilton to the Warren Court. Indianapolis: The Bobbs-
    Merrill Company, 1967.

Nelson, Harold L., and Dwight L. Teeter, Jr. Law of Mass
    Communications. Mneola, NY: Foundation Press, 1982.

New York Public Library. Censorship: 500 Years of Conflict.
    New York: New York Public Library, 1984.

Nordenstreng, Knark. In Mass Media Declaration of UNESCO.
    Norwood, NJ: Ablex, 1984.

Olsen, Kenneth E. The History Makers: The Press of Europe
    from its Beginnings through 1965. Baton Rouge, LA:
    Louisiana State University Press, 1966.

Overbeck, Wayne, and Rick D. Pullen. Major Principles of
    Media Law. New York: Holt, Rinehart, and Winston,
    1982.

Padover, Saul K., editor. The Writings of Thomas Jefferson.
    New York: The Heritage Press, 1967.

Padover, Saul K., editor. The Complete Madison: His Basic
    Writings. New York: Harper, 1953.

Papmehe, K.A. Freedom of Expression in 18th Century Russia.
    The Hague: Nijhoff, 1971.

Parks, Stephen. The English Book Trade, 1660-1853. New York
    and London: Garland Publishing, Inc., 1974.

Payne, George H. History of Journalism in the United States.
    New York: Appleton-Century-Crofts, 1920.

Pember, Don R. Mass Media Law. Dubuque, IA: William C.
    Brown Company, 1981.

Peterson, Theodore. Magazines in the Twentieth Century.
    Urbana, IL: University of Illinois Press, 1964.

Potter, Elaine. The Press as Opposition: The Political Role
    of South African Newspapers. London: Chatto and
    Windus, 1975.

Purvis, Hoyt H., The Press, Free and Responsible? Austin,
    TX: Lyndon B. Johnson School of Public Affairs, 1982.

Rips, Geoffrey. The Campaign Against the Underground Press.
    San Francisco: City Lights Books, 1981.

Rutland, Robert Allen, The Birth of the Bill of Rights.
    Chapel Hill, NC: University of North Carolina Press,
    1955.

Salmon, Lucy Maynard. The Newspaper and Authority. New
    York: Oxford University Press, 1923.

Schlesinger, Arthur M. Prelude to Independence: The
    Newspaper War on Britain, 1764-1776. New York: Alfred
    A. Knopf, 1958.

Schroeder, Theodore. Freedom of the Press and Obscene
    Literature. New York, NY: The Free Speech League,
    1906.

Schroeder, Theodore. Our Vanishing Liberty of the Press.
    New York: Free Speech League, 1906.

Schulte, Henry F. The Spanish Press 1470-1966. Urbana, IL:
    University of Illinois Press, 1968.

Schwartz, Tony. Media: The Second God. New York, NY:
    Random House, 1981.

Seldes, George. Freedom of the Press. Garden City, NJ:

Garden City Publishing Company, 1937.

Shaaber, Matthias A. Some Forerunners of the Newspaper in England, 1478-1622. Philadephia: University of Pennsylvania Press, 1922.

Shackleton, Robert. Censure and Censorship. Austin, TX: University of Texas Humanities Research Center, 1975.

Shapiro, Andrew. Media Acess. Boston: Little, Brown, and Company, 1976.

Siebert, Frederick S. Freedom of the Press in England, 1476-1776. Urbana, IL: University of Illinois Press, 1952.

Siebert, Frederick S. Theodore Peterson, and Wilbur Schramm. Four Theories of the Press. Champaign, IL: University of Illinois Press, 1963.

Simmons, Howard, and Joseph A. Califano, eds. The Media and the Law. New York, NY: Praeger, 1976.

Smead, Elmer E. Freedom of Speech by Radio and Television. Washington, DC: Public Affairs Press, 1959.

Smith, Anthony. The Newspaper: An International History. London: Thames and Hudson, 1979.

Smith, J. M. Freedom's Fetters. Ithaca, NY: Cornell University Press, 1956.

Speaking of a Free Press. Washington, DC: American Newspaper Publishers Association, 1974.

Spencer, Dale R. Law for the Reporter. Columbia, MO: Lucas Brothers, 1980.

Stein, M. L. Freedom of the Press. New York, Messner, 1966.

Steinberg, S. H. Five Hundred Years of Printing. London: Faber and Faber, 1959.

Stevens, John D. Shaping the First Amendment. Beverly Hills: Sage Publications, 1982.

Strickland, Stephen P. Hugo Black and the Supreme Court. Indianapolis, IN: Bobbs-Merrill, 1967.

Sullivan, Alvin. ed. British Literary Magazines. Westport, CT: Greenwood Press, 1983. (Two Volumes).

Sutherland, John. Offensive Literature. Totowa, NJ: Barnes and Noble Books, 1982.

Symonds, R. V. The Rise of English Journalism. Exeter, England: A. Wheaton and Company, Ltd., 1952.

Tebbel, John. A History of Book Publishing in the United States. New York: R. R. Bowker, 1972-1978 (Three Volumes).

Tebbel, John. The Compact History of the American Newspaper.
    New York: Hawthorn Press, 1963.

Tebbel, John. The Media in America. New York: Thomas Y.
    Cromwell Company, 1974.

Thomas, LL.D., Isiah. The History of Printing in America.
    Edited by Marcus A. McCorison and arranged for by the
    Reprint Society. New York: Weathervane Books, 1970.

Tindal, M. et al. Freedom of the Press, 1698-1709. New
    York: Garland (Reprint), 1974.

de Tocqueville, Alexis. Democracy in America. New York: J.
    and H.G. Langley, 1840.

Todorov, Dafin. Freedom Press. Prague, Czechoslovakia:
    International Organization of Journalists, 1978.

Tribe, David H. Questions of Censorship. London: George
    Allen and Unwin, Ltd., 1973.

Trager, Robert and Donna L. Dickerson. College Student Press
    Law. Revised Edition, Memphis, TN: College Media
    Advisers, 1979.

Van Alstyne, William W. Interpretations of the First
    Amendment. Durham, NC: Duke University Press, 1984.

Varlejs, Jana, editor. The Right to Information. Jefferson,
    NC: McFarland, 1984.

Weiner, Joel H. Radicalsim and Free Though in Nineteenth
    Century Britian. The Life of Richard Carlile.
    Westport, CT: Greenwood Press, 1983.

Wickwar, William Hardy. The Struggle for the Freedom of the
    Press, 1819-1832. London: George Allen and Unwin,
    Ltd., 1928.

Williams, Chester Sidney. Liberty of the Press. Evanston,
    IL: Row, Peterson, and Company, 1940.

Wortman, Tunis. A Treatise Concerning Political Enquiry, and
    the Liberty of the Press. New York: G. Forman, 1800.

Index

Abelman, Paul, 341
Abrams, Floyd, 337, 360, 371
Abrams, Jacob, 236
Acharya, G.N., 313
Lord Acton, 204
Actors, Peter, 14
Adair, James, 146
Adams, Abigail, 135, 153
Adams, Abijah, 136
Adams, Henry, 209
Adams, John, 94, 102, 105,
   109, 131, 135-8, 140, 147,
   154, 155, 162
Adams, Sam, 94, 105
Adams, Samuel H., 223
Adams, Thomas, 136
Adams, W.E., 198
Addison, Joseph, 77
Adler, Julius, 288
Adler, Victor, 220
Administrative Procedures
   Act, 271
Adolphus, King Gustavus II,
   34
Advertising, 10, 268, 291,
   301, 310, 324-6, 328, 330,
   332, 333, 338, 339, 349,
   362, 365, 369, 372, 374,
   376, 386
Advertising Court Decisions:
   American Civil Liberties
      case, 382
   Arizona Bar Association
      case, 349.
   Associates and Aldrich
      case, 326
   Bigelow case, 345
   Committee for Impeachment

case, 330
Contraceptives case, 349
Drew case, 291
Federal Trade Commission
   case, 339
First National Bank case,
   349
Maryland Pharmacy case,
   333
Pittsburgh Human Relations
   case, 334
Public Issues case, 374
Readers Digest case, 361
Schreiber case, 360
Shuck case, 259
Suffolk case, 350
Supreme Court and
   Commercial Speech, 357
Valentine case, 268
Affleck, James, 177
Afghanistan, 379
Africa, 340, 355, 381, 383
African Congo, 11
Agenda for New World Order
   of Communications, 329
Agents Identities Protection
   Act, 364
Agnew, Spiro, 313, 323, 325,
   328, 331
Aguirre, Horatio, 380
Altken, Robert, 108
Albania, 20
Albee, Edward, 30, 335
Aldunate, Wilson, 380
Alexander, James, 92, 93
Pope Alexander VI, 15
Alexander, Rae, 365
Tsar Alexander I, 179

Alexandria, 617
Algeria, 217, 317, 342
Ali, Muhammed, 181
Allen, Donald, 365
Allen, John, 131, 136
Almon, John, 113, 115
Alsapp, Bernard, 45
Alvardo, Juan, 341
American Antislavery
    Society, 185
American Association of
    Schools and Departments of
    Journalism, 273
American Bar Association,
    288, 304, 305, 347, 371
American Civil Liberties
    Union, 236, 311, 332, 361,
    371
American Defense League, 233
American Federation of
    Labor, 237
American Library
    Association, 225, 275,
    360, 368
American Medical
    Association,   286
American Newspaper Guild,
    259, 262
American Newspaper
    Publishers Association,
    240, 257, 259, 305
American Protective League,
    233
American Railway Literary
    Union, 188, 209
American Society of
    Newspaper Editors, 240,
    270, 283, 291, 303, 345
Americanism Protective
    League, 240
Amir, Ibn Abi, 8
Anabaptists, 18, 47, 50
Anarchy, 222, 227, 230, 252,
    264, 283
Anderson, Jack, 266
Anderton, James, 355
Anderton, William, 60
Andnes, de Alma, 33
Andros, Edmund, 71
Anglicans, 27, 30, 58, 86,
    87, 176
Angola, 381
Queen Anne, 61, 76-8
Annet, Peter, 113
Antifederalists, 123, 124,
    130, 154
Aquinas, Thomas, 8
Arabia, 7, 9, 181
Archer, Jerome, 365
Archer, Thomas, 38

Areogapitica, 46-48, 60, 62,
    83, 94, 269
Aristophanes, 239
Arius, 7
Armenia, 4
Armenian Baptists, 56
Argentina, 340, 380, 382,
    383
Asgill, John, 76
Ashbee, Henry, 215
Ashton, John, 43
Asian Mass Communications
    and Research Center, 354
Askew, Rubin, 352
Asner, Ed, 362
Assembly of God, 363
Associated Press case on
    press monopoly, 271
Association for Education in
    Journalism and Mass
    Communications, 357
Association for Preservation
    of Liberty, 143, 145
Association for Repeal of
    Taxes on Knowledge, 196
Assyria, 4
Athens, 5
Atheism, 257
Atheistic Depot, 196
Audley, Thomas, 50
Augereau, Antoine, 18
Augustine, Aurelius, 12
Austin, Ann, 68
Austin, Robert, 53
Australia, 173, 181, 201,
    217, 218, 241, 279, 280,
    317, 318, 340, 341
Austria, 5, 10, 11, 33, 40,
    98, 100, 122, 145, 149,
    180, 181, 202, 204, 205,
    220, 245, 247-9, 278

Babylon, 4
Bache, B.F., 137
Bacon, Francis, 31, 36, 39
Bacon, Roger, 13
Bagdikian, Ben, 322, 336,
    344
Bagshaw, Edward, 55
Bailey, Samuel, 172, 174
Bailey, William, 185, 188
Bainham, James, 24
Balancing of rights theory,
    353
Balancing of press rights
    court decisions:
    Brodhurst case, 312
    Douds case, 284
    Konigsberg case, 300
    Penthouse case, 350

Watson case, 262
Baldwin, James, 317
Baldwin, Luther, 138
Baldwin, Roger, 231
Balzac, Honore, 254
Banvard, John, 187
Baptists, 59, 67, 145
Barbados, 103
Barker, Robert, 39, 43
Barkley, John, 175
Barnes, Henry, 53
Barnett, Robert, 193
Barnum, Phineas, 183
Barrett, Richard, 193
Barron, Jerome, 314
Barton, Elizabeth, 24
Bascon, John, 209
Bastwick, John, 41, 74
Batista, Fulgencio, 295
Baudelaire, Charles, 203
Bavaria, 245
Baxter, Richard, 59
Bayer, Abel, 74
Bayfield, Richard, 21
Bayle, Pierre, 64
Beacon Firers, 53, 54
Beacon Quenchers, 53
Beadle, Irwin, 189
Beauharnais, Joseph, 287
Becourt, M. de, 162
Bedborough, George, 216
Beecher, Edward, 188
Beecher, Henry, 207, 208
Begeaud, General, 217
Belgium, 10, 13, 17, 33,
    200, 201, 204, 245
Belin, J.P., 149
Bell, Robert, 107
Bell, William, 32
Bellamy, Paul, 262, 335
Benbow, William, 171
Pope Benedict IV, 100
Bennet, H.G., 173
Bennett, John, 142
Bent, Andrew, 201
Bent, Silas, 253
Bentham, Jeremy, 192
Benton, William, 272
Berger, Victor, 238
Beria, Lavrentia, 295
Berkeley, William, 69
Berkenhead, John, 44, 49
Bern, Lou, 327
Bernard, Francis, 102, 104,
    105
Bernstein, Leonard, 335
Berquin, Louis, 17
Berry, Walter, 147
Berthelet, Thomas, 24
Besant, Annie, 192, 214

Best, W.D., 173, 175
Biddle, John, 54
Bill of Rights (see U.S. Bill
    of Rights)
Billboard regulations court
    decisions:
  Bern Broadway case, 327
  Metromedia case, 375
  Ohio and Maryland cases,
    375
Bilney, Thomas, 24
Bingley, William, 114
Birney, James, 185
Bismarck, Otto, 204, 218,
    219, 247
Blacaw, Rev., 172
Black, Hugo, 266, 269, 271,
    286, 289, 293, 299, 300,
    307
Blackstone, William, 105,
    113, 128, 133, 143, 153-5,
    229
Blackwood, William, 193
Blair, Montgomery, 190
Blanchard, Margaret, 252,
    357
Bland, Margot, 296
Blasi, Melvin, 367
Blasi, Vincent, 359
Blasphemy:
  In the United States, 134,
    207, 209, 224, 230, 232,
    237, 257
  In the American Colonies,
    67, 90
  In England, 53-5, 57-9,
    61, 76, 77, 79, 90, 93,
    113, 146, 166, 167, 168-
    72, 174, 175, 183, 192,
    194-6, 199, 214, 215,
    248, 355
  Elsewhere, 7
Blasphemy court decisions:
  Kneeland case, 183
  Mockus case, 232
  Reynolds case, 209
Blount, Charles, 48, 57, 60,
    61
Blatty, William, 365
Blume, Judy, 365
Board of Movie Censorship,
    252
Board of Rites, 8
Boccacio, Giovanni, 212, 222,
    239, 254
Bodenheim, Maxwell, 237
Bodenstein, Andreas, 17
Bohan, Edmund, 60
Bohemia, 218, 230, 247, 248
Boileau, Albert, 190

Bok, Curtis, 286, 289
Boleyn, Ann, 24
Bolinbroke (Henry St. John),
    77, 78, 81, 83
Bollan, William, 104
Bolts, William, 121
Bonald, Louis, 178
Bonneville, Madame, 166
Book Censorship Abolition
    League, 280
Boorstein, Daniel, 368
Booth, George, 268
Borah, William, 237
Borchard, E.M. 234
Bostwick, Arthur, 225
Botany Bay, 145
Botswana, 381
Bourne, Henry, 215
Bourne, Nicholas, 40, 42, 43
Bowler, James, 40
Bowles, John, 145
Bowdler, Thomas, 168
Boyd, James, 43
Boyle, Humphrey, 175
Bradford, Andrew, 90, 91
Bradford, William, 65, 70,
    71, 91, 93
Bradford, William III, 103
Bradlaugh, Charles, 192,
    213, 214
Bradshaw, Michael, 270
Bramston, James, 83
Brandeis, Louis, 237, 254,
    257, 265
Brandenburg, Clarence, 314
Branting, Hjalmar, 219, 220
Brautigen, Richard, 365
Bray, William, 43
Brazil, 15, 319, 380, 382,
    383
Brennan, William, 134, 292,
    304, 327
Brewster, Thomas, 56
Bridge, Peter, 332
Bridges, Harry, 266
Brisbane, Thomas, 187
British Bureau of Film
    Censorship, 341
Britnell, Albert, 243
Broder, David, 352
Brooke, Gerald, 317
Brooker, William, 87
Brooks, Nathan, 56
Broughan, Henry, 194
Brouse, Paul, 220
Brown, Arthur, 276
Brown, Claude, 336
Brown, David, 154
Brown, Henry, 221
Brown, Heywood, 261

Brown, Stephan, 281
Browne, Andrew, 130
Browne, Edward, 232
Browne, John, 65
Browne, Samuel, 65
Brucker, Hubert, 323
Bruno, Giordino, 32, 214
Bryan, Samuel, 124
Buchanan, Pat, 328
Buchanan, Robert, 210
Buck, Pearl, 335
Duke of Buckingham, 53
Buckingham, Joseph, 181, 185
Buckler, William, 116
Buckley, Amendment, 347
Buckley, Samuel, 73, 83
Buckley, William, 323
Buckner, John, 69
Bulgaria, 202
Bulwar, Edward, 193, 195
Burdett, Francis, 174, 175
Burger, Warren, 332, 345,
    350, 357, 365, 369
Burgess, Anthony, 335, 365
Burk, John, 137
Burke, Edmund, 143, 144, 244
Burleson, Albert, 233, 234,
    236, 238
Burnett, William, 88
Burnside, Ambrose, 190
Burr, Aaron, 137, 155, 158
Burroughs, William, 307, 365
Burton, Henry, 41, 42
Busher, Leonard, 37
Butler, Jacob, 190
Butler, Samuel, 44
Butler, William, 190
Butter, Nathaniel, 38-40, 42,
    45
Bye, George, 259
Byelorussia, 342

Cable television regulation
    court decisions:
    Carter Transmission case,
        302
    Fortknightly case, 312
    Cable Monopoly case, 377
    Southwestern cable case,
        312
Caball, Branch, 240
Cabell, James, 238
Cadoo, Emil, 302
Caesar, Julius, 7
Caldwell, Earl, 329
Caldwell, Erskine, 258, 260,
    286, 335
Caldwell, J.B., 211
Callender, James, 135, 136,
    147, 158

Callimachus, 6
Calvert, Giles, 54
Calvin, John, 18, 19, 26
Calvinism, 87
Camera in Courtroom, 304,
    353, 365, 371
Campbell, John, 87
Campanello, Tommaso, 33
Camus, Albert, 291, 335
Canaan, 4
Canada, 106, 218, 219, 233,
    243, 245, 249, 250, 281,
    372, 379, 381
Canning, Charles, 203
Canning, George, 173
Canons of Journalism, 240
Capello, Hannibal, 21
Care, Henry, 58
Carey, Matthew, 125
Carlile, Jane, 170, 172
Carlile, Mary, 172, 175
Carlile, Richard, 169-73,
    175, 176, 193, 194, 214
Carlin, George, 351
Queen Caroline of
    Denmark, 121
Carolus, Johann, 32
Caron, Pierre, 179
Carpenter, William, 193
Carrington, Edward, 124
Carter, Hodding, 331
Carter, William, 28, 29
Carthage, 7
Cartwright, Thomas, 27, 147
Case, Herbert, 286
Lord Castlereagh, 167, 171
Queen Catherine, 24
Tsarina Catherine, 100, 149
Catholics and Catholic
    church, 3, 7, 10, 16-20,
    26, 27, 32-4, 42, 57-9,
    63, 64, 98, 99, 122, 142,
    166, 173, 180, 201, 204,
    213, 217, 225, 228, 230,
    231, 245, 257, 259, 318,
    363, 379
Catholic National Office for
    Decent Literature, 291
Catledge, Turner, 300
Cato, 89, 91, 92, 172
Cave, Edward, 82, 85
Caxton, William, 13
Cayman Islands, 380
Cellier, Elizabeth, 58
Censorship:
    In the United States, 134,
    138, 152, 184, 185, 188,
    189, 191, 208, 210, 212,
    221, 225, 226, 228-33,
    235, 237, 238, 240, 252,
    254-8, 260-4, 267, 269,
    271, 273-7, 281, 286,
    287, 289, 291, 292, 295,
    301, 305, 306, 309, 311,
    314, 322-4, 326, 330,
    331, 334, 344, 346, 350,
    358, 362, 365, 370, 375,
    376
    In the American Colonies,
    68, 70, 89
    In England, 25, 27, 36, 42,
    46, 56, 61, 70, 73, 75,
    166, 169, 215, 383
    Elsewhere, 6, 8, 10, 16,
    17, 33, 34, 64, 99, 100,
    120-2, 145, 151, 178,
    180, 181, 200-4, 217,
    218, 220, 241-5, 247-50,
    278-283, 316, 317, 319,
    341, 342, 378-80
Censorship Bulletin, 290
Censorship Commission for
    Books and Periodicals, 280
Censorship court decisions:
    Business Executives case,
    326
    Cox case, 306
    Death of a President case,
    309
    Meyer case, 324
    Mills case, 307
    Moseley case, 330
    Near case, 257
    Nebraska Press case, 348
    SEC case, 376
    Sunshine Banks case, 348
    Wilson case, 292
Central Conference of
    American Rabbis, 252
Central Intelligence Agency
    Information Act, 367
Chad, 379
Chafee, Zachariah, 131, 305,
    306, 313
Channing, William 185
Chaplinsky, Walter, 267
Chappell, Warren, 63
Charlemagne, 12
Charles, Edward, 281
Charles I, 39, 40, 42,   51
Charles II, 47, 55-9, 68, 70
Charles V, 17
Charles IX, 20
Charles X of France, 201
Chase, J. Frank, 253
Chase, Samuel, 138, 140, 154
Chaucer, Geoffrey, 239, 335
Chauncey, Charles, 68, 93
Chateaubriand, Francois, 200
Che, Su, 8

Checkley, John, 87, 90
Cheetham, James, 166
Cheih, Wang, 7
Chekov, Anton, 241
Chicago Police Bureau of
   Censorship, 286
Chicago Police Red Squad,
   323
Chi-Chao, Ling, 220
Chidley, Samuel, 53
Child, Robert, 67
Childress, Alice, 365
Childs, Marquis, 299
Chile, 340, 380, 382, 383
China, 4, 6-8, 9, 63, 64,
   220, 235, 238, 241, 242,
   244-6, 249-51, 278-84,
   294, 298, 319, 340, 383,
   384
Churchill, John, 61
Churchill, Winston, 294
Cicak, Ranka, 382
Cicero, Marcus, 7
Citizens Choice Commission
   in a Free and Responsible
   Media Dialogue, 362
Citizens for Decent
   Literature, 291
Claflin, Tennessee, 207
Clap, William, 161
Clapham, Michael, 9
Clark, Tom, 288
Clark, William, 228
Clarke, John, 82
Clarke, Walter, 335
Clarke, William, 175, 176
Clarkson, Laurence, 50, 52
Classification Act, 272
Clay, Cassius, 187
CLEAN project, 291
Clean Books League, 252
Clear and Present Danger
   Rule, 236, 254, 252, 266,
   274, 285, 353
Cleaveland, John, 49
Cleaver, Elbridge, 155
Cleaver, Eldridge, 355, 366
Cleland, John, 164, 172
Clemenceau, Georges, 245,
   249
Clinton, George, 94
Clowes, John, 53
Coalition for Better
   Television, 360
Cobb, Irvin, 303
Cobbett, William, 135, 147,
   168, 171, 193
Cobell, Samuel, 135, 136
Cockburn, Alexander, 199,
   213, 295

Code, Michaud, 34
Cohen, Levy, 193
Coke, Edward, 30, 90
Colden, Cadwallader, 102
Coleman, Edward, 57
Coles, Francis, 45
Colledge, Stephen, 59
College student publications
   court decisions:
   Antonelli case, 323
   Bazaar case, 332
   Channing club case, 327
   Endress case, 347
   Howe case, 352
   Joyner case, 333
   Milliner case, 375
   Muhlenberg case, 377
   Norton case, 315
   Panarella case, 334
   Papish case, 330
   Schiff case, 346
   Stanley case, 376
   Trujillo case, 328
Collet, C.D., 196
Collier, John 230
Collins, Anthony, 81
Collins, Harker, 373
Colman, John, 88
Colonels Sexby and Titus, 54
Columbia, 380, 383
Combe, Abram, 176
Commission on Freedom of the
   Press of the University of
   Chicago, 273-75
Commission on Obscenity and
   Pornography, 322, 338
Commission for the
   Bicentennial of the U.S.
   Constitution, 369
Committee for Constitutional
   Government, 289
Committee for Plundered
   Ministers, 52
Committee of the Militia, 50
Common Law, 36, 57, 61, 68,
   75, 81, 105, 106, 108, 110,
   114, 130, 135, 137, 138,
   140, 144, 153, 158, 161,
   162, 167, 182, 224, 229,
   266, 305
Communications Act of 1934,
   269
Communists, 256, 259, 266,
   301, 302
Comstock Act, 207, 212, 230
Comstock, Anthony, 207-9,
   211, 212, 222-4, 230, 239
Conference on Freedom of
   Information, 284
Confidentiality of News

Sources, 227, 229, 327, 352
Confucius, 6
Congress (see U.S. Congress)
Conservative Political
  Action Conference, 374
Constant, Benjamin, 217
Constant, Henri, 180
Emporer Constantine, 7, 9
King Constantine, 248
Constantinople, 9
Constitutional Association
  of England, 172, 173, 175
Constitutional Association
  for Opposing Sedition (in
  England), 173
Contempt rulings and court
  decisions:
  Boise _Capitol-News_ case,
    228
  Callender case, 154
  Farr case, 327
  Fox case, 227
  Lawless case, 183
  Sheldon case, 182
  Supreme Court ruling, 188
Coode, John, 70
Cook, Alfred, 328
Cook, Samuel, 192
Cooley, Thomas, 207, 210,
  262
Cooper, James, Fenimore,
  185, 187
Cooper, Samuel, 105
Cooper, Thomas, 138, 140,
  154
Coote, William, 215
Copernicus, Nicolaus, 19,
  33, 34
Copyright, 23, 99, 129,
  230, 312, 347
Copyright Court decisions:
  Schnapper case, 350
  Sony case, 376
Coray, M., 164
Cordon, Charles, 363
Cornell, Greg, 329
Cosby, Bill, 335
Cosby, William, 92
Costa, Joseph, 371
Costa Rico, 354, 381-3
Coster, Lawrence, 9
Coswell Court Decisions
  about video games, 375
Cotten, Godwin, 163
Cotter, Bessie, 284
Coughlin, Charles, 265
Council of Europe, 341, 355
Council of Nicea, 7
Council of State, 53-5
Court of High Commission of

England, 27, 37, 40, 42
Cousins, Norman, 270
Coverdale, Miles, 26
Cox, Walter, 168
Coxe, A.C., 188
Craddock, Ida, 222
Craggs, James, 79
Cranach, Lucas, 17
Crandall, Reuben, 185
Crane, Stephen, 221, 335
Creel, George, 232
Crete, 4
Criley, Robert, 334
Criminal Code Reform Act, 334
Criminal libel court
  decisions:
  Armao case, 329
  Ashton case, 306
  Barnum case, 292
  Beauharnais case, 287
  Blanding case, 182
  Croswell case, 157
  Nugent case, 161
Criminal Syndicatism Act, 254
Croatia, 10
Cromwell, Joan, 52
Cromwell, Oliver, 44, 47, 49,
  51-4
Cromwell, Thomas, 24, 25
Cronkite, Walter, 375
Croope, John, 54
Croswell, Harry, 157, 158
Cuba, 295, 359, 380-2
Culpepper, Thomas, 69
Cumings, E.E., 335
Curll, Emund, 81, 82
Curtis, Jane, 58
Cushing, Thomas, 105
Cushing, William, 131
Cushman, Robert, 268
Czechoslovakia, 10, 13, 218,
  246, 249, 280, 284, 296,
  319

Dalby, Thomas, 171, 172
Dale, George, 253
Dalton, David, 336
Dalton, Isaac, 78
Dalton, Mary, 78
Daly, Lar, 292
Damascus, 8
Dana, Charles, 210
Daniel, Yuli, 318
D'Aquino, I. Toguri, 348
Daumier, Honore, 201, 220
Davidson, Donald, 254
Davies, John, 31
Davison, Thomas, 173
Daye, Stephen, 66
Deay, Dwight, 336

Declaration for Freedom of
the Press (English), 145
Declaration of Independence
(see U.S. Declaration of
Independence)
Declaration of Mass Media,
356
Declaration on Mass
Communications Media and
Human Rights, 356
Defoe, Daniel, 62, 73, 74,
77 78, 279, 291
DeGaulle, Charles, 318
DeGaulle, Mrs. Charles, 318
DeJonge, Dirk, 262
DeLacey, James, 252, 257
DeLaune, Thomas, 59
Delvalle, Gonzalez, 380
Denmark, 18, 34, 35, 121,
122, 201, 282, 316, 354
Dennett, Mary, 256
Dennie, Joseph, 155, 163
Dennis, Geoffrey, 281
Denton, William, 58
Dering, W.A. 319
Descartes, Rene, 35, 99
DeTocqueville, Alexis, 184
Devanant, Charles, 73
Dewey, Tom, 259
DeWolf, Richard, 230
Dicken, Arthur, 16
Dickens, Charles, 186, 197
Dickinson, John, 103
Dickey, James, 335
Diderot, Denis, 99, 100, 121
Dillingham, John, 50
Disraeli, Benjamin, 213
Disruptive Content court
decisions:
    Columbus Free Press case,
    329
    LeBaron case, 276
    Starr case, 290
    Winters case, 276
Distribution court
decisions:
    Ad World case, 374
    Chong case, 359
    Esquire case, 273
    International Krishna
    Society case, 353
    Katzen case, 293
    Lovell case, 263
    Lyons case, 312
    Martin case, 268
    McMillan case, 333
    Olson case, 249
    Rumely case, 289
    Schmid case, 376
    Schneider case, 264

United Steelworkers case,
310
Dix, John, 191
Djilas, Milovin, 295, 317
Dodd, William, 117
Dolban, Gilbert, 77
Dominican, Republic, 383
Dongan, Thomas, 67
Donne, John, 57
DosPassos, John, 280, 290
Dostoevsky, Fyodor, 334
Doublet, Madame, 99
Douglas, William O., 289,
300, 306, 330, 388
Dover, Simon, 56
Dreiser, Theodore, 228, 254,
256
Drennan, Dr.,
(proclamationist), 196
Drummer, William, 87
Duane, William, 150, 154, 159
Dubcek, Alexander, 319
Dudge, Amos, 82
Dudley, Thomas, 66
Dufief, M., 162
Duke, James, 75
Dunlap, Andrew, 183
Dunne, F.P., 257
Dunster, Henry, 68
DuPont, Pierre, 178
Durrell, William, 154
Dutton, Anne, 85
Dworkin, Andrea, 359
Dylan, Bob, 335

Eagleton, Thomas, 331
Baron Earlsfort, 143
Eastman, Max, 232
Eastman, Newton, 225, 226
Eaton, Daniel, 147, 167
Eckhardt, Christopher, 324
Ecudor, 34, 383
Eddy, Mary Baker, 238
Edes, Benjamin, 96, 101, 102
Edmonds, George, 170
Edward I, 13
Edward VI, 25
Effingham (Francis Howard),
70
Egypt, 4, 6, 7, 218
Ehrenburg, Ieya, 294
Egerton, John, 41
Eisenhower, Dwight, 288, 289,
303
El Salvador, 362, 380, 383
Lord Eldon, 146, 169, 171
Eliot, Andrew, 95
Eliot, John, 68
Queen Elizabeth, 27-31, 36,
116

Lord Ellenborough, 165, 167
Elliot, Roland, 335, 337
Ellis, Edward, 189
Ellis, Havelock, 216
Ellison, Ralph, 335, 336
Ellsberg, Daniel, 327
Ellsworth, Oliver, 125
Elwall, Edward, 90
Emerson, Ralph Waldo, 186,
    207
Emerson, Thomas, 323, 326
Emlyn, Thomas, 78
Enaeo, Olof, 34
Endress, Paula, 347
Engels, Fredereich, 219
England, 12, 14, 21, 23-6,
    28, 29, 37-9, 41-5, 50-8,
    60, 61, 67, 68, 70, 73,
    78, 79, 81-3, 87, 88, 91-
    4, 96, 97, 101-3, 105-9,
    112, 113, 116-8, 137, 138,
    140, 142-7, 163, 165, 168,
    169, 172, 173, 181, 182,
    192, 193, 195, 198, 200,
    202, 204, 213, 215, 216,
    218, 220, 222, 224, 229,
    242-4, 246-8, 250, 251,
    260, 266, 278, 283, 285,
    295, 318, 319, 341-3, 355,
    356, 378, 379, 381, 384,
    387
English Bill of Rights, 60,
    61
English Common Law
    Procedures Act, 198
English Race Relations Act,
    318
Equal Access (or time) rule,
    302, 315, 344, 352
Erasmus, Desiderius, 17, 26
Erskine, John, 73
Ervin, Sam 336
Ervin, Thomas, 547
Espionage, 292
Espionage Act of 1917, 231-3
Escott, T.H.S., 243
Euripedes, 4
Everett, Ernest, 247

Fairness doctrine, 293, 315,
    325, 332, 334, 337, 350,
    352, 367, 368
Farewell, John, 59
Farr, William, 327
Farrell, James, 263, 286,
    288
Faques, William, 23
Fast, Howard, 335
Faulk, John Henry, 302
Faulkner, William, 286, 290

Fawcett, Thomas, 45
Federal Common Law, 161
Federal Communications Act of
    1934, 260, 290
Federal Communications
    Commission, 269, 270, 272,
    293, 301-3, 308, 312, 324,
    325, 330, 334, 350-2, 359,
    362, 365, 367, 368, 371,
    375, 387, 388
Federal Election Campaign Act
    of 1971, 325
Federal Employees Salary Act,
    301
Federal Radio Commission,
    255, 256
Federal Security
    Administration, 286
Federal Trade Commission,
    263, 268, 339, 362
Federalists, 123, 126, 129,
    135, 141, 155, 157-9
Felker, Clay, 328
Fenno, John, 135
Ferguson, Robert, 147
Fereos, Rigas, 149
Ferlinghetti, Lawrence, 366
Field, John, 27
Fielding, Henry, 85
Findley, William, 125
Finerty, Peter, 147, 167,
    196
Finland, 20, 319, 342
Finlay, Thomas, 196
First Amendment (see U.S.
    Constitution, First
    Amendment)
First Amendment Congress,
    357, 364, 370, 388
First Amendment dimensions
    court decisions:
    Adult World bookstore
      case, 358
    Aumiller case, 349
    Barenblatt case, 293
    Brandenburg case, 314
    Buchanan case, 346
    Chaplinsky case, 267
    Deerfield Medical case, 360
    Douglas case, 268
    Edwards case, 349
    Fritz case, 338
    Gaspor case, 348
    Georgia case, 299
    Griswold case, 307
    Johnson case, 338
    Kerner case, 270
    Medrano case, 353
    Miami Herald case, 346
    Milky Way Productions

case, 315
Minnesota case, 375
Naked City case, 353
Peck case, 292
Philadelphia case, 376
Pioneer Press case, 265
Reporters Committee, 352
Thomas Case, 270
Thompson case, 348
Thompson case, 338
Tornillo case, 338
Tribune-Review case, 292
Universal Amusement case,
  352
Visual Educators case, 330
Williamson case, 286
Fish, Simon, 24
Fisher, Mary, 68
Fisher, Vardis, 261
Fitzgerald, F. Scott, 335
Fitzherbert, Maria Ann, 142
Fitz-Harris, Edward, 58
Fitzhugh, Peregrine, 168
Flaubert, Gustave, 220, 254
Fleet, Thomas, 93, 94
Flexnor, Stuart, 335
Flindell, Thomas, 171
Flint, George, 78
Flint, Mary, 78
Flower, Benjamin, 165, 230
Fonda, Jane, 362
Fontblanque, Albany, 195
Food and Drug Act of
  1916, 223
Foote, George, 215
Ford, Werthington, 233
Foreign Agents Registration
  Act, 364
Forster, Joseph, 194
Forum theory, 310, 328
Foscarini, Paolo, 33
Fourteenth Amendment (see
  U.S. Constitution)
Fourteenth Amendment
  Incorporation of the Bill
  of Rights court decisions:
  Arnold case, 289
  Gitlow case, 252
  I.W.W. case, 254
  Near case, 258
  Patterson case, 224
  Slaughterhouse case, 207
  Winters case, 276
Fowle, Daniel, 95, 103, 107
Fowler, Mark, 362, 363, 371
Fox, Jay, 227
Fox, W.J., 169
France, 10, 18, 22, 32-4,
  38, 61, 63, 64, 75, 78,
  79, 82, 95, 96, 99, 100,
  114, 117, 120-2, 136, 141,
  142, 144-6, 149, 150, 179-
  81, 200-4, 209, 217-20,
  226, 235, 242, 243, 245-50,
  278, 284, 290, 291, 295,
  296, 306, 317, 341, 343,
  379
King Francis, 17, 18
Francis II of Holy Roman
  Empire, 150
Francklin, Richard, 83
Frank, Ann, 335
Frank, Reuven, 325
Franke, Ludwig, 181
Frankfurter, Felix, 265, 269,
  299
Franklin, Benjamin, 89-93,
  95, 103, 105, 107, 108, 132
Franklin, James, 88-90
Fransecky, Roger, 323
Frate, Edward, 230
Frederick II, 98
Frederick III, 11
Frederick the Great, 100
Frederick William, 203
Free Press Defense Committee,
  216
Freedman, Ronald, 306
Freedom House, 382
Freedom of Expression Act of
  1983, 372
Freedom of Information, 275,
  301, 307, 308, 329, 330,
  333, 363, 367, 372
Freedom of Information Act,
  305, 342
Freedom of Information court
  decisions:
  Goodfader case, 300
  Mink case, 382
  Tennessean case, 330
  Zemel case, 307
Freedom of the Press Day,
  368
Freeman, Edmund, 143
French Declaration of the
  Rights of Man, 149, 150
Frend, William, 145, 147
Freneau, Philip, 133, 134
Freud, Sigmund, 280
Frick, Helen, 309
Frick, Henry, 309
Friends of Liberty of the
  Press, 145
Frothingham, David, 140
Fry, John, 52
Fryer, Peter, 319
Fullbright, William, 345
Fuller, Walter, 266
Furneaux, Phillip, 105

Prince Fushimi, 242
Fust, John, 10

Gaine, Hugh, 95
Gaines, Ervin, 309
Galella, Ronald, 375
Galilei, Galaleo, 34, 35
Gallatin, Albert, 138, 153
Gallagher, Wes, 311
Gandhi, Indira, 355
Gandhi, Mahatma, 251, 282
Garfield, James, 208
Garfield, John, 55
Garrison, William, 184
Gathing Committee Report,
   288
Gautier, Theodore, 201, 238,
   239
General Council of the
   (English) Press, 284
Gentz, Fredereich, 180
George II, 82, 84
George III, 112
George IV, 142
German Basic Law, 284
Germany, 9-12, 15-20, 24,
   32, 33, 35, 63, 170, 200,
   203, 204, 209, 217-20,
   238, 242, 244-51, 263,
   264, 279, 280, 282, 284
Gerry, Elbridge, 123, 141
Gertz, Elmer, 338
Giannone, Pietro, 98
Gibson, Milner, 198
Gilbert, William, 242
Gill, John, 96, 102, 107
Ginsberg, Allen, 242, 365,
   366
Ginsberg, Sam, 312, 321
Ginzburg, Ralph, 310
Girodias, Maurice, 316, 317
Gish, Thomas, 344
Gitlow, Benjamin, 1, 252
Glasgow court decision on
   scurrilous language, 227
Glasgow, Wesley, 227
Glemp, Jozef, 379
Glorious Revolution of
   England, 52, 60
Glover, Joseph, 66
Goddard, William, 109, 110
Godfrey, Howard, 312
Goebbels, Paul, 280, 281
Gold, Herbert, 335
Goldberg, Arthur, 303
Golding, William, 335
Goldman, Emma, 230
Goldschmidt, E.P., 9
Gomphers, Samuel, 237
Goodale, James, 347

Goodman, Christopher, 26
Goodwin, John, 53, 59
Goose, Elizabeth, 94
Gordon, George, 142
Gordon, Thomas, 79, 80, 91
Gordon, William, 110
Gorki, Maxim, 220, 280
Gorkin, Daniel, 68
Gorton, Samuel, 67
Gospel Workers of America,
   226
Gott, J.W., 248
Gottwald, Klement, 284
Gough, John, 23
Govermnent in Sunshine Act,
   347
Grafton, Richard, 25
Graham, Kathleen, 332, 337
Grant, James, 196
Grant, W.L., 250
Gravel, Mike, 330
Greece, 5, 6, 122, 149, 219,
   248, 249
Greeley, Horace, 187
Green, Samuel, 69
Greensberg, Henry, 286
Greenleaf, Joseph, 106
Greenleaf, Ann, 140
Greenspan, Benjamin, 258
Greer, Germaine, 341
Gregory, Francis, 61
Pope Gregory XIII, 32
Grenada, 363, 370, 380
Grenville, George, 79
Grey, Anthony, 319
Grey, Zane, 335
Griffen, Susan, 359
Griffin, Charles, 196
Griffin, John, 335
Grigorenko, Pyotr, 341
Grosz, Geog, 279
Grotius, Hugo, 22, 34, 91
Guatamala, 18, 383
Guesde, Jules, 220
Guirand, Paul, 99
Gutenberg, Johann, 9, 10, 13
Guyana, 380, 383

Hackluyt, Parson, 50
Haines, Henry, 84
Haiti, 380
Hakam, Al, 8
Halborn, Louise, 16
Haldeman-Julius, Emmanuel,
   240, 257
Hale, Matthew, 57, 81
Hall, Arthur, 28
Hall, G. Stanley, 226
Hall, Oakley, 206
Hall, Radclyfte, 256

Hall, Robert, 145
Halleck, Henry, 189, 190
Halsey, Raymond, 232
Hambling, William, 338
Hamilton, Alexander, 107,
    110, 129, 138, 140, 155,
    158
Hamilton, Andrew, 91, 92
Hammerskold, Dag, 354
Hammond, George, 134
Hancock, John, 105
Hand, Learned, 228, 231,
    265, 299
Handyman, Richard, 341
Hanham, Robert, 53
Hannegan, Robert, 273
Hanrahan, William, 292
Harden, Maxmillan, 246, 247
Harding, Warren, 239
Hardwicke, Lord Chancellor,
    86, 112
Hardy, Thomas, 146, 216
Harlan, John, 224
Harmon, Moses, 210
Harris, Benjamin, 58, 70, 71
Harris, Frank, 278
Harris, John, 52
Harris, William, 40
Harrison, Austin, 242, 246
Hartlib, Samuel, 43
Hartman, Sadakichi, 212
Harvard College, 66, 68, 71
Haselden, Kyle, 311
Haslam, Charles, 195
Hassendever, Peter, 103
Lord Hastings, 180
Hastings, Warren, 122
Haswell, Anthony, 138, 139,
    154
Hawthorne, Nathanial, 188,
    335
Hay, George, 139
Hays Code of Movie
    Censorship, 257
Hays, Rutherford, 209
Hayter, Thomas, 85, 116
Hayward, John, 36
Head, Ann, 335
Herbert, Jacques-Rene, 150
Heller, Joseph, 335, 366
Hell-fire club, 89
Helsinki Conference of
    Security and Cooperation
    in Europe, 342, 354
Helvetius, 100
Hemingway, Ernest, 280, 290,
    335
Henderson, Archibald, 230
Henry III, 12, 13
Henry IV, 36

Henry VII, 14
Henry VIII, 18, 23-25
Hentoff, Nat, 335
Heresy, 7, 13, 25, 26, 34,
    36, 37, 40, 59, 66-9, 76,
    99, 214, 286
Hern, John, 40
Herne, Richard, 43
Herrick, Robert, 250, 256
Hersey, John, 335
Hervey, John, 85
Hetherington, Henry, 194, 195
Heyward, Ezra, 209
Hickengill, Edmund, 58
Hickey, James, 122
Hicklin rule, 199, 212, 213,
    228, 256, 292, 295
Hicks, Dan, 321
Hierta, Lars, 201
Hill, Alexander, 224
Hindmarsh, Joseph, 59
Hinton, S.E., 335
Hitler, Adolf, 250, 251, 280,
    281
Hitton, Thomas, 24
Hobart, Peter, 67
Hobbes, Thomas, 57, 59
Hocking, William, 274
Hodges, William, 186
Holbach, Paul-Henry, 121
Holbrook, David, 318
Holland, 9, 10, 22, 34, 35,
    41, 42, 49, 63, 64, 121,
    122, 149, 180, 201, 219,
    246, 247
Hollis, Thomas, 94
Holmes, Marjorie, 300
Holmes, Oliver Wendell, 224,
    236, 237
Holmes, Peter, 164
Holmes, William, 175
Holt, Charles, 154, 157
Holt, Daniel, 146
Holt, Francis, 169
Holt, John, 75, 162, 188
Holy Roman Empire, 15, 17,
    18, 21, 98, 150
Holyoake, George, 196, 199
Honduras, 383
Hone, William, 168-71
Hoover, Herbert, 240
Hoover, J. Edgar, 311, 313,
    326
Hopkinson, Francis, 107, 133
House of Burgesses, 65, 87
House of Commons, 28, 39,
    43, 44, 49, 50, 58, 60, 61,
    73, 74, 76-8, 80, 81, 83,
    84, 86, 113, 115, 116, 166,
    171-3, 193, 196-8, 354

Ickes, Harold, 264
Immigration Act of 1903, 222
Indecent and hateful ideas
  court decisions:
  Aiello case, 358
  Kingsley case, 293
  Sandeling case, 334
  Vollmar case, 307
India, 121, 122, 150, 178,
  180, 181, 201, 203, 205,
  217, 218, 220, 235, 242-4,
  248, 250, 251, 279, 281,
  282, 284, 294, 296, 355,
  382
Indianapolis court decision
  about violence against
  women, 359
Indonesia, 355
Pope innocent IV, 8
Inquisition, 28, 32
InterAmerican Press
  Association, 278, 340,
  342, 383
Internal Security Act of
  1950, 285
International Commission for
  the Study of
  Communications Problems,
  355, 378
International Communications
  Agency, 350
International Convention for
  Suppression of Obscene
  Publications, 243, 251
International Economic
  Powers Act, 359
International Press
  Institute, 340, 379, 381
International Program for
  the Development of
  Communications, 378
International Publishers
  Congress of 1937, 263
International Publishing
  Company, 286
International Workers of the
  World, 227, 240, 254
Iran, 352
Iredell, James, 131
Ireland, 76, 78, 86, 118,
  119, 168, 196, 213, 215,
  223, 244, 247-51, 279,
  281, 283, 319, 343, 383
Irwin, Leonard, 277
Islam, 8
Israel, 280, 381-4
d'Israeli, Isaac, 151
Italy, 4, 10, 13, 18-21, 33,
  35, 64, 179, 203, 204,
  237, 246, 249-51, 264,

277, 278, 286, 317
Ivan the Terrible, 20
Iyengar, K.R. Srinvasa, 295
Jones, Andrew, 163, 184
Jackson, Holbrook, 258
Jackson, Robert, 266, 270
Jacobellis, Nico, 304
Jamaica, 380
Jacobins, 146
James I, 37, 38
James II, 57, 59, 67, 71, 75
James, Thomas, 39
Janeway, Richard, 60
Jankowski, Gene, 370
Jankowski, Henry, 382
Japan, 7, 33, 217, 218, 235,
  242, 243, 245, 246, 249,
  250, 278, 282, 295, 342
Jay, John, 129
Jeans, Alexander, 242
Jefferson, Thomas, 106, 107,
  110, 124, 130, 132-5, 139,
  141, 152-64, 286, 289, 388
Jeffries, Abell, 30
Jehovah's Witnesses, 263,
  267-9, 290
King, John, 12, 84
Johnson, Burgess, 238
Johnson, Colin, 355
Johnson, Eric, 299
Johnson, Lydon, 304, 308
Johnson, Marmaduke, 69
Johnson, Robert, 166
Johnson, William, 161
Johnson, Samuel, 59, 84, 86,
  117, 118
Jones, David, 81
Jones, James, 335
Jones, Jefferson, 246
Jones, William, 39
Jones, William, 118
Jong, Erica, 336
Joseph, Helen, 317
Joyce, Edward, 373
Joyce, James, 254, 260, 265
Joyce, Jeremiah, 146
Juan de Zumapraga, 18
Judge, M.H. 223
Judicial Conference of U.S.,
  364
Julio, Pedro, 380

Kafka, Franz, 280
Kahn, Ann, 371
Kalb, Marvin, 313
Kallen, Horace, 326
Kandel, Lenore, 305
Kassuth, Louis, 202, 220
Kata, Elizabeth, 335
Kaufman, Irving, 344

Kaufman, Stanley, 294
Keach, Benjamin, 56
Keith, George, 71
Kekkonen, Urho, 342
Kell, John, 343
Keller, Helen, 280
Kempis, Thomas, 69
Kendall, Amos, 184
Kennedy, Crammond, 208
Kennedy, Jacqueline, 309
  (see Onassis, Jacqueline)
Kennedy, John F., 298, 300,
  307, 311
Kenedy, M.D., 263
Kennedy, Robert, 301
Kent, Frank, 252
Kent, James, 157, 160
Kenya, 340
Kenyon, Judge, 143-7, 229
Kepler, Johann, 33
Kesey, Ken, 366
Ketaltis, William, 135
Key, Francis Scott, 185
Keyes, Francis, 335
Keyworth, George, 374
Kidgell, John, 112
Kilgore, Bernard, 285
Kimball, Edmund, 176
Kinlock, George, 173
King, Martin Luther, 314
Kippis, Andrew, 116
Kirschwey, George, 253
Lord Kithener, 246
Kitalaer, Nicholas, 10
Klaus, Robert, 350
Klein, Herb, 313
Klu Klux Klan, 253, 314
Kneeland, Abner, 183
Knell, Robert, 82
Knight, John, 292, 309
Knowles, Fred, 225
Knowles, John, 335
Knowlton, Charles, 183, 192,
  214
Knox, John, 59
Koen, Ross, 298
Korea, 8, 9
Krapac, Ben, 183
Kropotkin, Peter, 220
Kruschev, Nikita, 296, 317
Kutsiev, Manlen, 317
Kypreos, Christopher, 341

LaFarge, Oliver, 305
Lafayette, Marquis de, 164
LaFollette, Robert, 238
Lagash, 4
Lamb, John, 108
Lambert, John, 145
Landau, William, 301

Landis, Simon, 207
Lang, George, 264
Laprade, William, 261
Larrick, Nancy, 366
Lasher, Albert, 260
Laski, Harold, 281
Latin America, 340, 354, 355,
  381, 382
Latvia, 320
Laud, William, 40, 41, 43, 50
Laurence, Robert, 322
Laurents, Arthur, 335
Laurie, Warner, 296
Lavin, Garcia, 380
Lawless, Luke, 182, 184
Lawrence, David, 252, 254,
  270, 279, 299, 317
Leach, Francis, 45
League of Left Wing Writers,
  279
League of Nations, 251, 278,
  279
Lebanon, 317
Lebknecht, Karl, 220
Lebknech, William, 220
Lee, Charles, 110, 111, 138
Lee, Harper, 335
Lee, Richard, 123, 130, 161
Leech, Edward, 235
Leept, Gerardus, 10
Lefevre, Jean, 19
Leggett, William, 184
Legion of Justice, 322
Legrand, Louis, 219
Leigh, Robert, 275
Leighton, Alexander, 39
Lemon, Denis, 355
Lemontov, Michael, 220
Lenin, Nikolai, 244, 247,
  250
Pope Leo X, 16
Leslie, Charles, 76
Lester, Julius, 365
L'Estrange, Roger, 55-8, 74
Levellers, 42, 50, 51, 53,
  143, 145
Levin, Ira, 335, 366
Lewis, W.G., 170
Lewis, G.C., 187
Lewis, Sinclair, 254
Libel:
  In the United States, 106,
    107, 124, 127, 128, 130,
    131, 133-40, 152, 154,
    155, 157-9, 182, 187,
    210, 220-2, 226, 228,
    230, 239, 260, 268, 287,
    293, 302, 304, 306, 307,
    311, 326, 327, 329, 338,
    367, 369, 375

In the American Colonies,
  69, 70, 89-92, 94, 95,
  97, 101, 102, 104-6
In England, 13, 27, 29, 31,
  36, 37, 41-4, 49, 53, 55,
  57, 58, 60, 61, 75-8, 80-
  3, 112-4, 116-8, 142-5,
  147, 165-76, 192-6, 198,
  213, 214, 248, 295, 355
Elsewhere, 4, 33, 122,
  151, 242, 246, 280, 281,
  319, 320, 343
Libel court decisions:
  Apple Tree case, 374
  Blasi case, 367
  Bose case, 374
  Buckingham case, 164
  Chicago-Tribune case, 239
  Cooper libel suits, 187
  Freeman case, 133
  Gertz case, 338
  Jurkowski case, 361
  McCall case, 361
  New York Times v. Sullivan
    case, 304
  Rosenbloom case, 257
  Sharon case, 367
  Time case, 328
  Tribune-Republican case,
    361
  Walker case, 301, 310
  WDAY case, 293
  Westmoreland case, 367
  Woodhull case, 207
Library of Congress, 276
Liber, B., 235
Liberty of Conscience Party,
  54
Licensing of Press or Media:
  In the United States, 126,
    128, 133, 152, 227, 230,
    231, 240, 255, 256, 258,
    263, 265, 269, 287, 301,
    302
  In the American colonies,
    67-71, 88, 89, 101, 104
  In England, 24-7, 29, 30,
    36-42, 44-6, 49-51, 53,
    55-62, 73, 74, 84, 115,
    116, 148, 341
  Elsewhere, 121, 181, 203,
    317, 380, 382-4
Licensing court decisions:
  Jones case, 268
  Kunz case, 287
  Schneider case, 264
Lilburne, John, 41, 42, 44,
  49, 50, 52, 53
Lillie, J.S. 155
Lincoln, Abraham, 189-91

Lind, Scott, 382
Lingan, James, 161
Lippman, Walter, 290, 306
Lipsyte, Robert, 335
Lipton, Laurence, 291
Lithuania, 16
Little, Arthur, 384
Liverwright, Horace, 237,
  239
Livingston, Maturin, 166
Livingston, William, 95
Lochford, Thomas, 66
Locke, John, 48, 60-2, 91
Locke, Thomas, 53
Lockridge, Ross, 335
Lombarde, William, 23
London Association for Repeal
  of Advertising Duty, 196
London Correspondence
  Society, 146
London, Jack, 280
Long, Huey, 261
Lord Campbells' libel act,
  196
Louaillier, Louis, 163
Loudon, Samuel, 108
Louis IV, 64
Louis VIII, 149
Louis XVI, 149
Louis XVIII, 178
Louis-Phillipe, 201
Louys, Pierre, 254
Lovejoy, Elijah, 184, 185
Lovell, Alma, 263
Lowden, John, 79
Lower, Elmer, 325
Lucas, Charles, 86
Luce, Clare, 305
Lust, 377
Luther, Martin, 16, 17, 23,
  24, 26, 209
Luxembourg, Rosa, 220, 280
Lord Lynhurst, 196
Lyon, Matthew, 137-9
Lysenko, Trofim, 341

Macbride, Sean, 356, 378
MacCarthy, Desmond, 255
Macauley, Thomas, 143
MacDonald, William, 253
Macedo, Antonio, 64
Machiavelli, Niccolo, 16, 21
MacIntosh, James, 165
MacQueary, Howard, 211
Maddon, Edwin, 223
Madison, James, 107, 123,
  124, 129, 130, 132, 134-40,
  152, 364, 388
Magazine Censorship Board,
  254

Magna Carta, 12, 13, 39, 49, 61, 70
Magee, John, 143, 168
Mahoney, Dennis, 190
Malamud, Bernard, 366
Malaya, 384
Malherbe, Francois, 120
Manchester, William, 309
Mandeville, Bernard, 98
Mann, James, 173
Mann, Patrick, 366
Mansfield, William, 86, 112, 114, 115, 118, 143, 148, 229
Manson, Charles, 327
Manwaring, Roger, 39
Mao-Tse-Tung, 294
Marchetti court decision on classified information, 338
Marchetti, Victor, 338
Marcos, Ferdinand, 355
Mark, Percy, 254
Markin, J. Robert, 381
Marks, John, 338
Marlowe, Christopher, 31
Marshall, Mr. and Mrs. Andrew, 173
Marshall, John, 138
Martin, John, 212
Martin, F.X., 161
Martin, Gregory, 29
Martin, Jean, 34
Martin, Thelma, 269
Martin, William, 37
Marx, Karl, 200, 202, 217, 219, 280
Queen Mary, 26, 27
Mary of Orange, 60, 61
Mary, Martin, 363
Masaryk, Thomas, 218, 249
Maseres, Francis, 144
Mason, George, 107, 123
Mason, Steve, 134
Mathias, King Corvinus, 10
Mather, Cotton, 67, 88, 89
Mather, Jepeosa, 67
Mather, Increase, 89
Mather, Richard, 67
Matthews, John, 79
Matthews, Augustine, 39
Matzan, Melchoit, 35
Maugham, W. Somerset, 288
Maule, Thomas, 71, 72
May, A.W., 223
Mayflower Compact, 65
Mayhew, Jonathan, 94, 95
Mayle, Walter, 6
Mazzarallo, Juvencio, 382
McCarthy, Joseph, 289
McCarthy, Mary T. 288
McClellan, George, 226

McClelland, William, 189
McCormick, Robert, 257, 260, 286
McDougall, Alexander, 101, 107, 108
McFadden, Bernarr, 223, 225
McKean, Thomas, 130, 135, 157
McKinley, William, 222
McKuen, Rod, 335
McLeod, Gilbert, 173
McNamara, Robert, 300
Mead, William, 91
Mealmaker, George, 145
Mearne, Sam, 56
Medieval Scandalum Magnatum, 8, 13, 26
Medvedev, Juares, 341
Meiklejohn, Alexander, 299
Mein, John, 105
Melville, Arabella, 355
Melville, Herman, 335
Mencken, H.L., 253
Mendel court decision limiting U.S. Congressional powers, 327
Mendelssolin-Bartholdy, Felix, 280
Menders, Tricis, 320
Mentelin, Johann, 10
Meredith, James, 310
Merrian, Eve, 366
Mesopotamia, 4
Metcalf, Charles, 201
Methodists, 166, 170
Metternich, Klemens, 122, 181, 202
Mexico, 4, 18, 187, 246, 248, 283, 380, 382, 383
Michnik, Adam, 383
McGavin, William, 173
Michener, James, 335
Mihajlov, Mihajlo, 318
Mill, John Stuart, 199, 213, 214
Mill, James, 172, 174
Miller, Arthur, 335
Miller, Henry, 295, 301, 335
Miller, John, 116
Miller, Samuel, 110, 156
Milton, John, 39, 46-48, 59, 60, 62, 83, 94, 269
Minoa, 4
Minor, Demonthenes, 130
Miss America Pageant court decision about satire, 360
Mist, Nathaniel, 82
Mitchell, A.G., 331
Mitchell, Jonathan, 68
Moceri, Louis, 64
Mockus, Michael, 232

Moltke, Joachim, 35
Monroe, James, 163
Monroe, William, 97
Montagu, Richard, 39
Montague, Gilbert, 261
Montalvo, Eduardo, 340
Montalk, Potocki, 280
Montesquieu, Charles Louis, 99,
  100, 121
Montgomery, James, 146
Moor, Georga, 254
Moore, William, 95
Morley, Felix, 309
Mormons, 186, 238
Morris, Desmond, 335, 366
Morris, Lewis, 92
Morocco, 243
Morsing, Peter, 34
Mort, John, 208
Morton, J. Thomas, 66
Motion Picture Association,
  299, 305, 362
Motion Picture court decisions:
  Bill case, 375
  Censorship case, 304
  Chant d'Amour case, 306
  Freedman case, 306
  Heller case, 333
  Jacobellis, case, 304
  Jenkins case, 338
  The Miracle cases, 289
  Paramount Pictures case, 273
  Pathe Exchange case, 238
  Silkwood case, 350
  Swope case, 377
  Times-Film case, 301
Motion Pictures Producers
  Association, 239, 259, 305
Motion Picture Production Code,
  256, 291
Motion Pictures, 220, 225-8,
  230, 233, 238-40, 244, 246,
  248, 251, 252, 257, 259, 273,
  275, 278, 279, 281, 286-9,
  295, 300, 301, 306, 307, 311,
  313, 316, 321, 322, 333, 334,
  336, 350, 377
Mottelier, Julius, 219
Moxon, Edward, 195
Mozambique, 381
Muddiman, Henry, 54, 56
Muggleston, Lodowick 53, 57
Muir, Thomas, 145
Mulford, Samuel, 88
Mundt, Karl, 272
Munro, William, 263
Murray, Thomas, 259
Murrow, Edward, 299
Musgrave, Phillip, 88
Mussolini, Benito, 249, 251,

278

Nairobi, 355
Napoleon III, 198, 201
Napoleon Bonaparte, 151, 160,
  178-80, 201, 202
Napoleon, Louis, 203, 204
Nathan, George, 256
Nation, Carrie, 223
National Association of
  Broadcasters, 239, 287
National Association of
  Manufacturers, 227, 266
National Civil Liberties
  Bureau, 231
National Coalition Against
  Citizenship, 365
National Commission on
  Obscenity, 308
National Commission on
  Violence, 313, 314
National Conservative
  Federation, 368
National Council for Public
  Morals, 216
National Council of Editorial
  Writers, 345
National Council of Teachers
  of English, 305
National Council on Freedom
  from Censorship, 258
National Defense Association,
  208
National Endowment for the
  Humanities, 362
National Labor Relations Act,
  262
National Labor Relations
  Board, 262
National League of Decency,
  259
National Liberal League, 223
National News Council, 321
National Newspaper
  Association, 362
National Organization for
  Decent Literature, 290
National Purity Congress,
  212
National Security, 327, 366,
  370
National security court
  decisions:
  Ellsburg case, 327
  Josephson case, 274
National Union of (English)
  Journalists, 284
National Viewers and
  Listeners Association of
  England, 318

National Vigilance
  Association, 215
Natural human law and rights,
  6, 8, 9, 34, 37, 50, 62,
  73, 76, 77, 81, 82, 86, 93,
  103, 106, 108, 110, 116,
  117, 126, 130, 134-6, 150,
  169, 224
Nearing Scott, 235
Nedham, Marchamont, 49, 50, 54
Nehru, Jawaharlal, 281, 282,
  316
Neogy, Uganda president, 340
Neuborne, Burt, 371
Newberry, Nathaniel, 37, 38
Newman, Frances, 254
Newspaper Stamp Abolition
  Committee, 196
Newton, Isaac, 163
New International Communist
  Order, 341
New York Board of Regents, 286,
  287
New Zealand, 243, 316, 317, 341
Nicaragua, 380-3
Nicholas, John, 153
Nigeria, 382
Ninevah, 4
Niuwenhuis, Domela, 219
Nixon, Richard, 313, 322, 328,
  331, 334, 351, 357, 376
Nixon, Robert, 82, 84
Non-Partisan League, 227
Normandy, 12
Norris, Frank, 335
Norton, Bonham, 39
Norvell, John, 159
Norway, 9, 180, 319
Novello, Don, 337
Novikov, Nikolai, 100
Nugent, H.P., 161
Nutt, Richard, 82

Oates, Titus, 57
Oates, Williams, 295
Oath ex officio, 27, 41
Oboler, Eli, 344
Obote, Milton, 340
Obscene Literature Advisory
  Commission, 292, 472
Obscene Publications Act of
  England, 318, 319
Obscenity and Pornograph
  In the United States, 153,
    164, 183, 186, 191, 206,
    207, 209-12, 222-32, 235,
    239, 240, 252-4, 256, 257,
    260, 263, 265, 267, 268,
    272, 275-7, 286, 289, 291-
    3, 300-310, 312, 314, 315,
    317, 321, 322, 324, 326,
    327, 333, 334, 336, 338,
    348, 350, 351, 359-61, 365,
    368
  In England, 36, 76, 81, 112-
    4, 117, 165, 167, 172, 192,
    194, 198, 199, 213, 214,
    279, 295, 317, 319, 341,
    343, 354-6, 378, 379
  Elsewhere, 8, 21, 32, 64,
    100, 203, 218, 242, 280,
    316, 318, 343, 379
Obscenity court decisions:
  Alberts case, 292
  Bantam Books cases, 289,
    302
  Body Beautiful case, 263
  Butler case, 291
  Caldwell case, 255
  Carrie Nation case, 223
  Clark case, 228
  Cabell case, 240
  Comstock case, 212
  Craddock case, 222
  Delacey case, 257
  Dennett case, 256
  Devil Rides Outside case,
    291
  Eastman case, 225, 226
  Fanny Hill cases, 164, 306
  Ferber case, 374
  Flower case, 230
  Forever Amber case, 277
  Frate case, 230
  Friede case, 256
  Furuyama case, 360
  Ginsberg cases, 272, 312
  Ginzburg case, 310
  Goldman case, 230
  Gordon case, 286
  Griffen case, 361
  Grove Press case, 299
  Hagar Revelly case, 228
  Halsey case, 232
  Hambling case, 338
  Harmon case, 210
  Healthy Lust case, 377
  Heywood case, 209
  Curious Yellow case, 314
  Interstate circuit case,
    312
  Isenstadt case, 271
  Joyce case, 260
  Junction City case, 303
  Kaplan cae, 333
  Kingsley case, 293
  Klaus case, 307
  Knowlton case, 183
  Landis case, 207
  Lapatossu case, 229

Leaves of Grass case, 208
Life case, 213
Liverwright case, 237
Madamoiselle de Maupin
    case, 239
Manual Enterprises case,
    301
Marcus case, 300
McFadden case, 226
Mencken case, 253
Miller case, 253
Misc. Pornography case, 361
Naked Lunch case, 307
Open City case, 315
Pinkus case, 351
Paris Adult Theater case,,
    334
Parmalee case, 265
Reed Enterprises case, 310
Roth case, 292
Rowan case, 324
Schimmelpfenning case, 353
Seltzer case, 239
Shame Agent case, 310
Smith case, 350
Social Democrat case, 227
Stanley case, 315
Stopes case, 258
Tropic of Cancer case, 301
Waisbrooker case, 212
Wilson case, 212
O'Conner, Daniel, 196
O'Donnell, Peador, 267
O'Flower, Benjamin, 230
O'Hara, Frank, 290, 366
O'Higgins, Harvey, 233
Oldenburg, Henry, 57
Olmecs, 4
Omar, 7
Onassis, Jacqueline, 375
    (see Kennedy, Jacqueline)
Ongania, Juan, 340
Open trials court decisions:
    Gannet case, 352
    Kobli case, 277
    Nebraska Press Association
        case, 348
    Richmond Newspapers case,
        358
Orchard, William, 314
Orczy, Emmuska, 335
Oreglin, Erhard, 15
Organization for Economic
    Cooperation and
    Development, 356
Orr, William, 196
Orwell, George, 279, 283
Osgood, James, 221
Oswald, Eleazar, 127, 130
Otis, Harrison, 137

Otis, James, 94, 102, 105
Ould, Herman, 269
Overton, Richard, 50
Ovid, Publius, 31
Owen, Robert, 198
Oxford University, 38, 48,
    51, 56, 59, 168

Pablos, Juan, 18
Packwood, Robert, 367, 372
Pain, William, 59
Paine, Thomas, 108, 142-6,
    160, 167, 170, 176, 177,
    218
Pai-Shui, Lin, 278
Pakistan, 379
Palm, August, 220
Palmer, A. Mitchell, 237
Palmer, Elihu, 170, 176
Palmer, Thomas, 145
Panama, 340, 379, 381, 383
Panartz, Arnold, 10
Paoli, Giovanni, 18
Pappas, Paul, 329
Paraguay, 380-3
Pareus, David, 38
Parker, Isaac, 164
Parker, James, 94, 96, 101
Parks, William, 95
Parlement, 18, 19, 99, 100,
    120-2
Parliament, 13, 27, 28, 37,
    39, 41-5, 48-55, 57-62, 74-
    6, 80, 82-6, 103, 109, 112,
    114, 115, 118, 143, 146,
    167, 169, 171-3, 196, 213,
    215, 244, 248, 356, 379
Parsons, C.J., 161
Pasternak, Boris, 294, 296
Pascal, Blaise, 254
Pasic, Nicolas, 219, 220
Patriots, 107-9
Patterson, Thomas, 196
Patterson, Senator Thomas,
    224
Patterson, William, 134,
    138
Patterson, W.D., 287
Patton, Frances, 335
Pope John Paul II, 373
Pope Paul III, 18
Tsar Paul I, 100, 150, 151,
    179
Paz, Gainza, 294
Peacham, Edmond, 40
Peck, James, 183
Pemberton-Billing, Noel, 248
Penhallow, Mattie, 222
Penn, William, 70, 91
Pennypacker, Samuel, 221

Penry, John, 30
People for the American
  Way, 362
People's Charter Union, 196
Pergamum, 6
Peron, Juan, 294
Perry, James, 145
Perry, Stuart, 258
Peru, 341, 380, 381, 383
Peter the Great, 98
Peters, Richard, 138
Peterson, Morris, 325
Patterson, Morris, 325
Petition of Right, 59
Petty, William, 50
Pfeffer, Leo, 286
Philipon, Charles, 201
Phillips, William, 38
Philippines, 212, 235, 355
Phipps, Williams, 71
Phoenicians, 4
Piggot, Richard, 213
Pilgrims, 66
Pinckney, Charles, 123
P'io-p'ing, Shao, 278
Piri, Thomas, 360
Pitt, William, 147
Pope Pius V, 21
Plato, Aristocies, 6, 264,
  335
Plath, Sylvia, 366
Plattes, Gabriel, 35
Plehue, V.K., 241
Pickington, John, 342
Poiter, Louis, 201
Poland, 10, 16, 64, 122,
  379, 382, 383
Polewski, Maciej, 383
Polin, Johann, 179
Pollack, Channing, 231
Pollack, Theodora, 236
Polo, Marco, 8
Pope, Alexander, 112
Pornography (see Obscenity)
Portugal, 11, 35, 64
Postal regulation and court
  decisions:
  Greenberg case, 358
  Lamont case, 307
  Second class mail
    statement, 228
Pound, Ezra, 276, 277
Powell, Thomas, 106, 108
Poynder, John, 172
Presbyterians, 30, 44, 49,
  53, 54, 59
Price, Richard, 366
Prime time, 325
Prior restraint, 61, 94,
  113, 137, 138, 140, 153,

167, 224, 231, 235, 244,
  255, 258, 260, 292, 296,
  301, 332, 339, 342, 348,
  352, 359
Prior restraint court
  decisions:
  Aclin case, 358
  Aryan case, 352
  Bertot case, 346
  Goldblum case, 351
  Grosjean case, 262
  Marchetti case, 330, 338
  New York case, 352
  Overseas Media case, 307
  P.A.M. News Corporation
    Case, 346
  Pelczynski case, 339
  Rockwell case, 353
  Rosemont Enterprise case,
    339
  United Artists Case, 339
Privacy, 221, 307, 314, 316,
  346
Privacy court decisions:
  Briscoe case, 326
  Frick case, 309
  Galella case, 375
  Gilbert case, 360
  Lust Pond case, 310
  McNutt case, 346
  Narcotics Agents case, 314
  Spahn case, 310
Privy Council, 13, 25, 27,
  28, 30, 37, 62, 66, 75, 76,
  83, 96, 97
Proclamation Society, 142
Production Code
  Administration, 259
Proffat, John, 208
Protection of Children
  Against Exploitation Act,
  348
Protestants, 26, 27, 32, 34,
  62, 70
Proudhon, Pierre-Joseph, 203,
  204
Prussian, 98, 100, 158, 159,
  202, 203, 219
Prynne, Hester, 252
Prynne, William, 40-2, 49,
  252
Public Bodies Act of England,
  316
Public records court
  decisions:
  Beacon Press case, 330
  Cox case, 346
  Henneman case, 348
  Kent State case, 361
  Nixon records case, 351

Nixon Tapes case, 376
Pufendorf, Samuel, 91
Pullen, Ricky, 337
Pulitzer, Joseph, 223, 226
Puritans, 27, 30, 41, 42, 46,
    51, 66
Puskin, Alexander, 220
Pymatt, Joseph, 52
Pynchon, William, 68
Pyson, Richard, 23

Quakers, 54, 67, 68, 70, 71,
    91, 96
Quebec Declaration, 106
Quidde, Ludwig, 220
Quincy, Joseph, 94, 105, 164

Rabelais, Francis, 18, 19,
    222, 280
Rabi, Isidor, 299
Radio, 227, 229, 239, 240,
    255, 256, 258, 260, 269,
    277, 285, 287, 289, 293,
    299, 301, 302, 311, 315,
    330, 331, 334, 343, 347,
    359, 367, 375, 387
Radio Act of 1212, 227
Radio Act of 1917, 255
Radio court decisions:
    FCC radio regulation case,
        375
    Henry case, 301
    KQED case, 348
    Mayflower case, 265
    NAB case, 269
    PBS-NPR case, 375
    Pacifica Foundation case,
        351
    Peck case, 292
    Pennekamp case, 287
    Red Lion case, 315
    Yale Broadcasting case,
        334
Radio forum use, 258
Radischev, Alexander, 150
Radulescu, Ion, 200
Raleigh, Walter, 30
Randolph, Edmund, 123
Ranters, 52
Raskin, A.H., 309
Ratcliffe, Ebenezer, 106
Rawle, William, 182
Raymond, Henry, 206
Raynal, Guillaume-Thomas,
    122
Read, John, 90
Reardon Report, 305
Reagan, Ronald, 360, 363,
    366, 368, 370, 372-4
Redick, David, 127

Reed, Whitelaw, 206
Reedy, George, 336
Reeves, John, 146
Reineke, Chuck, 358
Remarque, Erich, 279
Renaudot, Theophaste, 34
Renault, Mary, 335
Reporters Committee, 322,
    344, 358
Reporter's privileges court
    decisions:
    Anderson case, 351
    Branzburg case, 329
    Bridges case, 332
    Forest Hill Utility case,
        333
Reporters Shield cases,
    227, 228, 323
    Wirges case, 311
    Ziegler case, 377
Reventlow, Count von, 247
Reynolds, C.B., 209
Rhodesia, 340
Rice, Elmer, 277
Richelisu, Cardinal Duc, 34
Richmond, Duke of, 168
Richard, Grabriel, 166
Rickman, Thomas, 144
Ridpath, George, 75, 77
Right to Read court
    decisions:
    Collins case, 329
    Lubie case, 330
    Package of Magazines case,
        303
    Pico v. Island Trees case,
        374
Riley, J.J., 248
Ritzch, Timotheus, 63
Rivas, Fernando, 381
Rivers, John, 363
Rivington, James, 107
Roalfe, Matilde, 196
Robb, John, 196
Robbins, Harold, 256
Roberts, William, 143
Robertson, James, 147
Robinson, Arthur, 260
Robinson, Henry, 45
Roberts, William, 143
Rocheport, Henri, 203, 204
Rodriguez, Luis, 381
Rogers, Abigail, 50
Rogers, Bruce, 250
Rogin, Lawrence, 257
Rome, 4, 6, 7, 9, 12, 14, 20
Roosevelt, Franklin, 259,
    261, 267
Roosevelt, Theodore, 222,
    223, 226, 228, 233

Rosen, Lou, 212
Rosenberg, Ethel and Juluis,
   304
Rosenbloom, George, 327
Ross, Albert, 211
Ross, Edward, 230
Rossellini, Robert, 288
Roth, David, 297
Rounsavelt, Nathaniel, 161
Rous, George, 115
Rousseau, Jean-Jacques, 100,
   120
Rowen, Archibald, 196
Royal Commission on the
   (English) Press, 284
Royalists, 49-52
Royster, Vermont, 323, 337
Royston, Richard, 50
Rudd, Jack, 52
Rumania, 15, 200, 242
Rumely, Edward, 289
Ruppel, Berthold, 10
Rush, Benjamin, 153
Russell, Bertrand 246, 296
Russell, Joseph, 169, 170
Russell, Walter, 117
Russia, 16, 20, 98, 100,
   150, 151, 179, 217, 218,
   220, 231, 236, 241-5, 247,
   249, 264, 279-81, 294-6,
   317, 319, 340-2, 355, 379
Russian Union of Writers,
   319, 320

Sabine, Waldo, 280
Sainsbury, Timothy, 379
Salinger, J.D. 335
Salisburg Oath, 12
Salmon, Lucy, 240
Saltonstall, Richard, 66
Samarakand, 8
Samizdat, 340
Sandburg, Carl, 237
Sandage, Charles, 325
Sandwell, B.K., 287
Sanford, Edward, 252
Sanger, Margaret, 229, 230,
   233
Sarp, Paolo, 64
Sare, Richard, 76
Sasser, Michael, 337
Saxons, 12, 17, 102
Schanen, William, 322
Schenck, Charles, 236
Schenkkan, P.M., 337
Schieffer, Bob, 370
Schmertz, Herbert, 372
Schmid, Chris, 376
Schmidt, Stephen, 382
Schoeffler, Peter, 9

Schofield, Harry, 229
Schon, Erhard, 17
School court decision:
   Gambino case, 351
   Reineke case, 358
   Salvail case, 353
   Tinker case, 324
Schroeder, Theodore, 227,
   229, 272
Schultz, George, 374
Schwartz, A., 365
Schweinheim, Conrad, 10
Scotland, 12, 21, 23, 26, 42,
   44, 173, 196, 246
Scotland Yard, 318, 356
Scott, John, 108
Scott, Walter, 117
Scroggs, William, 57, 58
Scully, Denis, 168
Searchers, 52
Sears, Isaac, 107. 108
Seawall, Samuell, 69
Second Class mailing, 208,
   221, 223, 227, 228, 238,
   256, 272, 273
Sedition
   In the United States, 124,
      131, 135-40, 152-54,
      158,161, 226, 229, 230,
      234, 261, 265
   In the American colonies,
      65-7, 70, 71, 88, 91, 92,
      97, 101, 102, 104-7
   In England, 25, 26, 36,
      37, 42, 43, 45, 53-6, 59,
      60, 75, 76, 78-80, 83,
      86, 112-4, 116-8, 144-7,
      165, 167, 168, 171-5,
      192, 193, 196, 213, 215,
      244, 245, 317
   Elsewhere, 145, 217, 242,
      251
Sedition court decisions:
   Abrams case, 230
   Adams case, 136
   Baldwin case, 138
   Berger case, 238
   Burk case, 137
   Cobbett case, 135
   Cobell case, 135
   Cooper case, 140
   Dennie case, 155
   Gilbert case, 232
   Gitlow case, 252
   Greenleaf case, 140
   Haswell case, 139
   Herold case, 235
   Lillie case, 155
   Lyon case, 137
   Pierce case, 237

Schenck case, 236
Steelik case, 238
Trachtenberg case, 286
Sedition Act of 1798, 228,
  285, 327
Sedition Act of 1917, 229,
  234, 236, 238
Sedition Slammers, 233
Segal, Erich, 326
Sejon, King, 9
Selby, Hubert, 319
Selden, John, 60
Seldes, George, 267
Seltzer, Thomas, 239
Senate, 131, 134, 182, 207,
  208, 229, 260, 270, 323,
  369
Senegal, 380
Serbia, 18, 121, 219, 220,
  243, 245
Settle, Mary, 335
Setzer, Johannes, 18
Seward, William, 187
Pope Sextus, 21
Seymour, Thomas, 160
Shakespeare, William, 31,
  84, 279, 335
Sharon, Ariel, 367
Shaw, Frederick 316
Shaw, George Bernard, 223,
  279, 280
Shebbeare, John, 86
Sheldon, John, 182
Shelley court decision about
  voluntary associations,
  276
Shelley, Percy Byssche, 168,
  175, 177, 195
Sheng, Pi, 8
Sheppard, Sam, 308
Sheridan, Richard, 166
Sherman Act, 271
Sherman, Roger, 123, 127
Sherman, William, 189, 190
Sherwin, English publisher,
  170, 171, 173
Shipley, William, 118, 144,
  118
Shippen, William, 127
Shively, Governor, 96
Shokutu, Empress, 7
Short, William, 161
Lord Sidmouth, 168, 169, 171
Silva, Costa, 319
Simmons, Steven, 350
Simon, Sidney, 350
Sinclair, Upton, 254, 280
Singleton, Hugh, 28
Sinyavsky, Adrei, 318
Skirving, William, 145

Slander, 26, 57, 98, 104,
  116, 131, 228, 246, 342
Sleiden, Johann, 19
Slovakia, 242
Slovenia, 19
Smilie, John, 127
Smith Act, 265, 286
Smith, Francis, 58
Smith, Hedrick, 313
Smith, Huston, 335
Smith, James, 137
Smith, Joseph, 186
Smith, Lillian, 271
Smith, Pauline, 254
Smith, Wallace, 281
Smith, William, 95-7, 313
Snyder, Harry, 334
Sobeloff, Simon, 291
Social responsibility theory,
  274
Socialist party, 227, 252,
  254, 353
Society Opposed to Vice and
  Immorality, 147
Society of Professional
  Journalists, 275, 330, 357,
  363, 364, 367, 373
Society for Promoting Useful
  Knowledge, 193
Society for the Reformation
  of Manners, 60
Society for the Suppression
  of Vice, 165, 169, 170,
  175, 192, 199, 207, 212,
  214, 223, 231, 238, 239,
  256
Socinians, 47
Socrates, 5
Soekarno, President, 355
Sokolsky, George, 290
Solzhenitsyn, Aleksander,
  319, 320, 342
Sons of Liberty, 101, 107,
  109
Sorbonne, 10, 17-19
South Africa, 295, 317, 319,
  340, 342, 380, 381, 383
Southey, Robert, 169
Southwell, Charles, 195, 196
Spahn, Warren, 310
Spain, 8, 10, 18, 19, 22, 33-
  5, 40, 58, 64, 134, 150,
  166, 179, 181, 241, 243,
  248
Sparke, Michael, 39, 40, 43
Spellman, Henry, 65
Spence, Thomas, 146, 147,
  165
Spencer, Herbert, 216, 219
Spender, John, 280

Speyer, Johann, 10
Spinoza, Benedict, 214
Spotswood, Alexander, 90
Sri Lanka, 354
Stafford, Simon, 30
Stagg, Bessie, 337
Stalin, Josef, 280
Stamp (or knowledge) taxes,
    74, 76-8, 86, 90, 96, 102,
    103, 110, 116, 168, 193-5,
    197-9, 213
Stansby, William, 38
Stanton, Edwin, 189, 190
Stanton, Frank, 342
Star Chamber, 14, 26, 27,
    29, 39-41, 44, 45, 53
Stargess, John, 54
Starkie, Thomas, 167
Stationers, 13, 25-30, 38,
    41, 43-5, 49, 50, 56, 58,
    59
Stead, W.T., 215
Steele, Richard, 77, 78, 81,
    114
Steinbeck, John, 335, 336
Steiner, George, 305
Stephens, Alfred, 267
Stephens, Leslie, 213
Stern, J. David, 303
Steven, Marcus, 305
Stevens, Sylvester, 309
Stevenson, E.R., 267
Stewart, Kenneth, 272
Stewart, Potter, 293, 345,
    350, 353
Stockdale, John, 143, 166
Stocker, Bram, 225
Stockwin, Harvey, 355
Stoicism, 6, 9, 11
Stolz, Mary, 335
Stone, 268, 271, 335
Stone, M.E., 215
Stone, William, 146
Stopes, Marie, 223, 258
Storey, Wilbur, 206
Story, Joseph, 222
Stow, John, 27
Strackbein, O.R., 311
Strand, John, 28
Strauss, Leo, 287
Strauss, Walter, 302
Stringer, William, 275
Structural Concept of Press
    Freedoms, 345, 350
Struenesse, Johann, 121
Stuart, Archibald, 132
Stubbes, John, 28
Student Press Law Center,
    354
Sullivan, Alexander, 213

Sullivan, Arthur, 242
Sullivan, James, 154
Sullivan, John, 303
Sullivan, L.B., 304
Sulzberger, Arthur, 271,
    273, 298
Sumeria, 4
Summer, John, 223, 230, 239,
    256
Sun-yat-sen, 244
Supreme Court (see U.S.
    Supreme Court)
Suriname, 383
Sussman, Leonard, 349
Sutherland, George, 262
Swaggert, Jimmy, 363
Swann, Joseph, 170
Swancara, Frank, 257
Sweden, 10, 20, 34, 63, 121,
    122, 178, 179, 201, 219,
    220, 314, 319
Sweeney, Lawrence, 103
Swift, Jonathan, 77
Switzerland, 10, 19, 20, 33,
    98, 120, 121, 151, 200,
    201, 204, 219, 247, 249,
    381
Swope, Herbert, 285
Sydney, Algernon, 59
Symonds, H.D., 144
Syndicialism, 240, 254, 262,
    266
Syndicalism court decisions:
    De Jonge case, 262
    International Workers of
      World case, 254
    Wood case, 266
Syria, 4
Szilagy, Richard, 311

Talley court decision on
    anonymous publication, 299
Talmadge, DeWitt, 210
Talmadge, Herman, 267
Tanzania, 381
Tao, Feng, 8
Tarsis, Valery, 317
Taticus, 7
Taylor, George, 137
Taylor, W.S., 261
Television, 239, 278, 289,
    293, 297, 298, 302, 304,
    312, 313, 315, 317-9, 322-
    4, 328, 330, 331, 336, 342,
    347, 348, 351, 358, 362-5,
    367, 375-7, 380, 383, 387
Television Code of Good
    Practices, 287
Television court decisions:
    Buckley case, 347

CBS case, 358
Chandler case, 358
FCC cases, 315, 334, 351
Hanby case, 324
Hastings case, 375
Home Box Office case, 351
Red Lion case, 332
TX Pix case, 321
Writers Guild case, 348
Lord Tenterden, 192
Te-pai, Kung, 278
Terhorst, S.F., 344
Terrible Threateners, 233
Terry, Fernando, 380
Teukesbury, John, 21
Thackery, William, 199
Earl of Thanet, 147
Thatcher, Margaret, 356
Thelwell, John, 147, 173
Theresa, Maria, 100
Thomas, Helen, 254
Thomas, Isaiah, 103, 106, 110
Thomas, John, 42
Thompson, Denys, 264, 276
Thompson, Dorothy, 276
Thompson, John, 154
Thompson, Nathaniel, 59
Thornbecke, Premier, of Holland, 203
Thorsen, Danish film maker, 354
Thwaites, Edward, 24
Thichte, Johann, 150
Tillinghost, Charles, 127
Timmerman, Jacobo, 382
Timothy, Lewis, 93
Tindal, Matthew, 61, 62, 73, 74, 77
Tinker children, 324
Ti, Shi Huang, 11
Tocker, Mary, 169
Todd, Helen, 267
Tooke, John Horne, 114, 116, 146, 147
Toland, John, 62, 73, 78
Tolkien, J.R.R. 335
Tolstoy, Leo, 211, 220, 237
Tories, 55, 73, 78, 107, 147, 172
Tourtellot, Arthur, 269
Toussaint, Francis, 99
Towers, Joseph, 145
Towle, Charlotte, 286
Trachtenberg, Alexander, 286
Trading with the Enemy Act, 232, 239
Transylvania, 12
Treason, 25, 26, 36, 42, 43, 50, 53, 55, 56, 58-60, 65, 74, 75, 78, 85, 93, 107, 116, 119, 146, 168, 190, 198, 242, 266, 277, 285
Trenchard, John, 79, 80, 81
Trial interference court decisions:
    Arkansas Gazette case, 358
    Bridges case, 266
    Calley case, 347
    Nye case, 266
    Sheppard case, 308
Tricoupis, Charilaos, 219
Trigg, Frank, 211
Trotsky, Leon, 249, 266, 280
Truman, Harry, 285
Tucker, St. George, 153, 155, 156
Tunstall, Cuthbert, 23
Turberville, George, 127
Turkey, 9, 15, 20, 121, 122, 150, 249, 381, 382
Turnbill, George, 288
Turnbridge, William, 176
Turner, Alan, 364
Turner, Nat, 183
Turner, Ted, 367
Tutchin, John, 73, 75
Twain, Mark, 209, 211, 335
Tweed, William, 206, 207, 211
Twentieth Century Fund Task Force, 329
Twyn, William, 56
Tydings, Millard, 266
Tyler, Robert, 192
Tyndall, John, 219
Tyndale, William, 24, 26

Udall, John, 30
Uganda, 340, 384
UnAmerican, Activities Committee, 291
Underground newspapers, 312, 313, 321, 322, 328, 330, 350
Underground Press Syndicate, 350
United Kingdom, 384
United Nations, 283, 284
UNESCO, 283, 284, 318, 341, 349, 354-6, 362, 363, 380, 383, 384
UN Committee on Peaceful Uses of Outer Space, 318
Union Society of England, 170
Unitarians, 54, 78, 90, 145, 169, 185, 232
United Order of Blasphemers, 196

U.S. Bill of Rights, 3, 123–
5, 183, 207, 252, 300, 303,
308, 327, 331, 345, 368,
386, 387
U.S. Committee on Public
Information, 232
U.S. Congress, 1, 123-9, 131–
40, 127, 129-31, 133, 137,
152-4, 162, 183, 184, 187,
207, 222, 225, 228, 236,
237, 252, 255, 260, 263,
269, 275, 291-3, 298, 305,
307, 308, 322, 327, 331,
332, 363, 364, 367, 368,
387, 388
U.S. Constitution, 1, 2, 3,
123-32, 134, 137-9, 141,
153, 156, 221, 225, 237,
255, 262, 268-71, 303,
311, 312, 337, 368, 369,
388
  First Amendment, 1, 2,
  129, 131, 137-40, 153,
  212, 224, 227, 230, 252,
  258, 262-4, 266, 268,
  270, 271, 273, 275,
  276, 286, 288-93, 300-7,
  310, 312, 315, 321, 323,
  324, 326-33, 337, 338,
  343, 344, 346-53, 357–
  62, 368, 372, 374, 376,
  377, 387, 388
  Fifth Amendment, 270
  Sixth Amendment, 277
  Fourteenth Amendment, 1,
  206, 207, 224, 225, 252–
  5, 257, 258, 262, 264,
  268, 269, 289, 292, 301,
  304, 315
U.S. Customs, 186, 254, 256,
259, 260, 291, 308
U.S. Declaration of
Independence, 2, 107, 108
U.S. Information Agency, 366
U.S. Justice Department,
308, 364, 365, 368
U.S. Newspaper Program, 362
U.S. Supreme Court, 1, 2,
134, 138, 161, 188, 207,
212, 224, 227, 232, 238,
240, 252-4, 258, 262-4,
266-8, 273, 285, 287, 289–
92, 299, 300-4, 306-8,
310, 312, 314, 315, 324,
327, 329, 330, 332, 333,
338, 339, 346, 348, 349,
351, 353, 357, 358, 359,
374, 375, 387
Universal Declaration of
Human Rights, 283, 342

Uraguay, 380, 382, 383
Uris, Leon, 319
Urukagina, King of Lagash, 4

Vance, Earl, 271
Vane, Henry, 53
Van Thieu, President of
Vietnam, 318, 354
Varus, 12
Varvaez, Ramon, 180
Vatican Index of Prohibited
Books, 318
Vendome, Louis, 34
Vendotis, George, 122
Vendotis, Polis, 122
Venzuela, 383
Verblen, Thorstein, 238
Verhoven, Abraham, 32
Verne, Jules, 335
Verlione, Paul, 280
Veuillot, Louis, 201
Vian, Boris, 295
Vidal, Gore, 340
Vietnam, 318, 322, 325, 327,
350, 354, 361
Vincent, Antoine, 63
Vines, Henry, 68
Vinson, Fred, 285
Vizetelly, Henry, 215
Vlack, Adrian, 42
Voltaire, 99, 100, 121, 122,
180, 279, 281
Von Hertling, Chancellor,
249
Vonnegut, Kurt, 335, 366
Vorpe, W.G., 266

Waddington, Samuel, 176
Wagner, Robert, 305
Waisbrooker, Louis, 212
Wakeman, George, 58
Wakeman, Thaddeus, 223
Walker, Edwin, 310
Walker, Frank, 273
Walker, Henry, 44
Walker, Thomas, 43, 140
Walley, Henry, 45
Walpole, Horace, 85
Walpole, Hugh, 282
Walpole, Robert, 76, 82-84,
94
Walter, John, 143, 147
Walter, John II, 192
Walwyn, William, 46, 51
Ward, Artemus, 188
Ward, Roger, 30
Warren, Earl, 337
Warren, Fred, 226
Warren, Joseph, 104, 105
Washington, George, 107, 109,

110, 134-6, 158
Watch and Ward Society, 207,
   221, 226, 252, 253
Watkins, Hezakiah, 96
Watson, James, 176
Watson, Morris, 262
Watson, Thomas, 230
Waxman, Stephanie, 366
Wayte, James, 53
Webster, Daniel, 183, 186,
   187
Webster, Francis, 168
Webster, Noah, 133, 183
Webster, Pelatiah, 128
Weinberger, Harry, 232
Welch, Robert, 338
Wellesley, Arthur, 166, 168
Lord Wellesley, 178, 180
Duke of Wellington, 168, 193
Wentworth, Harold, 335
Wentworth, Peter, 28
West, Henry, 237
West Indies, 122
Westmoreland, William, 367
Weyman, William, 96
Wharton, George, 50
Wheble, John, 115
Wheelwright, John, 67
Whigs (English), 58, 73, 77,
   78, 84, 113, 146, 166
White, Byron, 329
White court decision about
   newspaper picketing, 239
White, Edward, 30
White, Edward (Chief
   Justice, 234
Whitehead, Clay, 329, 331
Whitehill, Robert, 128
Whitehouse, Mary, 341, 356
Whitgift, John, 27, 29
Whiting, William, 124
Whitman, Walt, 208, 209, 221
Whitney, Anita, 254
Whittier, John, 185
Wickes, Edward, 209
Wickham, John, 56
Wickliffe, John, 82
Wiggins, James, 288, 303
Wilberforce, William, 142
Wilcocks, Thomas, 27
Wilde, Oscar, 215
Wildman, Donald, 360
Wilhelm, Crown Prince, 249
Wilhelm, Kaiser, 245
Wilkes, John, 105, 112, 114-
   6
Wilkins, Mike, 370
Wilkins, Thomas, 142
Wilkinson, Clennell, 251
William III, 116

William III of Holland, 219
William the Conqueror, 12
William of Nassau, 201
William of Orange, 52, 60,
   61, 71
Williams Committee on
   (English) Obscenity, 356
Williams, John, 176
Williams, Joseph, 275
Williams, Oliver, 55
Williams, Oscar, 335
Williams, Thomas, 147
Williamson, Arleigh, 274
Willingham, Colder, 286
Willkie, Wendall, 265
Wilson, Charles, 366
Wilson, Edmund, 272
Wilson, George, 212
Wilson, James, 128, 134
Wilson, John, 193
Wilson, Woodrow, 235, 245,
   246, 249
Windsor, Kathleen, 277
Winslow, John, 71
Winthrop, John, 66
Wither, George, 37, 38
Withers, Philip, 142
Wirges, Eugene, 311
Wirth, Timothy, 364
Wise, Andrew, 30
Wise, John, 70
Wolfe, Bertram, 243
Wolfe, John, 28, 36
Wolfe, Thomas, 265
Wood, Ida, 266
Wood, Ina, 237
Wood, Robert, 237
Baron Wood, 167
Woodfall, Henry, 114, 116
Woodhull, Victoria, 207, 212
Woodruff, Clinton, 225
Wooler, Thomas, 168, 170,
   171, 173
Woolsey, John, 257, 260
Woolston, Thomas, 82
Workman, Benjamin, 128
World Administrative Radio
   Conference, 355
Wortman, Tunis, 152, 154
Wrenn, R.C. Carter, 367
Wright, Richard, 288
Wright, Susannah, 172
Wroe, James, 170
Wycliffe, John, 13
Wyse, Andrew, 30

Yancey, Charles, 163
Yeats, William, 279
Young, James, 208
Yuan, President, 245

Yucatan, 380
Yugoslavia, 279, 317, 318,
   382
Yu-Wei, K'ang, 220

Zambia, 381
Zeigler, Ron, 325
Zenger, John Peter, 83, 91-
   3, 115, 144, 158
Zeno, 6
Zimbabwe, 381
Zirpoli, Alfonso, 323
Zola, Emile, 215, 220, 290
Zweig, Arnold, 280
Zweig, Stefan, 280

About the Author

LOUIS EDWARD INGELHART is Professor Emeritus of Journalism at Ball State University, Indiana. He is the author of *Freedom for the College Student Press*, and *Press Law and Press Freedom for High School Publications* (Greenwood Press, 1985, 1986).

Lightning Source UK Ltd.
Milton Keynes UK
UKOW03n0654020417
298081UK00008B/96/P